TRACKS & SIGNS
OF THE BIRDS OF BRITAIN & EUROPE

TRACKS & SIGNS
OF THE BIRDS OF BRITAIN & EUROPE

Second Edition

ROY BROWN, JOHN FERGUSON,
MICHAEL LAWRENCE AND DAVID LEES

COLOUR PLATES BY
DAVID QUINN AND CHRIS SHIELDS
LINE DRAWINGS BY MICHAEL LAWRENCE

CHRISTOPHER HELM
LONDON

Published by Christopher Helm, an imprint of A & C Black Publishers Ltd.,
37 Soho Square, London W1D 3QZ

Copyright © 1987 and 2003 Roy Brown, John Ferguson, Michael Lawrence and David Lees
Colour plates by David Quinn and Chris Shields
Line Drawings by Michael Lawrence

This paperback edition published in 2003

ISBN 0-7136-5382-5

A CIP catalogue record for this book is available from the British Library

A & C Black uses paper produced with elemental chlorine-free pulp, harvested
from managed sustainable forests.

Printed through Colorcraft Ltd.,Hong Kong

Produced and designed by Fluke Art, Cornwall.

10 9 8 7 6 5 4 3 2 1

Contents

Acknowledgements

Many people have helped directly and indirectly with the production of this work and we gratefully acknowledge them all. In particular we thank our long-suffering ladies Doe Brown, Vanessa Lawrence, Patricia Lees (Mrs Ferguson) and Phyllis Lees. They have given moral and practical support, and for many months have not been too sure what they would find next in the deep freeze. Simon Brown, Maria and Terry Lees, V Arancio, Rosena Down, Peter Ottoway, Elizabeth and Terry Dorer, Terry Holder and Brian Simpson have all helped by collecting material. Many organisations and individuals have helped in specific ways. We thank Neville Wilby and Jackie Golder of Flamingoland, for help with feathers, droppings and tracks; The Hancock Museum, for skulls; The British Museum (Natural History) Bird Section at Tring, in particular Mr I Galbraith (retired), Mr G Cowles, Dr Philip Burton and Mr Derek Read; Mr R Raymont of Stagsden Bird Gardens, for providing large numbers of specimens; the management and staff of the Norfolk Wildlife Park, in particular Julie Dixon; Rosemary Crawford, for generously allowing access to her feather collection for illustrative purposes; the Wildfowl Trust, particularly at Slimbridge and at Washington; the head librarian RSPB.

Colour plates on pp. 18, 112, 117, 118, 140, 157, 175, 177, 183, 189, 195, 199, 209, 223, 237 (part), 253, 261, 267, 272 and 285 are by Chris Shields. All other colour plates are by David Quinn. The line artwork is by Michael Lawrence, with additional drawings by David Henderson.

The following individuals and organisations provided invaluable assistance with the preparation of the second edition: Jose F Pillar, David Amy, David Revell, Elizabeth Sugden, Janet Hornby, Paul Johnson, Dr. John Day, R.B. Treleaven, Tom Bain, Robert Worrall, Stewart Taylor, Paul & Laura Fasce, Ron Downing, T. Barker, Desmond Dougan, Joyce Pope, Derek Yalden, Mick Marquiss, Richard & Julie Kemp, Jemima Parry-Jones, Bob McGowan (National Museums of Scotland), Dr. Robert Preys-Jones (British Museum of Natural History), Flamingo Park, Whipsnade Wildlife Park, Zoological Society London, Dr. Eulalia Moreno (Estacion Experimental de Zonas Aridas, CSIC), Drs Josefina Barreiro, Carmen Martinea, Manuel Carrasco Redondo & Maria Jesus Sanchez (Soler Park Nacional Tablas de Deimiel), Jesus Hernando Vulture Sanctuary, Jose Gutiere (Museo Nacional de Cieucias Naturales), Dr. Ian Wyllie, Prof. Zdzislaw Pucek (Polish Academy of Sciences).

Apologies are due if we have inadvertently overlooked any individual or organisation. We are very grateful for all the assistance we have received from every quarter.

Chapter 1

INTRODUCTION

The Study of Bird Signs

Across Europe, the observation and study of birds interests more people than any other aspect of natural history. As a group birds are widespread and numerous, and are often very conspicuous. Many are colourful or boldly patterned, many more have distinctive songs or calls, and most possess highly idiosyncratic behavioural traits. They exhibit a great range of morphological and behavioural adaptations, enabling them to pursue various different lifestyles and to exploit virtually all habitat types. Birds are therefore valuable ecological indicators as well as interesting creatures in their own right. Some require a fairly specific set of habitat conditions, whilst others are much more versatile. Migratory species breed and overwinter in different environments which may be a few tens or thousands of kilometres apart. There are also seasonal changes in habitat utilisation amongst some non-migratory species. All of this makes the field study of birds and their habits fascinating as well as scientifically valuable.

There are many excellent books on ornithology (a selection is listed in the Bibliography) covering bird identification, habits, song and sometimes nests and eggs. However, some species are secretive, rare or may occupy habitats which are not easily accessible and in these cases it is not so easy to observe the birds themselves. All birds moult, leave feeding remains, evidence of breeding and droppings. Road casualties, not only the ubiquitous Pheasant, are common and corpses in various states of decomposition are a common find in habitats such as the sea-shore. Such finds often yield intact skulls, which enable identification to species or genus. This book concentrates on these indirect signs which enable the field naturalist to identify species and also to collect information on patterns of activity without necessarily ever seeing the bird itself.

About the book

The layout and contents of this book are unique and provide the field naturalist with a comprehensive guide to bird signs. The book is intended for field use over the whole of Europe, but is also designed as a reference source to enable more in-depth analysis of signs and their interpretation. Much of the material is totally original and is organised into self-contained sections dealing with one particular type of sign. The number of individual species and amount of material included varies according to the accuracy with which signs can be identified, and is also conditioned by the frequency with which a species is likely to be encountered. (That is not to say that rarities and the unexpected are excluded – for instance the authors have collected the remains of a Cory's Shearwater from the shores of Crete, an Arctic Skua road casualty in North Yorkshire, a Flamingo corpse on the west coast of Scotland and the feathers of a Great Bustard in the Orkneys). The chapter on droppings, for example, is brief since it is possible to identify many birds only to group or family level from the structure and content of faeces. In contrast the vast majority of species or genera can be identified from their skulls or unique feather structures/markings, so the chapters covering these aspects include the majority of European species. As far as possible, colour photographs or plates have been used to facilitate field identification. The exceptions to this are the systematic track/trail and skull chapters where black and white drawings enable key identification features to be recognised. All illustrations are backed with descriptive text, quantitative information and, where helpful, simple statistical analysis.

This introduction outlines the scope of the following chapters in the book and the range of habitats in which signs of bird activity are likely to be encountered, with a brief discussion on associated species. The welfare of the birds is paramount and is backed by stringent legislation in most countries. A short guide to good practice concludes the introduction, backed by a more comprehensive Code of Conduct, summary of relevant legislation to protect and manage birds and list of contacts and websites in the backmatter.

Outline of Chapters and How to Use the Book

Field methods and analysis

This chapter deals with methods of collecting evidence in the field, recording and analysing the information. It explains how to record and measure tracks and trails; how to analyse and record the information from droppings, pellets and other feeding signs; feather collecting and recording (see Best Practice p17); and skull preparation and storage. Tools for and methods of tracking and recording in the field are discussed, ranging from the long established notebook, tape measure, conventional still photography and plaster casting through to thermal imaging and radio telemetry. It has to be said that such high-tech methods are beyond the reach of many people using this book and in any event the satisfaction derived from the personal input into conventional methods is not easy to replace. Birds, as with all of nature, show much variation even within a single species. In the case of Curlew skulls, for instance, the absolute length of the bill varies by more than 60%, but bill-length to cranium-length ratios and other distinguishing features lie within a limited range. A basic understanding of simple measuring and statistical principles is important and these topics are introduced with the emphasis on practical application rather than theory.

Tracks and trails

Over 70 individual species are illustrated in this chapter with many additional measurements of species tracks. Whilst bird tracks do not generally show the variety in morphology of their mammalian counterparts, many species or closely related groups of species can be identified from their tracks/trails/associated marks on the ground if careful examination is carried out. With this in mind the variation in track type, related to species, size, activity, ground conditions and season amongst other factors is analysed before the individual birds are described. The tracks illustrated cover many common European birds as well as some of the rarer ones. Illustrations are based on size and morphological similarities. Unusual behavioural trail types, such as birds taking off on soft ground or pouncing on prey in the snow, are illustrated along with examples of standard gaits, eg walking, running, hopping, fluttering. Where diagnostic, trails of individual species are also shown.

Nests and roosts

Bird nests are a common sign. The main types of nest are illustrated and described in relation to shape, material and method of construction. Many species nest in more than one habitat type and a comprehensive series of examples are discussed by habitat. Some bird nests can be confused with those of mammals, such as squirrel dreys. Invertebrate activity, such as complex webbing associated with defoliating caterpillars, or even vegetation such as clumps of mistletoe in tree branches, can also resemble bird nests. Examples are illustrated and discussed. There is brief reference to eggs (which are also discussed in the context of feeding and behavioural signs) but this is kept to a minimum since comprehensive coverage is beyond the scope of this book. There are several reference works in existence, *and it is not the wish of the authors to encourage people to look for or at nests which are in use* (see Best Practice p17).

Feeding and behavioural signs

Birds leave a wide range of feeding and other activity signs. In this chapter there is a systematic approach to the various categories. This is organised around different sources of food such as growing plants (foliar and woody material), soft fruits, seed heads and flowers, nuts, cones, fungi, and animal remains, both vertebrate and invertebrate. In addition to food remains signs of feeding activity (e.g. moss turned over by a flock of starlings searching for Tipulid larvae in the topsoil) and breeding behaviour (e.g. display areas such as Capercaillie leks) are described. When confusion with mammal activity is likely examples are shown to allow identification. While as much individual information as possible is presented here it is important to be aware that signs left by closely related species or those with similar habits, such as some of the finch family, are very similar and only generic differentiation is possible.

Pellets

Regurgitated hard remains of food in the form of pellets are a common sign. Many species produce pellets, and these can provide a great deal of information about the species responsible, dietary preferences and food availability. Owls are probably the best known pellet producers, but raptors, crows, gulls, waders, herons and shrikes also regurgitate the hard and indigestible parts of their food in distinctive forms. Even some of the insectivorous and seed-eating species produce pellets. Closely related species produce similar pellets. The morphology, contents and location of pellets from over 50 species/groups are discussed and illustrated. The analysis of pellets is discussed in detail in '*Field Methods and Analysis*'. Pellets can be confused not only between bird species but also with the droppings of some carnivorous and insectivorous mammals. These are illustrated to highlight differences.

Droppings

Bird faeces, which consist of both solid waste and uric acids, fall into a number of distinct categories dependant on morphology and composition, which is in turn related to diet. Location is an important secondary identification factor. The droppings range from the liquid 'squirts' of birds of prey, which regurgitate or digest all the hard parts of their food, to the solid, compressed faeces produced by gamebirds feeding on fibrous vegetation. Even within the same species different types of dropping are produced throughout the year or even the day depending on diet, activity or breeding condition. While the droppings of some species are not diagnostic, many are because of their morphology, content and location. A number of examples are discussed and droppings of mammals which could be confused with those of birds are illustrated for comparative purposes.

Feathers

These are perhaps the most commonly collected 'nature objects' after sea shells. Many of us have tried to match an unusual feather we have found with a whole bird picture in a field guide. Excellent though these illustrations may be they rarely allow the identification of individual feathers, which are often more varied than the overall rather drab appearance of some species suggests. Unless reference is made to specialist sources, which are often not readily available and cover only a limited range of species anyway, then identification of the single feather is impossible.

There are about 500 species of bird recorded regularly from Europe. Some are very similar, particularly in immature or winter plumage, and it is often not possible to distinguish individual species from single feathers. Many species are, however, readily identifiable by the colouration and patterning formed by the plumage – their individual feathers carry some part of this overall pattern and are equally easy to identify. The aim of this guide is to provide a scheme of identification for flight and control feathers (remiges and rectrices) on a systematic basis for all of the readily identifiable species and similar small groups. Other types of feather from the body are included in the illustrations, but not systematically. This chapter introduces the study of feathers and moult cycles in a way which has not been tackled elsewhere. It has not been possible to cover all 500 species here, although a good proportion have been covered, as it would be necessary to illustrate 5000 outer flight feathers alone. By describing and illustrating the size, shape, colour and type of marking of each of a large sample of feathers, a sufficiently comprehensive framework is presented to enable the naturalist to arrive at a very brief shortlist of potential species. Over 250 species are illustrated and/or described in detail. This chapter brings together a range and depth of material which cannot be accessed elsewhere and this is one of the major original contributions this volume makes to the study of birds as a whole.

Skulls

Skeletal remains of birds are common in certain conditions, such as the shoreline (particularly after heavy weather). Intact skulls and long bones from birds and mammals are frequent in regurgitated castings, particularly owl pellets. Skulls are the most reliable structures for species identification. This chapter is based on key diagrams to skull structures and differentiation of bird skulls from those of other vertebrates. It illustrates major groups systematically, in relation to size and morphology rather than on a taxonomic basis. The skulls of some closely related species are very similar and in these cases a single representative species is illustrated, although further information is given in the text. Altogether about 255 species or closely related small groups are dealt with. In addition to line drawings to allow easy identification there are a series of 'in the field' illustrations, as the skulls are rarely found detached from the body and in a perfectly clean condition. Some preparatory work, as described in chapter 2, is normally necessary, but the results are very informative. If collecting and keeping the remains of skeletons and feathers, it is important to be aware of the strict laws which apply in the UK and elsewhere in Europe (see Best Practice p17).

Back matter

The final sections provide information on European organisations, both government and NGO, along with websites, legislation and code of practice, references and further reading, acknowledgements and finally a comprehensive index by both common and scientific names.

Geographical Terms of Reference

Map 1 identifies the geographical scope of this book, which covers the whole of Europe. This map includes capital cities, major rivers and upland areas as basic reference points.

Key

1	Netherlands	9	Moldova	17	Corsica
2	Belgium	10	Slovenia	18	Sardinia
3	Luxembourg	11	Croatia	19	Sicily
4	Switzerland	12	Bosnia-Herzegovina	20	Crete
5	Austria	13	Serbia & Montenegro	21	Cyprus
6	Czech Republic	14	Macedonia	22	Georgia
7	Slovakia	15	Albania	23	Armenia
8	Hungary	16	Balearic Islands	24	Azerbaijan

Map 1

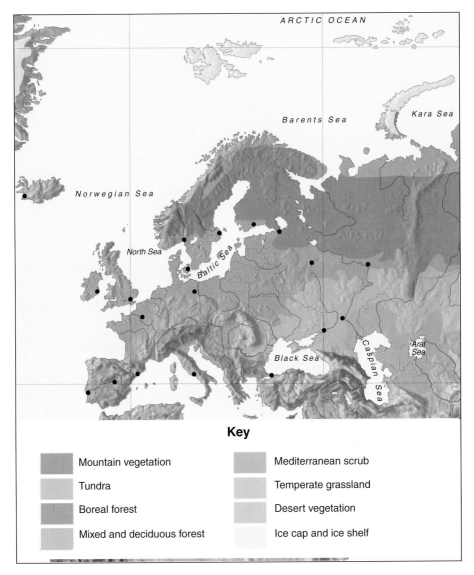

Map 2

Bird Habitats

Map 2 indicates the primary range in habitat from the Mediterranean woodlands, scrub (maquis) and even semi-desert, through to the mixed woodlands and grasslands of central and eastern Europe. Further west, deciduous woodlands predominate. These habitats in turn grade into the boreal coniferous forests, and ultimately the Arctic habitats of the far north of the range. Mountainous regions in all parts of Europe show an equivalent pattern of gradation of habitat type as altitude increases. There is a west-east and north-south climatic gradient impacting on ambient temperatures, humidity, exposure and day length. Freshwater rivers and coastal habitats impart yet further variations and finally the degree of human intervention and management may be the overriding factor on habitat type and structure in many parts of the continent. The following examples pick up on some of the key habitats and their particular interest in the context of biodiversity and bird activity in particular.

1. Mediterranean scrub or maquis, which may be degraded into sparse scrub, grassy or even semi-desert areas, consists of a combination of aromatic bush and herb vegetation which provides shelter and food for a range of species, including finches, larks and raptors. Feeding remains are common signs.

2. Mediterranean forests consist of various pines, junipers and cedars. These are important for a wide range of birds and provide nesting habitats for some of the larger predators, such as Black Kites. Feeding remains (including pellets and nests) can be found, also tracks in damper areas.

3. Dehesa is a traditional Mediterranean agricultural system derived from undercropping or retaining grazing amongst cork oaks or nut trees. Along with some other Mediterranean agricultural systems such as traditional olive groves and orchards these habitats contain a tremendous diversity of birdlife with species such as Cattle Egret, other herons, Hoopoes, smaller raptors, a wide variety of passerines and various woodland edge specialists. Many types of sign may be found here.

4. Wetlands cover a range of freshwater conditions from peat bogs and valley mires (marshes) to streams and rivers, canals, ponds and larger freshwater bodies. They provide many habitat niches depending on surrounding vegetation and geographical location, the presence of foreshore or bankside, and the style and intensity of land management. Freshwater reed-bed areas are important for many warbler species and certain other passerines, whilst the larger marshes carry harrier, heron, wader and gull populations. River banks are nesting sites for species such as Kingfisher, Sand Martin and Bee-eater, and arctic wetlands provide breeding grounds to many waders and wildfowl species. Large freshwater bodies/wetland areas in southern Europe may be particularly important on migration routes (eg. Majorca, the Camargue in France, and the Marismas del Guadalquivir in Spain). Key areas, especially where there is open space and bare soil, for all signs and actual bird observation.

5. Mountains cover a range of habitats including Alpine species-rich pastures and bare rocky areas which are particularly important for the larger birds of prey such as the eagles, vultures and larger owls. Lower sub-montane areas may carry managed moorland which is important for ground-nesting waders and gamebirds as well as harriers, Merlins and owls. Many feeding and breeding signs and, under the right ground conditions, tracks and trails.

6. *Broadleaved woodland and scrub ranges from the beech/poplar elements in southern Europe to the oak/ash/hazel associations of northern soils and the pioneer birch/mountain ash combination colonising habitats at the tree-line level. Heathland scrub exists on many more sandy areas in northern Europe and is important for warblers, chats, larks, smaller birds of prey and a range of ground-nesting birds. On the heaths, hawthorn, gorse and the heathers are dominant. There are of course many other associated plant species in both woodland and scrub areas. These woodland areas with their associated ground flora provide a rich range of food sources from the tree fruits and seeds, as well as shelter and nest sites. Many birds are associated, e.g. woodpeckers, a range of owls and many passerine species. Frequently there are grasslands, wetlands or agricultural areas associated and these again generate great edge area diversity. Good for most signs, especially where wetter areas are present.*

7. *Boreal forest/northern coniferous forest is represented mainly by pine-, larch- and fir-dominated woodland, as well as many of the man-created or -modified plantations. This habitat supports a characteristic avifauna including various finches, tits, gamebirds and larger owls. Feeding and nesting remains.*

8. Sub-Arctic/Arctic habitats contain the open tundra, colonising tree line and some of the sub-montane and higher moorland/heath. Waterfowl, waders and birds of prey are important groups, and signs include nests, tracks and feeding remains.

9. Coastal habitats cover a wide range of conditions, including marshes and mudflats, beaches and shingle areas (including intertidal zones), cliff faces, estuary complexes and the open sea. The salt pans of Spain and France are also included here. Latitude and longitude affect the range of species using these areas, as does human modification, especially of salt marshes and estuaries. Species found vary from the breeding colonies of auks and tubenoses associated with cliff-faces and clifftops, to the great numbers of wildfowl and waders which congregate on marshland and estuaries on passage and through the winter. These huge concentrations inevitably attract birds of prey, and many upland passerines winter in coastal habitats. Excellent locations for tracks, feeding remains and some breeding activity as well as observing the birds themselves. Ecologically, these are sensitive areas and should be treated as such.

10. Steppes/grazed grasslands. The true steppes of the east, which are the natural grasslands on deep soils (chernozems) of eastern Europe, have generally been agriculturally modified, and extensive pastures, mainly in the uplands, are secondary habitat systems. However, they are important breeding/feeding areas for waders, gamebirds and raptors. Feeding, feathers and nesting signs mainly.

11. Traditional agriculture is associated with low-intensity crop and grazing patterns which have created a mosaic of habitats and carry a wide variety of birdlife conditioned by general location/habitat type/geographical region. The Dehesa (3 above) is a specific example of these increasingly less common areas. Current changes in agricultural management priorities are leading to a gradual return of lower external inputs in the very intensive agricultural areas which have developed in the last 40 years. This is bound to have a beneficial effect upon birdlife in the long term. Passerines, smaller raptors, corvids, larks, buntings and pigeons are favoured along with many location-specific species. Tracks, feeding and breeding signs.

12. *Built environment and intensive agriculture habitats do not, in general, support the same number and diversity of birds as other habitats. Buildings, roads and quarries, for example, severely modify or entirely destroy existing habitat. However, the new niches created may favour other bird species, and derelict industrial, mined or quarried land may be even more diverse. In the UK for instance, valuable and species-rich wetland sites include flooded gravel pits or areas of mining subsidence which have become waterlogged. In intensive agriculture, the loss of non-cropped habitat (hedges are a vital woodland edge substitute), the effects of monoculture and associated chemical inputs have depressed both the food source and activity potential for birds referred to in 11 above. However, typical farmland birds do still persist in some areas, and current changes to redress the balance will have a positive effect. Throughout Europe, even where crop yield is maintained at a high level, if there is a good ratio of non-cropped to cropped area (4 to 8% under hedge, grass or flower margin, ditch, water margin scrub or set-aside) then overall biodiversity can be moderate and bird activity can be high. Feeding and breeding evidence.*

Best Practice

- Always put the welfare of birds, other wildlife and the habitat first.

- Keep disturbance to a minimum and do not damage or trespass in any way.

- Do not collect anything other than discarded remains, photographic images and notes.

- Be aware of relevant legislation and do not infringe it.

- Communicate information carefully – do nothing to put any wildlife under human pressure.

- Respect the countryside and the needs of all those who use it.

Pellets

Short-eared Owl

Merlin

Whole carcases/wings

Goldfinch

Skulls – range of size and structure

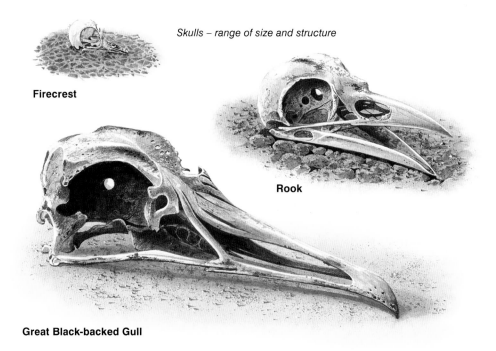

Firecrest

Rook

Great Black-backed Gull

Examples of field signs which can be used in species identification (life size).

Chapter 2

FIELD METHODS AND ANALYSIS

This chapter explains how to collect, record and analyse information. It is essential to glean as much information as possible from the signs which birds leave, and this can best be achieved by a systematic approach.

Tracks

Tracks can be recorded by drawing and measuring, by photographing and by taking plaster casts. It is true that some species spend little time on the ground, but most do spend some time, often searching for food or nesting materials, and bird tracks are more common than most people realise. They are most frequently found on very wet, muddy paths, on river banks, and on estuarine mudflats and intertidal areas. Snow is a good tracking medium since even the smallest of tracks show, and it is otherwise rare to find the tracks of small perching birds, except in soft silt. Muddy fields often yield the tracks of larger birds which have been searching for food, but it is not recommended to go searching for tracks on newly seeded fields! Cow pats sometimes provide a valuable source of tracks when birds search for the invertebrates living in them, and even roadside dust can be a useful, if temporary, source of material.

Recording

When a track is found, the area around it should be examined for other signs of activity. The soil conditions, weather, date and time as well as the precise location should be noted. It is surprising how long some tracks will persist on undisturbed ground and, if they are being used as an aid to activity studies, it is important to know which tracks appeared when. If a trail is present this should be carefully drawn to scale, noting and measuring the features shown in the diagram. The gait (e.g. walking, hopping, running or jumping) should be recorded. If droppings, remnants of feeding activity, feathers or other signs are found near the trail these should be sketched and, ideally, photographed *in situ*. Only then should they be disturbed, if needed, for further analysis. Once the trail has been examined as a whole, then individual tracks should be drawn to include the information on the diagrams. It is best to describe several tracks, not just the 'perfect' ones which show every feature clearly.

Photographs of tracks and trails are a useful and convenient way of storing information, but there are limitations. Other than on sandy or silty shores, the muddy soils in which tracks are found tend to be dark. Photography therefore requires a fast film, good oblique lighting conditions (flash pictures of tracks are rarely successful), and a tripod to hold the camera vertical over a single track or oblique along a trail. Many tracks are small and close-up facilities are useful; modern macro-zoom lenses in the range 35mm to 90mm are most satisfactory. It is important to include an indication of scale in photographs, and finally it is essential that they are clearly labelled.

A reference collection of plaster casts is invaluable. It is a time-consuming business to take a cast properly, but casts show details such as segmentation and tubercules on toes which it is not possible to see in the tracks themselves, nor in drawings or in photographs.

Surgical plaster should be used for casts. First, prepare the area for taking the cast by pushing a frame into the ground around the track and sealing it with softened soil outside. Use a frame large enough to allow at least 10mm clearance around the track. Card can be used, and plastic flower pots cut to a depth of 50–70mm, make excellent 'casting rings'; the sloping sides allow easy removal of the cast. Enough plaster of Paris should be mixed to cover the whole area inside the frame to a depth of about 20mm. When mixing the plaster always add the powder to the water, gradually

1. Making a plaster cast; plastic ring around track

2. Plaster poured into ring

3. Cast roughly cleaned in the field

4. Cast cleaned, inked and labelled

increasing the amount until the correct consistency is reached. The plaster should be mixed to the consistency of thin cream and poured gently into the track. The frame should be gently tapped to dislodge air bubbles. Always leave the cast until the plaster has become warm and cooled down again (normally 15 to 20 minutes) before attempting to lift the cast. Gently clean excess soil from the cast in the field and then wrap the cast in newspaper; this protects it and helps to absorb moisture. Gently clean the track when it is completely dry. This is best done with a soft brush under running water. Label the back and pick out the details of the track in black.

The best soil medium for casting is damp, but not waterlogged, mud/silt. Sand, if it is coarse and dry, gives a poor impression, and snow melts.

Features to measure in bird tracks and trails

1. Great Black-backed Gull Track: Left foot, $^1/_2$ life size

A – Overall length
B – Overall width
C – Length of centre toe (toe III)
D – Metatarsal area

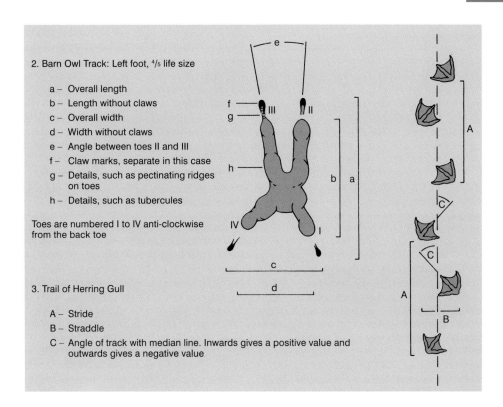

2. Barn Owl Track: Left foot, 4/5 life size

  a – Overall length
  b – Length without claws
  c – Overall width
  d – Width without claws
  e – Angle between toes II and III
  f – Claw marks, separate in this case
  g – Details, such as pectinating ridges on toes
  h – Details, such as tubercules

Toes are numbered I to IV anti-clockwise from the back toe

3. Trail of Herring Gull

  A – Stride
  B – Straddle
  C – Angle of track with median line. Inwards gives a positive value and outwards gives a negative value

Pellets

Chapter 6 illustrates the great variety of pellets regurgitated by different species of birds. The remains in pellets of some species, such as Kestrels, can be identified only by microscopic examination and detailed knowledge of the small hard parts of invertebrate as well as vertebrate prey. The owls, some other birds of prey and scavenging species produce pellets in which the fragments are much larger, and indeed whole bones and skulls may be found. Chapter 9 keys out bird skulls, and *The Country Life Guide to the Animals of Britain and Europe* (by two of the current authors) keys out mammal skulls. Our bibliography contains references to keys of other vertebrate, invertebrate and plant material likely to be found in pellets.

The locations of pellets, especially if large accumulations are found away from an obvious nest site, should be logged since these indicate feeding or roosting sites or less obvious nesting sites. Regular collection and analysis of pellets can give information about the habitat use and feeding preferences of the bird, as well as qualitative and quantitative assessments of prey populations, especially small mammals.

Most often, the interest in pellets lies in analysing their contents, but it is useful to have a reference collection of whole specimens. Pellets containing animal remains are susceptible to attack by invertebrates such as moth larvae, beetles and mites. Some of the mixed, or vegetation-based pellets crumble and fall apart when dry. The best method of keeping them whole is to spray them with an insecticide and then coat them with a spray lacquer. They are best kept in labelled screw-top plastic specimen tubes.

All pellets should be collected in batches as far as possible. They should be weighed as a batch and then individually. The length and circumference of each pellet should be taken and the dimensions and contents on analysis recorded on separate sheets for each pellet. There are various methods of recording pellet data. The example shown overleaf is a comprehensive data sheet which individual naturalists will wish to modify according to their needs. It is worth keeping comprehensive and systematic records over the years.

i. Pellets should be gently teased apart with the fingers.

ii. Forceps and a dissecting needle are used to divide the pellet further.

iii. Bone and other hard parts should be gently eased out of the matrix of fur, feather and other soft material.

iv. The bones should be cleaned of matrix material.

v. The bones should be sorted into types – crania (skulls), denteries (lower jaws), long and innominate bones. The matrix should be carefully sifted before being discarded, there may be invertebrate hard parts which throw even more light on the feeding behaviour of the individual.

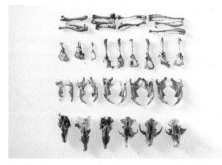

vi. The bones should be systematically laid out (useful to record an image at this stage) and identified to species. Often the skulls and denteries give the final total of individuals, but in this case there are six skulls (shrew, mouse and vole) but only five sets of lower jaws.

Owl pellets should be gently teased apart to remove the bones and other hard parts, both plant and animal, which can be identified. There are generally large fragments present and a detailed examination of the matrix is not always necessary but a x 10 hand lens is very useful. Dry pellets can be gently teased apart over a white surface, but it is best to soak them in water in a shallow while dish and to separate the bones from feather and fur once these have softened. Older, decomposing pellets, especially from some of the larger owls, can be unpleasant to deal with and are best soaked in a 30 per cent alcohol solution, which reduces odour and kills off any unwanted invertebrates.

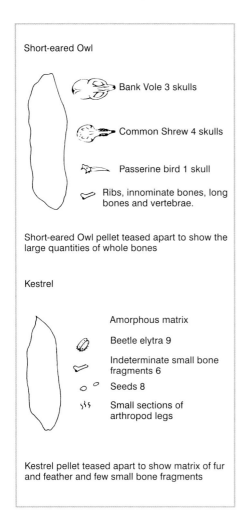

Short-eared Owl

Bank Vole 3 skulls

Common Shrew 4 skulls

Passerine bird 1 skull

Ribs, innominate bones, long bones and vertebrae.

Short-eared Owl pellet teased apart to show the large quantities of whole bones

Kestrel

Amorphous matrix

Beetle elytra 9

Indeterminate small bone fragments 6

Seeds 8

Small sections of arthropod legs

Kestrel pellet teased apart to show matrix of fur and feather and few small bone fragments

Contents of actual pellets

PELLET ANALYSIS RECORD SHEET

Species producing pellets: Date of analysis:

Location:

Number of pellets in sample:

General composition of pellet:

TOTAL BONE FRAGMENTS		
Mammals:	Birds:	Other:
Crania:	Crania:	
Mandibles:	Mandibles:	
Long bones:	Long bones:	
Innominate:	Innominate:	

INVERTEBRATES

INDIVIDUAL SPECIES	Crania	Right mandible	Left mandible	Minimum individuals
Mole				
Common Shrew				
Pygmy Shrew				
Water Shrew				
Bank Vole				
Field Vole				
Water Vole				
Harvest Mouse				
Wood Mouse				
Yellow-necked Mouse				
House Mouse				
Brown Rat				
Black Rat				
Common Dormouse				
Edible Dormouse				

TOTALS				
Birds				
Reptiles				
Amphibians				

Notes

Sample pellet analysis record sheet

Kestrel pellets are more tedious. The pellet should be crumbled gently between the fingers, taking a note of the percentage composition of the matrix (e.g. fur, feather remains, plant fragments, sand). Small particles of identifiable material should then be separated from the matrix and identified. A x 10 lens is essential and, ideally, a binocular microscope with a x 10 or x 20 capability should be used. It takes at least 30 minutes to deal with each pellet because the fragments are small.

Droppings

For many species, little can be gained from a detailed analysis of the droppings. The exceptions to this are the seed-eaters, those feeding on more fibrous vegetation, insect-eaters and some of the scavenging species. Work carried out on droppings of Choughs, in which small hard parts do pass through the digestive tract, has shown this species' diet to range from exclusively insectivorous to a mixed one of carrion, grain and even figs and oranges. Many droppings are distinctive by virtue of their size, shape and structure, so that detailed measurements, notes and photographs are the best method of keeping records unless a very detailed analysis is going to be undertaken on the same basis as pellet analysis.

MEASUREMENT RECORD SHEET

Species:	Ref:
	Locality:
	Date:

Bird length:	Tail length:
Wing length (l):	Wing length (r):

Longest primary (l):	Longest secondary (l):	Longest primary (r):	Longest secondary (r):

Bill length:

Tarsus length (l):	Tarsus length (r):

Bill colour:	Leg colour:	Mouth colour:

Eye colour:	Eye rim colour:

Claw length:	
Left	Right
1	1
2	2
3...... 8	3...... 8

Moult
Tail:
Right:
Left:

Left wing:	Right wing:
Alula:	Alula:

Primaries:	
11	11
10	10
9	9
8...... 1	8...... 1

Secondaries:	
1	1
2	2
3	3
4...... 20	4...... 20

Tail (l)	Tail (r)

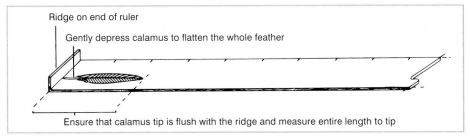

Ridge on end of ruler

Gently depress calamus to flatten the whole feather

Ensure that calamus tip is flush with the ridge and measure entire length to tip

Measuring a feather against a ruler

Feathers

Chapter 8 gives detailed keys to feather identification and to the location of various feather types on the body. The time, place and weather conditions may have a bearing on the identification process and, since it may be some time before a feather is examined, it is important to record such details at the time of collection.

If a wing, or a whole carcase, is found, then the feathers should be removed from the tail and wing and mounted on paper in order. It is useful to keep one wing intact and to use the other to remove individual feathers. Wings can be preserved by removing them from the body and pinning them open on a board in a warm, dry place. They can be stored in large envelopes or paper bags and will periodically need dusting with combined insecticide-fungicide preparations.

Individual feathers may not always be in good condition if they have been on the ground for any length of time. Wet feathers deteriorate rapidly, especially if they are stored in polythene bags. As soon as possible after collection they should be gently dried out. Paper bags are most useful for storage at this stage, since they let the feathers 'breathe' and they can be written on. If the feathers are caked with sand or mud, they may be 'swished' in warm water with a little washing-up liquid added. More stubborn spots, such as the tar too often found on beaches, should be gently massaged with a little hair shampoo (soap is of limited effectiveness, especially in hard-water areas). Soft-vaned or downy feathers should not be wetted since they will lose their structure. After washing, the feathers should be rinsed in clean water and allowed to drip dry in a warm, dry place, such as an airing cupboard. Once they are dry, a little gentle 'preening' may be necessary to repair splits in the webs.

It is important to take accurate measurements. This is best done by placing the feather on a ruler, ideally with a stop ridge at the 0 end, with the tip of the calamus (shaft) on the 0. Gently smooth the feather so that it lies flat on the ruler, and take the reading of length from the tip.

The process of identification is discussed in detail in Chapter 8. After identification and preparation, the feathers may be stored by mounting them on light card. They can either be attached by cutting insets into the card, or be stuck down with gum or gummed paper (but never self-adhesive tape). The cards – grey ones are best – can be stored in a cardboard box or a loose-leaf filing system, with one or two mothballs to inhibit moth and mite attack.

Skulls

Bird skulls are generally very delicate and care has to be taken with their preparation. There are a number of ways of cleaning and separating the skull from the carcase. It is rarely worth retaining a whole skeleton, since this is difficult to store or mount because of its fragility. Carcases or heads can simply be left to rot in a jar of water for a few weeks. This is messy and smelly but is effective. The carcase can be left on top of a board in a fine-mesh bag or under a heavy pot, leaving small cracks for small organisms to get in and out. This again takes several weeks. More robust skulls may be cleaned by gentle simmering in boiling water. This can also be used as a final stage on skulls partially cleaned by the other methods, and is aided if a little washing soda is added to the water. To remove the oils and make the skulls white, bleaching is required. This can be done using dilute household bleach or by leaving the skulls exposed to strong sunlight. If a skull has a highly coloured bill sheath this should be protected in strong sunlight by covering with masking tape and the skull should not be boiled or chemically bleached.

Skulls must be labelled with a tie-on tag. It is a good idea to tape the lower jaw to the upper with drafting tape to prevent separation and loss.

Feeding Remains

The nature of feeding remains varies considerably, and the best universal method of recording is a scaled, colour photograph. Pellets and feathers have already been considered and it is not recommended that feeding remains from carnivores should be collected. Hard parts of plants such as nuts and cones, which have been opened in a particular way are easily kept. They need to be dried in a warm atmosphere. Smaller items can be mounted on labelled card; larger ones should be tagged and kept in boxes. Much of this may seem to be common sense and unnecessary, but a reference collection of nuts opened by different species of birds and mammals can help to avoid confusion in the field.

It is worth underlining the need to keep a systematic notebook in the field and to transfer one's notes regularly into a flexible permanent system.

An A5 spiral-bound shorthand notebook is the most useful in the field, and it is essential that all information is clearly recorded, including date and location. A tape measure, small ruler or scale bar, and snap-closing polythene bags for specimens are essential, and binoculars and a single-lens reflex camera are most useful. It is not within the scope of this volume to discuss technical aspects of photography or sound recording, both of which are useful aids in bird study that do not necessarily involve sightings of the birds. References are given in the bibliography. A computer-based data system is now being adopted by many naturalists for location and sighting records. Both single image and video digital equipment can now be used instead of conventional photography and have the advantage that images can be downloaded directly and stored on disc, CD or DVD. Sign material, however, is complicated and it will be some time before the rewarding process of human interpretation is replaced for this aspect of study.

| Wood Mouse | Bank Vole | Water Vole | Great Tit | Nuthatch |

Collection of hazelnuts eaten by different birds and mammals. These can be stored in specimen tubes or by sticking them on to small card squares.

Chapter 3

TRACKS AND TRAILS

Introduction

Many birds are small and light and spend little, if any, time on the ground. Despite this, the range of tracks likely to be found is considerable, provided there is suitable soft ground such as river silt/mud, snow or mudflats. There is a great deal of variation in tracks, and the careful observer can use them not only for species identification, but to interpret activity patterns as well. This chapter does not suggest that every species can be identified from its tracks, and in some cases the illustrations and notes refer to a type or group of tracks rather than to those of individuals.

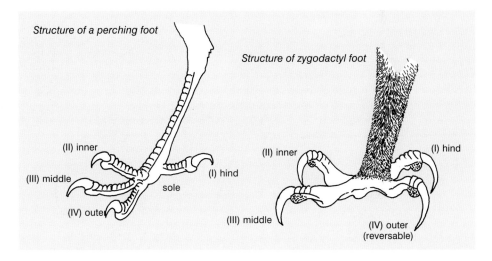

Track Morphology

The shape of a track is related to the foot structure. Almost all birds have four toes radiating around the base of an enlarged and fused metatarsal bone. Toe I, which may be reduced, points backwards; toe II is closest to the body; toe III is normally the longest; and toe IV is furthest from the body. Toes II to IV are normally forward-facing. In a track the metatarsal area leaves an impression, the toe pads covering the toe bones (phalanges) leave impressions, and finally the claw impression, which may be attached to or separate from the toe impressions, are often visible. The track structure varies according to the main purpose of the feet, e.g. perching, killing, wading or swimming.

Number of Toes in Track

The majority of tracks show four toes, but often toe I is small and may be set high on the metatarsal bone so that it only just shows. On hard ground, the impression of a moderate-length toe I may be very faint or absent.

Toe Length

Generally, toe III is the longest and toe I is the shortest, except in some wading (e.g. heron) and perching (e.g. sparrow) birds, where it is very long. The last lobe on toe I is called the hallux and may be very pronounced on some species, e.g. the hawks. In most birds with toes II to IV pointing forward toe II is the second shortest and toe IV the second longest. This varies on specialist feet such as those of woodpeckers and kingfishers, where I and II are shorter than III and IV.

Track identification features. This diagram shows track types in association with other factors that aid identification and, taken with the central toe measurement, toe angle, latitude and physical surroundings should enable an identification to be made. Always be sure to provide a scale in a photograph or sketch to assist identification at a later time. Refer to p29 (opposite) for illustration of each track type.

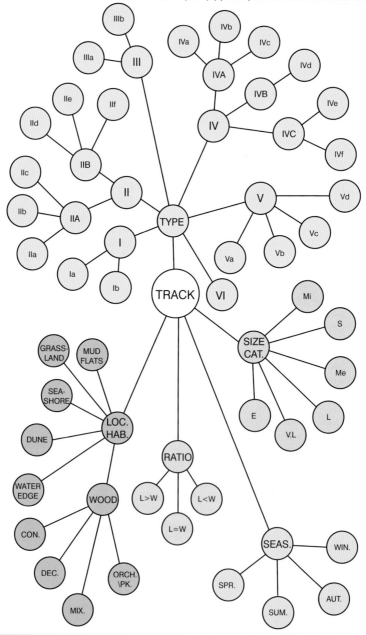

LOC.	Location	ORCH/PK.	Orchards and Parkland	WIN.	Winter
HAB.	Habitat	SEAS.	Seasons	L>W	Length greater than width
CON.	Coniferous woodland	SPR.	Spring	L<W	Length less than width
DEC.	Deciduous woodland	SUM.	Summer	L≈W	Length and width
MIX.	Mixed woodland	AUT.	Autumn		approximately equal

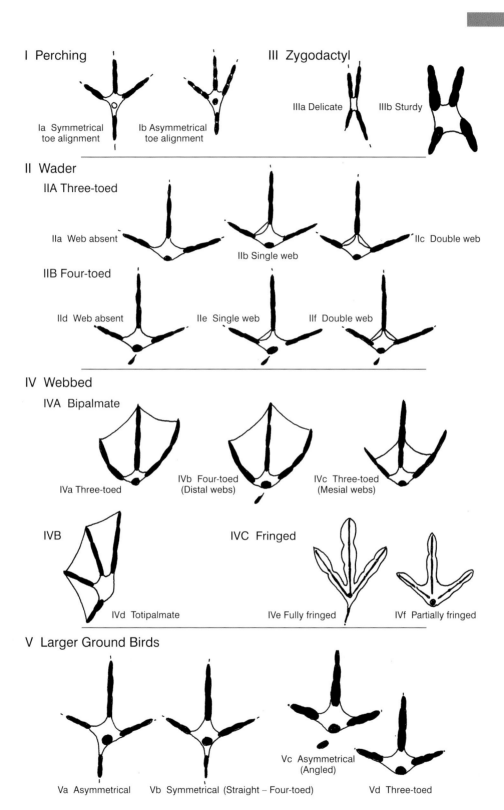

I Perching

Ia Symmetrical toe alignment
Ib Asymmetrical toe alignment

III Zygodactyl

IIIa Delicate   IIIb Sturdy

II Wader

IIA Three-toed

IIa Web absent
IIb Single web
IIc Double web

IIB Four-toed

IId Web absent
IIe Single web
IIf Double web

IV Webbed

IVA Bipalmate

IVa Three-toed
IVb Four-toed (Distal webs)
IVc Three-toed (Mesial webs)

IVB

IVd Totipalmate

IVC Fringed

IVe Fully fringed
IVf Partially fringed

V Larger Ground Birds

Va Asymmetrical
Vb Symmetrical (Straight – Four-toed)
Vc Asymmetrical (Angled)
Vd Three-toed

Toe Arrangement

Commonly, toe I points backwards and II to IV forwards, with a wide splay (up to 120°) between the forward toes in wading birds but less splay (90°) in perching birds. Sometimes toe I may lie sideways (e.g. pelicans). In some species, toes II and III point forwards in parallel and may be held in parallel by tissue. Such syndactyl tracks are found in woodpeckers and kingfishers. In specialist tree-climbing species, toe IV may often face backwards; in owls, it may lie to the side or face backwards. Birds with two toes pointing forwards and two back are zygodactyl. Three-toed Woodpeckers have toe I completely missing, but are still syndactyl. In some species, there are ridges running across one of the claws on the underside (normally toe III); such pectinated claws are used in preening, and under certain conditions the details will show in tracks.

Symmetry

In some species, it is possible to draw a line down through toes III and I (if present) and for the track to mirror itself on either side of the line. In others there is asymmetry, and this can be a major diagnostic feature.

Webbing

Webbing provides valuable identification characteristics. Simple webbing stretches between toes and may be distal, mesial or proximal to the metatarsal area. Normally only toes II to IV are connected, but where I to IV are linked, as in the pelicans or cormorants, the foot is termed totipalmate. In some waders, a small area of webbing is present between III and IV only.

Lobed webbing may consist of discrete, simple lobes on each toe (grebes), discrete indented lobes (coots), or simple indented lobes connected by proximal webbing (phalaropes).

Track Size

To help with identification, the tracks are presented in six size categories and then subdivided by morphological characteristics in each size group. The six categories of length are:

0–25mm	Minute (Mi)	26–50mm	Small (S)
51–75mm	Medium (Me)	76–100mm	Large (L)
101–125mm	Very Large (VL)	>125mm	Enormous (E)

Track Analysis

The quality and amount of detail visible in a track vary greatly according to ground conditions. In very soft ground, species which have a reduced toe I and webbing between toes II and IV (e.g. the ducks) will leave a track showing all the toe outlines, webbing and claws. In harder ground, only the four toe impressions and partial web will show, while in very hard ground only the impressions of the three front toes will be seen.

The track will also vary with speed of movement. When they move quickly, many of the smaller, lighter perching birds tend to impress less deeply, whereas the heavier ground dwellers will leave tracks with some very deeply impressed sections.

There can be considerable variation in the appearance of tracks from the same species, but there are often key characteristics which make identification to track type, if not species, possible. The COOT illustrates this variation very well. The track is very big, always four-toed with toe I being offset and carrying a fairly large claw. This toe is not contained within the lobed webbing so apparent on the other toes, and its form and position are diagnostic of the species. There can, however, be very great differences, as the illustrations show.

Figure A shows the perfect track, with all the details of the lobes, claws and toes complete and distinguishable. Such a track is rare (see p68). B shows a track where only the more solid inner lobe is apparent, and C shows how the position of the outer lobe can be inferred in such a track. Frequently, on wet leaf mould for instance, only the general outline of the whole track without any internal details present will be seen (D), but again the missing details can be interpolated (E). In all of the tracks, the form of toe I is clear. In the final example (F), which occurs occasionally on a firm surface, only the toe outlines appear. In this condition the track could be confused with that of PURPLE GALLINULE, except that toe I is longer, more slender and centrally placed in the latter species (see p86).

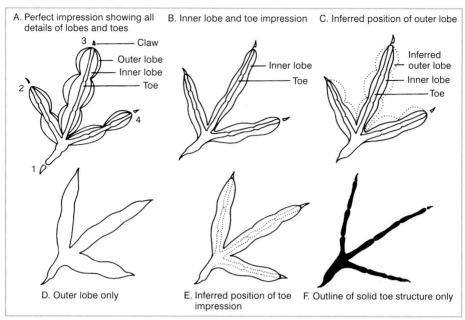

A. Perfect impression showing all details of lobes and toes

3 — Claw
— Outer lobe
— Inner lobe
— Toe
2
4
1

B. Inner lobe and toe impression

— Inner lobe
— Toe

C. Inferred position of outer lobe

Inferred outer lobe
— Inner lobe
— Toe

D. Outer lobe only

E. Inferred position of toe impression

F. Outline of solid toe structure only

Anatomy of Coot track.

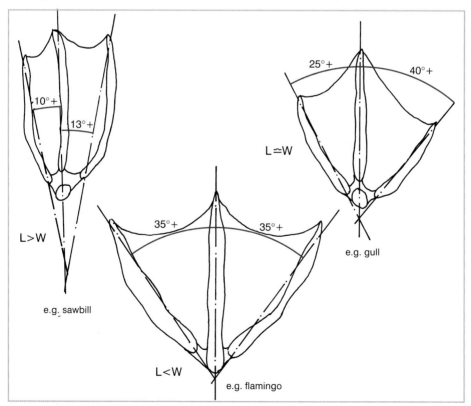

10°+
13°+

L>W

e.g. sawbill

25°+   40°+

L≃W

e.g. gull

35°+   35°+

L<W

e.g. flamingo

Ratios of bipalmate tracks with distal webs

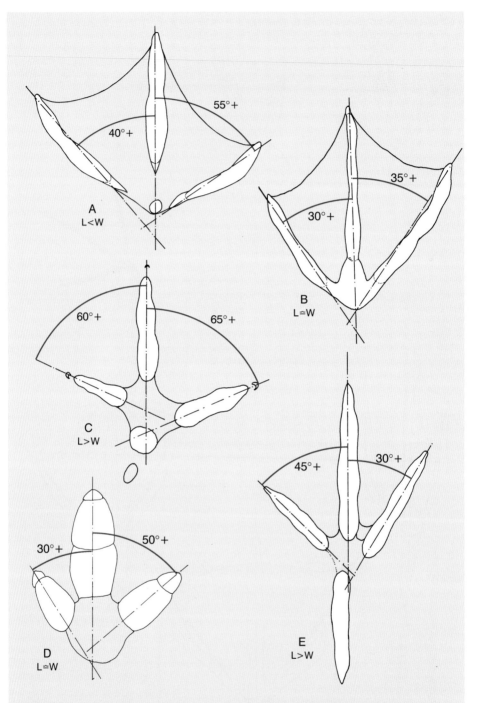

Measuring toe angles. Make a tracing or accurate scaled drawing of the track. On the copy, draw a line vertically down through the centre of toe III, from the centre of the tip to the centre of the base. Repeat for toes II and IV and continue each line downwards until the three lines intersect. Measure the angles produced at the point of intersections.

Trail Morphology

Bird trails are easy to interpret because only two feet are involved with occasional accessory marks, such as wing and tail feather drag. Three main gaits may be identified: (i) Walking, (ii) Running and (iii) Hopping.

Walking At this pace, the tracks may appear in a straight line, more or less astride the median line, as in the pheasants (see A below). In some species the tracks are distinctly straddled, as in pigeons (B), giving two rows. Sometimes the tracks are only slightly straddled, as in gulls (C). Unless the ground is very soft, accessory marks and toe drag are not seen at this pace.

Running The stride increases and toe drag marks are frequently present. Again, the single file or splayed variations may be seen depending on species, although straddle tends to decrease as speed increases.

Hopping In this gait, the tracks are paired directly opposite each other and normally close to the median line. This type of movement (D) is common among the crows.

The position of the tracks relative to the median line varies. Perching birds leave trails with tracks which are parallel to, or turn only slightly towards, the median line. Duck and pigeon tracks point markedly inwards (E), while some species of long-legged wader and some gulls leave tracks which are parallel to the line or even point slightly outwards. Some species move in straight lines, e.g. the gamebirds, while others follow an erratic, weaving course, e.g. wagtails. The actual gait adopted varies within genera and species. Some individuals alternate between walking/running and hopping gaits. Most birds break into a run when they are taking off, and if the ground is soft enough wingtip marks may be seen. Some species with longer tails (e.g. pheasants) may leave drag marks as they walk (F) if the ground is soft, but more often than not bird trails consist simply of tracks.

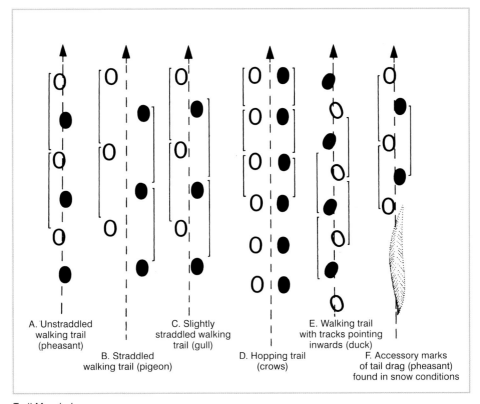

A. Unstraddled walking trail (pheasant)

B. Straddled walking trail (pigeon)

C. Slightly straddled walking trail (gull)

D. Hopping trail (crows)

E. Walking trail with tracks pointing inwards (duck)

F. Accessory marks of tail drag (pheasant) found in snow conditions

Trail Morphology

Lark tracks

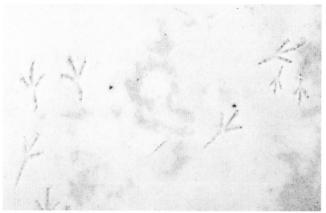

Blackbird and Chaffinch tracks

Carrion Crow and Magpie tracks

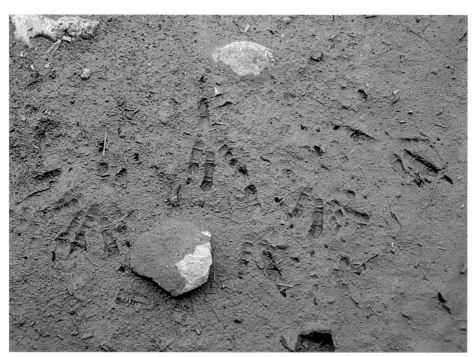

Carrion Crow tracks

Woodpigeon tracks

Turtle Dove tracks

Track descriptions by species

In the following section track descriptions are grouped according to the toe arrangement of the species concerned. The basic groupings are:

I	Perching	**III**	Zygodactyl	**V**	Larger Ground Birds
II	Wader	**IV**	Webbed	**VI**	Miscellaneous (toe arrangements

which do not fit other categories, e.g. Swift, Three-toed Woodpecker)

In some instances tracks have been placed out of their group because of other considerations e.g. size, likely locations etc. For example, Raven (see p73) is placed with group V, as its size is comparable with the other members of that group.

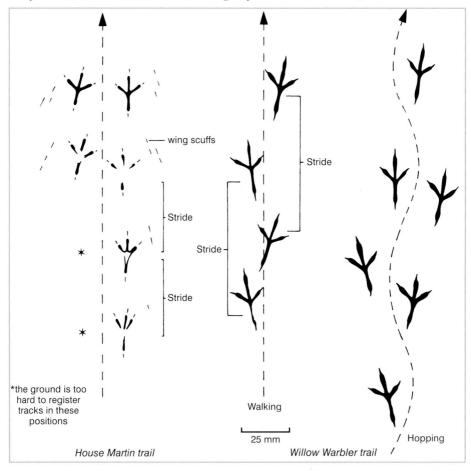

House Martin trail · wing scuffs · Stride · Stride · Stride · *the ground is too hard to register tracks in these positions* · Stride · Stride · Stride · Walking · 25 mm · *Willow Warbler trail* · Hopping

Perching I

House Martin Ia (Mi)

Track Nearly symmetrical. Four-toed. Overall length 20mm; width 15mm excluding small, short, separate claws. Toes III and I about 8mm long. Angle between II and IV about 90°. Very slender tracks and toes, central metatarsal area not very apparent. *Trail* A cross between a clumsy walk and a hop. Wing marks frequently present. The widely straddled tracks turn slightly inwards and a stride of about 40mm is taken. Often found, like Swallow, when collecting mud for nest building.

Willow Warbler Ia (S)

Track Symmetrical. Four-toed. Overall length 28mm, width 18mm. Slender tracks, with toe ends

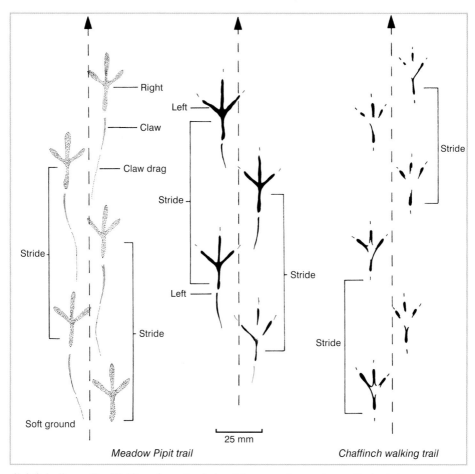

slightly bulbous. Toe III 12mm long, toe I about the same. Long, sharp attached claws, especially on toe I. Angle between II and IV less than 90°. Whole track tends to be uniformly impressed. *Trail* Walks quickly on ground. Tracks slightly straddled and tend to point outwards. Stride about 35mm.

Meadow Pipit Ia (S)

Track Symmetrical. Four-toed. Overall length up to 35mm, width 20mm without claws. The claws on II to IV are very elongated, slender and separate. The claw on I is extremely long and curved. In certain conditions the whole claw, which may be 20mm long, will show, while in others just the extreme tip is apparent as the hard-ground example shows. Toes III and I are about 15mm long, while II and IV are about 12mm long, although in a track without claw marks all toes tend to be of a fairly similar length. Toes may appear fairly broad in soft conditions, or very slim on harder ground. *Trail* Often a fast walk. Tracks straddled, but parallel to the median line. Claw marks often dragged in soft material. Stride 40–45mm, but the very long claws make the tracks appear close together.

Chaffinch Ia (Mi–S)

Track Symmetrical. Four-toed. Toes long and slender. Claws fairly long and detached. Overall length 25–30mm, width 12–15mm. Toe I is up to 12mm long without the claw, while toe III is 10mm long. The central metatarsal area is not deeply impressed, but the toe pads and claws are clear. Tracks are fairly common as the bird spends a lot of time on the ground. *Trail* Normally moves with a fast walk in which short strides are taken. Tracks are only slightly straddled and parallel to the median line. The stride is 35mm. Sometimes hops, leaving paired tracks 50–55mm apart.

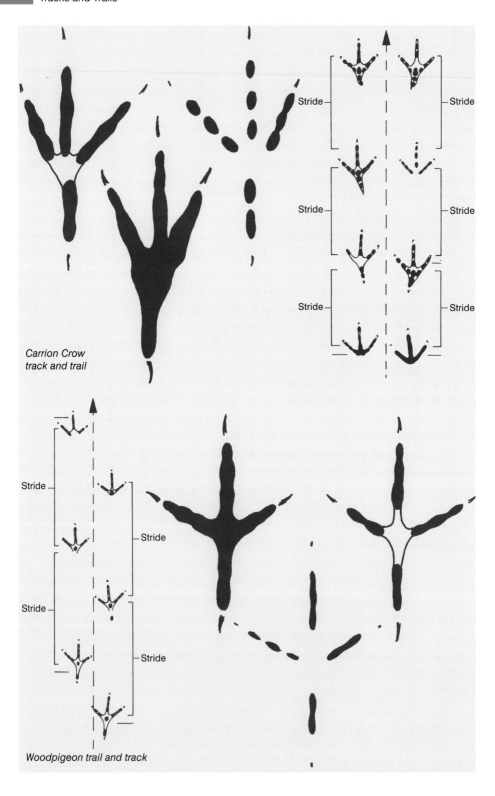

Carrion Crow
track and trail

Stride

Stride

Stride

Stride

Stride

Stride

Stride

Stride

Stride

Stride

Stride

Stride

Woodpigeon trail and track

Crow Ib (Me)

Track Asymmetrical. Small, always four-toed. Toe I slightly offset from central line and approximately 25mm long, against the 30mm of toe III. Overall length 65mm, width 35mm excluding claws. Toes show phalangial and interphalangial pads, central metatarsal area small. Angle between toes II and IV less than 70°. Three forward toes have small, pointed detached claws while the claw on toe I is very long and sharp. *Trail* Either a walking or a hopping gait, with the tracks distinctly paired. Stride 300–500mm when hopping. Toe III tends to turn under and inwards, and this is very obvious in the trail.

Woodpigeon Ib (Me)

Track Asymmetrical. Four-toed. Toe I set to one side. Overall length 60mm, width 40mm without claws. Toe III up to 30mm long, toe IV up to 25mm. Toe imprints fairly broad, claws long and detached but rounded. Central metatarsal area fairly large, phalangial and interphalangial lobes often clear. Angle between II and IV less then 70°. *Trail* Normally a walk with the tracks straddled and pointing distinctly inwards towards the median line. Stride 60–130mm.

Kestrel Ia (Me)

Track Symmetrical. Small, always four-toed. Overall length up to 45mm; width 25mm without the short, sturdy, sharp detached claws which are present on all four toes. Toe III about 15mm long, toe I about 18mm. Toes II and IV relatively short. Small central metatarsal area is not prominent, phalangial pads are distinct and deeply impressed. Track long, narrow and rather slender. *Trail* In common with most other raptors, little time is spent on the ground and only odd groups of tracks will be found, normally in a straddled walk or hop.

Kestrel track

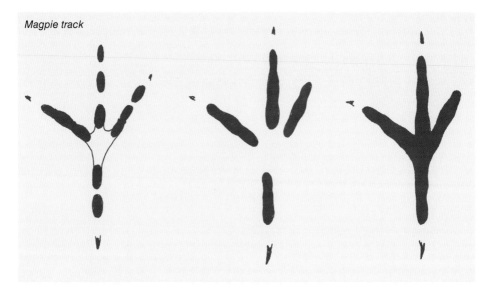

Magpie track

Magpie Ib (S)
Track Asymmetrical. Track four-toed, toe III tending to turn under and inwards as in other crows. Overall length up to 50mm, width 30mm. Toe III up to 20mm long, toe I up to 15mm. Phalangial pads distinct on all toes. Angle between II and IV very small. Claw marks small, sharp and detached on II to IV, very long, sharp and detached on I. *Trail* Walk or hop. Similar to all other crow trails, tracks tending to turn inwards. Stride 150–230mm.

Sparrowhawk Ia (Me)
Track Almost symmetrical. Four-toed. Overall length, including claws which normally show, 65–70mm; width 35–40mm. Toe III very long (30mm) and slender; toe II (15–18mm) slightly shorter than IV (20mm). Toe I short (10mm) and relatively thick, with a very well-developed distal lobe or hallux. All claws long, slender and detached, with claw I exceptionally long. Toes II to IV have a well-developed distal pad, with an even larger one on the phalanx below. This is often deeply impressed. The central metatarsal area often shows – in common with other birds of prey – as a very broad impression. Central area is often deeply impressed. Toe pads and claw tips are always obvious. *Trail* Little time is spent on the ground. The gait is a clumsy walk with partial hopping motion. Stride 120-150mm. The example here shows a range in quality of tracks as the bird crossed from dry sand through very wet silt. The long hind claw and toe I may be displaced sideways.

Blackbird Ia (Me)
Track Almost symmetrical. Four-toed. Very slender. Overall length up to 55mm, width 30mm. Toe III over 20mm, toe I about 20mm. No obvious metatarsal impression, all toes slightly curved with central pad areas and tips most deeply impressed. Very small attached claws on the three forward-pointing toes. Claw on toe I longer and detached. *Trail* Walk, run or hop. Slightly straddled, with toes III and I tending to turn slightly inwards. Stride about 70mm; hopping stride up to 100mm.

House Sparrow Ia (Mi–S)
Track Symmetrical and four-toed. Toe II only slightly shorter than IV. Overall length 25-30mm, width about 15mm. Toe I about 12mm long, as is toe III. The track is characterised by very slender, elongated toes with short, blunt claw marks. The central metatarsal pad and distal pads are prominent. Although this species spends a lot of time on the ground it is extremely light and, while individual and small groups of tracks are common, trails are less so. *Trail* The normal gait is a hop. At a slow pace the stride is 50-70mm, but at speed 110mm may be cleared. The paired tracks are straddled and parallel to the median line.

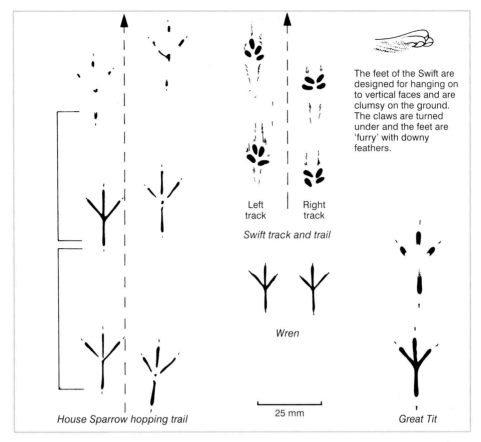

The feet of the Swift are designed for hanging on to vertical faces and are clumsy on the ground. The claws are turned under and the feet are 'furry' with downy feathers.

Left track | Right track

Swift track and trail

Wren

25 mm

House Sparrow hopping trail

Great Tit

Great Tit Ia (Mi)

Track Symmetrical and four-toed. Overall length about 25mm without the long, pointed detached claw marks, and up to 35mm with them. The central metatarsal area does not often show, and the distal toe pads are slightly lobed. Difficult to distinguish from most other tits and, indeed, from small passerine species in general. *Trail* Hopping gait, leaving paired tracks 50–70mm apart in an indistinct trail.

Wren Ia (Mi)

Track Small, symmetrical and four-toed. Despite the small size, it is relatively large for such a tiny bird. Toe I is relatively short compared with other small passerine tracks. Overall length 20–25mm including the short, sharp claw marks. Although the bird spends a lot of time on the ground, tracks are not common because of its small size and the leafy substrate on which it spends much of that time. *Trail* Hopping trail with a stride of 40–60mm, although the bird often 'flits', landing and then flying on before landing again, so that often only single pairs or even solitary tracks are found.

Miscellaneous VI

Swift VI (Mi)

Track Very rare, as the bird will not land on the ground through choice. The track consists of the tops of four strong turned-under claws, which appear like four irregular commas covering an area of about 8mm by 8mm. All toes point forward, and no other details of the feather-covered feet show. *Trail* The bird is almost helpless on the ground, and partly hops and partly drags itself with its wings. It is not possible to discuss gait or stride. Claw and body marks are apparent on very soft ground, but it is extremely rare to find tracks since the bird is at home in the air and the hooked feet are really designed for hanging on to vertical faces.

Wader IIA

Ringed Plover IIa (S)

Track Slightly asymmetrical. Three-toed. Overall length about 24mm, width 28mm. Toe III 18mm long. Small central metatarsal area not always prominent, toes relatively broad. Angle between II and IV over 120°. Very short, blunt claw marks joined to track. *Trail* Walking trail typical of other waders. Tracks parallel to median line, slightly straddled and about 50–80mm apart.

Curlew IIba (S/M)

Track Nearly symmetrical. Usually three-toed, with an angle of over 120° between II and IV. Toe III is 35-40mm long. Overall length 55mm, width 60mm; toes II and IV of similar length (30mm), and an equal angle between II and III and IV and III. In soft ground the entire track outline shows, including a sometimes well-developed proximal web between toes III and IV. The toes are slender, slightly lobed and do not taper. The central metatarsal area is small and does not show on hard or dry ground. Claw marks obvious, very slender, elongated and attached. *Trail* Walk or run, with the tracks in a straight line, slightly straddled but not pointing inwards. Stride up to 250mm.

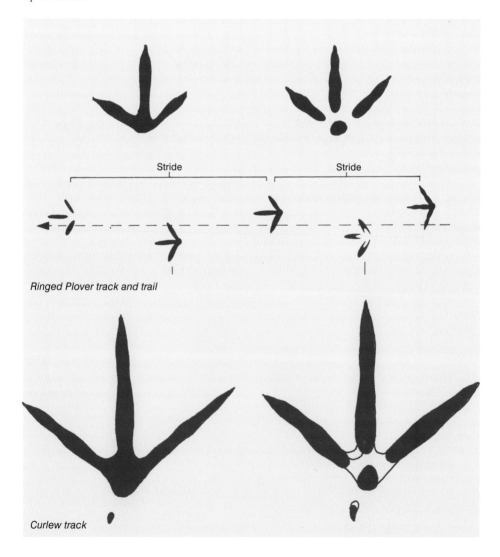

Ringed Plover track and trail

Curlew track

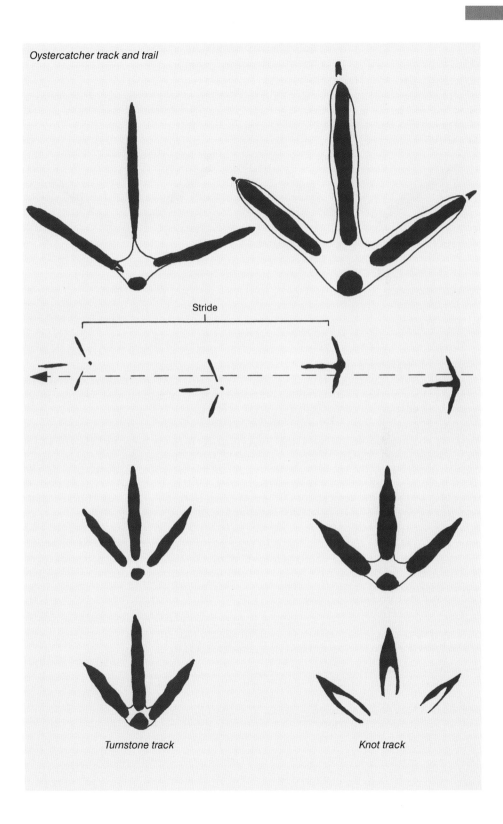

Oystercatcher track and trail

Stride

Turnstone track

Knot track

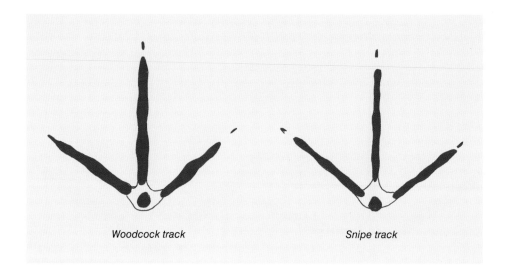

Woodcock track   Snipe track

Shanks and larger sandpipers (*Tringa*) IIa (S)
Track Symmetrical. Normally three-toed, although the much-reduced toe I may occasionally show. Very broad toes, tips deeply impressed. Heel rounded and not pronounced. Overall length 45mm, width 35mm. Toe III over 30mm long. Angle between toes II and IV about 70°. Toes spread out at distal ends, with very small pronounced and attached claws. *Trail* Tracks tend to lie on median lines, with no inward turn and little straddle. Normal gaits are walk and run. Stride variable, but normally less than 200mm.

Oystercatcher IIb (S)
Track Symmetrical. Small, with three toes. Angle between II and IV over 150°. Overall length 45mm, width 60mm. Toe III 30-35mm long, toes II and IV 25mm long. Very small central metatarsal area, which may be obvious in wet conditions but missing on hard ground. Toes very slender and slightly lobed. Very slim, elongated and separate claws sometimes show, as does the very small proximal web between toes III and IV. *Trail* Normally a fast walk. Tracks slightly straddled across median line, but parallel to it. Stride between 100mm and 200mm.

Turnstone IIa IIb (S)
Track Symmetrical; three- or four-toed. Overall length approximately 30–40mm. Width 30–35mm. Toe III 25mm, the long metatarsal pad shows well. Webs absent, toes flattened, and broad angle between toes II and IV (about 80°). Short blunt claw marks attached to toes, inner toe slightly smaller than outer.

Knot IIa IIb (S)
Track Symmetrical; three-toed. Length 35mm; width, 45mm. Toe III 24–26mm long. Metatarsal pads often show webs present between toes II, III and IV. Toes are broad and flattened, angle between toes II and IV 110°. Short blunt claws, inner toe slightly smaller than outer.

Woodcock IIa (Me)
Track Three-toed symmetrical track. Toe III up to 43mm. Overall length 45mm, width 50mm. Angle between toes II and IV 105°. Webs absent, toes long and slender, metatarsal pad small and prominent. Outer and inner toe very similar in length (although inner marginally smaller) – both are smaller than central toe.

Snipe IIa (Me)
Track Three-toed symmetrical track. Toe III up to 39mm, overall length approximately 40mm, width 50mm. Angle between toes II and IV 100°. Webs absent, toes long and slender. Metatarsal pad small and prominent, outer toe longer than inner toe. Claw marks sharp and narrow.

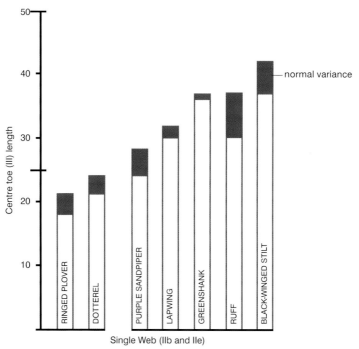

Centre toe III length of waders

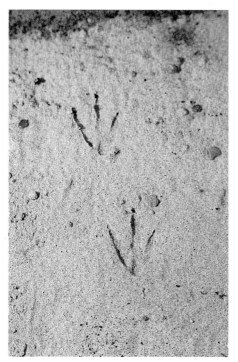

Curlew trail

Oystercatcher trail

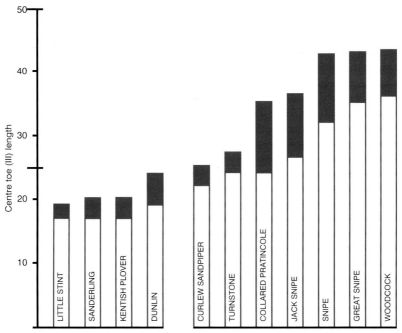

Centre toe III length of waders

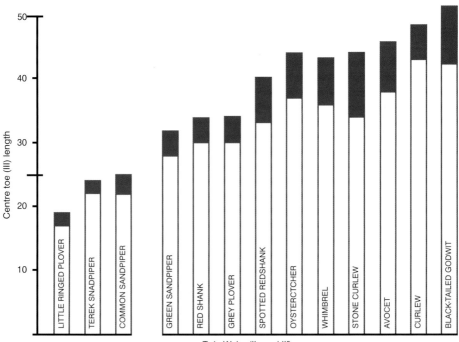

Centre toe III length of waders

Zygodactyl III

Osprey IIIb (Me)
Track Asymmetrical. Four-toed with toes II and III diverging. Phalangeal pads large and distinctive and in exceptional conditions tubercules are very prominent on the toes. Claw marks long and slender. Length 55–65mm, width 30–35mm without claws

Barn Owl IIIb (S)
Track Asymmetrical. Four-toed zygodactyl. Toe IV rotates backwards from a side position, so that the tracks show toes II and III pointing forward and toes I and IV pointing backwards. Length up to 45mm; width up to 30mm without the rounded, elongated separate claws. Phalangial pads and tubercules prominent on toes. Large central area between toes not deeply impressed in track. ***Trail*** Little time spent on ground. When a trail is found the tracks are close behind each other, but widely splayed and tending to turn outwards. Stride up to 70mm.

Tawny Owl IIIb (S)
Track Track and trail very similar to those of Barn Owl, although the dimensions are marginally greater. In the splayed walking trail, the tracks follow a curving course with a stride from 65mm to about 130mm. The tracks point slightly outwards.

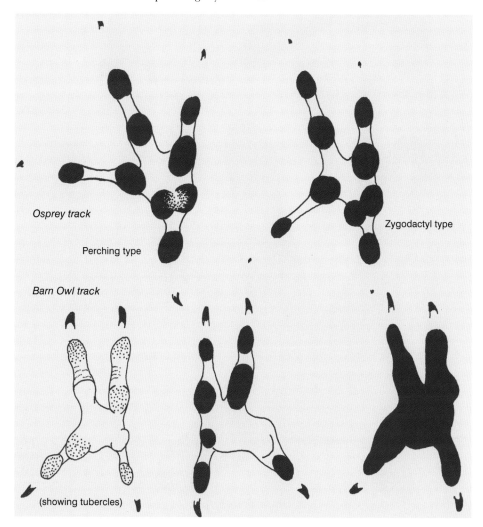

Osprey track

Perching type

Zygodactyl type

Barn Owl track

(showing tubercles)

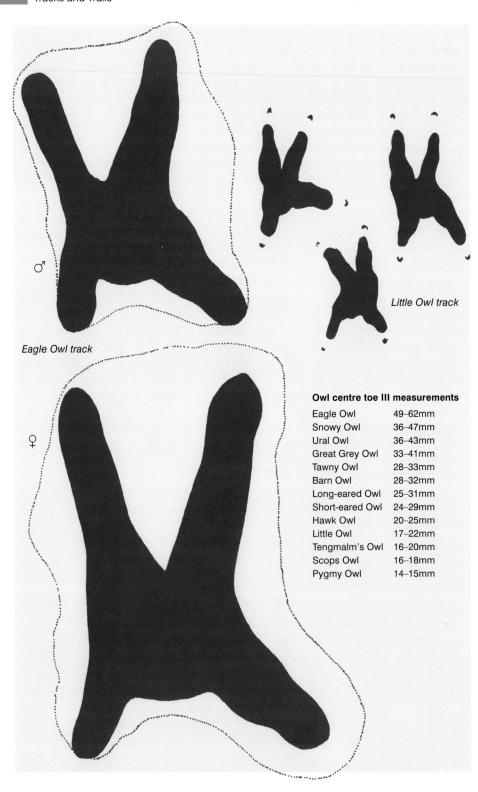

♂

Eagle Owl track

Little Owl track

♀

Owl centre toe III measurements

Eagle Owl	49–62mm
Snowy Owl	36–47mm
Ural Owl	36–43mm
Great Grey Owl	33–41mm
Tawny Owl	28–33mm
Barn Owl	28–32mm
Long-eared Owl	25–31mm
Short-eared Owl	24–29mm
Hawk Owl	20–25mm
Little Owl	17–22mm
Tengmalm's Owl	16–20mm
Scops Owl	16–18mm
Pygmy Owl	14–15mm

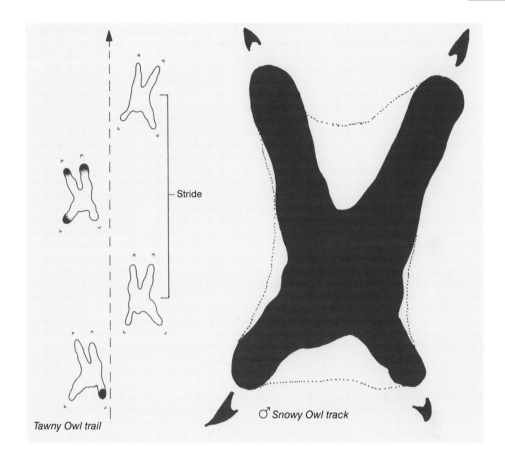

Stride

Tawny Owl trail

♂ Snowy Owl track

Little Owl IIIb (Mi–S)
Track The tracks, which are minute to small, are very similar to those of other owls and, as in all other owl species, are not common. Overall length 25-35mm. Toe IV frequently almost at right angles to the other toes, rather than distinctly pointing backwards as in many other species of owl. Claws distinct, but short.

Snowy Owl IIIb (L)
Track Asymmetrical. Four-toed. The splay between toes II and IV is wide. Toe IV is large and set back. Overall length up to 100mm (female), up to 80mm (male). Claws do not always impress, since they are short and emerge from the top of the distal pads, which are deeply impressed. The track often appears very large, and shows few details because of the masses of feathers covering the feet. Sometimes only the toe pads are distinct in a large depression. Feather marks are common in soft soil and snow. *Trail* Little time is spent on the ground, but both a running and walking gait are adopted. In the run, the widely straddled tracks are up to 480mm apart in the female, slightly less in the male. In the hopping trail, the paired tracks are about 350mm apart.

Eagle Owl IIIb (L–E)
Track Asymmetrical. Four-toed, with toes II and III diverging. Toe IV long and set to one side. Overall length up to 105mm without the long separate claw imprints. The claws are very long and curved on toes II to IV. Toe I and claw are sometimes indistinct, with claw almost missing. The distal pads are prominent, but other details tend to be obscured. The central metatarsal area is not obvious. *Trail* Trails sometimes found in snow in northern boreal forests. The tracks tend to be dragged and obscured when the bird first lands. The normal gait is a running hop, with the straddled tracks almost in pairs and strides of 150mm to 400mm between them.

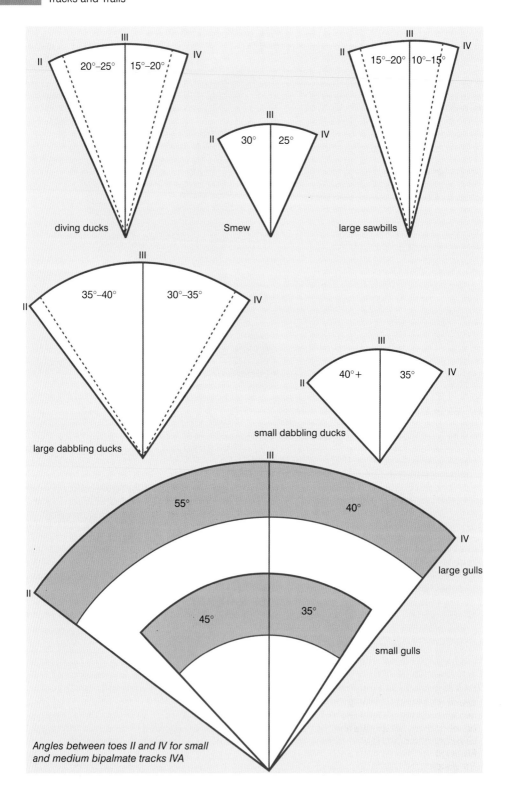

Angles between toes II and IV for small and medium bipalmate tracks IVA

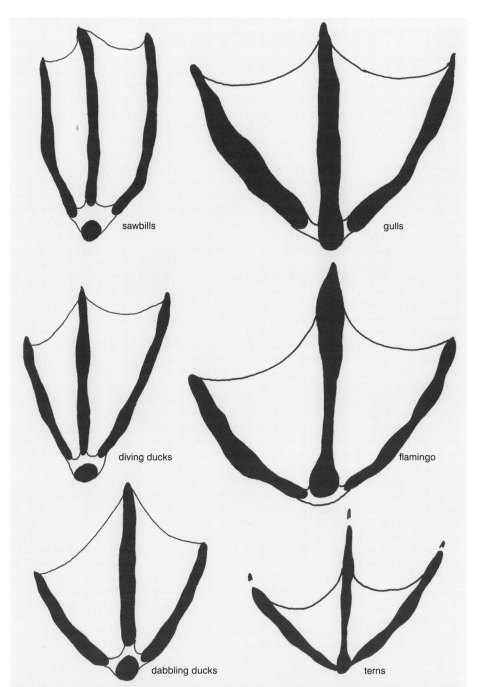

Web track types. Reveals the diversity of web angle within bipalmate tracks. In order of increasing angle the sawbills are the narrowest group, followed by diving ducks, large dabbling ducks, small dabbling ducks, small gulls and large gulls. These are all distal webbed tracks. Geese compared to similar sized gull tracks are obviously narrower than gull tracks. Terns have mesial webbing and the Flamingo has an intermediate form. Totipalmate tracks have webbing between toes I, II, III, and IV. Continued on page 52.

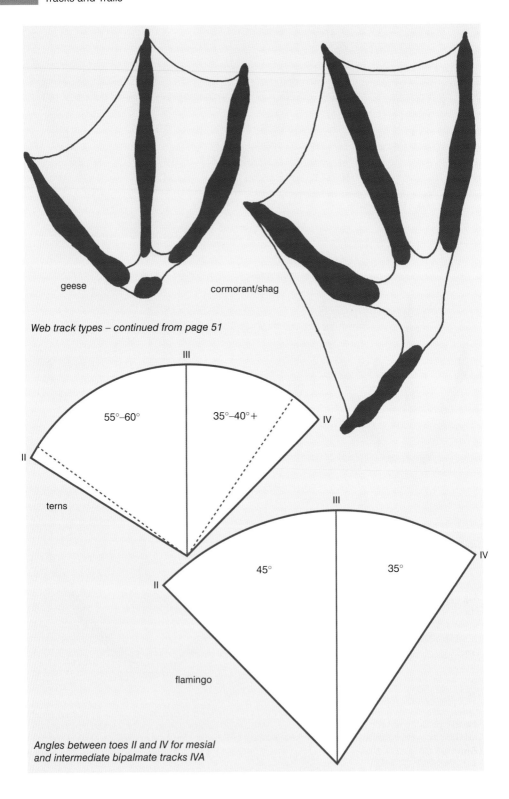

geese

cormorant/shag

Web track types – continued from page 51

terns

55°–60°   35°–40°+

II

III

IV

flamingo

45°   35°

II

III

IV

Angles between toes II and IV for mesial
and intermediate bipalmate tracks IVA

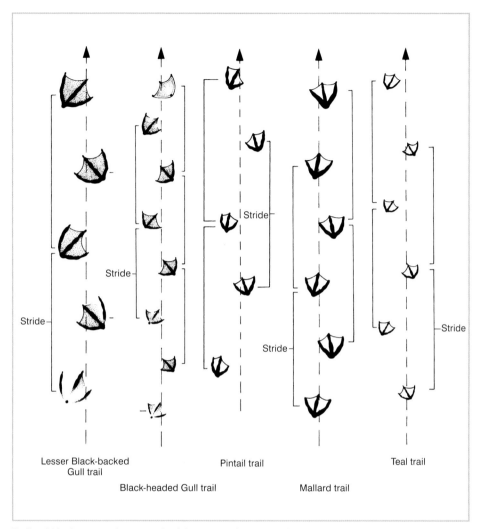

Trails of bipalmate tracks – note the 'pigeon-toed' position of the tracks

Webbed IVA

Wigeon and Pochard IVa (S–Me)
The Wigeon, which is a surface-feeding vegetarian, and the Pochard, which dives and concentrates on crustaceans, are of very similar size, as are their tracks. Those of Pochard tend to be more slender, but this is not always evident in the field.
Track Asymmetrical. Three- or four-toed. Toe I much reduced. Overall length without toe I about 55mm, width 50mm. As with all ducks, toes II and IV tend to become parallel towards the front. There is a well developed web between toes II to IV. *Trail* The gait is a walk or waddle, with the tracks straddled and pointing inwards. Stride about 180mm.

Pintail IVa (Me)
Track The tracks and trail of this large duck are not diagnostic to species, but tend to be large with heavy features, although detail, e.g. lobing on the toes, is not coarse. Overall length up to 65mm without the minute toe I; width about 60mm. *Trail* A walk or fast waddle, with strides of up to 250mm.

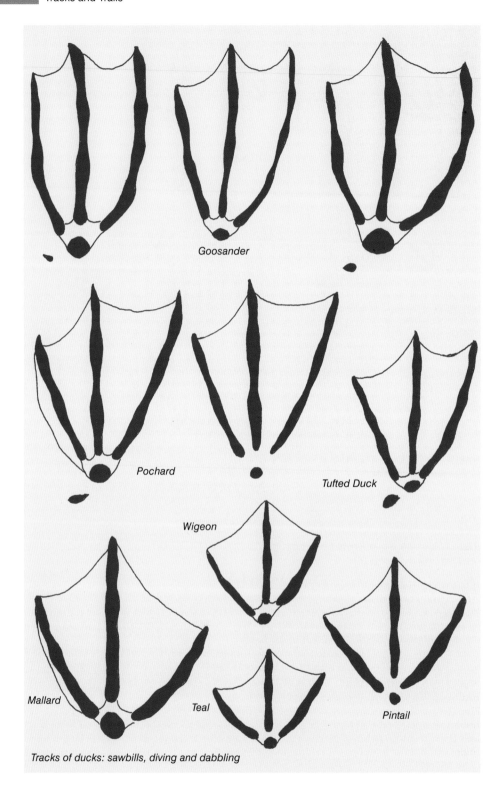

Goosander

Pochard

Tufted Duck

Wigeon

Mallard

Teal

Pintail

Tracks of ducks: sawbills, diving and dabbling

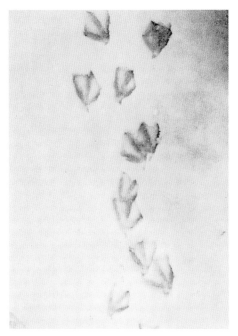

Mallard tracks   Black-headed Gull tracks

Teal IVa (S)

Track Slightly asymmetrical. Three- or four-toed track. If toe I is present, it is very reduced and rather elongated. Concave webs are present between toes II to IV. Overall length 45–50mm (excluding toe 1), width about 55mm. Very small metatarsal area, and the toes slender with II and IV tending to curve inwards towards the front. The small, rounded and attached claws are normally obvious and protrude beyond the web. *Trail* Usual, straddled, duck walk with the tracks turning distinctly inwards. Tracks evenly spaced, with a stride of 180–240mm.

Goosander IVa (Me)

Track Slightly asymmetrical three- or four-toed track. Angle between toe II and IV 25°; II & III 10°; III & IV 15°. The fourth toe sometimes shows as a small depression. Toe III 40–45mm, outer toes gently curving inwards. Length of track 60mm, width up to 35mm.

Mallard IVa (Me)

Track Asymmetrical. Three- or four-toed; toe I much reduced. Overall length about 60mm without toe I, width 55–60mm. Toe III about 50mm long. Toes very slightly lobed, with II and IV curving distinctly at the back so that the tips are almost parallel with an angle of less than 70° between them. Distal web, which is asymmetrical as the area between II and III is larger than that betwwen III and IV. The whole toe area is deeply impressed, and the claws are very small, but often distinct. *Trail* Normally a walk or waddle, with the tracks straddled and distinctly inward-pointing. Stride about 200mm.

Webbed IVA–IVC

Terns IVc (S–Me)

Track Asymmetrical, but only slightly. Normally three toes, rarely four. Some variation in the size between species, but as a general guide the overall length is about 50mm and width about the same. Toe III is elongated, although only the distal end is deeply impressed. The length from the very distinct metatarsal is over 40mm, while II and IV are less than 30mm. A web runs from the tips of toes II and IV which joins toe III in a mesial position so that 10–15mm of the toe extends clear of the web. Claws short and attached, angle between II and IV more than 120°. *Trail* Tracks straddled, pointing slightly inwards, and about 80mm to 150mm apart in the normal fast walking gait.

Black-headed Gull IVa (S)

Track Symmetrical. Three-toed. Overall length 35–40mm, width 40–45mm. Toe III 25–30mm. Toes II to IV at an angle of more than 120°, and do not curve inwards towards their tips. Distal web, joining the tips of the slightly lobed toes, has a straight edge, giving the track a trapezoid shape. Claws small, attached and protrude beyond the web. Small metatarsal area, toes always deeply impressed but web sometimes absent. *Trail* A walk or run, with the tracks fairly close together. Slightly straddled across the median line, the tracks tend to point inwards. Stride 60–130mm.

Godwits (*Limosa*) IVc (Me)

Track Slightly asymmetrical. Sometimes four-toed, but toe I is much reduced and is often absent. Overall length 40-45mm, width 40mm. Toe III, up to 30mm, is elongated as in the terns, but II and IV are not relatively so short. The web occupies a similar mesial position to that in the terns, but does not always appear right to the tips of II and IV. Web area is small, the toes are rather elliptical in shape, and the very short, attached claws are not always apparent. *Trail* Similar to tern, although slightly less straddled and the stride is longer.

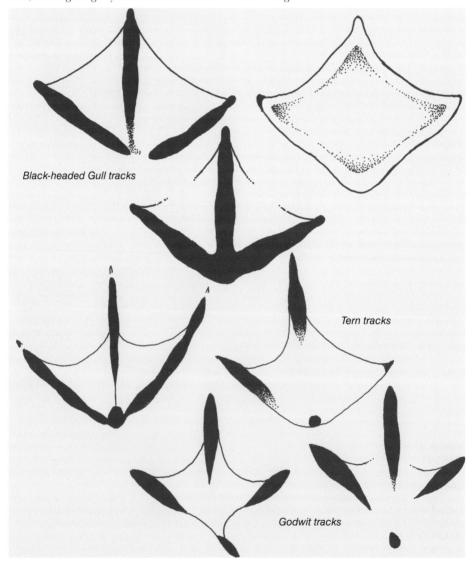

Black-headed Gull tracks

Tern tracks

Godwit tracks

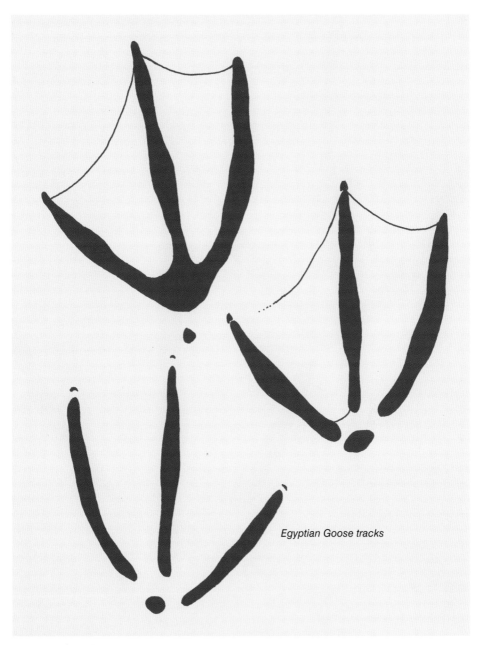

Egyptian Goose tracks

Avocet IVd (Me)
Track Symmetrical and with strong mesial webbing extending from between 2nd and 3rd phalanges of toes II and III, and III and IV. Central toe length between 38–46mm. Hind toe absent in track.

Egyptian Goose IVa–IVb (L)
Track Medium to large track, toe III being between 65–75mm. 80mm long by 65mm wide. Strong distal webbing distinguished from gull of similar size (e.g. Lesser Black-backed) by being relatively narrow.

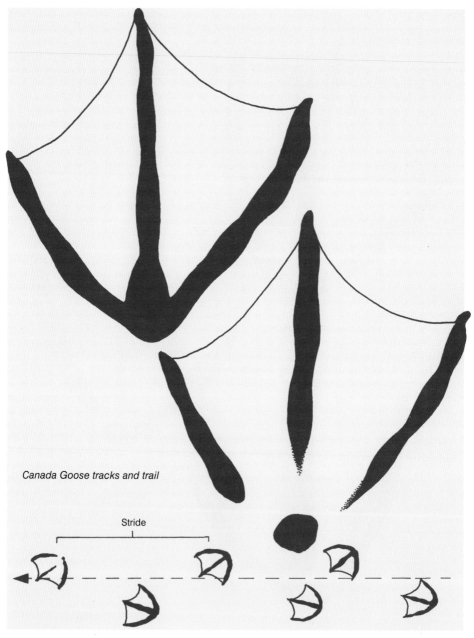

Canada Goose tracks and trail

Stride

Canada Goose IVa (L–E)

Track The asymmetrical tracks lie on the boundary of medium and large. Three-toed, with concave webbing present between toes II to IV. Overall length about 100mm, width 90–95mm. Toe III up to 85mm long, toe IV to 80mm. The toe prints are distinctly lobed, especially at the base of al which merges into the small metatarsal area. Toes II and IV tend to converge at front, the angle between them about 70°. Tracks are generally heavy and deeply impressed, with heavy, rounded and attached claws present. *Trail* Irregularly spaced, heavily straddled and inturned tracks are seen in the normal slow walking trail. The stride is fairly short relative to the size of the bird, being 200–350mm.

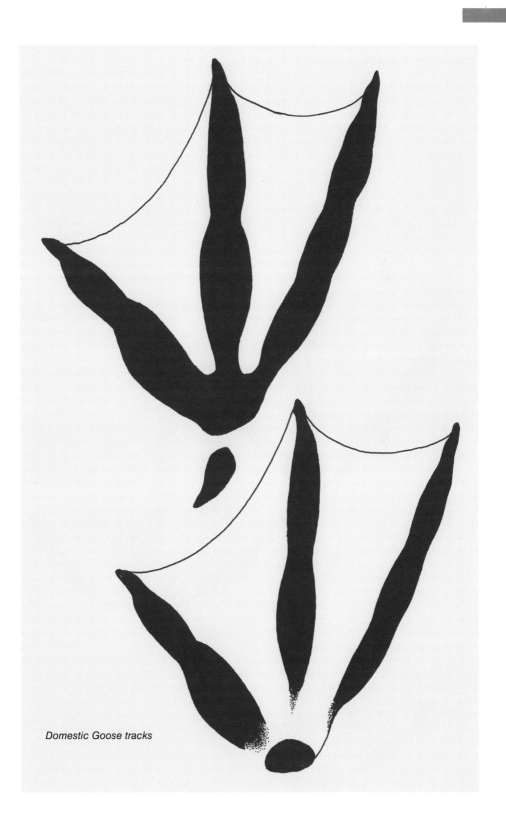

Domestic Goose tracks

Domestic Goose IVb (L–E)

Track Asymmetrical. Toe II is distinctly smaller than IV, and toe I is a small 'comma' no more than 20mm long. Heavy track showing all four toes in soft ground, three on harder conditions. Toe IV is of similar length to III (e.g. 85mm). Overall length up to 120mm, width 90mm. The forward-pointing toes make an angle of less than 90°. Distal webbing is present between toes II to IV, and is wider between II and III than III and IV. Toes are heavy, with small, broad, slightly pointed attached claws. *Trail* Toes turn inward at either the walk or the run. Stride varies from 100mm to 250mm, increasing as the pace increases.

Lesser Black-backed Gull IVa (Me)

Track Asymmetrical. Three-toed. Length 60-65mm, width 70-75mm. Toe III up to 50mm, toe IV only a little shorter. Angle between toes II and IV less than 90°. Tips of toes are straight or only slightly convergent. Central metatarsal area very small. Toes lobed, tending to be thicker at centre than at base or tip. Distal webbing, present even on fairly firm ground, is slightly concave on the margins. The claws are outside the web, and normally show as attached and slightly elongated. *Trail* Walk or run. Tracks close to median line, but tend to point inwards. Stride from 170mm to 450mm.

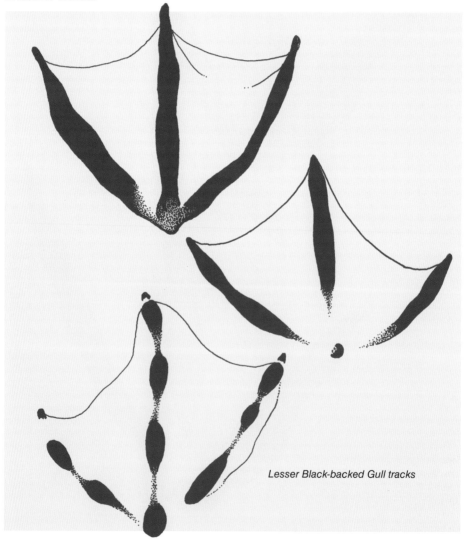

Lesser Black-backed Gull tracks

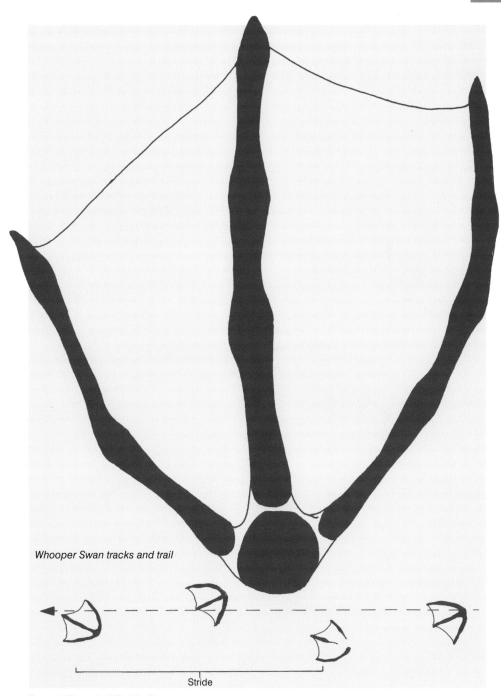

Whooper Swan tracks and trail

Stride

Swans (*Cygnus*) IVb (E–G)

Track Slightly asymmetrical, with toe II a little shorter than IV and the spacing between II and II greater than III and IV. Three- or four-toed tracks. In all swans, the web between II and III is distinct, distal and concave. The toes are long, slender and deeply impressed, with II and IV curving slightly inwards. The claws are short and tend to be rounded and attached. The central metatarsal area is very small. In the Whooper Swan toe I is small (10–20mm), turns inwards and shows only in very soft conditions. The overall length of track is up to 180mm and width to 170mm. Toe III is 150mm long. By contrast, the slightly larger Mute Swan has a track up to 200mm long, toe III up to 160mm and toe I, if present, 20–25mm. Toe III of the smaller Bewick's Swan is up to 120mm long. *Trail* At a walking pace, the tracks turn inwards towards the median line. In Whooper and Mute Swans a stride of 250–350mm is taken. The feet are not lifted far above the ground, and in very soft silt or snow toe III drags, leaving a mark.

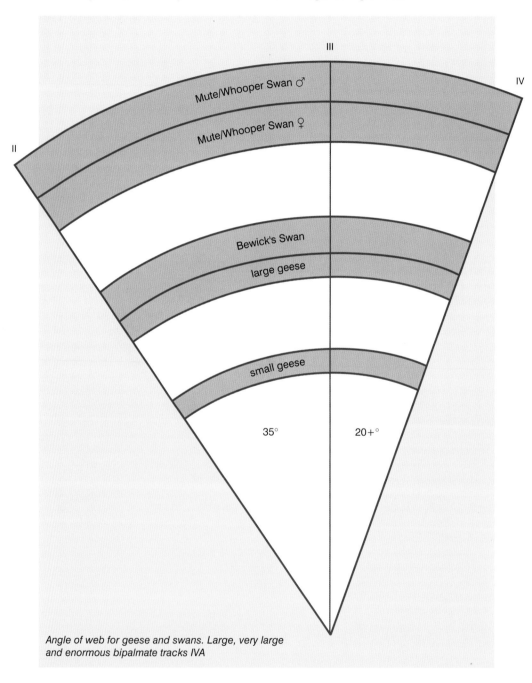

Angle of web for geese and swans. Large, very large and enormous bipalmate tracks IVA

Great Black-backed Gull IVa (L–E)

Track Asymmetrical, very large 'duck' shaped track. Three-toed. Length 85mm; width 110mm, giving a very wide-looking track. Toe IV slightly smaller than II. Angle between toes II and IV 100°. Outer toes curved slightly inwards. Toe III up to 70mm. Claws short and blunt and within web outline.

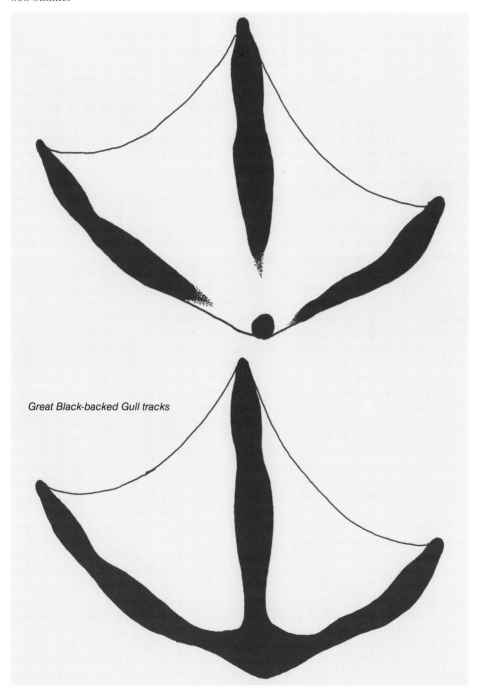

Great Black-backed Gull tracks

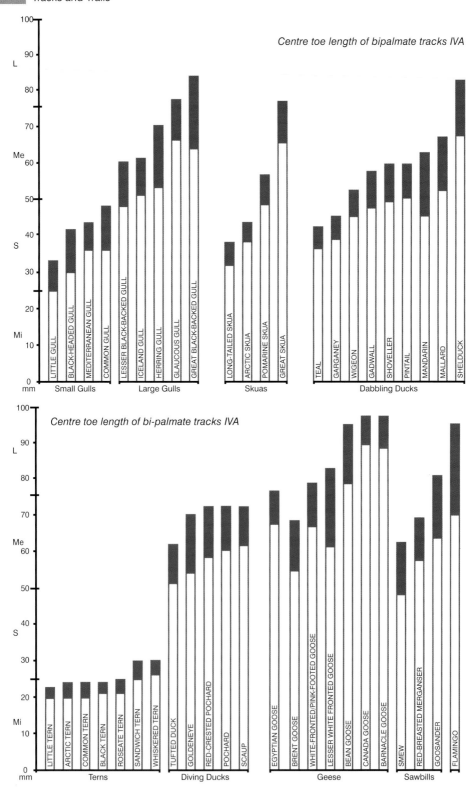

Centre toe length of bipalmate tracks IVA

Centre toe length of bi-palmate tracks IVA

Totipalmate IVB

Pelican IVd (E)

Track Strongly asymmetrical with strong distal webbing between toes I, II, III and IV. Length of entire track from tip of first toe to tip of third up to 150mm, and is therefore in group E enormous. Width from II to IV greater than 90mm. The toe prints are relatively slender.

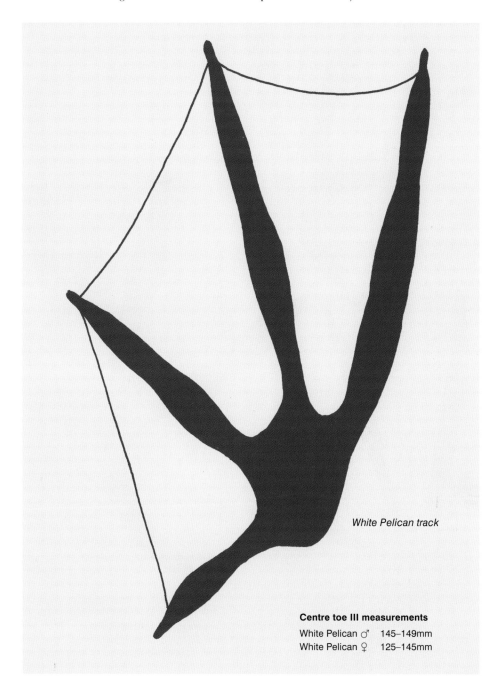

White Pelican track

Centre toe III measurements
White Pelican ♂   145–149mm
White Pelican ♀   125–145mm

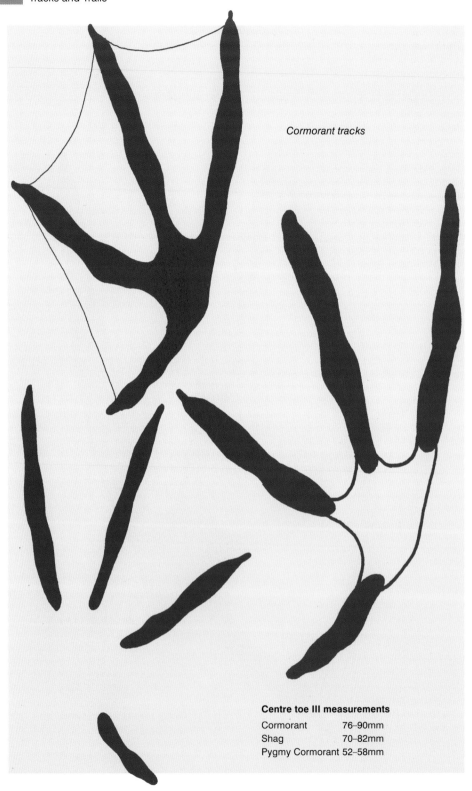

Cormorant tracks

Centre toe III measurements

Cormorant	76–90mm
Shag	70–82mm
Pygmy Cormorant	52–58mm

Cormorant IVd (VI)

Track Asymmetrical and four-toed. Toe I lies to the side of the track, and all toes are linked at their distal ends by webbing (totipalmate). Overall length up to 130mm, width 120mm. Toe IV is the longest (e.g. 110mm) rather than III (e.g. 95mm), as in most species. There are long, pointed detached claws outside the web on all toes. Toe imprints are extremely long and slender, the toes being straight. The metatarsal area is medium in size. SHAG tracks are similar, but slightly smaller. ***Trail*** It is not common to find a trail, since the birds are not at home walking on dry land. If one is found, the tracks are close together and turn slightly inwards. The stride is rarely more than 250mm.

Fringed IVC

Coot IVc (E)

Track Asymmetrical. Large/enormous tracks, almost always showing four toes. Toes very slender, toe I curving inwards. Overall length 140–150mm including the long integral claw on toe 1, but not the smaller, pointed and often detached claws on II to IV. Track width 110–120mm. Toe III is 100–110mm, toe I 35–45mm long. Very small metatarsal area. ***Trail*** The tracks lie very close together and often in a meandering line. They do not point inwards and are sometimes partially registered.

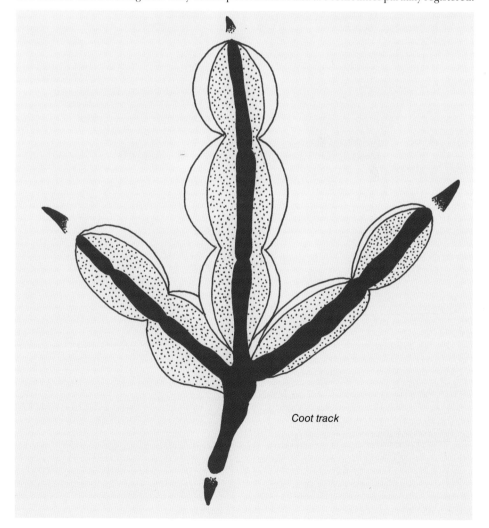

Coot track

Great Crested Grebe IVc (Me)

Track Highly asymmetrical. Length 75mm; width 65mm. Toes broad and flat and relatively smooth-sided without the deep separate lobes of the Coot. Toe IV usually appears longest, but sometimes III looks longer. Claw marks short and blunt. In exceptional circumstances toe I will show (see photo).

Grebe tracks

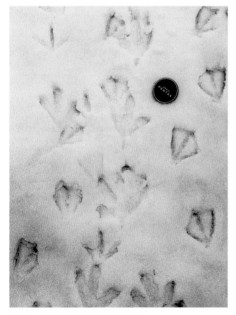

Duck, grebe and Coot tracks

Coot tracks

Larger Ground Birds V

Red Grouse Vc (S)

Track Almost symmetrical in three-toed track, but asymmetrical if the offset toe I is present. Tracks 35mm by 35mm in young. Toes slender with parallel sides. Toe III over 20mm long. Very large, deeply impressed metatarsal area. Small, separate sharp claws show distinctly. Residual proximal web may show between III and IV, more rarely between II and III. ***Trail*** Walking gait shows, as in adult, slightly straddled alternate tracks which do not turn inwards. Stride about 130mm.

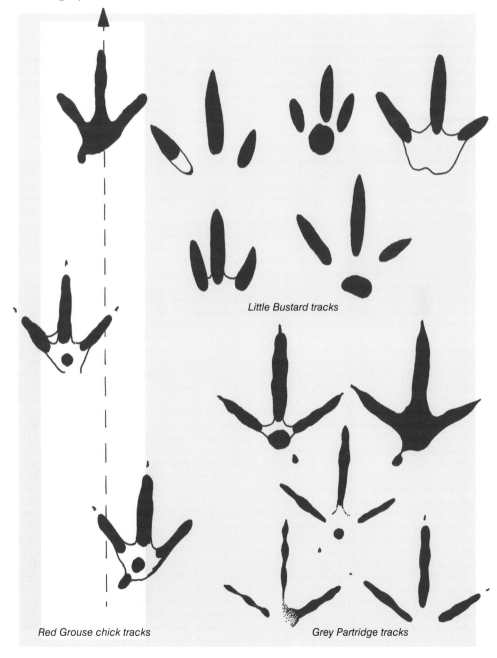

Little Bustard tracks

Red Grouse chick tracks

Grey Partridge tracks

Pheasant Vc (Me)

Track Asymmetrical, with toe II distinctly shorter than IV. Toe I very reduced, lying to one side and sometimes absent. Overall track length 65–75mm and width 60–65mm. Toe III 40–45mm long. Toes fairly slender and very slightly lobed, often with distinct, pointed and fairly large claw marks. Large metatarsal area, which is nearly always distinct when the bird is moving slowly. Tracks often distinct because of high ratio of weight to foot size. *Trail* Walk or run. Tracks astride the median line, or only slightly straddled, tend to point slightly inwards and are often dragged in soft soil or snow. Stride varies according to speed from 90mm to 200mm. At fast speed, only the toe marks show.

Grey Partridge Vc–Vd (S)

Track Four-toed; asymmetrical, symmetrical when only three toes show. Toe I when visible is small and divergent. Overall track length 25–40mm, width 30–35mm. Toes relatively slender with lobed appearance, central toe 39–44mm. Small proximal webs between front toes. Metatarsal pad usually prominent, and claws marks fine and slender.

Little Bustard Vd (S)

Track Three-toed, asymmetrical. Length up to 45mm, width 30mm. Central toe up to 40mm. Track short and deeply-impressed with broad flattened toes. Claws short and blunt and often merge with the toe tip. Sole very distinct, often giving a hand-like appearance.

Great Bustard Vd (L)

Track Slightly asymmetrical. Always three-toed. In common with other terrestrial species, the track is very robust. The toes are thick and tapered and there is a large metatarsal area. Overall length up to 90mm, width 95mm. Toes II to IV at an angle of almost 100°. Toe III up to 60mm long. Broad, slightly pointed and detached claw marks often show. Detail ranges from complete outlines with distinct 'heel' marks in very soft material, to toe and metatarsal impressions in harder material, and toe only tracks when the bird is moving at speed across hard ground. *Trail* Straddled walk or run, with tracks anything up to 900mm apart.

Pheasant tracks

Great Bustard tracks

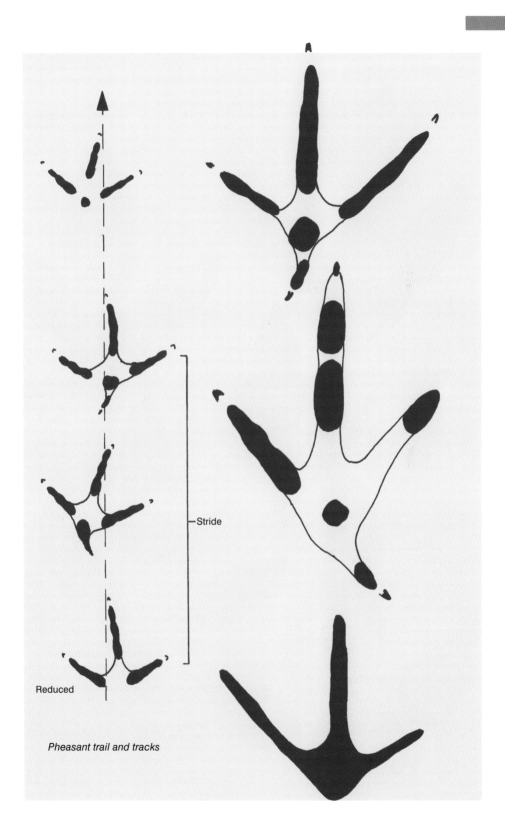

Stride

Reduced

Pheasant trail and tracks

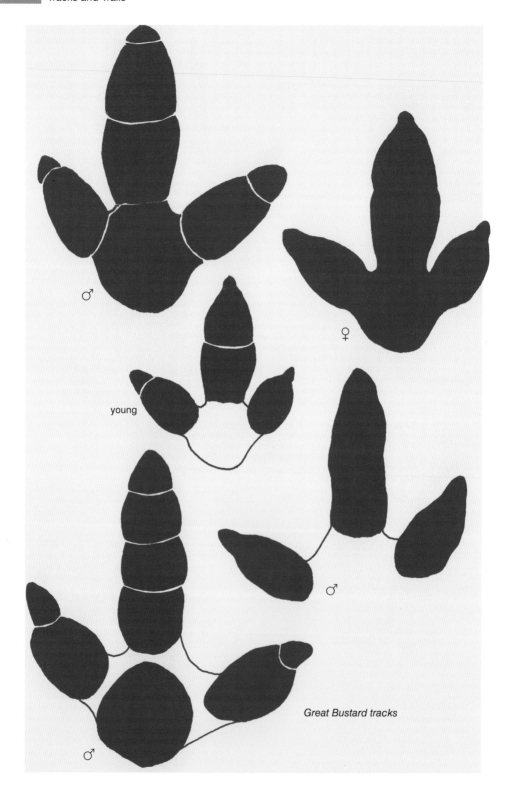

♂

young

♀

♂

♂

Great Bustard tracks

Raven tracks

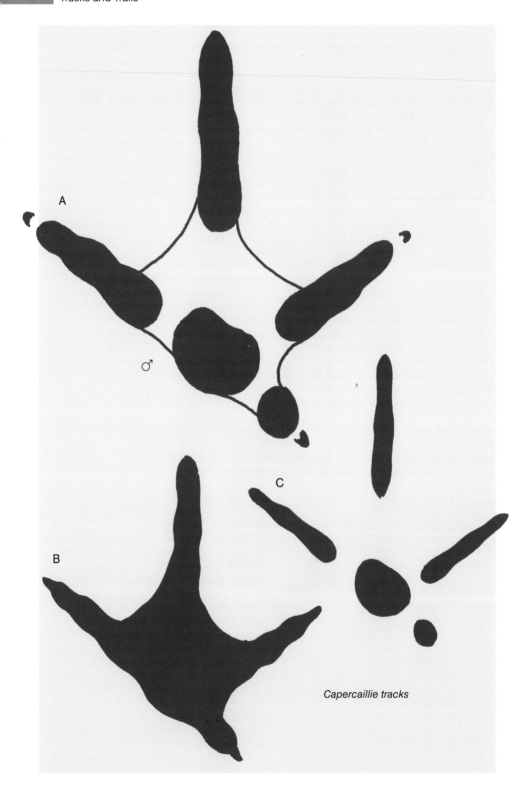

A

♂

C

B

Capercaillie tracks

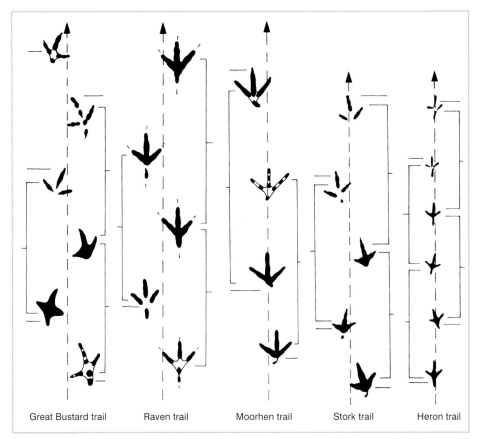

Trails of walking birds (V) to scale

Great Bustard trail	Raven trail	Moorhen trail	Stork trail	Heron trail

Raven Ib (L)
Track Almost symmetrical. Large/medium four-toed tracks which may be up to 140mm long, 70mm wide including the very large pointed separate claws. Toes I and III are very long, up to about 60mm each. Well-developed phalangial and interphalangial pads show clearly in the tracks because the toes tend to close and impress deeply. Angle between toes II and IV less than 90°. Metatarsal area small. *Trail* In a walking trail, the tracks occur singly in a curving line with a stride of 400 to 650mm. A hopping trail, with the tracks in pairs, generally shows the groups about 500mm apart.

Capercaillie Vc (L–E)
Track Asymmetrical. Sometimes with three, but normally with four toes. Whole track very square, with a large central area. Large metatarsal pad, with toe I very short and set distinctly to one side, under toe II. In soft conditions all toes show, with distinct broad pads and small, heavy, detached rounded claws (A, p74). Complete tracks in the larger males are up to 110mm square, in females the same tracks are about 60–70mm square. Toes are short relative to the metatarsal area, being no more than 60mm long (male). Toes II and IV are about 150° apart. On harder ground only the toe-pad outlines and metatarsal pad show (B), and when the bird moves at speed only the three front toes show. In very soft soil or thin snow, the track may appear as a featureless black outline (C). *Trail* At a walking pace, the tracks are close together with a stride of 200–300mm. The tracks are slightly straddled across the median line and turn inwards. The outlines may be blurred in soft conditions. In mating displays the male moves around quickly, dragging wing feathers, so the tracks may become confused and furrows be left by the wings.

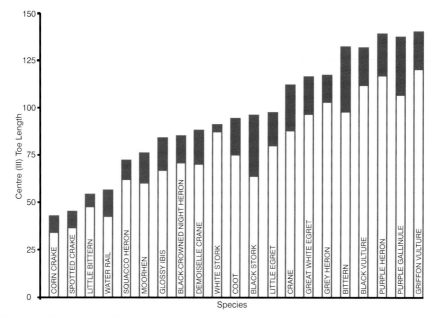

Centre toe lengths of walking group V

Raven tracks

Grey Heron tracks (the larger set)

Wild Turkey Vc (L–vL)

Track Four toes normally present. Toes II to IV almost symmetrical, but the reduced toe I is set to one side. Very long and heavy toe III. In the larger male the overall track is 135mm long, 85mm wide, with toe III 90mm long. Toe I is 25mm long, but very broad. Track of female 125mm long, up to 100mm wide. Toe III 75mm long, and toe I 25mm long, but very narrow. In the male toe III is very heavy. The angle between toes II and IV is less than 100°. Rounded heavy attached claws are normally present in the track. The metatarsal pad is not pronounced. *Trail* Erratic, curving lines of widely straddled tracks from walking or running gaits. Tracks point straight forward, and a stride of 150mm to 400mm is taken.

Night Heron Va (Me)

Track Asymmetrical. Medium/large. Normally four-toed, although toe I may be missing on hard ground. Toe III 55-65mm long, toe I 25-35mm. Overall length up to 110mm, width 55mm. Toes II and IV point distinctly forward. Small proximal web often present between III and IV. Metatarsal area relatively small, and may be deeply impressed or absent depending on soil conditions. Claws not always apparent, but if present are long, narrow, slightly pointed and detached. *Trail* Tracks in a straight line at the walking gait, do not straddle the median line. Tracks point straight forward, and strides of between 400mm and 500mm are taken at a slow walk, increasing to 800mm if the bird moves at speed.

Little Bittern Va (Me)

Track Asymmetrical, the hind toe is markedly offset from the line of toe III. Overall track length 70mm, width up to 60mm. There is a small proximal web between toes III and IV, toe III length 45-54mm.

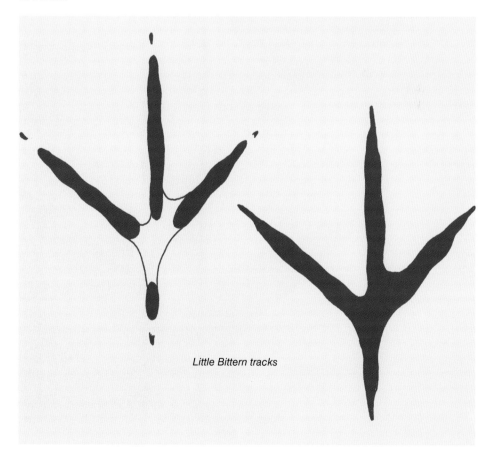

Little Bittern tracks

Wild Turkey tracks

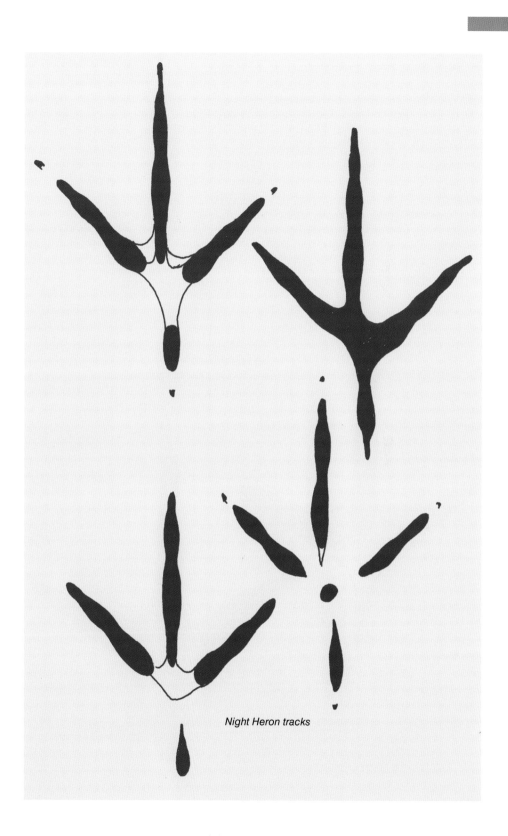

Night Heron tracks

Glossy Ibis Vb (Me–L)

Track Very similar to those of the Night Heron and Little Egret. Nearly symmetrical. Normally four-toed. Toe I relatively long. Angle between toes II and IV about 120°. Toe III about 50mm long, toe 1 25-35mm long. Overall length 80-90mm, width 65-70mm. Claws small, blunt and attached. In soft ground the entire track outline shows, including a small proximal web between toes III and IV. The toes are slender and only slightly lobed, tending to be largest at the distal ends. Generally, all parts of the track are uniformly deeply impressed. *Trail* The normal gait is a walk or run. Tracks slightly straddled, but parallel to the median line. Stride between 200mm and 400mm depending on pace.

Little Egret Va (L)

Track Similar morphologically to other heron tracks. Asymmetrical and four-toed. Medium to large. Overall length up to 120mm, width to 85mm. Toes II to IV point distinctly forward. Small proximal webs are sometimes present between toes III and IV. Metatarsal area is normally deeply impressed. The claws are long, narrow, pointed and detached. *Trail* Normally moves at a slow walking, or stalking pace, although can move at high speed. Tracks are slightly straddled, but are parallel to the median line. At a slow walk the stride is 350-450mm; at higher speeds it may be over 650mm.

Glossy Ibis tracks

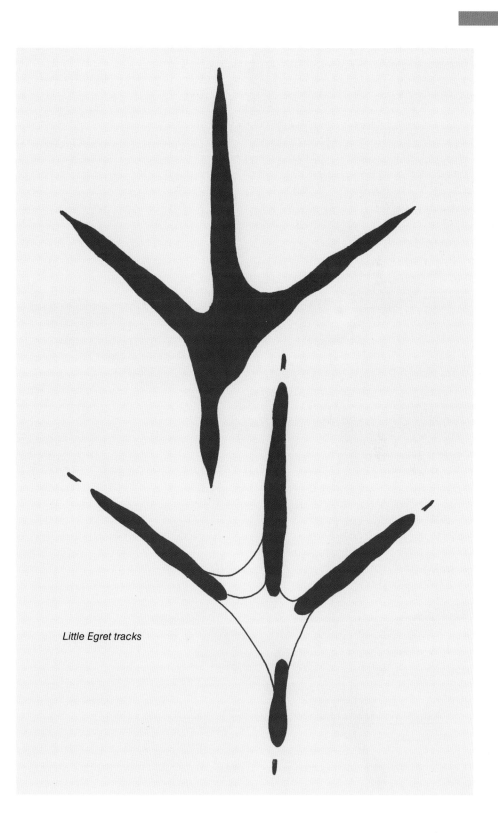

Little Egret tracks

White Stork tracks

White Stork Vc (vL)

Track Asymmetrical. Large, showing three or four toes. Toe I much reduced and blunt. Toe III 70mm long. Length of entire track greater than 140mm, very wide (120mm) with toes II and IV very nearly at right angles to III. Toes II and IV very similar in length, with II slightly smaller. Central metatarsal pad may show in deep tracks. Claws rounded, blunt, normally attached. *Trail* Erratic line of tracks about the median line. Tracks tend to point inwards. Enormous variations in stride depending on speed of movement, normally 100–400mm at a walk but over 1,500mm at speed.

Moorhen Vc (vL)

Track Slightly asymmetrical in three-toed track, distinctly so in four-toed track, with the small, rounded toe I (up to 15mm) pointing inwards. Overall length up to 95mm, width to 80mm. Toes slender and sometimes lobed. Angles between toes II–III and IIIV are similar. Toes II to IV point distinctly forward, with less than 90° between them. The central metatarsal area is small, but often distinct. The claws do not always show, but may show as small, rounded and attached or separate. *Trail* Tracks placed one in front of the other on the median line. Stride at normal walking gait is 120-140mm, increasing to 160mm at a run. The median line may be straight or curved.

Grey Heron Va (E–G)

Track Asymmetrical. Large to enormous. Normally four toes show. Toe III greater than 75mm, normally 80mm plus. Toe I very long, often more than 50mm. Overall track length 130mm to 170mm plus. Width normally 80-90mm, with toes II and IV pointing distinctly forward. Often small proximal web between III and IV. Toe II smaller than IV. Metatarsal area relatively small. Claws very small, blunt and attached. *Trail* In a walking gait, the tracks are in 'a straight line' and do not straddle the median line. Tracks tend to point straight forward, and the stride varies from 500mm to 600mm at a walk to over 1,000mm when the bird is moving at speed on the ground (not a common event).

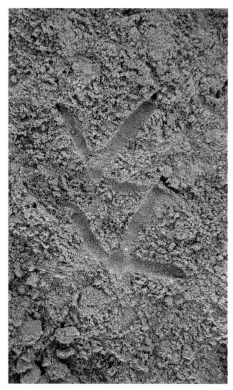

Moorhen tracks

Common Crane tracks

Moorhen tracks

Grey Heron tracks

Purple Gallinule tracks

25 mm

Purple Gallinule Vb (E)

Track Symmetrical. Four- or occasionally three-toed tracks on hard ground. All toes long and slender, with an angle of more than 110° between II and IV. Toe I, if present 50–60mm long; toe III 85–110mm long. Overall track length 160–170mm, width 140–160mm. Central metatarsal area small, but deeply impressed. The claws, if present, are narrow and pointed. There is considerable variation in the amount of detail, as the examples show, depending on the surface conditions and the individual bird, but the very slender toes, symmetrical structure and high width-to-length ratio of track dimensions are characteristic of this species. *Trail* Curving lines, with tracks nearly touching at a slow gait. At speed, the stride increases to 300mm. Tracks do not turn inwards.

Purple Gallinule track

Common Crane Vb (E)

Track Asymmetrical. Tracks always three-toed with toe I being absent. Very broad, robust tracks up to 160mm long and 180mm wide. There is an angle of 120° between toes II and IV. Toe III is up to 110mm long, and toe II is much shorter than IV. The heavy pads on the outer phalanges always show distinctly, even in hard ground (C), as does the very heavy metatarsal pad unless the bird is moving at speed (B). Toe prints are very broad and heavy, the claws rounded and attached in a deeply impressed track, slightly separated on harder ground. In a total outline, a small skin flap or 'web' may show between toes II and III (A). *Trail* Walks or runs. The tracks tend to be in distinct straight lines, with strides of over 600mm being taken. The prints are slightly splayed across the median line, but do not turn inwards.

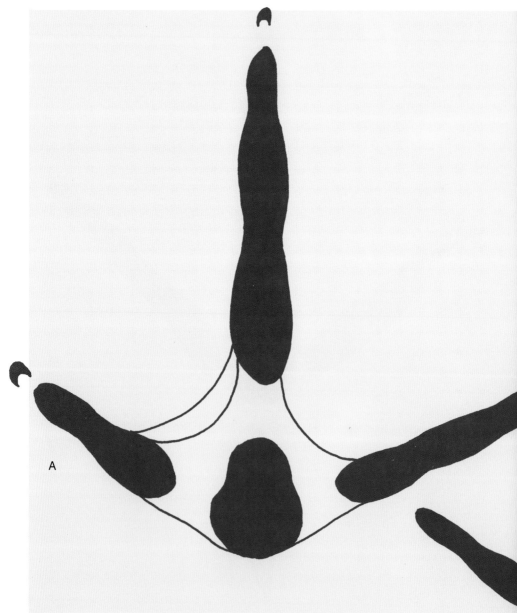

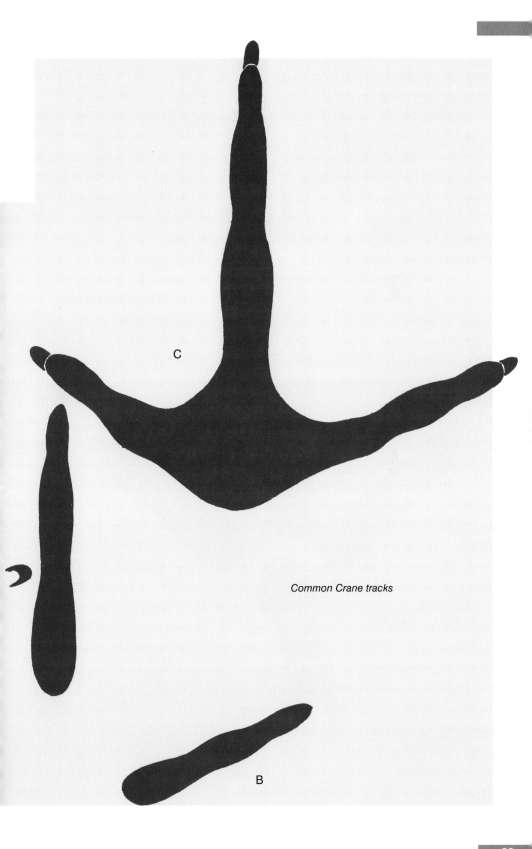

C

B

Common Crane tracks

Black Vulture Vc (E)

Track Large and slightly asymmetrical. Four-toed. Toes very robust, and metatarsal area relatively small but distinct. Overall length about 130mm, width 120mm. Toe I offset and 25-30mm long. Toe III 80mm long. Only about 90° between toes II and IV. In soft ground, a small skin flap may register between toes II and III and the long, sharp and separate claws are distinct. In harder ground details may be missing, but the distinctive elliptical rear lobe of toe I, known as the 'hallux' and so characteristic of the birds of prey and scavengers, is always clear. *Trail* May walk, run or hop on ground, with wings partially open for balance. Feet widely straddled and tracks often incomplete. Stride at running gait up to 900mm. At hopping gait the paired tracks are 500–700mm apart.

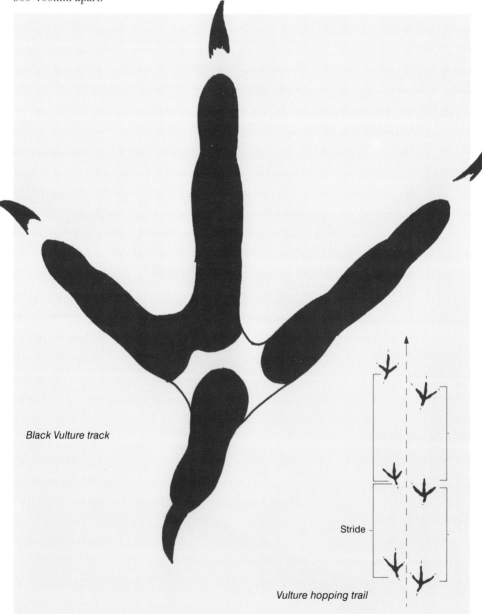

Black Vulture track

Stride

Vulture hopping trail

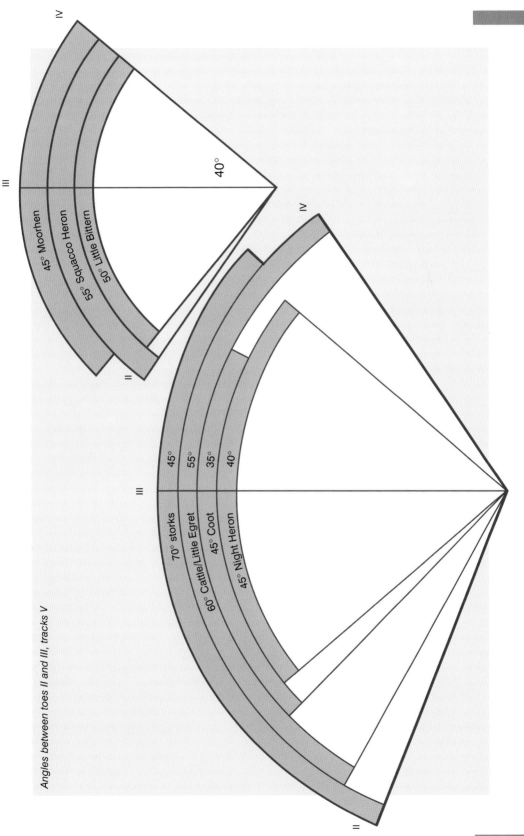

Angles between toes II and III, tracks V

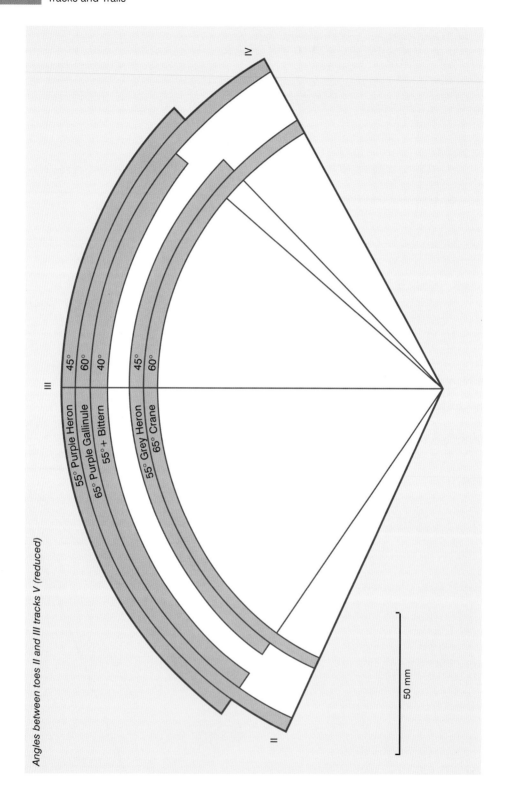

Angles between toes II and III tracks V (reduced)

45° 55° Purple Heron
60° 65° Purple Gallinule
40° 55° + Bittern
45° 55° Grey Heron
60° 65° Crane

50 mm

Chapter 4
NESTS AND ROOSTS

Introduction

Most birds do not have homes as such. Some may use semi-permanent shelters, some may return to the same nest annually, some use more than one nest at a time for breeding purposes, but the majority construct temporary structures on an annual basis for breeding only. It must be remembered that some birds do not build nests of their own. A number of birds of prey, such as Hobbies and Kestrels, take over other nests from birds such as pigeons and crows or even old squirrel dreys. The Cuckoo parasitically lays its eggs in other birds' nests, while shearwaters may take over existing rabbit burrows.

Nests are useful signs of bird activity, but it is essential that they are not disturbed at any time when they are in use, be this at the construction stage, when the eggs are being incubated or when there are young. A number of countries have strong legislation and this must be respected. It is not the purpose of this chapter to encourage naturalists to disturb nests, but nevertheless nests are often found. The following pages act as a brief guide to the major nest types and locations, since a book on tracks and signs is incomplete without such reference. There is deliberately no attempt to deal with eggs in a systematic way, and for those interested the bibliography carries references to those works which do.

Two interrelated factors need to be considered. These are nest types, and the location and habitats in which they occur.

Nest Types

The elements involved are nest shape, materials used in construction, and method of construction. Using these criteria, the following main types may be identified. It is difficult to identify species involved in types 1 to 3 unless an adult bird, eggs or down are present.

1. Simple depression or scrape in vegetation, soil or shingle. Sometimes lined or surrounded by a few shells or twigs, e.g. Oystercatcher.

2. Depression or scrape, sometimes lined with down or feathers, e.g. duck.

3. Shallow, lined bowl in ground. Often under a bush or concealed by a clump of vegetation, e.g. Lapwing.

4. Raised cup of dried mud, e.g. flamingo.

5. Floating platform made with masses of aquatic vegetation, e.g. grebe.

6. Platform with a depression or bowl, made from sedges, reeds or rushes and located on a fallen tree, clump of reeds or rushes, or on the water edge, e.g. Moorhen (not illustrated).

7. Domed nest, the interior consisting of woven vegetation, e.g. Willow Warbler (not illustrated).

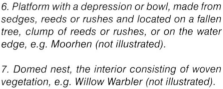

8. Platform consisting of twigs, branches or reeds, e.g. Mute Swan.

9. Platform consisting of twigs or branches, with a dome constructed of twigs, e.g. Magpie.

10. Ball-shaped nest, generally located in the fork of a branch in a tree or bush. Made from lichen, down, moss and spiders' webs, e.g. Long-tailed Tit.

11. Bowl, may be shallow or deep, generally constructed in the fork of a branch in a bush or tree. Woven from vegetation, e.g. Blackbird.

12. Nest in the form of a cradle suspended from the fork of a tree or bush branch, e.g. Golden Oriole (not illustrated).

13. Woven pouch hanging from the extreme tips of branches, e.g. Penduline Tit.

14. Made from aggregates of mud, with some vegetation, bound together with saliva, e.g. Crag Martin.

15. Very deep cup attached to stems of reeds or bushes, e.g. Reed Warbler.

16. Tunnel excavated in soil or soft rock, e.g. European Bee-eater.

17. Bowl-type nest under rock, in a crevice, cave, tree hole, at the end of an existing tunnel or under roof tiles, e.g. Jackdaw.

18. Cavity deliberately excavated in tree trunk. May be partially lined, e.g. woodpecker.

19. Naturally occurring, irregular cavity in a tree trunk and also cracks in coarse bark. May contain lined nest, e.g. Treecreeper (not illustrated).

False Nests and Confusion between Bird and Mammal Structures

Large masses of parasitic mistletoe in the crowns of deciduous trees may look like nests of some description from a distance. Similarly, debris left in bankside vegetation after the waters of a swollen river have subsided may look like simple platform nests. Moth larvae feeding webs in bushes may look like small nests e.g. Long-tailed Tit. Close inspection will reveal the true identities in all cases, but mis-identification from a distance is very easy.

Platform stick nests in trees are nearly all bird constructions. The domed nests of Magpies can sometimes be confused with grey squirrel dreys, although the nest is more open on the top and tends to be less tightly woven. Some birds do take over abandoned squirrel dreys (birds of prey may even eat the original owner!) and confusion may arise. When the drey is being used by the squirrel it is a distinctly rounded, dense structure and there will be other signs such as bark stripping and gnawed nuts and cones. Taken over by a bird (commonly a raptor or pigeon) it becomes more flattened in appearance and there are normally droppings, both in the nest and below it.

Common dormouse nests are small structures woven from stripped bark and often located at a relatively low height in the scrub layer. They can be distinguished from the nests of small bush nesting birds by their globular structure, as opposed to generally open cup and small twig/grass structure, and evidence of stripped bark close by.

Mistletoe (cf. rookery)

Caterpillar feeding web (cf. tit or finch nest)

Flood debris (cf. Dipper or Moorhen nest)

Squirrel drey (cf. Magpie or crow nest)

From a distance, the spherical breeding nests of harvest mice can be confused with warbler nests in the reedbeds or ditch-side coarse grass where both may be found. The mouse nest, however, is globe-shaped and without an obvious entrance hole, whereas those of the warblers are deep cups on closer inspection. The construction of the mouse nest is also unique, since the leaves of the plants in which it is built are split lengthways and incorporated into the nest without being removed from the plant.

Scrapes in the ground can also be confusing. A mountain hare form can be confused with a Capercaillie lek in the heather, although the latter tends to be associated with more scrubby areas. The plants themselves tend to be compressed and chewed in the hare form whereas the lek is worn away.

Locations and Habitats

Some species are habitat-specific in terms of their nest building, but the majority will utilise more than one habitat. Many species do use specific locations within different habitats. The following examples are based around major habitat groupings and illustrate a large number of the habitat/location/nest type categories to be found in Europe.

Woodland – Including both Broadleaved and Coniferous Species

This habitat offers a wide range of nesting environments for many species.

1. Deciduous and Mixed Woodland

A. Canopy Many species which nest in a closed canopy of trees will also use the tops of isolated trees. SPARROWHAWKS build their nests at variable heights in the canopy. An old nest of another species, such as a crow, may provide a base. It is a roughly constructed, flattish structure of dry twigs with a sparse lining of leafy twigs. WOODPIGEONS may also nest on rock ledges, but in tree branches they construct a thin twig platform some 250mm across. This may be based on the nest of another species. The GREY HERON tends to nest high in the branches of tall trees near to water, although reedbeds and rock faces are also used. The birds are colonial and there may be several nests in one tree, which will become heavily stained with faeces over the years. In tree branches, the nest is a large horizontal twig platform with a shallow central dip in which there is a thin twig/root lining. The platform is added to annually. Various members of the CROW family build their rough stick and muddy earth nests in the treetops. The JAY builds in a fork at any height above 2m. The cup-shaped nest is made from twigs, stems and muddy earth, the neat inner cup being lined with fine roots and hair. The MAGPIE nest has a loose dome of twigs, while the ROOK produces a bulky cup of twigs in the outer, uppermost branches. Smaller birds, such as the MISTLE THRUSH, nest up to 10m above the ground in a fork in a bush or tree towards the edge of woodland. The nest is a cup of grass, stems, roots, leaves and moss, often consolidated with earth. There is a well-formed internal cup lined with grass.

Black Kite, note the use of paper as a lining

Mistle Thrush

Rook   *Thrush*

B. Tree trunks and major branches (i) Holes. Many species make use of natural holes, or excavate their own in rotten or even sound wood. STOCK DOVES sometimes make use of large existing holes with a lining of twigs, roots and dead leaves at the bottom. TAWNY OWLS will nest in natural or artificial holes in tree trunks. They will also take over squirrel dreys and the nests of other birds. The nest is a shallow unlined hollow. WOODPECKERS are perhaps the best-known wood excavators. The BLACK WOODPECKER uses large mature trees in broadleaved or coniferous forests. Cavity often excavated in sound wood. The entrance hole is 6 to 10m up, hole diameter 120mm x 100mm, cavity in tree 200-230mm wide and up to 600mm deep. Nest unlined, or with a few wood chips. The GREEN WOODPECKER tends to use open woodland or woodland fringes. The trunk may be sound or rotten, and the cavity is excavated at any height above 1 m. Entrance hole diameter 60mm x 75mm, cavity in tree 150mm wide and up to 400mm deep. Unlined. GREAT SPOTTED WOODPECKERS use closed or open woodland. The entrance hole, sited from 3m upwards and 55mm x 55mm in diameter, links a small tunnel to a cavity 120mm wide and about 300mm deep. Nest unlined. LESSER SPOTTED WOODPECKERS also use a wide range of tree habitats, but tend to nest in softer, decayed wood, often in a side branch, from a low level to the top of the tree. The entrance is 35mm x 35mm, and a short tunnel leads to an elongated nesting chamber 75mm wide and about 230mm deep. Unlined. The WRYNECK nests in a wide range of natural and artificial holes, but does not excavate its own and may dispossess smaller birds.

SPOTTED FLYCATCHERS nest in a wide range of woodland and hedgerow tree situations. The nest may be close to the trunk on a branch, or in a hole or crevice. It is up to 10m above the ground and consists of a cup made from grass, thin twigs, roots, lichens, plant down, fibres and spiders' webs, lined with small feathers and down. Many species of TIT nest in tree holes, some even excavating their own holes in rotten wood. The GREAT TIT produces a thickly lined nest containing much moss, and may occupy abandoned large nests, squirrel dreys and nestboxes. The NUTHATCH tends to take over a natural crevice or hole, often where a rotten branch has fallen, and reduces this to the required size by plastering it with mud. The inner nest is a crude cup of moss, bark flakes or feathers. ROBINS often nest in holes in tree stumps, crevices in tree-root systems or around buildings. The nest is a small neat cup, often in a cavity which makes it appear to have a roof. STARLINGS may take over holes made by other birds, and these may be used for nesting and roosting. The nest is an untidy cup of stems, leaves and other plant material, lined with feathers, wool and moss. JACKDAW nests in holes or branch forks are large, untidy accumulations of twigs.

(ii) Crevices. TREECREEPERS nest in large trees in woodland or more open situations. The nest is concealed behind loose bark, in a crevice or in accumulated debris between large branches. It is a loose cup of twigs, roots, moss and grass, lined with fine bark, feathers and sometimes wool. It is small, about 75mm across.

C. Bushes and shrubs WRENS nest in almost any suitable hollow, but tend to be associated with the low cover of the shrub layer. The nest is a small, stout dome of leaves, moss and grass, lined with fine feathers. Many FINCHES use the bush layer in woodlands or hedges. The CHAFFINCH, for example, builds into the fork of a taller shrub and produces a very neat moss cup which also contains lichen, grass roots, feathers and spiders' webs. The LONG-TAILED TIT nests in brambles and thick scrub between 1m and 4m. The nest is usually close to the main stem or a branch, and consists of a distinctive large, compact, elongated dome of moss and lichen bound with spiders' webs and hair. It is 60–75mm across and up to 130mm long. SONG THRUSHES also nest close to the main stem at between 1m and 4m. The nest is a cup of grass, thin twigs, roots and moss with dead leaves and lichen. It is neatly constructed, and has a smooth inner cup of rotten wood pulp or mud.

D. On the ground (i) Below bushes. NIGHTINGALES nest on a slightly raised site on litter and fine twigs under shrubs. The nest is a loose, bulky cup of dead leaves and grass, lined with fine grass and hair. The WILLOW WARBLER makes a domed, spherical nest with a side entrance from plant stems, grass, rotten wood and roots. It has an inner cup of finer vegetation and feathers, and is placed on the ground beneath bushes.

(ii) Ground layer WOODCOCKS nest in low cover in a variety of woodland situations, as well as in tall heath. The nest is a hollow, lined with dead leaves and other nearby plant material.

(iii) Open ground. NIGHTJARS use many open areas in woodlands, new coniferous plantation and heath, as well as dunes and beaches. The nest is a lightly scraped hollow, usually near a piece of wood or a stone as a marker. PHEASANTS nest on the ground in a very wide range of habitats. The nest is a shallow hollow, which may be unlined or lined with grass and dead leaves. The droppings of this species are a useful indicator of nesting or roosting sites, which, with current sporting trends in Europe, tend to be increasingly in woodland.

2. Coniferous Woodlands, Forests and Plantations

A. Canopy. LONG-EARED OWLS frequently nest in coniferous plantations, as well as in smaller copses and on open areas of marsh and heath. They often use a large, old nest of another species or a squirrel drey. The owl simply nests in the existing structure. The GREAT GREY OWL uses the broken tops of tall conifers or again the nests of other species. CROSSBILLS nest in branches from 2m to 20m up. The base cup of the nest consists of pine twigs, built up with grasses, moss, lichen and often wool. The finer inner cup is of grass, hair, fur and feathers. WAXWINGS nest in conifer and birch woods, normally between 2m and 7m up, in trees close to the forest edge, a clearing or water. The nest is a cup of conifer twigs, reindeer moss and grass, lined with hair and down. GOLDCRESTS build a nest suspended in a fork of twigs under foliage near the end of a conifer branch. The deep, thick cup is built tight against the leaves and twigs, so access to the small internal cavity is restricted. The nest is bound to the supporting twigs with moss, lichens and spiders' webs. It is lined with feathers, and measures 70-100mm across.

Crossbill

B. Tree trunks. HAWK OWLS nest in natural holes or old woodpecker holes. The cavity is unlined. TENGMALM'S OWL occupies similar holes but often uses Black Woodpecker holes and will utilise nestboxes. CRESTED TITS excavate holes in a rotten stump or a partly dead tree or sapling. Sometimes they will use an old drey or nest. A neat moss-lined cup nest is constructed in the cavity or old nest. COAL TITS normally nest in tree holes although they will occasionally use the forest floor. The nest is thickly lined with moss and spiders' webs.

C. On the ground. HAZEL HENS nest beneath trees, bushes or in low cover. The nest is a shallow scrape with a little green or dead plant material and sometimes twigs. The large

CAPERCAILLIE nests on the open forest floors, in juniper scrub or heather moorland. In addition to the nests, which may be taken over from other species and consist of shallow hollows lined with local vegetation, the males' mating displays result in worn circular areas known as 'leks'.

Obviously, woods and forests contain other nesting habitats, many of which are discussed elsewhere. The use of trees, crags, large rocks or even buildings by BONELLI'S EAGLE to build its enormous twig nest, which is re-used annually, is a good example of this variation.

Meadows, Hedgerows, Arable Land, Woodland Edge and Human Habitation

This may seem a wide-ranging category, but in reality many species make use of numerous different nesting locations, as the range of examples here shows.

WHITE STORKS usually nest in or near human settlement, where they are traditionally welcomed. They form colonies in trees, buildings and ruins and even on specially erected poles with a platform on. The nest is a large structure of branches, sticks, grass tufts and earth which is 900–1,500mm across and is re-used annually. It contains a shallow cup lined with debris and feathers. The HOBBY lives in open country with scattered trees or on the woodland edge. It normally takes over the twig nest of another, larger bird or a squirrel drey and will use it as it is or even remove material. The commoner KESTREL nests on suitable ledges or outcrops and even in trees over a wide range of landscapes. It may

White Stork

make a slight hollow on a suitable ledge and incorporate local vegetation, but more often than not it takes over an old stick nest of another species, such as one of the crows. Both the GREY PARTRIDGE and the QUAIL nest in grassland, among crops in coarse hedgerow and woodland-edge vegetation and occasionally in heathland. The nests are shallow hollows lined with local vegetation, the partridge nests more often sheltered by taller plants. The GREAT BUSTARD is completely terrestrial and nests in open grassland and cultivated fields. The nest is a simple bare scrape and the birds show no nest-building behaviour at all.

COLLARED DOVES are widespread in cultivated and built-up areas. They use trees and ledges on buildings, where they construct a thin platform of fine twigs and plant stems as a nest. The BARN OWL is widely distributed and breeds in holes in trees, on ledges in buildings, and in crevices in rocks, on cliff and quarry faces. The nest is a shallow hollow in existing debris and may be partly lined with pellets. LITTLE OWLS are associated with parkland, cultivation and open country. They will use a hole or crevice in a tree or building, a crevice in a cliff or quarry, and even a burrow in the ground in open conditions. The nesting cavity may be completely unlined or use may be made of an old bird nest already there.

The SWIFT is very widespread and makes use of many nesting sites, including holes and crevices in buildings, cliffs and rock outcrops; woodpecker holes; House Martin nests; and nestboxes. The nest itself consists of a shallow cup, sometimes on a small ledge or existing nest structure of another species, made from stems, leaves, other plant debris and feathers collected from the air on the wing and stuck together with saliva. SWALLOWS use a variety of habitats, often near water and frequently close to man. The nest is a mud structure stuck against a vertical surface with support. Rafters, girders, bridges and occasionally trees are favoured. The nest is an open shallow cup of mud pellets, vegetable fibres and plant fragments some 100–130mm across. It is sparsely lined with feathers. HOUSE MARTINS build in rocky areas and on buildings near water. They often form loose groups and the nests may abut one on to another. The nest is a rounded half cup built on a vertical surface close to or against an overhanging projection. It consists of mud pellets and some plant fibres and is lined with feathers, dry grass and other plant fragments. There is a narrow opening at the top and frequently large accumulations of droppings on the ground below. PIED WAGTAILS nest in a wide range of hollows and cavities,

Swallow

Pied Wagtail

but will frequently take over old Sand and House Martin nests, adding their own cup of stems, small twigs, leaves, roots and moss lined with hair, feathers and even wool.

HOOPOES tend to nest in open areas of scattered trees and buildings. The nest is a hole in a tree, old wall, building, stone heap or nestbox. The cavity may be unlined, or sparsely lined with plant remains, feathers, wool or rags. Droppings are allowed to accumulate in the nest, which consequently becomes foul-smelling. The LARKS nest in a range of open and cultivated habitats. SHORT-TOED LARKS are found in dry pastures, cultivated sandy soils, sparse scrub and saltmarsh. They nest on the ground in loose colonies with deep cup nests of dry grasses, stems and roots lined with down, hair, wool and feathers. Small pebbles and pieces of soil may be used to build up the exposed edge of the nest. The more familiar WOODLARK is found in cultivated areas, heathland, scrub with scattered trees, woodland edges and on hill and mountain slopes. It nests in areas where there are taller features to use as singing posts. The nest is sheltered and well-concealed on the ground, and consists of a well-built cup with a lining of fine grasses and tufts of hair inside the grass and moss exterior.

The RED-BACKED SHRIKE nests in open places with scattered scrub, heath-land, grassland, hedges and thickets. The nest is 1-3m up in the branches of a shrub. It is a bulky cup 120–150mm across made from grass stems, plant stems and moss and lined with hair, rootless, wool or down. WHITETHROATS and DUNNOCKS also nest in hedges and thickets. The Dunnock builds, or takes over abandoned nests, in shady sites at levels from 60cm to 3m. The nest is a firm cup of twigs, stems, moss and roots and is lined with hair, wool and fine mosses. The Whitethroat nests at heights of up to 5m, constructing a loosely made deep cup of twigs and stems with a lining of grass and hair. The nest is wedged between the twigs or stems and not attached to them. BUNTINGS nest chiefly in open habitats, constructing a well-concealed cup nest on or near the ground. The YELLOWHAMMER, for example, usually uses tall ground vegetation against a hedgerow or bank, but will sometimes nest at up to 2m in a thick bush. The nest is a cup of grass, stems and moss with a lining of grass and hair. HOUSE SPARROWS are closely associated with man, but will also nest in trees and bushes. The nest in trees is an untidy dome with a side entrance. In a building it is a crude cup. In both cases it tends to be built of stems, straw and rubbish, lined with feathers and wool. Many other groups, such as the finches, thrushes, tits and pipits, are widespread in this range of nesting habitats, but examples of their nests are given elsewhere.

Open Land – Including Mountain, Moorland, Tundra and Arid Areas

Many of the birds of prey nest in more open areas. The EGYPTIAN VULTURE inhabits dry open country, building its nest in crevices in rock faces and outcrops or, more rarely, in buildings or trees. The nests are bulky structures of twigs, lined with debris, skin, fur and rags, and are plastered with droppings. The nests are re-used and added to, so they become very large. LAMMERGEIERS inhabit mountainous regions, building their nests in rocky niches, cavities or caves in the faces of rocky crags. Large narrow ledges may also be used, and the sites are normally under overhangs. The nest is a platform of twigs and branches, with a hollow lined with animal bones. Nest heavily marked with droppings. The BLACK VULTURE lives at the tree limit in mountainous regions. Large isolated trees or rock ledges are used as nest sites. The nest, which is re-used, is large when new and becomes enormous as years go by. It is made from large sticks, and lined with leafy branches, bark and skin. The GOLDEN EAGLE nests on trees, on cliffs and on rock ledges in mountain areas. Several nests may be built in a territory. New nests on ledges are thin platforms, but these thicken with re-use in successive years and become massive. The nests are built from thick branches, twigs and plant stems and are lined with green leafy twigs, including pine sprigs. BUZZARDS may be classed as birds of open country and frequently nest in trees, cliffs, rock outcrops or, rarely, on the ground. Some nests are re-used, some are used only once. Frequently, nests of other species are used. The nests are bulky and made from sticks, twigs and stalks. They are decorated with green material, which is constantly renewed. PEREGRINE FALCONS will nest on a cliff ledge, rock outcrop or even a tall building. Occasionally, a raised mound on open ground or an old tree stump is used. The nest is a hollow scrape with no material added to it. Perhaps the most characteristic of the moorland-nesting birds of prey is the MERLIN. It will also nest in rough pasture, dunes, marshes, on the coast and sometimes in trees, but it is most at home nesting on the ground among tall heather. The nest is generally a bare hollow, although it may have some grass lining, and in trees the nests of other species are normally used.

The WILLOW GROUSE and its British subspecies the RED GROUSE are moorland species. The Willow Grouse inhabits willow, birch and juniper scrub, often in boggy places. The Red Grouse uses open heather moor and grassy heath. The nest is a shallow hollow in ground vegetation, covered by small bushes or heather tufts, and may be partially lined with grasses, moss and heather stems. PTARMIGANS live in arctic tundra and high mountain areas. The nest is on open ground, open slightly sheltered by a rock or tub of vegetation. It is a shallow hollow or scrape scantily lined with bits of grass, other plant material and a few feathers.

Many waders and their allies nest in open land. GOLDEN PLOVERS favour open moorland, but range from the arctic tundra in the north to grassy areas in the south. The nest is on the ground, sometimes among short heather and sometimes in the open. In the north of the British Isles, newly burnt heather moorland is a particularly important nesting area. The nest is a shallow scrape, lined with locally available material. DOTTERELS nest in a wide range of open conditions, from the tundra and bare hills of the sub-arctic in the north to Dutch polders and mountains in southern Europe. Again, the nest is a shallow hollow on the ground, which may be lined or unlined. LAPWINGS are found on moist moorland, meadows, rough pastures, marshes and open cultivated land. The nest is a shallow hollow on the ground, sometimes slightly raised in wet areas, and may consist of a thick pad of local vegetation. DUNLINS nest either on moorland with pools and bogs or on lowland wet grassy areas and coastal saltmarshes. The nest is a distinct cup in grass tussocks, lined with leaves or grass. GREENSHANKS use open moist moorland or open forest areas. The nest is on the ground close to an object, such as a log, and again consists of a hollow, but is lined with debris as well as other plant material. The CURLEW is a large wader which nests in a variety of habitats ranging from large forest clearings, through rough grassland, moor and heath to marsh and dunes. The nest is a shallow hollow, lined with local

Griffon Vulture

Hen Harrier

plant material. STONE CURLEWS are found on bare ground, open heaths, short grass, bare sand and shingle, scrub or scattered trees and arable land. The nest is normally on the ground and is a shallow scrape which is open lined with debris, including small stones and rabbit droppings. The various species of SAND-GROUSE, although their nest is only a simple undistinguished scrape, are of note because they tend to live in dry areas and the males soak their breast feathers in water to bring it to the young.

Some of the larger OWLS are characteristic nesting species of open ground. SNOWY OWLS nest in the arctic tundra, high fell and mountain areas. The nest is on the ground,

Short-eared Owl

sometimes in a slightly elevated position, and consists of a hollow scrape, sometimes lined with moss and a few feathers. EAGLE OWLS use a wide range of habitats and nesting locations. Steep hillsides, crags, gorges and cliffs are inhabited. The nest site may be in a crevice, cave or large hollow tree. Sometimes, large old stick nests of other species are taken over. On open ground, the nest is a shallow, unlined scrape. SHORT-EARED OWLS are more characteristic of the heather moorland, and make their unlined shallow hollow in the shelter of heather, tall grasses, reeds or bushes.

STONECHATS and WHINCHATS nest on or near the ground. The nest is a cup of grass or other plant material, lined with grass, hair and feathers. It is usually located in a hole or hollow under rocks, under stones or in thick herbage. WHEATEARS nest on drier hillsides, wasteland dunes, or in walls. The nest is in a hole or burrow, and the entrance may be reduced in size by the birds accumulating small pebbles or rock fragments in a low rampart.

The Coast

This is an important nesting-habitat complex. There is a need to be close to the food source, namely the sea, and many species such as the Gannet, Manx Shearwater, storm petrels, Black-headed Gull and Guillemot are colonial mainly because of limited nesting space.

1. Cliffs

On high cliffs, the GUILLEMOTS and RAZORBILLS nest on the open ledges and lay their eggs on bare rock. The young of both these species jump into the sea before they are fully fledged, and so vertical cliffs are favoured. KITTIWAKES nest on cliff and rock ledges, building a solid nest of mud, vegetation, moss and seaweed. The whole forms a well-defined hollow about 300mm across. FULMARS nest on ledges with some soil, and the eggs are laid in depressions scraped in

Kittiwakes

Fulmar

the earth. GANNETS build on steep faces and sometimes on more gently sloping clifftops. The nests are rounded mounds of seaweed, plant material, feathers and debris, and are spaced at slightly more than pecking distance apart. The HERRING GULL is a good example of a cliff-nesting gull, although it will use a wide range of other habitats, including human habitation. The nest is a rough accumulation of plant material, debris and seaweed in a suitable hollow or sheltered area. While ROCK DOVES are frequently associated with man (our Feral Pigeons), they also nest in large numbers on sea cliffs. The nests are often in crevices or even holes, and are a scanty layer of fine stems, roots, twigs and pieces of rubbish. The WHITE-TAILED EAGLE often nests in rocky areas or in large trees on the coast. There may be several nest sites in the territory, each nest consisting of a massive accumulation of branches and twigs with a central cup lined with green plants, leafy twigs and often wool.

2. Rocky Coasts and Islands
SHAGS generally nest on low rocky cliffs and in hollows under boulders on rocky shores. The nest is an accumulation of seaweed and other plant stems, with a central hollow, normally lined with finer material. CORMORANTS nest either in a rocky situation at the coast or in trees by fresh water. A seaside nest is a heap of seaweed and sticks 450-600mm across. Inland nests are more solid structures of sticks, lined with leaves, grasses, water plants and debris. The nests are often close together and trees are heavily stained or even killed by droppings. The GREAT BLACK-BACKED GULL nests in island situations and on inland moors. It is colonial. The nests are large accumulations of sticks, heather, seaweed, grass and feathers according to location.

3. Soft Cliff and Soil Areas
PUFFINS nest in turf slopes and soft clifftops. They use burrows which may be taken over from a shearwater or a rabbit, or excavated by the Puffin itself. Sometimes, a natural rock crevice or hole is used. The nest is a shallow hollow some way inside the tunnel, and plant materials and feathers are carried into the burrow, but not arranged as lining material. MANX SHEARWATERS live in colonies in turf burrows or natural crevices in fallen rocks. The burrow may be excavated to a length of up to 1m and contains some plant material and feathers. LEACH'S PETREL inhabits turf or rocky slopes on islands. It excavates burrows up to 2m long in soft soil. There may be several chambers in these burrows occupied by separate pairs. Debris is accumulated in the chambers.

Bempton Cliffs, in northern England, show a range of nesting conditions on sheer chalk cliffs with softer material on top. Large numbers of Guillemots, Kittiwakes, Razorbills, Puffins, Fulmars and Gannets make use of the space available.

4. Shingle and Sandbars
OYSTERCATCHERS nest on open coastal beaches, among rocks, on islands, in dunes, on grass banks along rivers and around lakes and lagoons. The nest is a shallow hollow, unlined or with pieces of dead plant, small stones, rabbit droppings and other debris. RINGED PLOVERS often use shingle and sandbars. The simple scrape may be exposed or sheltered, and is sometimes lined with tiny pebbles, debris or plant material. Perhaps the TERNS are most commonly associated with this nesting habitat. The LITTLE TERN makes a shallow hollow which is unlined or has fragments of plant material, small pebbles or shell. The COMMON TERN produces hollows lined with a little local vegetation and a few feathers in a coastal location, but inland may produce vegetation nests which may even float in their fresh water situation. Some terns nest on grass slopes, and the BLACK TERN is found in large colonies in fresh water marshes and lagoons in parts of Europe. The SHELDUCK often nests on coastal sandbanks and mudflats. It will nest in hollows under dense vegetation or even under buildings, but frequently in old rabbit burrows where the nest is 2–3m inside and consists of a hollow, lined with down and feathers. The down tufts are large, pale grey, brown-tinged and variably tinted, appearing mottled. EIDERS nest in exposed shore sites by the coast, as well as in lake and riverside situations. The hollow is lined with nearby plant material and seaweed, large quantities of feathers and down. The down tufts are light greyish-brown with ill-defined centres and paleish tips.

5. Saltmarshes and Lagoons
FLAMINGOS are sociable birds nesting on the edges of lakes and brackish or saline lagoons They make distinctive small conical mounds (450mm x 450mm) of mud with a hollow in the

top. The material is scooped up and moulded with the bill, and may be built over an existing hard base. PELICANS use coastal and fresh water marshes and islands in lakes. The DALMATIAN PELICAN nests among vegetation. The nest is a heap of reeds, grass, sticks or stones. It is consolidated by droppings, and floating reed nests may settle and have to be added to as the young grow. LAPWINGS nest in coastal marshland, as well as in many inland pasture and moorland areas. They make a shallow hollow, often on slightly raised sites, and may line this with large quantities of local vegetation. The distinctive AVOCET nests on bare, dry mud, sand near water, or short vegetation near salt or brackish lagoons, on low islands, sandbars or mudflats. It is a colonial species, and creates shallow scrapes with little or no lining.

Fresh Water

This habitat, which includes open water, bank complexes, marshy areas and woodland fringes, is a major breeding-habitat complex for many species.

1. Open Water and Emergent Vegetation in Water

The GREBES make nests which are accumulations of soggy, rotting vegetation which is often floating. The GREAT CRESTED GREBE nests by fresh water lakes, and builds its large shapeless structure among reeds or similar plants at the water's edge. The nest may float or rest in shallow water. The LITTLE GREBE builds up heaps of aquatic vegetation above water level in shallow water among lake, pond and riverside vegetation.

2. Reedbeds, Bankside Vegetation, Marsh, Fens and Fresh Water Islands

DIVERS nest close to the water's edge in northern areas of Europe. They cannot walk well. The GREAT NORTHERN DIVER nests on bare promontories and small islands, where the nest will be a hollow scrape with little lining. In reedbed sites, a large mound of vegetation may be assembled. RED-THROATED DIVERS build similar nests, but favour the edge of pools in wooded areas. LITTLE BITTERNS are solitary birds nesting in reeds and thickets around fresh water. They may nest on low branches, floating vegetation or on the ground, where a shallow saucer of sedges, reeds and other plant stems is built. The nest is about 450mm across and is lined with fine plant material. The familiar MUTE SWAN builds a large waterside heap of vegetation, which has a slight depression and may be lined with a little down. By contrast, the WHOOPER SWAN, which also builds large mounds in its arctic and sub-arctic breeding grounds, lines the nest with large quantities of white down and small feathers. The GEESE generally construct some form of a scrape with lining close to water. GREYLAG GEESE nest in marshes and swamps, as well as on moorland and offshore islands. On dry sites they make scrapes, but in reedy situations the nest will be an accumulation of reeds or rushes. The down lining is thin, the small tufts having grey, light centres. The BARNACLE GOOSE nests in arctic valleys in colonies, and the scrape nests are characterised by the large quantities of feathers and down, which is dark grey with whitish centres. The nests are re-used. In common with those of the geese, many DUCK scrapes can be identified positively only by their down lining. The widespread MALLARD provides a general example of a typical duck nest. This is a hollow, often in standing vegetation, lined with plant debris, leaves, grass, feathers and down. The down has pale centres and tips and is used to cover the eggs when the nest is unattended.

The MARSH HARRIER nests on the ground in fens, marshes and reedbeds, sometimes over shallow water. The nest is a large mass of sticks and reeds, lined with grasses. It is re-used each year. CRANES prefer extensive areas of marsh for breeding. The COMMON CRANE normally constructs its large heap of plant material on the ground close to wooded areas. The nest is re-used and is 1,200-1,500mm across. WATER RAILS build a bulky cup of dead leaves of reeds and waterside plants in reedbeds, swamps and streamside vegetation. The nest is often raised above ground level in the thick lower growth

Common Sandpiper

of reeds and rushes. COOTS nest on the ground or in branches at water-level in waterside vegetation of lakes, large pools and slower rivers. The nest is a bulky cup of dead stems and leaves, often well raised, and there may be 'runs' through the vegetation linking with extra nest platforms for the young to rest on. SNIPE use a range of moist habitats at varying altitudes. They nest on the ground, producing shallow grass-lined hollows normally in a clump of vegetation. This may be partly pulled over to cover the site. Many of the TERNS nest in fresh water sites. The WHISKERED TERN uses swampy areas, where it forms colonies. The nests are flimsy structures of aquatic weed, the central hollow without obvious lining. They float on the water and are anchored by weeds.

REED WARBLERS and MARSH WARBLERS nest by or over water. The latter uses overgrown thickets from 0.3m to 3m above ground. The nest is a tapering cylindrical cup with the rim extending to handles on the plant stems. It is 100mm across, with a loose outer construction and a tight, well-formed inner cup. The PENDULINE TIT uses willow and poplar thickets in marshes. The nest, at up to 11m, is a domed structure with an entrance tube at the side. It is made from willow and poplar material and is 125mm across.

3. Exposed Banks

The KINGFISHER makes a tunnel with its bill, normally in a bank over slow-moving water but sometimes inland, and kicks the soil out with its feet. The tunnel is 300–900mm long and rises slightly to a rounded, unlined nest chamber which is 125–1150mm across. Castings of fish bones are present in the tunnel. BEE-EATERS are colonial and will nest in dry banks and road cuttings, as well as those over water. The horizontal tunnel slants into the bank and is 1–3m long. There is a rounded, unlined nest chamber, and castings containing insect remains are present in the tunnel. SAND MARTINS are colonial and nest in burrows in vertical banks, often close to the ground in the north of their range. Existing artificial holes may be used. The tunnel ends in a rounded chamber, lined with plant stems and feathers.

4. Walls, Bridges and Rock Faces

Wagtails are open associated with rocky areas close to water, but perhaps the DIPPER is the best example to choose. This species tends to favour upland streams. The nest site overlooks water and may be on an overhung bank, a rock face, under a culvert or bridge or behind a waterfall. A bulky domed structure of moss is made, with an internal cup of moss and grasses. The canopy of the dome overhangs the cup to form a downward-pointing entrance directed towards the water.

Dipper

5. Bushes and Trees

The LITTLE EGRET nests on raised sites near marshes and rivers. The nest of thin twigs is shallow and about 300mm across. It may be located in reeds, bushes in marshes or trees near water. The EGYPTIAN GOOSE may nest on the ground, among rocks, on rocky ledges, and also take over old nests. It will also use large holes in trees. The nest is lined with pale grey down. SPOONBILLS are often colonial and nest in marshes, reedbeds, bushes or trees. In trees a rough platform of twigs and branches is made, while the reedbed nests are a crude platform of reed stems and debris. The vegetation is often trampled down around the mound, which is 300–450mm high. MOORHENS nest in many waterside locations, sometimes choosing dense scrub or an abandoned nest in a tree. A bulky platform of dead plant material and debris is used, and there may be other brooding nests in the territory.

The OSPREY normally chooses a treetop or rocky-outcrop location close to lakes, rivers, estuaries and coasts. It may be solitary or colonial, and several nests may be built in a territory. A massive platform of sticks and debris is constructed. The inner cup is lined with finer stems and grasses. The nest is re-used and extended in successive years. PALLAS'S FISH EAGLE is associated with large rivers and lakes, often at high altitude. It builds its massive nest of sticks, reeds and debris in trees, reedbeds or on the ground. The nest has a sparse lining of green branches and grass, and is re-used annually.

Chapter 5
FEEDING AND BEHAVIOURAL SIGNS

Introduction

Birds feed on a wide range of plant and animal material and make use of almost every habitat to obtain their food, some even feeding on the wing. Some species have a unique way of dealing with a particular food type, and remains can be used for specific identification purposes. In most cases, the remains suggest the type of bird responsible, e.g. a raptor, a woodpecker or a wader. Detailed examination of such remains, their precise location, and other signs such as tracks, droppings and roosts may make species identification possible. The following examples, based around type of remains and habitat, illustrate the range of material and the best locations to look for it.

Berries and Soft Fruits

GREENFINCHES peck out the flesh from hips to reach the carpels, removing small wedge-shaped sections. CROSSBILLS occasionally peck a large section of flesh out of large fruits, such as apples, to reach the carpels and leave the discarded flesh scattered around. By contrast, BLACKBIRDS and THRUSHES peck out and eat the flesh from the larger fruits, leaving only the outer skin.

Hips pecked out by seed-eating birds have only small areas of flesh removed, whereas those eaten by BANK VOLES have large areas of flesh gnawed out.

Flower and Thistle Heads

GOLDFINCHES peck out flower heads, especially thistles, concentrating on one side of the plant. The remains are left littered below once the bird has extracted the seeds. GREENFINCHES behave in a similar way. TWITES also feed on thistle and flower heads, but tend to break up the whole head.

Rose hip eaten by finches

Yew berries eaten by finches

Grazed Vegetation

Geese graze off low-growing vegetation, including grass, and leave large, irregular, closely cropped areas. BRENT GEESE graze on saltmarshes, concentrating on sea grasses, e.g. *Zostera*. WHITE-FRONTED GEESE will graze on a potato crop, taking both the green shoots and the tubers, a habit which makes them unwelcome.

Nuts and Seeds

Nuts and seeds are important elements of the autumn and winter diets of many birds and mammals. Some species have clearly identifiable ways of opening their food.

FINCHES open walnuts by making large irregular holes, especially when the nuts are freshly fallen and still moist. GREAT TITS punch small neat holes into walnuts, hazelnuts and acorns. These often carry fine beak marks. Again, the behaviour is restricted to fresh, moist nuts. NUTHATCHES often jam nuts into coarse bark and hammer them open by making irregular, large holes, but small beak marks are again often obvious. Sometimes whole walnuts are tackled in their outer casing on the ground or still hanging from the tree. The end of the casing and soft shell is pecked out so that the seed inside can be reached.

WOODPECKERS may also wedge nuts into bark, but the holes are very untidy, often with large beak marks, and the contents are completely cleared out. MAGPIES chip open hazelnuts and walnuts, leaving large, heavy peck marks. JACKDAWS hold the nut down and break it with repeated blows. The holes are quite small, but are irregular. In common with the Woodpigeon and the Jay, this species may store nuts, although none of the birds buries them in the same way as squirrels do. HAWFINCHES split open small nuts and hard seeds, such as cherry stones, with their powerful bills. The shells are neatly split in two.

Several species of MAMMALS tackle nuts. Squirrels normally split acorns and hazelnuts neatly in two, but large teeth marks are apparent on the apex of the shell. Wood mice gnaw fairly neat holes, with small teeth marks on the outer rim of the hole. Bank voles leave a neat, slightly rough-rimmed hole without teeth marks, while hazel dormice leave a very neat, rounded hole which is almost polished on the rim and quite distinctive.

Woodpeckers and Nuthatches split beechmast to reach the kernel, but it is impossible to distinguish between species. Several species of finch feed on beechmast in winter. The husks are irregularly pecked open and pieces of the white kernels may be found in small piles.

Thrushes eat yew berries whole, digesting the flesh and passing the seed through in the droppings. The Hawfinch pecks into the flesh to reach the seed, which it splits for the kernel, but discards the flesh itself. Nuthatches will wedge yew seeds into bark crevices to split them. Some species of tit take the whole yew fruit to a feeding branch and squeeze out the nut, leaving the discarded flesh stuck to the branch.

Almonds eaten by Azure-winged Magpie

Peàr with flesh pecked by Blackbirds

Hips pecked open by finches to reach the carpels

Blackbirds have left only the skin of this windfall apple

Thistle flower head pecked out by Goldfinches

Cones

The seeds from spruce and pine cones are major constituents in the diets of some species. Many birds and mammals have a distinctive way of breaking through or removing the outer scales to reach the seed.

CROSSBILLS shear the scales on spruce cone lengthways, and accumulations of cones may be found beneath a tree that has been visited by flock of birds. The scales on pine cones are split and pressed outwards to reach the seed.

WOODPECKERS frequently jam cones into rough bark, or a rock crevice. Spruce-cone scales are opened irregularly, pine cones are pecked open lengthways. The twisting and tearing action gives the cone a rough, torn appearance. Large accumulations may occur beneath favourite feeding places, which are known as 'anvils' or 'workshops'.

NUTCRACKERS have strong bills and peck the scales off, often working on the top of a tree stump or flat stone. They do not leave rough edges as the woodpeckers do, and again there may be large accumulations below a preferred feeding place.

Among the MAMMALS, the squirrels gnaw the scales off and leave a roughly denuded central core of the cone, be it spruce or pine. The remains are often found in large quantities. Mice gnaw the scales off very neatly, leaving the top, non-seed bearing scales intact.

The PINE GROSBEAK has a very strong beak and tends to concentrate on the tougher pine cones, the scales of which it splits very effectively, while the Crossbill with its weaker beak sheath generally opts for the thinner scales of spruce cones.

Fungi

Several species, including the THRUSHES and STARLING, will peck at fungi. Frequently, they are taking invertebrates as much as the flesh itself. Birds leave distinct peck marks and holes whereas mammals always leave teeth marks (mice, voles, squirrels and rabbits will all feed on fungi) and slugs leave shallow surface trenches often with associated slime trails.

Bracket fungus pecked by Starlings

Insects and Invertebrates

Very often the evidence for feeding activity on these groups consists of disturbance to the habitat rather than actual remains.

STARLINGS, for instance, will break up mossy areas on heath and tundra, on lawns and even on roofs, to get at the invertebrates living in them. BLACKBIRDS will throw material out of roof guttering to reach the invertebrates, a very annoying habit if there is a freshly washed car on the drive! In more exposed environments, the impact of a flock of foraging birds can be considerable.

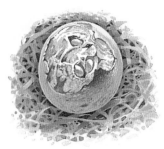

Fresh walnut pecked open by a Nuthatch. Many finches tackle the shell in a similar way.

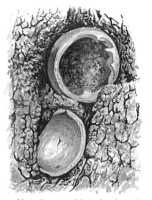

Nuts jammed into bark and hammered open by Nuthatch.

Neat holes punched in acorns by a Great Tit.

Hazelnuts opened on a branch by woodpeckers. Note the large irregular holes.

Hazelnuts opened by Grey Squirrel. These are almost completely split in two.

Cones stripped by a Crossbill.

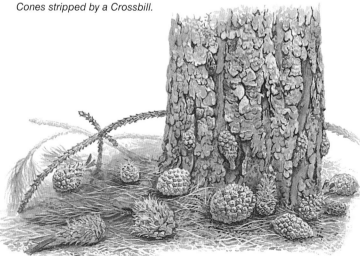

Cones under a woodpecker 'workshop'.

Spruce cone with the scales gnawed down by a squirrel.

Mouse

Squirrel

Squirrel

Crossbill

Mouse

Mouse

Squirrel

Cones opened for seeds by mammal and bird species

Moorland moss area turned over by Curlews searching for larvae.

Wasp nest broken open by Honey Buzzard. The insects have all been eaten.

Green Woodpecker feeding at the base of a rotten stump.

CURLEWS also turn over mossy areas on moorland, but their approach is more systematic and often results in a mini ridge-and-furrow appearance of the surface. Cranefly (*Tipulidae*) larvae are an important food source in such areas. Some birds peck into the ground at a specific point to reach a known buried quarry, and this activity is described under 'Feeding Environments' below.

WOODPECKERS and WRYNECKS peck into rotten wood to get at the invertebrates, particularly grubs, inside. GREEN WOODPECKERS often 'beat up' fallen trees on the ground; they will also peck open wood-ant nests to get at the insects, and seem unaffected by the formic acid retaliation.

HONEY BUZZARDS also sometimes feed on the ground. They break open wasp and bee nests for the insects, and leave the honey and combs largely intact. By contrast, nests broken open by Badger, or even Brown Bear, have the honey comb destroyed and eaten but the insects largely disregarded.

Many birds which are herbivores as adults rear their young on invertebrates. Grouse, Chaffinches and Yellowhammers are examples. Remains are limited, but may be confusing when associated with the nests in which the adults are known to be plant-feeders.

BEE-EATERS feed on insects, including bees, first removing the stings. Occasionally, accumulations of such stings will be found beneath wild-bee nests in trees.

Molluscs and Crustaceans

Several species have developed specialised feeding techniques to deal with shelled invertebrates. EIDERS crush freshwater mussels and the broken remains are found in reedbeds. SHELDUCKS feed on marine molluscs, crustaceans, worms and especially the snail *Hydrobia*. Feeding remains generally consist of the fragmented shells of the larger molluscs.

OYSTERCATCHERS are adapted to opening mussels in one of two ways. One group, with a probing bill, prises open the valves, leaving marks on the edges. Another group, with a blunter bill, hammers the shells and breaks them open. The differences in approach can be seen clearly in a mussel bed worked by a flock of Oystercatchers.

THRUSHES extract snails by holding the lip of the shell and knocking it against a hard surface to expel the occupant. The stones, or 'anvils', used for this purpose frequently have the remains of many shells around them. Bank Voles, by contrast, nibble down the spiral of snail shells. Large numbers of shells attacked by voles may be found on woodland edges or paths, but there is no sign of an anvil and the gnawed spirals are quite distinct.

Thrush 'anvil'

Feathers

Obviously feathers are a valuable means of species identification, as later chapters will show, but the way in which they have been removed from a bird is obvious from their condition. Individual feathers with the quill and plume intact have normally been moulted. A mass of feathers, even if the rest of the body is missing, often indicates the site of a kill, or at least where the predator has stopped to pluck the carcase.

BIRDS OF PREY pluck the feathers out with their sharp beak and leave a hole or broken section of quill. Small carnivorous mammals bite through the feather so that most of the quill is missing. Larger carnivores, like the foxes, pull the feathers out in mouthfuls, leaving the quills broken and the plumes damaged; smaller feathers are often matted together with dried saliva.

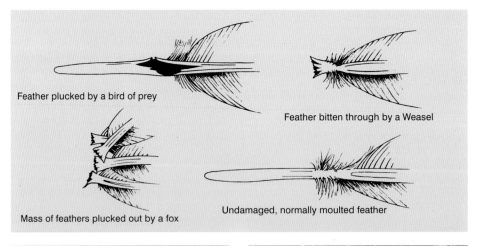

Feather plucked by a bird of prey

Feather bitten through by a Weasel

Mass of feathers plucked out by a fox

Undamaged, normally moulted feather

Gull feathers (Sparrowhawk strike)

Yellowhammer feathers

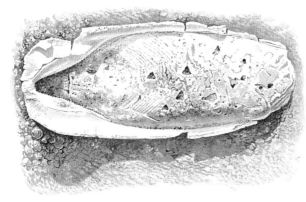

Entire snail shell on right contrasted, on left, with a shell gnawed round the spiral by a Bank Vole. Snails attacked by thrushes are more fragmented and are found close to hard objects, 'anvils'.

Cuttlefish bone showing peck marks from a Common Gull. The marks are triangular and distinct.

Naturally hatched egg showing neatly removed end.

Egg preyed on by Weasel.

Egg preyed on by gull showing the peck marks clearly.

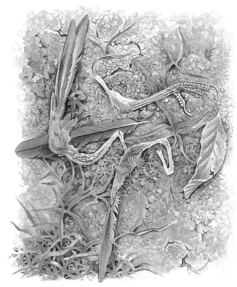

Brown Rat skull on Kestrel feeding place. The V-shaped marks left by the small sharp bill are distinct on the shattered cranium and on the back of the lower mandibles.

Sparrowhawk kill. Only the wings and legs are left, although other secondary predators may have cleared the carcase of this Thrush.

Carcases and Bones

It is not often possible to be species-specific in identifying a predator from a kill, but some useful guidelines may be obtained. The prey size and the habitat are useful clues. Most birds of prey pluck the feathers, and often decapitate their avian prey.

MERLINS use prominent points, such as large stones, fence posts or grouse butts, as places to pluck their prey. An examination of wings and feathers shows that they concentrate on small ground-nesting birds, but they will also take some larger species. An interesting variation has been found on a wet moor in the north of England where the main feeding remains found were the viscera of frogs and toads.

SPARROWHAWKS concentrate on the smaller perching birds, plucking the feathers and normally eating the breast muscles first. The example opposite shows the remains of a thrush eaten by a Sparrowhawk. Only the wings, legs and some body bones are left; the plucked feathers have blown away.

Prey species	Numbers	%
Meadow Pipit	896	61.9
Starling	146	10.2
Skylark	65	4.5
Yellowhammer	35	2.4
Chaffinch	34	2.3
Whinchat	34	2.3
Linnet	31	2.1
Snipe	25	1.7
Pied Wagtail	24	1.7
Red Grouse	23	1.6
Swallow	17	1.2
Golden Plover	16	1.1
Willow Warbler	15	1.0
House Sparrow	14	1.0
Blue Tit	12	0.8
Curlew	10	0.7
Great Tit		
Wheatear		
Lapwing		
Fieldfare		
Spotted Flycatcher		
Redstart		
Robin		
Nuthatch		
Dunnock		
Marsh Tit	51	3.5
Song Thrush		
Redshank		
Dotterel		
Swift		
Budgerigar		
Coal Tit		
Redpoll		
Greenfinch		
Redwing		
Total	**1,448**	**100.0**

The small ground-nesting birds are vital, but Starlings are also important at other times of year.

Merlin prey remains (long hind claw denotes pipit species).

Magpie killed by Sparrowhawk (head removed).

Rabbit found near Goshawk nest.

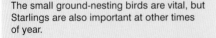
Merlin feeding remains. Avian prey from a large moorland sample taken in 1984.

PEREGRINES tackle their prey in the same way, but concentrate on larger birds such as pigeons, curlews and plovers.

BUZZARDS often turn the carcases of small mammals, such as rats and squirrels, inside out. Larger mammals, such as rabbits and hares, are often found with the skin and fur shredded.

Bones are very often eaten whole or broken into fragments. The LAMMERGEIER feeds on carrion, especially the marrow from large bones. These may be dropped from a height on to a hard surface to break them open.

Bird and mammal carcases left by MAMMALIAN PREDATORS normally show crushed bones and teeth marks. Often there is a strong musty smell if the kill is fresh.

Hen Pheasant killed by a fox

Eggs

It is not the purpose of this book to describe eggs in their own right, but naturally hatched and predated eggs are common finds under some circumstances. Naturally hatched eggs are opened in one of two ways. Some species neatly chip a line right around the shell towards one end and push the cap clear to hatch (e.g. pheasants). Others chip one or more irregular holes and then force their way out of the shell, leaving a series of irregular broken sections (e.g. Curlew). In either case the serrated edge tends to be pushed outwards rather than being pecked in and often the chorionic membrane is largely intact, even if it is dried and shrunken. Eggs preyed on by birds are pecked open with jagged holes, which are punched inwards, normally in the central area rather than the ends. The contents are cleared out but there are normally traces of membrane left. GULLS, SKUAS and CROWS are the main egg predators although raptors and owls may also take eggs.

Weasels and stoats bite into the eggshell and may even leave teeth marks. Even the larger mammal species such as foxes will often bite the ends off without crushing the rest of the shell. Rats and squirrels tend to break the shells into smaller fragments, but in all cases of mammal predation the shell content tends to be cleared out completely.

Specialist egg feeders, such as EGYPTIAN VULTURES, smash large eggs by picking up big stones in their beaks and repeatedly dropping them onto the shell until it cracks.

Predated shells may be found almost anywhere and nests where all the eggs have been predated *in situ* are sometimes encountered. Ducks are prone to nest predation by mink, whereas ground nesting waders (e.g. Golden Plover) and gamebirds (e.g. Willow Grouse) are prone to mustelid or crow attack. Hatched shells are not normally found very close to nests, since the adults carry them some way off or even eat them to avoid drawing predators' attention to the nest and the young.

Predated Song Thrush egg

Hatched Oystercatcher egg

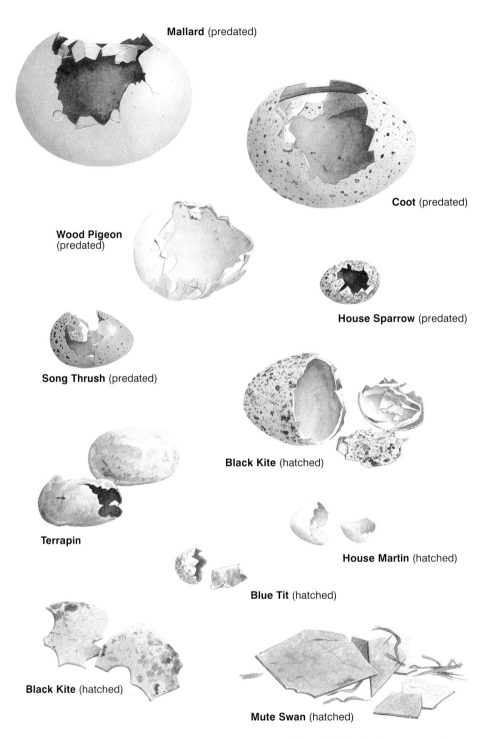

Mallard (predated)

Coot (predated)

Wood Pigeon
(predated)

House Sparrow (predated)

Song Thrush (predated)

Black Kite (hatched)

Terrapin

House Martin (hatched)

Blue Tit (hatched)

Black Kite (hatched)

Mute Swan (hatched)

Examples of hatched and predated eggs. Hatched eggs, e.g. House Martin, showing two neat pieces.

Hatched Kestrel egg

Hatched Rook egg

Hatched Magpie egg

Hatched Wood Pigeon egg

Predated Coot egg

Predated House Sparrow egg

Feeding Environment

Seashore

Seashores may be rocky, shingle, sandy or muddy. The upper and middle shore, where there are various lengths of exposure between periods of immersion with sea water, are varied and rich feeding environments for birds. The rocky areas yield many crustaceans and molluscs, while sandy and muddy shores are a valuable food source, especially to waders and gulls, which have adapted to reaching the enormous number of invertebrates living at different depths on and in the sand and mud.

While the gulls are rather clumsy, opportunist feeders, waders have evolved different bill lengths to seek out particular food species. The CURLEW has a 120–130mm bill to probe for the deeper-living species such as ragworm (*Nereis*) and lugworm (*Arenicola*). The REDSHANK has a 50mm bill which will reach intermediate sources such as tellin (*Macoma*). The RINGED PLOVER has a 10–15mm bill with which it takes superficially-living cockles (*Cardium*) and lever spire shells (*Hydrobia*).

The waders are further adapted by spending the winter on the shoreline, estuaries and mudflats where they feed on molluscs, crustaceans and marine worms, but in summer they move onto open and arable land where they breed and take Tipulid larvae, *Diptera*, *Chironimidae* and *Coleoptera*. OYSTERCATCHERS take a high proportion of earthworms in their diet under certain conditions on arable land in the summer.

The shoreline is a valuable place for feeding signs. OYSTERCATCHERS leave the broken remains of bivalves and cockles, but also probe into the soft substrates, leaving distinctive oval beak marks. The larger beak marks of CURLEWS are often found in almost semi-

Crab eaten by a Common Gull

circular groupings, as the bird tends to stand for several seconds and systematically probe its surroundings. By contrast, the tiny bill marks of the DUNLIN often lie in an erratic line, as the bird moves quickly forward probing the ground as it goes. SHELDUCKS also search the mud for food. They sift the ground with their broad beaks, searching for invertebrates, and moving their heads from side to side as they move slowly forward. This results in parallel, continuous semi-circular troughs in the ground.

Although their beaks are not specially adapted for digging, larger GULLS probe intertidal mud, silt and sand surfaces. The marks are not diagnostic of species, but can sometimes be identified from associated tracks. In one of the examples shown here, a gull has attempted to dig out a lugworm as the tide has receded and before the worm has drawn completely into its

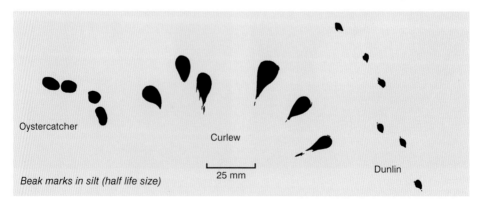

Oystercatcher

Curlew

Dunlin

Beak marks in silt (half life size)   25 mm

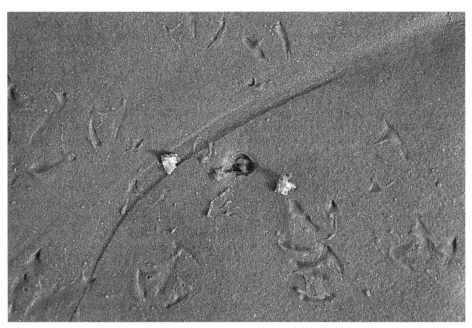

Marine worm attacked by Herring Gull. Note the tracks with long central toe clear of the web.

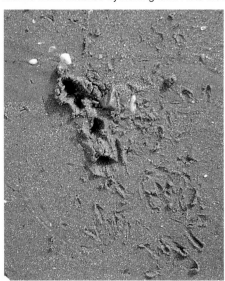

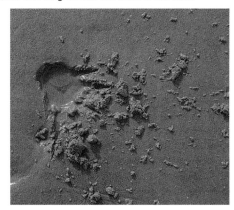

Above: A Lesser Black-backed Gull has attempted to dig out a lugworm, without success, as the tide receded.

Left: Great Black-backed Gull beak marks in intertidal sand.

burrow. In this case the attempt was unsuccessful. In the other example, a HERRING GULL has been more successful in dislodging a polychaete and the remains of the tube can be seen on either side of the hole. The tracks, ranging from toe prints alone to full web outlines, can be seen around the hole.

Other shoreline feeding signs include crab shells, cuttlefish bone, and dead fish and bird corpses carrying the beak marks of scavenging GULLS and SKUAS. Although they are difficult to spot and collect before being destroyed by the advancing tide, gull and wader pellets can give a great deal of information about feeding activity and are discussed in more detail in the next chapter.

Fresh Water

Generally speaking, signs of feeding activity tend to be less obvious. SHELDUCKS may leave the crushed shells of fresh water molluscs in reedbeds. OSPREY pellets containing fish remains are sometimes found below waterside perches in trees. The habit of wiping fish scales from the beak onto branches near the nest hole may give away the presence of KINGFISHERS to the trained eye. It is, however, sometimes difficult to distinguish bird feeding remains from those of mammals. Otters, mink and muskrats may all leave mollusc and fish remains by the water's edge. Waterside vegetation may be cropped down by both birds and mammals, but these signs are more easy to differentiate: geese and ducks tend to graze bankside herbs and grasses widely, while the close cropping of the water vole is restricted to smaller areas close to the water and around bankside burrows.

Woodland

Woodlands provide a great range of food sources. Birds have adapted to use a range of feeding environments, as the tabulated example shows.

Blue and Long-tailed Tits are canopy and shrub feeders. Nuthatches and Treecreepers are trunk feeders, Wrens are herb-layer feeders, while the Robin and Blackbird are ground feeders. Various signs of feeding activity will be found. Tree stumps in clearings or rides are used by birds of prey, such as SPARROWHAWKS, to pluck and eat prey. (See p115; a Brown Rat skull has been left on a rock. The cranium has been broken open and the lower jaw damaged. This is typical of prey killed either by a bird of prey or a small mustelid. This particular skull carries only small sharp V' marks caused by a raptor bill – in this case, a Kestrel.)

Nuts and cones are found in large quantities below branches and in particular feeding sites. Tree stumps are used by NUTCRACKERS to split cones. Woodpeckers and Nuthatches lodge nuts in bark. TREECREEPERS may dislodge pieces of bark where they are searching for invertebrates. Nuthatches do the same, and small quantities of fragmented bark may be found at the bases of trees. Woodpeckers leave large quantities of rotten wood and bark around a feeding site.

Accumulations of pellets below roosting places are common in woodlands.

GREAT SPOTTED WOODPECKERS some-times peck holes in rings around the trunk of a tree to feed on the nutritious sap which oozes out. They are particularly fond of lime species.

One specialised method of dealing with food leaves very distinctive signs in woods and hedges. SHRIKES store food on thorn bushes, barbed wire or jammed into the angles of branches. They do not have long talons to hold their prey while it is dismembered, which is one of the reasons for impaling or wedging in so-called 'shrike larders'. The other reason is storage. The GREAT GREY SHRIKE tends to wedge small mammals and birds between branches in bushes, while the REDBACKED SHRIKE impales invertebrates, amphibians, reptiles, and bird and small mammal prey directly on to thorns or barbs.

Shrike larder

Open Land

Signs of feeding activity specific to open land are limited. Wader and Starling workings of open peat areas for invertebrates have already been discussed. Pellets and carcase remains may be found around fence posts, on open moorland and tundra, especially on slightly raised ground and prominent rocks. Grazed heather shoots and other forms of low-growing vegetation in mountain and arctic areas are characteristic of the various grouse and their allies. The areas involved are small and cannot normally be confused with extensive areas grazed by deer, stock or even voles.

Improved Land

Gulls and waders pick over newly ploughed and seeded fields, leaving beak marks as they do on the shore. Traditional haystacks and circular bales are worked by sparrows, Starlings, crows and even gulls searching for both nest materials and invertebrates. Straw may be spread over a wide area.

GREENFINCHES often flock, and will totally strip large areas of farm weeds such as charlock (*Sinapis* spp.), persicaria (*Polygonum* spp.) and burdock (*Arctium* spp.). They also strip seed heads from cereals, hemp, flax, hops and sunflowers, leaving the remains under the plants, which may

be severely damaged. SERINS strip seeds from trees, and take buds from birch trees on the edge of cultivated land in Mediterranean woodland. They take various seeds from the fields, including brassicas and dandelions, especially in winter.

Muddy tracks on farms often have puddles used as bathing areas. Tracks are often present and the mud is smoothed around the water's edge. In dry soil, shallow dust baths are common. Often several species will use the same depression, although Pheasants tend to make large dust baths on field edges. Sparrows and finches are fond of dust baths and create small, deep depressions. In all cases droppings and feathers, along with any tracks present, will help with species identification.

Sparrow dust bath

Territorial Signs and Regular Routes

The main territorial signs are leks – regular display areas made by gamebirds such as CAPER-CAILLIE and other species of grouse. Cock birds move around in circles, dragging their wings. This leaves worn, flattened trenches in soil and vegetation. The GREAT SNIPE and RUFF also make communal leks.

Ducks produce well-established routeways in pond and riverside vegetation where the populations are stable. Reedbeds have narrow, but distinct paths. In very tall reeds or grasses duck trails take on the appearance of tunnels, in contrast with deer, otter or muskrat runs where the vegetation is completely flattened to form an open path.

In undisturbed riverside situations, ducks will roost in regular locations by the water's edge. Such roosts are often under the shelter of tree roots and consist of flattened areas of mud or vegetation, often with feathers, large numbers of droppings, and tracks in wetter conditions.

Mute Swan preening spot, note feather down and droppings

False Feeding Signs

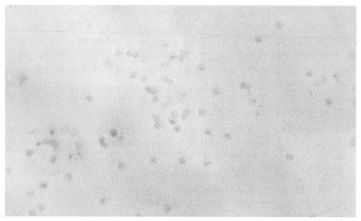

Raindrops on ice, not bill marks

Entrances to ant nest, not bill marks

Bark stripped by deer, teeth marks show

Chapter 6

PELLETS

Several groups of birds regurgitate the hard, indigestible remains of their food as pellets. The form, content and location of pellets can give a great deal of information about the species which has produced them and about the pattern of feeding activity. Perhaps the owls (*Strigidae* and *Tytonidae*) are the best known group of pellet producers. Since the owls tend to swallow their prey more or less whole, and have a relatively gentle digestive process, bones and other hard parts such as feathers and insect carapaces remain intact. Identification of feeding remains is very easy. All other birds of prey produce pellets, although the remains tend to be more fragmented. The herons, shrikes and kingfishers produce distinctive pellets, while the crows and gulls regurgitate pellets which are highly variable according to diet. Wader pellets consist largely of the hard parts of marine invertebrates. Some small omnivorous birds also form pellets, but these are very difficult to identify and in some cases can be confused with droppings.

It is not possible to distinguish between the pellets of closely related species without positive identification of the bird itself. Basic pellet types are, however, as the list below shows, easily identified and a detailed study of the pellets of a known species is often the only way to obtain knowledge of its feeding ecology.

OWLS Cohesive, dense and consisting of invertebrate remains, fur, feather and many intact long bones and skulls.

VULTURES, HAWKS AND EAGLES Form and size of pellet vary greatly with species. Cohesive, dense, mainly fur and feathers with only small bone fragments as the flesh is torn off the bones. Hawks pluck the larger feathers from prey.

FALCONS Pellets similar in many ways to those of hawks. Cohesive, dense, consisting of tiny bone fragments, fur and feather matrix with lizard scales, arthropod and earthworm remains present.

HERONS Cohesive, dense and mainly fur with few bones or other fish remains.

GULLS Generally not compacted, may be well or ill formed. Consist of various vegetable, invertebrate, vertebrate and inanimate remains.

HOBBY Although this is a falcon, the pellets are distinctive, tending to be loose, light, rounded and not cohesive, consisting almost entirely of insect remains.

SHRIKES Pellets small, very dense, elongated and cohesive. Contain small vertebrate and invertebrate fragments.

WADERS Small pellets, varied in shape but generally not very cohesive. Contain invertebrate remains and, in the coastal environment, a matrix and the hard parts of marine invertebrates. Mucous lining is sometimes present in the pellets of some species.

Barn Owl roost with pellets on ledges and in rough stonework

Distinguishing Pellets from Mammal Droppings

Pellets containing fur, feather and bone remains can be confused with some carnivore droppings especially those of fox. Fresh droppings, however have a particular smell and are generally found singly and in open country. The remains lie parallel to the long axis of the dropping, which is twisted with at least one tapering, pointed end. Pellets do not show the same twisting, and the remains are not always parallel to the long axis. Pellets do not smell musty and are frequently found in large quantities in buildings or under roosts in trees, or below a feeding post.

Pellets consisting of insect remains (e.g. Hobby pellets) can be confused with droppings of insectivorous mammals such as hedgehogs. The pellets tend to be globular, while the droppings are elongated, twisted and frequently much more cohesive.

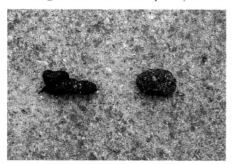

Hedgehog dropping (left) compared with Hobby pellet (right)

Fox dropping showing twisted form

Great Grey Shrike

Size range 20 to 30mm long x 10 to 15mm diameter. Pellets small, hard, compressed and dark. Elliptical and laterally compressed. Contain feathers, fur, bone fragments, insect remains and coarse vegetation particles. The remains are oriented parallel to the long axis and are normally very small. The pellets are found below feeding places, often close to 'larders'.

Great Grey Shrike pellet

Cuckoo

Size range 15 to 25mm long x 5 to 10mm wide. Small and compact. At certain times of year, a major element in the food is hairy caterpillars. The hairs are not digested and accumulate in large quantities in the stomach, to be regurgitated, mixed with other hard parts of invertebrates, as pellets.

Kingfisher

Size range 10 to 40mm long x 5 to 15mm wide. Ill-formed accumulations of fish bones, scales and mucus. Often large in relation to the bird. Normally these 'castings' are found in the nest tunnels, where they fairly rapidly break down into incohesive masses rather than distinct pellets.

Grebes

Size range 20 to 45mm long x 15 to 22mm wide. Although not commonly found in the wet, waterside nesting environment, the pellets of this group are distinctive. They consist of fish bones and insect remains. In the case of the young, they also contain large quantities of feathers, which are fed to them by the adult birds to help with digestion.

Crow Pellets

All members of the crow family produce pellets at some time. These contain a wide range of remains including small mammals, birds, invertebrates, egg shell, worms and various types of vegetable matter. Stones are a frequent constituent. It is not always possible to differentiate between the pellets of different species, since these vary greatly with diet, but all crow pellets tend to be cohesive and contain many small fragments of more than one material.

Crow pellets

Comparison of Jackdaw, Rook and Carrion Crow pellets

Carrion Crow

Size range 30 to 70mm long x 10 to 20mm diameter. Pellets medium to large, elongated and rounder but with pointed ends. Often laterally compressed. Lightly or tightly compacted depending on contents. Frequently contain seeds, insect and vertebrate remains, but these are rarely intact since the carcases are pecked to pieces rather than eaten whole or in large sections. Hard parts often fit parallel to the long axis of the pellet.

Rook

Size range 30 to 40mm long x 10 to 15mm diameter. Small pellets, elongated and slightly pointed at one end. Cohesive with mixed contents, including bone and feather fragments. Often with small stones and vegetation, especially seed. Large accumulations may be found below the communal nests.

Corn ears eaten by rooks

Rook pellets, consisting of corn husks

Jackdaw

Size range 25 to 30mm long x 10 to 15mm diameter. Pellets small, elongated, slightly pointed and laterally compressed. Light-coloured and cohesive but not dense. Often consist of hard parts of vegetation only, but small fragments of bone may be present.

Magpie

Size range 35 to 45mm long x 10 to 20mm diameter. Pellets small to medium. Elongated, narrow and pointed. Contain loose fragments of bone, fur, plant seeds and grit.

Gull Pellets

The pellets are generally well formed, but vary greatly in content according to the diet, since most gulls eat a wide range of food. They will often scavenge on waste tips, and pieces of polythene and string are common in pellets. Pellets are often rounded and globular.

Gull pellets   *Herring Gull pellets*

Herring Gull

Size range 25 to 50mm long x 15 to 20mm diameter. Small to medium pellets. In the example above, the bird had been feeding on a field of cereals and the pellet consists entirely of the husks. The pellets are light and often very loose. They may be round or elongated, and hard parts such as fish bones are not necessarily parallel to the long axis.

Great Black-backed Gull

Size range 35 to 55mm long x 15 to 25mm diameter. Pellets small to medium. They are rounded, light and loosely compacted. This example, which consists mainly of seed, is not very cohesive, but pellets which contain fish and other animal remains are denser and stay together more readily.

Wader Pellets

Almost all species produce pellets. Those of Redshank, Curlew, Knot and Oystercatcher are physically distinctive, whereas those of other species are less so. The example shows that even less easily distinguished pellets can give a great deal of information, provided they are collected from the shore in time.

Turnstone

As with many of the waders feeding in the intertidal area, the small and delicate pellets do not persist for very long and, unless a particular species is seen regurgitating, it is often difficult to say which pellet belongs to which bird. Detailed studies of this species have shown the following composition by volume:

Barnacle plates	60%
'Brown matrix'	17%
Littorina operculata (periwinkle)	12%
Crab remains	5%
Polychaete jaws ⎤	
Grit/sand ⎥	6%
Vegetable matter ⎥	
Feathers ⎦	

This is an interesting illustration that pellet remains can be misleading, because the remains of the crustacean *Gammarus*, which was observed to be a major food source when watching the birds feed, hardly featured in the analysis.

Owl Pellets

The prey is swallowed whole or in large sections, which results in cohesive pellets containing fur, feathers, bones and invertebrate hard parts. Whole small mammal and bird skulls are common.

Barn Owl

Size range 30 to 70mm long x 15 to 40mm diameter. Pellets large, smooth, cylindrical and rounded at both ends. Dark colour with a sheen when fresh. Large bone fragments not often

Barn Owl pellet (compacted/fur)

Barn Owl pellet (open/bones/fibrous material) a 'weathered' pellet

apparent at the surface. Highly compressed. Main prey species are small rodents and birds, but there is much variation between individuals and habitats.

	Habitat (roost)		
Prey species (% of total units)	Arable (barn)	Oak wood edge (stable)	Village (church spire)
Wood Mouse	8	47	13
House Mouse	18	12	19
Bank Vole	4	16	39
Field Vole	14	7	9
Starling	50	1	0
Others	6	17	20
*Based on 840 pellets analysed from northern England sample sites			

Table of vertebrate remains from barn owl roosts*

The preferred nesting/roosting sites are ledges or flat areas in barns, outbuildings, church spires and ruins.

Tawny Owl

Size range 20 to 50mm long x 10 to 25mm diameter. Medium-size pellets with a bumpy surface. Bones often protrude. Irregular in shape and tend to taper at one end. The pellets are compressed, light grey in colour, and consist mainly of vole and mouse remains with some bird and invertebrate material. Found mainly in groups under tree or post roosts.

Tawny Owl pellets

Short-eared Owl

Size range 30 to 60mm long x 15 to 25mm diameter. Medium to large pellets. Elongated, rounded at one end and tapered at the other. Rounded in cross-section. Grey with a slight sheen and highly cohesive, but light. Whole bird and mammal skulls common and clearly aligned with long axis. Small mammal, bird and invertebrate remains. Found individually or in groups under roosting points on open moorland or grassland. Pellets sometimes regurgitated on the ground in moorland or open hill land situations.

Short-eared Owl pellets

Long-eared Owl pellets

Eagle Owl pellet

Little Owl pellets

Little Owl pellet

Long-eared Owl
Slightly smaller pellets than those of Short-eared Owl, but elongated, irregular and very slender. Contain mainly small mammals, birds and invertebrates. Found in small numbers below trees of woodland or forest edge, particularly coniferous forests or plantations.

Little Owl
Size range 15 to 40mm long x 10 to 15mm diameter. Small to medium pellets. Elongated and pointed at one end. Colour, size and content depend greatly on diet. The pellets are light and may be compressed or very crumbly. Small rodents, birds, reptiles, insects and earthworms (although few remains of the latter are seen) are common. Large quantities may be found under fence and gate posts, as well as below tree roosts.

Eagle Owl
Size up to 150mm long x 40mm diameter. Very large pellets. Cohesive and containing a wide range of vertebrate remains, including rabbits, lizards and birds (even smaller owls). Large bones and near-complete skulls are common.

Snowy Owl
Size up to 120mm long x 35mm diameter. Very large, elongated, irregular and loosely compressed pellets. Large bone fragments from a wide range of prey, including lemmings, other rodents, rabbits and even birds as large as geese, ducks and gulls. Pellets found on nest ledges, in and under tree nests and roosts, and on open tundra ground.

Scops Owl
Size range 10 to 15mm long x 5 to 10mm diameter. Very small pellets. Rounded and consisting almost entirely of insect remains.

Snowy Owl pellet

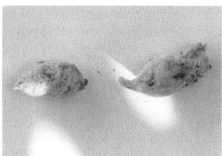

Scops Owl pellet

Tengmalm's Owl pellet

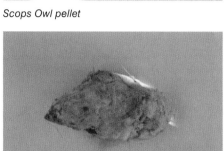

Ural Owl pellet

Hobby pellet

Tengmalm's Owl

Size range 30 to 35mm long x 10 to 15mm diameter. Small, irregular pellets. Often very light, but highly compacted. Bone fragments from small mammals and birds are very obvious.

Ural Owl

Size range 55 to 65mm long x 20 to 30mm diameter. Large and broad. Slightly tapered. Very compact and consisting of a mass of bones, fur and feathers, as well as insect remains.

Hobby

Size range 20 to 26mm long x 10 to 15mm diameter. Small pellets, fragile and slightly elongated but generally rounded. Contain the remains of small birds sometimes, but invertebrate remains such as those of large flying insects are common. This example consists almost entirely of beetle elytra.

Kestrel

Size range 20 to 40mm long x 10 to 25mm diameter. Small to medium pellets, rounded at one end and pointed at other. Very light, grey and often laterally compressed. Consist of fur/feathers with fragments of bone, invertebrate remains and sometimes vegetable matter. The most important single elements of prey are the field vole (*Microtus agrestis*) in the British Isles and the common vole (*Microtus arvalis*) in mainland Europe. Other rodents, young rabbits, other small mammals, small birds, frogs, lizards, worms and insects are elements of prey and can occur in any combination in pellets.

Kestrel pellets

White-tailed Eagle pellet

Booted Eagle pellet

Sparrowhawk pellets

Stork pellet

Grey Heron

Size range 45 to 80mm long x 25 to 40mm diameter. Medium to large pellets, variable in shape. The prey is eaten whole or in large segments. Highly compressed. Although fish are a large part of the diet, they are generally completely digested and the pellets consist of mammal and sometimes bird remains. There may be a few small bone fragments, hut generally only fur and feathers with some invertebrate hard parts are present. Often found in accumulations below nesting places, and by the water's edge at regular feeding places or roosting places.

Buzzard

Size range 45 to 60mm long x 25 to 30mm diameter. Large and elliptical. Pellets consist mainly of masses of tightly packed fur, sometimes with feathers. Very few, if any, bone fragments. The prey, other than small mammals, is stripped into very small pieces. Pellets found under posts and branches, sometimes below nests.

White-tailed Eagle

Size range 90 to 110mm long x 35 to 40mm diameter. Enormous pellets. Very broad and solid with rounded ends. Tend to be slightly flattened. Consist of much fur and feather remains, but there is virtually no bone and what there is consists of tiny fragments.

Booted Eagle

Size range 50 to 60mm long x 20 to 30mm diameter. Large and highly compacted. Consist of a rounded mass which is very solid and has round ends. Fur and feather remains from small birds and mammals, with very small bone fragments.

Sparrowhawk

Size range 25 to 35mm long x 10 to 18mm diameter. Small and compacted, although not dense.

Rounded at one end and tapered at the other. Consist mainly of feathers and sometimes some fur, but rarely any bone or other hard parts. In the example shown on page 132, the feathers are from a cock House Sparrow. The feathers are almost always small and downy, as the larger body, wing and tail feathers are plucked.

White Stork
Size range 40 to 60mm long x 25 to 35mm diameter. Medium pellets, often very dense, cohesive and sticky. Contain fur, feathers and invertebrate remains, and often a lot of soil from the earthworms which form a major part of the diet.

Golden Eagle pellets

Blackbird pellet

Vulture pellet, contains wool

Arctic Skua pellet

Eagle Owl pellets in 'casting' location.

Eagle Owl pellets, note on the left old and weathered showing bones and on the right a fresh pellet.

Chapter 7
DROPPINGS

Introduction

Generally, bird droppings consist of undigested food remains, which have passed through the gut mixed with urine, which is often in the form of a white paste. The urine mixes with the faeces in the cloaca. Many birds have undistinctive droppings which consist of amorphous, semi-liquid masses. A large number of species do, however, produce droppings which are distinctive because of their form, content and location. Deposits of droppings, which do not make species or even group identification possible, help the observer to locate nests and roosts. The droppings of some birds vary greatly with activity patterns and the breeding cycle, especially in some of the herbivorous species, and this underlines the need to treat identification with caution.

A number of basic types of dropping, taking account of contents, consistency and form, can be recognised. The droppings may be completely liquid, semi-liquid or solid. In form they may be amorphous/liquid; round and twisted/semi-firm; or cylindrical/firm. These combinations give rise to five major groups related partly to form and partly to diet.

Dropping Types

Amorphous
Many species produce droppings with no particular constant form (e.g. fowl). In other species, amorphous droppings indicate a particular phase of digestive activity (e.g. grouse).

Seed-eater
Generally small, well-formed droppings which can sometimes be confused with pellets. Contain seed and fruit remains (e.g. thrushes).

Plant-eater
(1) Elongated droppings consisting of coarse, fibrous plant remains, with (e.g. Pheasant) or without (e.g. grouse) a white capping of urine.
(2) Cylindrical semi-liquid masses, when diet consists largely of non-fibrous plants (e.g. swans).

Insect-eater
(1) Tubular droppings, often encased in a membrane (e.g. Green Woodpecker).
(2) Small, globular droppings, often found in masses below roosts (e.g. House Martin).
In both types of insect-eater droppings, the hard parts of the invertebrate remains are clearly visible.

Carnivore
The hard parts of prey are either digested or regurgitated as pellets, so that droppings consisting mainly of urine and liquid faeces are excreted. In the case of the raptors the tail is lifted and the faeces squirted as a jet (e.g. Merlin), while some of the scavenging species produce largely liquid droppings with some small hard parts in them (e.g. gulls).

Locations

Individual droppings are found at random, but accumulations around nesting, roosting and feeding places are useful signs. Large masses of dark droppings are found below HOUSE MARTIN nests under roofs. Roosting DOVES leave lines of light-coloured, semi-amorphous droppings under trees, bridges and the exterior of buildings. Trees used by nesting and roosting HERONS and CORMORANTS are often extensively stained white with liquid faeces and may be partially or even totally killed by them. Raptor feeding places, such as large isolated rocks, fence posts and telegraph poles, are often stained with liquid 'squirts' and have feeding remains, including

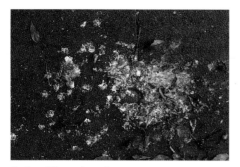

Collared Dove droppings

Thrush droppings, containing fruit 'stones'

pellets, littered around them. Such sites are used by Buzzards, hawks and owls. Droppings from finches, Blackbirds and thrushes are often found on and around seed- and berry-laden bushes; they are coloured by the berries which the birds have consumed. Bird tables, patios, and wall and fence-post tops are also useful places to look for droppings from small passerine seed-eating species.

Insect-eaters

Insectivorous birds leave hard, often dry, droppings containing the indigestible remains of chitin.

Barn Owl droppings and pellets

GREEN WOODPECKERS deposit elongated, cylindrical droppings of invertebrate remains encapsulated in a greyish membrane. Often the remains are almost exclusively of ants.

WAGTAILS produce small, globular droppings which may be found in large accumulations in and around nests. They are grey to black in colour, and contain highly comminuted invertebrate remains.

HOUSE MARTINS again produce small globular droppings containing invertebrate remains. They are very dark and do not have the greyish hue of wagtail faeces.

House Martin droppings

GOLDEN PLOVERS leave dark, coiled droppings with a white urine cap. These tend to be found singly on open moors in summer and in coastal areas in winter. The diet varies, but invertebrate remains can sometimes be seen. In general, the composition is more liquid than in other species which feed exclusively on insects, and the matrix is generally more amorphous.

Seed-eaters

Perching seed-eating birds produce droppings which are semi-cohesive, well formed, and often contain undamaged seeds. This fact is important for the propagation of some plant species. CHAFFINCH droppings are small, well formed and a good example of this type of faeces.

BLACKBIRDS produce more liquid droppings, full of seeds and pips, which are often stained with the juice of the fruit.

The diet of individual species varies considerably. Although gamebirds generally feed on the shoots of herbs, grasses and fibrous vegetation, they will occasionally eat seed heads. In this example, a RED GROUSE has been taking the stems and seeds of *Carex panicea* exclusively.

Blackbird dropping

Grouse droppings consisting of Carex *seed*

Birds Living on Soft Vegetation

SWAN droppings are cylindrical, flat-ended and often green. Up to 150mm long, they often contain plant remains and are found near nesting and roosting places by the shore.

GEESE produce cylindrical faeces, normally dark at one end and with a distinctive urine capping. They are often slightly coiled, and contain highly compressed plant fragments so to 80mm long and 10 to 15mm in diameter.

Vegetarian DUCKS produce droppings which may be cylindrical, smaller versions of goose droppings or may be amorphous circular deposits, depending on the diet and species involved.

Goose droppings

Birds Living on Fibrous Vegetation

A number of species, particularly gamebirds, graze on coarse vegetation. The droppings are tubular and pellet-like, containing the stems and seeds of the plants.

RED GROUSE faeces are normally tubular, brown, slightly curved and dry. A white urine capping is not always present. The droppings are 10 to 20mm long and about 6mm in diameter. They may be found singly, in groups on vegetation tussocks, or in resting scrapes in moorland vegetation. If a bird rests in one place for a long time, then the faecal contents of the caecal appendices are voided after all the fibrous material in the gut has been passed. Such droppings are semi-liquid, and dark in colour. They are up to 40mm in diameter. If a bird has rested overnight, normal and caecal faeces will be found together. Breeding females which remain on the nest for a long time produce large, blocky fibrous droppings (known as 'clockers') owing to prolonged inactivity and an enlarged cloaca. Such droppings are up to 50mm long and 20mm in diameter, and normally have a white urine cap.

Red Grouse droppings, showing the cylindrical shape and urine cap

Caecal droppings from a resting Red Grouse

Red Grouse 'clocker' dropping from an incubating female

Capercaillie droppings

Pheasant droppings in an overnight roost site

Ptarmigan droppings in snow

HAZEL HEN droppings are similar in size to those of grouse, but consist mainly of birch, alder and hazel catkins and fruits.

BLACK GROUSE produce larger droppings than Red Grouse (up to 10mm diameter). These consist mainly of birch buds in the spring. They are much paler in winter, turning darker with age.

CAPERCAILLIE droppings are large (up to 20mm diameter), but similar to those of the grouse. Large caecal faeces are produced which may be up to 70mm in diameter. Droppings are yellow-green when fresh, but turn brown-grey with age.

PHEASANT droppings are brownish-black-green and firm in winter. They are more liquid in summer, when lusher vegetation is being grazed. A prominent urine cap is present. Individual droppings are 20mm long, 4 to 5mm in diameter. They are often found in large groups in depressions in vegetation where the bird has been resting.

Carnivores and Scavengers

It is not possible to use the liquid or semi-liquid splashes of these birds to identify species. Other signs and geographical location will often give more clues to their identity.

Gull droppings are semi-amorphous, but often contain some hard parts. The GREAT BLACK-BACKED GULL dropping shown here contains a hard core of polychaete remains in the white matrix.

Wader and gull droppings and tracks are generally common on the seashore. In this example of HERRING GULL droppings,

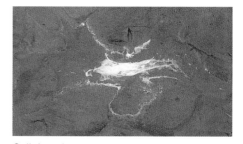

Gull dropping on wet sand

which are generally almost shapeless, there is also a range of tracks, showing toe III well clear of the webbing and helping with the identification of the species involved.

Merlin splashes on a rock perch

Sparrowhawk splashes

Dipper droppings

Tawny Owl droppings, note moulted feather

Amorphous Droppings

At certain times of year, and with variations in diet, many species produce almost shapeless droppings with no recognisable contents. DOMESTIC and ORNAMENTAL FOWL produce large blob-like faeces which take on the colour of the food.

These may contain some recognisable vegetable matter, but are generally without distinct shape.

Analysis

Analysis is of limited value, except in the case of some fibrous-plant- and seed-eating species. A good example of this exception is the CHOUGH. This species does not produce pellets, and much of the food passes through the digestive tract. Faeces have been shown to contain invertebrate remains, grain, lizards, carrion, rubbish, figs, and even oranges in Mediterranean countries. In other studies, beetles and cranefly have been important in autumn, swift moths in spring, ants in summer, and kelp flies and sandhoppers in late autumn.

Great Bustard dropping

If an analysis is undertaken, the droppings should be treated in the same way as pellets namely by teasing them gently apart after soaking in a water or alcohol solution. Seeds and fibres can then be identified with a hand lens or microscope using appropriate keys. The same is true of invertebrate remains, and a qualitative and quantitative analysis of diet can be attempted.

Wheatear droppings

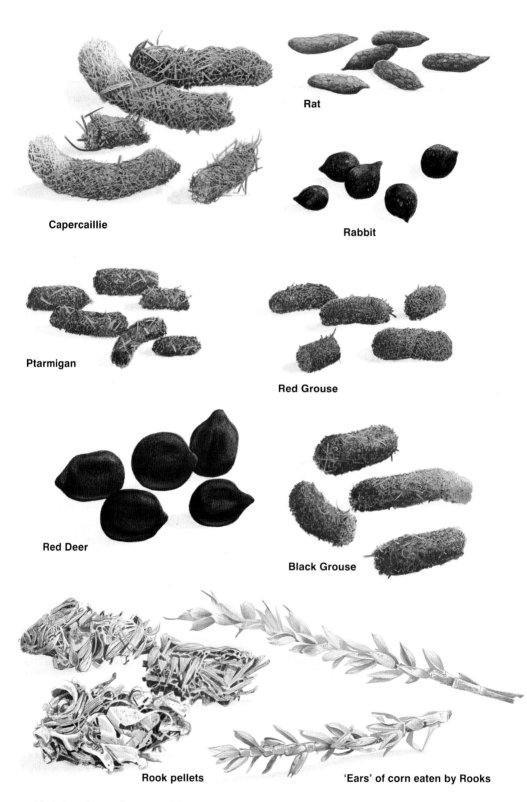

Capercaillie

Rat

Rabbit

Ptarmigan

Red Grouse

Red Deer

Black Grouse

Rook pellets

'Ears' of corn eaten by Rooks

Hard droppings pellets comprising vegetation

Chapter 8

FEATHERS

Discarded feathers, or even whole carcases, are found throughout the year. If a whole wing, or body, is picked up, then identification from existing reference material is easy. Single feathers, which are very common finds, can be another matter. Obviously, various factors, such as the time of year, the length of time the feather has been on the ground and the reasons it was lost (i.e. moulted or through predation), will determine its general condition. Many feathers, however, do carry distinctive patterns which make species identification possible even from a single, bedraggled specimen. This chapter sets out to explain how this can be done. Because of the numbers involved and the limitations of physical space explained in Chapter 1, only the flight and tail feathers can be systematically covered here.

The Functions of Plumage

The plumage, or feathery covering, of a bird serves a number of functions. Like mammals, birds are 'warm-blooded', needing to maintain a constant body temperature in changing environmental conditions. Plumage acts in the same way as fur, protecting the body against sun, cold, wind and rain. Being tough, yet soft within, it also provides some protection against injury.

The plumage forms the outer shape of the bird, which can be altered at need, from streamlined in flight to, for example, rounded and bulky if the bird is threatened. Being the visible covering, it also carries the colours and markings for display and camouflage. Additionally, the plumage supplies the large surfaces necessary for flight.

Feather Development

Feathers are made from **keratin**, in the same way as are the hair, horn and outer skin of mammals. Keratin is a complex of proteins, and is insoluble in water and resistant to enzymes. The **feather follicle** is a socket-like pit in the bird's skin, at the bottom of which lies a group of cells specialising in the production of a feather, usually once a year, throughout the life of the bird.

When a feather starts to form, the **germinal cells** begin to reproduce very rapidly, forming a tube which, covered by a dry sheath, soon projects from the follicle. Within this tube is a pulpy mass containing nerves and blood vessels. The cells of the tube, continuing their rapid division, form into rows which undergo the process of conversion to keratin, starting at their outer, free, ends. Typically, the rows unite in a thicker, central, multiple strand destined to become the rachis. The dried covering begins to break up at the tip, revealing the new feather tuft. At this stage the feather is said to be 'in pin', as is the bird.

After some days the developing 'pin' reaches its greatest length and sheds its covering, gradually exposing the completed feather while, within, the pulp dies back. At the base, keratinisation of the germinal tube itself produces the hollow root or calamus. The thin partitions inside mark the resting phases of the retreating pulp. With the production of a final cap, the **inferior umbilicus**, the feather is completed and the germinal cells become dormant.

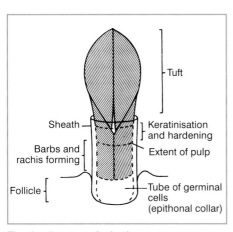

The development of a feather

Labels: Tuft; Sheath; Keratinisation and hardening; Barbs and rachis forming; Extent of pulp; Follicle; Tube of germinal cells (epithonal collar)

The developed feather resembles a tube, one side of which has been slit open lengthwise with part, at one end, being left intact. Where this slit ends, at the junction of the rachis and calamus and where the barbs emerge, there is always a small pit, the **superior umbilicus**.

Feather Type and Structure

The number of feathers on a bird depends mostly on its size. Among European species, there are from about 1,500 on the Swallow to 25,000 on the Bewick's Swan. However numerous the feathers, they all fall within a few well-defined types.

The primitive feathers of extinct birds were supported on two equal shafts, a condition still found in some flightless birds. It is thought that all other feathers have evolved from this prototype by the loss, or reduction, of one shaft. Many retain a small tuft-like 'aftershaft'.

The primary feather of a Red-legged Partridge is used to illustrate the topographical and structural features defined in the following paragraphs.

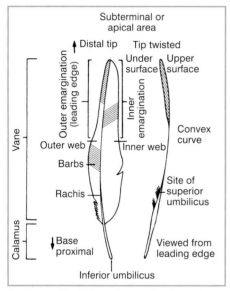

Red-legged Partridge primary, showing main feather structures

Down feathers have a small **calamus** (the shaft at the base of the feather) and a weak or absent **rachis** (the shaft between the barbs). The **barbs** (main branches) remain separate, with filamentous side branches – the whole being very light and fluffy.

The first feathers to be grown by the bird are those that comprise nestling down. This differs in fine detail from adult down, but has the same function, which is to trap warm air against the body. The adult down of some species slowly disintegrates to form a white powder which dusts the entire plumage. The plumage of hawks and owls is particularly well supplied with such down. It is not uncommon for owls to collide with large windows at night, leaving an imprint of the face and wings in powder on the glass. In extreme cases, a specialised continuously-growing **powder down** has evolved. Herons use powder from this down, which is located on the breast, flanks and rump, as an aid in removing fish slime, particularly that of eels, from the plumage.

Bristles are found on the head, particularly around the eyes and the corners of the mouth, in species such as Swifts and Nightjars. They resemble mammalian whiskers, consisting of a stiff rachis, naked or with only a few barbs near the base. Those at the corners of the mouth may help in the capture of flying insects.

Filoplumes are like fine hairs, sometimes tipped with a tuft of barbs, growing among other feathers of the plumage. One possible explanation of their function is that they aid the bird in positioning the outer feathers during preening. The root of the filoplume is well supplied with nerves.

The visible plumage of adult birds is composed of **contour feathers**. These have a well-developed rachis, with barbs linked together to form a flat sheet, the **vane**. At the base (i.e. towards the bird's body), the barbs are usually separate and downy. **Semiplumes** have a well-developed rachis, but no stiff vane, being entirely downy.

On the body, the tips of the massed contour feathers protect the down like overlapping roof tiles. They may augment the down by the possession, as in the pheasants, of a downy aftershaft. Nearly all contour feathers have a tuft of down at the site of the aftershaft.

Each contour feather carries a unit of the bird's overall colour and pattern, whether for display or camouflage. Sometimes the feather carries a marking, which makes it identifiable by itself, while often it is quite plain. By contrasting with its neighbours, however, it may form part of a strong pattern.

The most highly evolved contour feathers are the large feathers of wing and tail used for propulsion and steering. Here, the structure connecting the barbs to form the vane can be seen in its most developed state.

The barb of a **flight feather** is not a simple rod. It is a flat blade fixed to the rachis, with its sides facing its neighbours. Along its upper edge there are two fringes of short **barbules**. Those on the side towards the tip of the feather bear downwardly-directed hooks, **hamuli**, while those projecting towards the base are shaped like gutter troughs. The hooks engage with the edges of these 'gutters' and are prevented from becoming unhooked by forward-projecting spines. The barbs do not lie at right angles to the rachis, but are directed towards the tip at an angle. This angle is related to the stiffness required of each web. The more acute the angle, then, generally, the stronger and stiffer is the web.

Colour

The substances and structures which produce the colours of the completed feather are introduced during development.

White results from an absence of colouring agents in unusually pure keratin, and may be enhanced by structural devices. These may consist of a 'felty' surface, imparting a chalky whiteness; or of minute external or internal reflecting surfaces, giving added brightness. It is thought that the absence of coloured toughening agents results in the rapid wear of white feather material in species such as gulls.

Brown and black are produced by melanin. This substance, an almost universal vertebrate pigment, is deposited by special cells in the follicle and appears as tiny granules both within and on the surface of the feather material. It produces colours from buff to black, according to density.

Reds and yellows are produced by carotenoids, a range of substances derived from food and named after the red of carrots. The best-known example is the pink of flamingos, which is derived from the shrimps in their diet. The pigment may be unchanged or modified

Rapid wear in the white tip of a gull feather

by the bird's body chemistry before incorporation into the developing feather material, where it is dispersed rather than concentrated into granules. Yellows and reds may be enhanced by reflective structures, usually minute internal gas-filled spaces.

Blue is produced by colourless, translucent keratin over black pigment, not by a blue pigment. A similar arrangement with carotenoid in the translucent layer produces green.

Iridescence is well demonstrated by peacock 'train' feathers and by the **speculum** (coloured wing patch) of ducks. It is characterised by the production of metallic colours (e.g. gold) and by the tendency of the colours to change with the angle at which the surface is viewed. These effects are produced in the same way as the colours in an oil film but in the feather the extremely thin transparent layer needed is provided by scale-like surface structures. The underlying feather is usually densely pigmented with melanin to absorb any light not reflected by the special structures.

Wherever plumage colour is being enhanced by reflective devices, the background is usually black. A breast feather from a Great Tit, viewed in isolation, lacks almost any colour. The brightness of the bird's plumage is the effect of massing the yellow tips over a black downy background. Only light returning from tiny reflective 'bubbles' within the transparent yellow keratin reaches the eye.

Wear and Replacement

Once a feather has 'hardened' it is a dead thing, but it is subjected to external forces and changes continuously. During autumn and winter, the coloured breeding plumage of some male songbirds intensifies. It was once thought that this was due to an increase in pigmentation, but such changes are now ascribed to wear. If the tips of the feathers are dull and the mid sections brightly coloured, then the removal by wear of the tip of one feather, thereby exposing the mid section of its underlying neighbour, increases the visible colour.

There may be real changes in colour owing to staining (most noticeable in white, aquatic birds). Preen oil may eventually yellow white feathers or dull iridescent surfaces. A Mallard speculum feather displays a range of rich greens, purples and even browns, but, if it is washed in grease-removing solvent, it becomes a bright, even electric blue.

Birds constantly strive to keep the plumage in good order. Much time is spent in preening. Sparrows are often seen dust bathing, possibly to remove excess preen oil as well as parasites, and, as often, splashing in water, presumably to remove the abrasive dust. All this activity takes its own toll on the feathers.

Sunlight affects both the colour and the durability of the plumage, particularly of birds such as gulls which live out their lives under the open sky. By midsummer, black feathers usually bear the 'imprint' of an overlying neighbour. Outside of the shaded portion the pigment will have become faded and tawny. The keratin itself will also start to degenerate, making the feather progressively more brittle.

Courtship, nesting and the feeding of the young increase the rate of abrasive wear. This is partly because of the general increase in activity and partly through the enforcement of otherwise avoidable activities, such as fighting and crawling into nest holes.

By the end of the breeding season, most of the flight feathers will be worn out. Body-covering contour feathers, essential for keeping dry, will have lost much of their effectiveness. The downy underplumage may also be depleted on some species by having been used for nest lining. To survive approaching winter, the bird's plumage will need to be at peak efficiency in flight and weatherproofing. Hence the moult of the old and the growth of new feathers that occurs annually in almost all birds.

Feathers may be lost at any time of year, through injury, and are often (especially in the case of the tail feathers) replaced in a few days. **Moult**, however, is a complete renewal of plumage which is systematic in both sequence and timing. The onset of this event is triggered by seasonal changes in both the environment and the bird's metabolism. The actual mechanism of feather loss is said to be the pushing out of the old feather by its growing replacement.

A bird carries approximately 40 per cent of its dry tissue weight in the form of plumage, so that, in moult, it must replace a great deal of protein. In most of Europe food is abundant in summer and autumn, and it is at this time that the majority of adult European birds moult and that most feathers will be collected.

Moult

The main moult of the annual cycle is the one after the breeding season and this is a complete moult involving both the body feathers and the flight feathers. Any moult prior to the breeding season is a partial moult with the tail and flight feathers being retained.

There are two factors that determine the moult strategy in all birds and they are keeping the ability to fly and also having a successful breeding season. There is a short period between the end of the breeding season and the onset of winter or migration, when intensive moult is possible. Those species that over-winter in a cold wet climate do not moult during the winter. Migratory species that fly to tropical countries can arrest moult that has been started before they go and continue after they arrive in their winter quarters.

Each group of birds has its own way of performing moult successfully. All European passerines renew their plumage at least once a year, (although whether this is due to an actual need to replace worn feathers is uncertain). Large birds have different strategies that enable them to keep flying. This is mainly done by extending the moult period and taking as long as three years to complete all feathers. This is the case in species such as albatrosses and vultures. At the other extreme species such as ducks and geese drop all flight feathers together and are flightless for a period whilst the new feathers grow. Male ducks, which usually have bright and conspicuous plumage during the breeding season, moult into a dull, female-type plumage known as eclipse during the period of flightlessness. This cryptic plumage reduces vulnerability to ground predators.

After the breeding season is over juveniles will have new feathers and the adults will have worn feathers that will need to be replaced. This results in a timing difference between them for the moult. This has to be completed so that the juveniles will be able to moult as adults the following year. Juveniles have to moult after fledging because the juvenile plumage is less dense and robust. The bird also needs to acquire the patterning of the adult plumage to interact appropriately with its conspecifics. Generally it is only the body feathers which are moulted by the juveniles, the flight feathers being retained for just over a year.

Contour Feathers

In the illustration shown on page 147 of a Woodpigeon in flight, the wing and tail feathers are individually identified. The contour feathers covering the body are simply named according to their position: breast, rump, etc. In poultry and some gamebirds these have specialised names, such as 'saddle hackle' for cockerel rump feathers.

The **primaries** are attached to the 'hand' portion of the wing skeleton. There is a maximum of 11 full-sized primaries, as in the grebes. In other groups such as the gulls, waders and waterfowl, the outermost primary, though present, is minute. Pigeons, owls and gamebirds have 10 primaries, all of full size. In passerines, the large group of perching birds including warblers, finches and crows, the 10th is reduced or minute. They are numbered from the 'wrist', or **carpal joint**, outwards in the order of moult.

The outermost, full-sized primary has a narrow and hard outer **web**. Feathers in which the distal portion of one or both webs is reduced in width are said to be emarginated. When the wing is spread, the emarginations on adjacent feathers form a notch in the wing outline. The depth and number of these notches vary from a few shallow depressions in the Kestrel's wing, to the six deep notches in the Pheasant's wing. In the outer primaries, the inner web is three or more times wider than the outer web.

In general, each primary is narrower and more pointed than its inward neighbour, so that the outer primaries are quite different from the inner ones. Acutely pointed primaries are unusual, except in auks and some marine ducks which use the wing for swimming.

The inner primaries have webs which may approach equality of width in some species (e.g. cormorants). It is, however, unusual for the inner web to be much less than twice the width of the outer. The inner primaries are broad and parallel-edged with their tips angled rather than pointed, the outer edge extending further than the inner.

The rachis of all the outer flight feathers bends inwards (i.e. towards the tail on the extended wing). In the primary series, this curve is gentle and strongest in the middle of the feather. The distal third of the rachis may be straight, or even very slightly recurved in the outermost primaries. The calamus of the outer primaries is stout and long in strong fliers.

The 'forearm' part of the wing bears the **secondaries**, which are numbered inwards from the carpal joint. There are from 9 secondaries in most perching birds (passerines) to 40 in the Wandering Albatross. The innermost secondaries often form a distinct group, known as **tertials**. In some species (e.g. Pheasant), an additional small outer secondary, called the **carpal remex**, is present.

The outermost secondary may be distinguished from the innermost primary by one or more of the following factors. The inner web is usually less than twice the width of the outer, and in many species the two webs are of

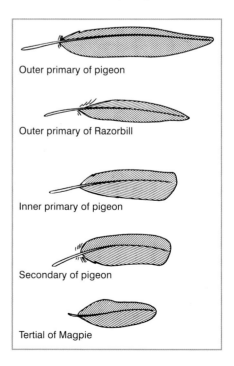

Outer primary of pigeon

Outer primary of Razorbill

Inner primary of pigeon

Secondary of pigeon

Tertial of Magpie

equal width. The tip may be rounded, square, concave or angled with the inner web projecting farther than the outer. The inward curve of the rachis is stronger than it is on the primary. The point of greatest curvature is closer to the base than the tip. The outermost secondaries of many passerines can be difficult to distinguish from the inner primaries. The most reliable indicator is to be found in the curvature.

Tertials, positioned close to the 'elbow' joint, lie one on top of the other and stiffen the inner end of the wing. They may have an outer web which is broader than the inner. The rachis curves diagonally across the vane towards the inner margin. The tertials are often leaf-shaped, and pointed at the tip. In some cases, such as on wagtails and ducks they may be longer than the other secondaries.

Most species have either 3 or 4 feathers attached to the 'thumb' remnants to form the **alula**. Some species have as few as 2 feathers, while others have as many as 7. The feathers of the alula lie on top of each other, with the longest at the bottom and the smallest uppermost, forming a stiff blade-like unit. The largest and most readily identifiable is pointed and stiff, with a narrow, hard outer web. The calamus is short and straight. An alula feather differs from a small primary in being, by comparison, relatively short, broad and robust.

Each primary has a **primary covert** attached close to its root. These coverts are very stiff, with a large calamus which is bent forwards at its junction with the rachis. The web-width ratios reflect those of adjacent primaries, while the vane itself is usually narrow and often gently pointed. Those which most resemble primaries in shape can be distinguished by their stiffness and by the very large calamus. There are interesting variations. The primary coverts of owls are broad and very rounded, while those of swifts are ribbon-like in shape. There are sometimes one or two more **secondary greater coverts** than secondaries. Rounder and softer than the primary coverts, they are visible when the wing is folded and are often strongly marked or brightly coloured. The calamus may be very short. **Median** and **lesser coverts** cover the remainder of the upper surface of the wing.

There is a similar arrangement of **underwing-coverts** on the underside of the wing. These are flat, or slightly concave, and of predominantly pale colours.

The **scapulars** grow from the 'shoulder' regions. They cover the folded wing, while in flight they close the gap between the body and the inner end of the wing. They are usually leaf-shaped and pointed. This is the case in the ducks, in which the scapulars resemble the tertials in shape and size. In colour and pattern they tend to resemble the body, rather than the wing feathers.

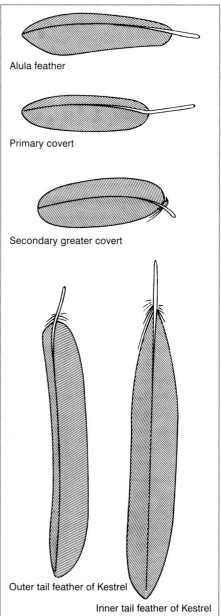

Alula feather

Primary covert

Secondary greater covert

Outer tail feather of Kestrel

Inner tail feather of Kestrel

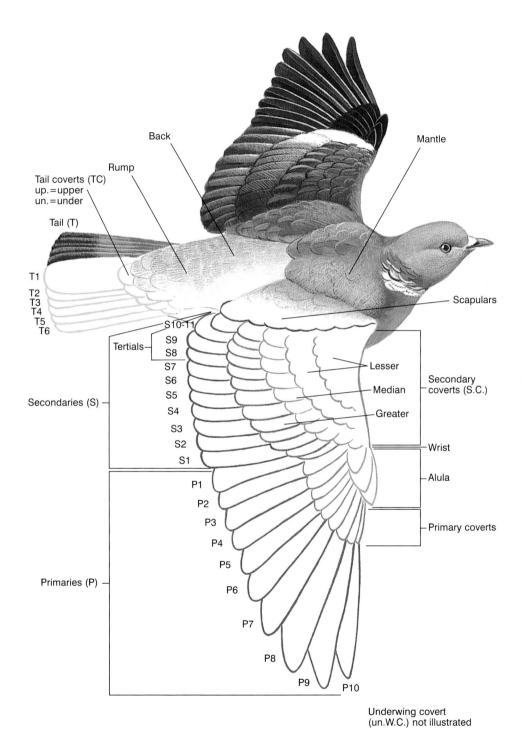

Flying Woodpigeon showing the location and nomenclature of feathers

Beneath the wing the scapulars are complemented by the **axillaries**, which are long, concave and soft.

Among European species, there are from 10 main **tail feathers** or **rectrices** in Cetti's Warbler and the Swift to 24 in the Mute Swan. The majority of species have 12, that is 6 pairs, numbered in this book T1 to T6 from the centre of the tail outwards. The rectrices are vestigial in the grebes. The outer tail feathers have narrow outer webs, similar to those of the outer primaries. Unlike primaries, the tail feathers are often broad towards the tip. The vanes of the outer feathers are frequently flat, or even of concave curvature, whereas the inner pairs are more often convex.

Tails are extremely variable, as a glance through the coloured plates will confirm. Large tail feathers, like those of the pheasants, are obvious. Those of short-tailed species, such as ducks, are less well known but are highly characteristic. Confusion is most likely to arise where tail feathers resemble those of the wing. In these cases, the calamus may appear rather short for the size of the feather. A bend in the rachis, close to its junction with the calamus, directs the latter inwards and downwards. The bulk of the rachis is straight, or even recurved (bent outwards). Often, the tip of the calamus bears a small, upwardly directed knob.

The central tail feathers appear very straight and symmetrical when viewed from above. From the side, the calamus is seen to be directed slightly downwards. The vane tends to be strongly convex.

Uppertail- and **undertail-coverts** smooth the body shape into the tail. In some cases, the central uppertail-coverts may be as long as the adjacent tail feathers (e.g. grouse). They are always convex, this being particularly marked in the undertail coverts, which press up against the underside of the tail. No one shape is characteristic of the tail-coverts of all species, but in many a broadly triangular vane, especially if strongly convex, is indicative.

Of all the above types of contour feather, the large primaries, secondaries and tail feathers are most likely to be encountered in the field. They are sufficiently tough to survive attack by insects and micro-organisms for long enough to be collected. They tend to lack striking colours, so that shape is often the main means of identification.

Flight and Feather Shape

The shape of a feather, particularly a flight feather, is dependent on function, while the function depends on the lifestyle of the bird. Recognising the adaptation of a feather to a particular environment, or flight speciality, is an important stage in identifying the bird from which it came.

Soaring Most birds will hang in an updraught such as is found at the edge of a cliff, if it is strong enough to support their weight. To take full advantage of the gentler uplift available from rising warm air requires a relatively large wing area and a low body weight.

The Buzzard, which is well adapted for thermal soaring, has a wing area of about 2,000 sq.cm and an average weight of 750g (2,800 sq.cm/kg). The outer primaries are deeply emarginated, the narrow portions being of aerofoil section. The remaining wing feathers are broad. There are 13 secondaries, not a high number. Much of the large wing area is provided by the inner primaries, which are particularly ample. The tail feathers, though large, are more elongate in form. In soaring, the wing is held steady, while the free distal sections of the outer primaries twist in the updraught, propelling the bird as the angled sails propel a windmill.

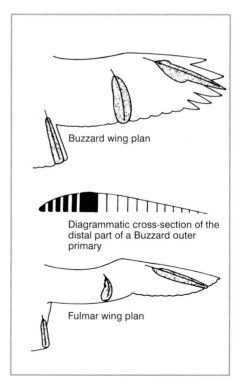

Buzzard wing plan

Diagrammatic cross-section of the distal part of a Buzzard outer primary

Fulmar wing plan

Gliding Seabirds, such as the Fulmar, alternately dive downwind, adding wind speed to acceleration due to gravity, then turn to gain ground and height upwind. At sea, the wind is slowed by contact with the surface and the bird uses this 'dead' air to gain ground in the direction it wishes to travel. Wing loading is higher than in soaring birds, about 1,300 sq.cm/kg in the Fulmar.

The deeper the chord (the shortest distance between leading and trailing edges of a wing), the slower the wing's natural speed. Therefore, the Fulmar's wing is narrow and long. It is also very 'clean', having a smooth outline free of notches or projections. The outer primaries taper, with no emargination, while the inner primaries are short. The 20 secondaries are also short, with the vane almost round. The square tail is short to reduce drag.

Powered Flight In powered flight, it is the 'hand' section of the wing, particularly the outer primaries, which acts as the propeller. When flapping, it moves farther, and at a higher speed, than does as the inner wing and can be thought of as driving the latter through the air. The outer wing, then, provides thrust and the inner wing lift.

The cormorants are regarded as fairly primitive birds. Their flight is most frequently low and straight, neither fast nor agile. Inland, in hot weather, they may at times be seen soaring. When diving, the wings are not used for underwater swimming. The Shag's 2kg are carried on 1,000 sq.cm wings (500 sq.cm/kg), a high wing loading though the wing is not very highly developed. The outer wing is relatively short, about equal to twice the length of the 'forearm'. Primaries and secondaries are similar in length and proportions. None of the feathers is very broad. Their webs, prone to limpness when wet, do not overlap greatly. The whole wing, including individual feathers, is strongly convex as if to counter its weak structure. The tail feathers are of very simple form. The rachis is straight and stiff, and the webs are narrow.

Ducks, in contrast, are fast, heavyweight fliers. The Eider's 2kg are carried on wings of about 700 sq.cm (350 sq.cm/kg). The wing-beat is rapid and shallow. The wing loading dictates a high landing speed and the familiar 'splash down'. Overall, the wing is rather flat. Its propulsive outer section is nearly three times the length of the forearm. As a whole, the wing is pointed and fairly narrow. The primaries are very stiff and highly differentiated from the secondaries. The undersurface edges of the barbs are flattened, extended and folded at right angles towards the rachis. By overlapping, they combine to form a sheet of material, the 'shiny patch' or tegmen, which turns the web into a 'box girder'. This modification, found in all ducks, geese and swans (and also in screamers), renders the primaries of these birds easily recognisable. The calamus is long and thick to cope with the strains of flight.

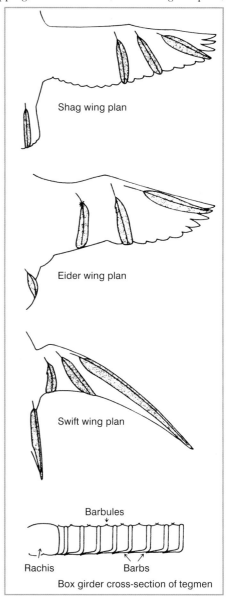

Shag wing plan

Eider wing plan

Swift wing plan

Barbules

Rachis   Barbs

Box girder cross-section of tegmen

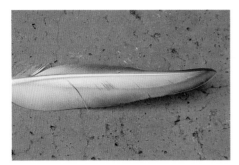

Duck tegmen ('shiny patch')

There are 17 or 18 secondaries in the Mallard, about the same number as in the Shag (18 or 19) – but the degree of overlap is much greater. The secondaries of the ducks, moreover, are of two different types. The outer 11 are short and broad while the remainder, designated 'tertials', are leaf-shaped, pointed and ascend in vane length to almost twice the outer secondaries. The tail is very short, composed of 18 to 20 stiff, blade-shaped feathers almost concealed among the tail-coverts.

A long hand section with a short forearm section (a combination also seen in the falcons) finds its extreme development in the Swift. In the Swift, the hand section (carpal joint to wingtip) is eight times the length of the forearm. The pointed primaries decrease in length by equal steps from the very long, thin outermost 3 to the innermost, which is very little larger than the 8 to 10 tiny secondaries. The tips of the secondaries are striking in that the inner web projects a good deal beyond the outer. In this species flight is no longer a sustained beat, but an alternation of powered phase and high-speed glide. The scissor-like tail can open for manoeuvring, but at speed it closes to shed drag.

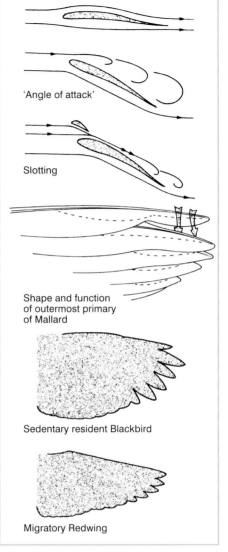

'Angle of attack'

Slotting

Shape and function of outermost primary of Mallard

Sedentary resident Blackbird

Migratory Redwing

In order to fly slowly enough to land safely, birds increase their '**angle of attack**'. The extra turbulence caused is reduced by **slotting**, raising the alula to 'squeeze' the air and increase its speed over the upper surface of the main wing. The outer primary may also have a short, twisted and emarginated distal section, capable of producing a second slot. This condition is found in the Mallard. In many species, such as crows and Sparrowhawk, the outermost primary is shortened, the better to form a 'second alula'. The swifts, which have a small alula and no other means of slotting, have an extremely poor low-speed performance.

Narrow, pointed wings are best suited to sustained rapid flight, while a shorter wing with deeper chord is more useful to a non-migratory forest dweller, whose average 'flight' may be as little as one metre and which also takes off and lands every few seconds when foraging among the branches. In such birds it is not the outer but the middle primaries which are the longest, resulting in a rounded wing. The secondaries are large, deepening the chord, and a longer-than-average tail increases manoeuvrability in pursuit or avoidance. Closely related species, the Redwing and the Blackbird, for example, demonstrate the long wing of the migrant and the rounded wing and long tail of the resident. Woodland species also display an increase in emargination, both in the extent and in the number of primaries involved. Ground-feeding birds, such as the Pheasant, subject to rushing attack by ground predators have carried such adaptations to the extreme. The 6 outermost primaries of the Pheasant are emarginated for three-quarters of the length of both the inner and outer webs. They are stiff and deeply convex. Apart from the short, outer secondary (the carpal remex) and the inner tertials, the 16 secondaries are large, with symmetrically rounded tips. The long inner tail feathers are distinctive. There are 18 in all, diminishing in size from the centre outwards.

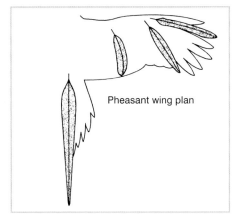

Pheasant wing plan

In steeply climbing take-off, the 'normal wing', of the Woodpigeon for example, gains some thrust during the backstroke from air venting through the opened primaries. During the more powerful downstroke, however, the primaries are closed each trapping the broad inner web of its outward neighbour. A great deal of movement is thus wasted in simply redeploying the wing at a propulsive angle.

The Pheasant's outer primaries, however, cannot lock together and are free to generate thrust throughout the full travel of both strokes. This type of wing, effective for rapid acceleration from a standing start, is found in most gamebirds and also, though in a less extreme form, in hawks. The latter can also use the arrangement for soaring, or by folding back the outer wing, close the slots for fast gliding. This versatility is common, only the most extreme products of evolution (swifts and albatrosses, for example), being committed to a single mode of flight.

Flight and Sound

A by-product of flight is noise. The rhythmic 'whooshing' of a flight of swans can be heard from up to a kilometre away. To owls, however, such noise would be a serious handicap, alarming their nocturnal prey. Owl feathers are instantly recognisable by their soft, furry upper surfaces which muffle the sounds of flight. The leading edge of each outer primary is also equipped with a soft fringe of curved tooth-like projections (see plate on p245).

The male Snipe deliberately employs the rush of air, to produce a loud noise. Such is the purpose of its curiously twisted outer tail feather. This display flight, called **drumming**, includes dives in which the tail is spread and the special feather is exposed in the airstream.

Other Special Feather Modifications

When swimming underwater, some diving birds (many ducks, the divers and the guillemots for example) steer with the feet. Others use the tail. Water is a much heavier medium than air, and this requires very strong, stiff feathers such as are found in cormorants and the Gannet. In the latter, the rachis is exceptionally thick and the web symmetrically tapered to form an acutely pointed vane, the tip of which is usually found to be abraded away, as the plate on p257 shows.

The tails of woodpeckers are composed of stiff, pointed feathers, strongly reminiscent of those of the Gannet. When a woodpecker is drilling, the tail bears much of the bird's weight, by pressing against the tree trunk. The end of the rachis is invariably missing, the barbs on either side giving the impression of a double tip (see plate on p233).

Identification

The information and plates which follow are designed to help identify isolated feathers. These have been laid out around size and colour, giving information on moult times and actual feather dimensions. To get the maximum benefit the following procedures should be adopted.

1. During identification, the feathers should be viewed against a dark background with

daylight coming from behind the observer. Alternative lighting and background may produce a different appearance.

2. Examine the feather and decide which type it is. Use the line-drawings in the preceding pages as a guide. If it is a primary, secondary or tail feather, proceed as suggested below. If it is not one of these, it may be illustrated – but locating it will be more laborious. Use the Index to see if the species you suspect of producing the feather is covered in the book (over 230 are).

3. Measure the length of the feather (Chapter 2) and refer to the size chart on p153. This will give a size/group number I to IX.

4. Turn to the pages which are devoted to the appropriate size group. Within these pages the examples are broadly arranged by colour and pattern.

5. Find the illustration which most closely resembles the feather in hand and consult the written account, particularly the measurements. A tolerance of at least 10 per cent should be allowed when applying the dimensions. If the feather does not fit, try adjacent size categories.

Note It must be made clear that living birds of any species should not be interfered with. Road casualties, zoos, and the seashore after storms may provide sources of materials, but there is no justification under any circumstances for killing or injuring birds in order to collect feather material.

Feather Size Chart for Flight and Tail Feathers

The chart opposite is based on measurements from 'typically' shaped wing and tail feathers. In assigning all birds to size groups, the largest primaries are given precedence. Obviously the feathers from some birds cover a wide range of size groups, but a base line has to be chosen for comparing species, and the size of the largest primary is as good as any.

The information accompanying the feather illustrations is laid out in the following general pattern.

Size category I to IX

Species The common name. Description of main flight and tail feathers, with others of interest sometimes included.

The bars below represent a 12-month calendar and show when birds of the species will be found in moult, at whatever stage. They are excluded if not well studied.

Adult moult	J	F	M	A	M	J	J	A	S	O	N	D
Juvenile moult	J	F	M	A	M	J	J	A	S	O	N	D
Primaries n feathers	P10	P9	P8	P7	P6	P5	P4	P3	P2	P1	
Secondaries n feathers	S1	S2	S3	S4	S5	S6	S7	S8	S9	etc	
Tail n feathers	T6	T5	T4	T3	T2	T1					

Feather measurements are given in millimetres, and feathers are arranged with the outermost on the left, in the numerical order shown. The number 'n' is a maximum, not found in all individuals.

There are 9 to 11 primaries, the outermost of which are often so reduced as to preclude measurement.

The secondaries are highly variable. Unless otherwise stated, missing measurements are from the inner part of the wing. A box with a diagonal line indicates 2 feathers with the same measurement. The total number of secondaries for some species of birds has yet to be finalised. Where this is so, the number of feathers following the word 'secondaries' has been omitted.

In the case of the tail, the number is for the whole (as in other publications), though measurements are only from the left half.

All measurements followed by 'M' have been taken from the specimens in the skin collection of the British Museum (Natural History). They must therefore be treated with caution, as it is difficult to get exact measurements from feathers *in situ*.

Constraints on the space available have made it necessary to omit some information and the secondary measurements, particularly where these are little different from the primary measurements, may have been omitted. The description of feathers tends to be taken from the adult male only, while juvenile plumages have not been included at all.

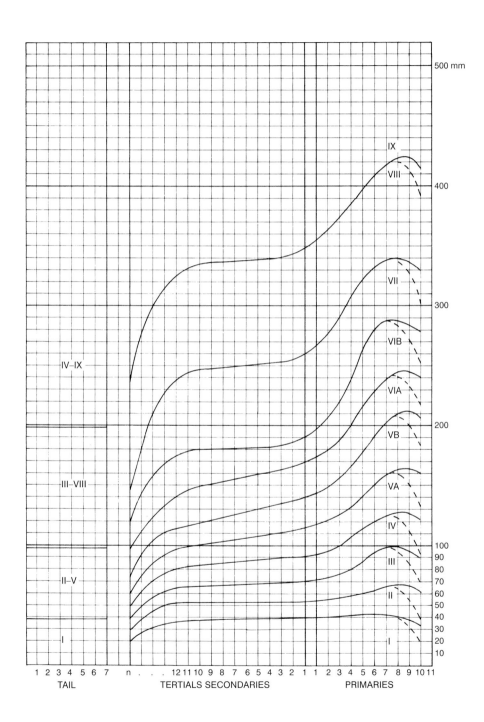

I

GOLDCREST The tail feathers are dark brown with the outer webs fringed yellowish-green. The flight feathers are dark brown, fringed white on the inner web. The first two primaries have outer webs brown, the next four have outer webs fringed yellow-green; the remaining primaries and the secondaries are the same, but with the outer webs as follows: basal portions greenish-yellow, then a band of black followed by yellowish-green. The tertials are greenish and tipped whitish, without the black band.

	J	F	M	A	M	J	J	A	S	O	N	D
Adult moult	J	F	M	A	M	J	**J**	**A**	S	O	N	D
Juvenile moult	J	F	M	A	M	J	**J**	**A**	S	O	N	D
Primaries 10 feathers	16	39	45	47	47	47	43	43	40	40		
Secondaries 9 feathers	39	39	38	36	35	34	31	25	20			
Tail 12 feathers	40	41	40	39	39	36						

FIRECREST Feathers similar to Goldcrest but the outer webs fringed clearer green.

	J	F	M	A	M	J	J	A	S	O	N	D
Adult moult	J	F	M	A	M	J	**J**	**A**	S	O	N	D
Juvenile moult	J	F	M	A	M	J	**J**	**A**	S	O	N	D
Primaries 10 feathers	21	43	49	51	52	51	48	45	45	43	M	
Secondaries 9 feathers	41	40	40	37	35	32	29	27	20	M		
Tail 12 feathers	43	45	45	45	43	43	M					

WREN The tail feathers are rufous-brown, finely barred black-brown. The flight feathers are brown-black with the inner webs narrowly edged whitish. The outer webs of the outer five primaries are barred whitish and rufous-buff, the sixth has more rufous, and the rest and the secondaries are rufous-brown with narrow brown-black bars. The innermost secondaries have both webs rufous-brown with narrow brown-black bars. The outer webs of P5–P8 are emarginated.

	J	F	M	A	M	J	J	A	S	O	N	D
Adult moult	J	F	M	A	M	J	J	A	S	O	N	D
Primaries 10 feathers	18	34	40	40	40	42	42	41	41	41		
Secondaries 9 feathers	40	40	40	38	36	35	31	27	20			
Tail 12 feathers	30	33	33	34	32	33						

MARSH TIT The tail feathers are black-brown with outer webs edged olive-brown, with a very narrow whitish outer line on outer pair. The flight feathers are black-brown, narrowly edged brown on the outer webs and white on the inner webs. The innermost secondaries are pale-brown. The outer webs of P4–P8 are emarginated.

	J	F	M	A	M	J	J	A	S	O	N	D
Adult moult	J	F	M	A	**M**	J	J	A	S	O	N	D
Juvenile moult	J	F	M	A	M	**J**	J	A	S	O	N	D

WILLOW TIT All feathers are the same as the Marsh Tit except that the innermost secondaries are edged whitish.

	J	F	M	A	M	J	J	A	S	O	N	D
Adult moult	J	F	M	A	M	**J**	J	A	S	O	N	D
Juvenile moult	J	F	M	A	M	**J**	J	A	S	O	N	D
Primaries 10 feathers	20	40	49	53	55	55	54	51	49	49		
Secondaries 9 feathers	48	48	47	45	43	40	36	26	19			
Tail 12 feathers	48	53	55	54	53	53						

COAL TIT The tail feathers are greyish-black, fringed olive-green on outer webs. The flight feathers are greyish-black, fringed olive-green, with the inner webs fringed white. The tertials have greyish-brown inner webs and whitish tips. The outer webs of P5–P8 are emarginated.

	J	F	M	A	M	J	J	A	S	O	N	D
Adult moult	J	F	M	A	M	**J**	J	A	S	O	N	D
Juvenile moult	J	F	M	A	M	J	**J**	A	S	O	N	D
Primaries 10 feathers	20	46	54	56	56	54	51	49	48	46	M	
Secondaries 9 feathers	44	40	40	38	38	36	35	29	21	M		
Tail 12 feathers	44	48	48	46	46	46	M					

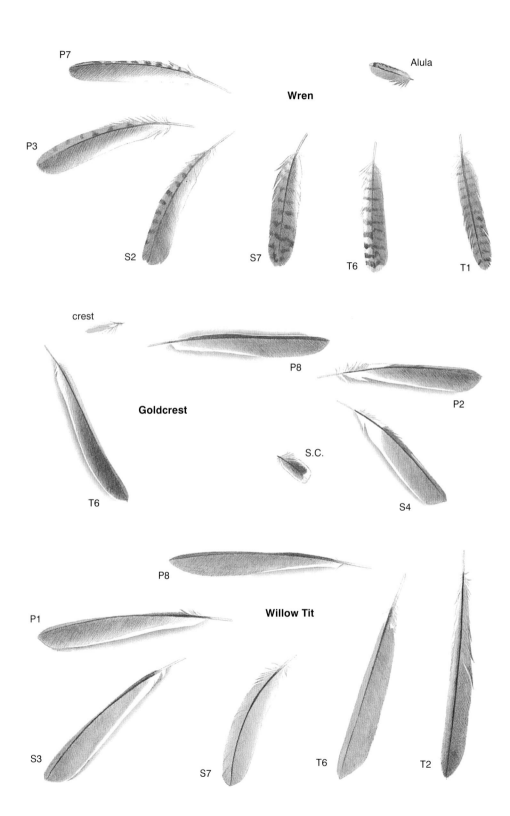

Wren

P7

Alula

P3

S2

S7

T6

T1

crest

Goldcrest

P8

P2

T6

S.C.

S4

P8

Willow Tit

P1

S3

S7

T6

T2

I–III

BEARDED TIT The tail feathers are tawny-chestnut with the tips slightly marked blackish; the central pair is more yellowish than the rest, and the outer pair has the outer web and tip of inner dusky white and the rest of inner web and base black; next pair with distal half of outer web dusky white. The primaries are black-brown, the inner webs white, P4–P8 with conspicuous white margins to outer web; the rest with yellowish-tawny margins. The secondaries have the margins of outer webs tawny, the rest of the outer webs becoming black on inner secondaries and the inner webs of these feathers becoming creamy-white. The innermost secondary is entirely creamy-white. The outer webs of P5–P8 are emarginated.

	J	F	M	A	M	J	J	A	S	O	N	D
Adult moult	J	F	M	A	M	J	**J**	**A**	**S**	**O**	N	D
Juvenile moult	J	F	M	A	M	J	**J**	**A**	**S**	**O**	N	D
Primaries 10 feathers	20	48	50	55	58	57	53	52	47	46		
Secondaries 9 feathers	46	46	45	45	44	42	42	35	30			
Tail 12 feathers	96	90	88	88	87	51						

GRASSHOPPER WARBLER Tail feathers are dark olive-brown, usually faintly barred dusky on T1 only. The flight feathers are dull black or greyish-black, the outer fringes of the flight feathers are narrowly but sharply fringed olive-brown or cinnamon-brown except for P9. The outer web of P8 and occasionally P7 is notched. The inner web of P9 is notched.

	J	F	M	A	M	J	J	A	S	O	N	D
Adult moult	J	F	M	A	M	J	**J**	**A**	**S**	O	N	D
Juvenile moult	J	F	M	A	M	J	**J**	**A**	**S**	O	N	D
Primaries 10 feathers	16	51	54	53	51	49	48	47	46	45		
Secondaries 9 feathers	44	43	42	41	40	39	38	31	23			
Tail 12 feathers	54	54	53	51	48	41						

PENDULINE TIT The tail feathers are dull black or brown-black with the outer feathers dark grey. The central pair have pale yellow-buff along both webs. The remainder have narrower and sharper pale yellow-buff fringes along the outer web and tip and an off-white border along the inner web. The flight feathers are dull black or greyish-black. The primaries are narrowly fringed pink-buff to off-white along outer web and tip. The secondaries have slightly wider and warmer tawny-buff fringes. Outer web of P5–P8 and the inner webs of P6–P9 are emarginated.

	J	F	M	A	M	J	J	A	S	O	N	D
Adult moult	J	F	M	A	M	J	**J**	**A**	**S**	O	N	D
Juvenile moult	J	F	M	A	M	J	**J**	**A**	**S**	O	N	D
Primaries 10 feathers	23	52	55	50	42	42	42	42	40	40		
Secondaries 9 feathers	58	55	55	54	50	45	40	35	28			
Tail 12 feathers	46	46	45	46	46	47						

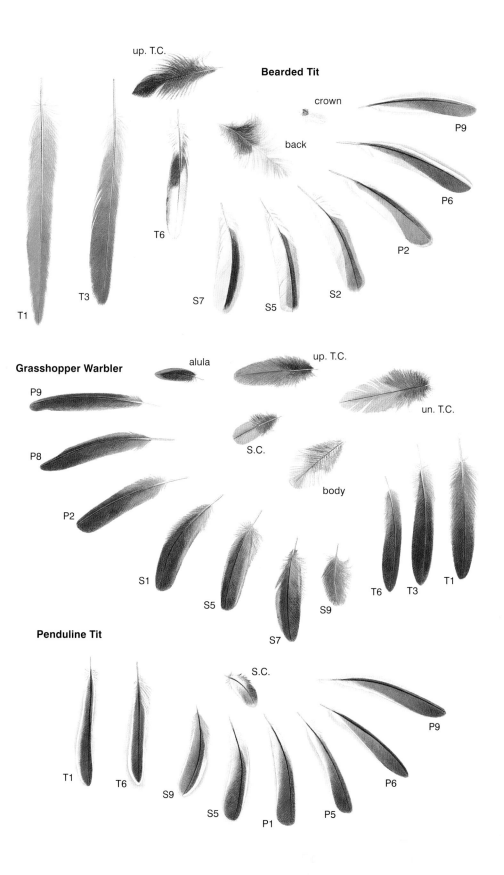

Bearded Tit

up. T.C.

crown

back

P9

P6

P2

S2

S5

S7

T6

T3

T1

Grasshopper Warbler

alula

up. T.C.

un. T.C.

P9

S.C.

body

P8

P2

S1

S5

T6

T3

T1

S9

S7

Penduline Tit

S.C.

P9

T1

T6

S9

P6

S5

P1

P5

I–III

DARTFORD WARBLER The tail feathers are blackish-grey with the central feathers having narrow light grey fringes. T4–T6 have a narrow sharp fringe along the outer web and tip. Flight feathers are greyish black or black with the outer web and tips narrowly fringed grey. Outer webs of P6–P8 are emarginated. Inner web of P9 notched.

	J	F	M	A	M	J	J	A	S	O	N	D
Adult moult	J	F	M	A	M	J	J	A	S	O	N	D
Juvenile moult	J	F	M	A	M	J	J	A	S	O	N	D
Primaries 10 feathers	18	38	45	45	48	47	47	47	47	45		
Secondaries 9 feathers	45	45	43	44	38	37	35	28	24			
Tail 12 feathers	65	65	65	66	69	69						

SARDINIAN WARBLER The central 5 pairs of tail feathers T1–T5 are black with a grey fringe along the outer web and tip. The inner webs of T3–T4 have a white spot or fringe on the tip. The tip of T5 has more extensive white. The outer web of T6 is white and the inner web is black with a white tip. The flight feathers are dull black or greyish-black, with the outer webs and tips narrowly fringed light grey. Outer web of P6–P8 emarginated. Inner web of P9 notched.

	J	F	M	A	M	J	J	A	S	O	N	D
Adult moult	J	F	M	A	M	J	J	A	S	O	N	D
Juvenile moult	J	F	M	A	M	J	J	A	S	O	N	D
Primaries 10 feathers	22	44	49	50	50	50	49	47	47	47		
Secondaries 9 feathers	48	48	48	45	41	40	35	30	25			
Tail 12 feathers	54	58	59	58	57	57						

ZITTING CISTICOLA The central pair of tail feathers are sepia brown with narrow paler buff-brown fringes along the sides. T2–T5 are dark sepia-brown or black-brown with paler buff-brown outer fringes. There is a black subterminal bar 3–4 mm wide with a pale grey-buff or off-white fringe along the tip. T6 is similar but has a paler brown ground colour and the bar is reduced to a spot. The flight feathers are dark grey-brown or sepia-black with the outer webs and tips narrowly fringed pale brown-buff to buff-white. The outer webs of P4–P8 and the inner webs of P6–P9 are emarginated.

	J	F	M	A	M	J	J	A	S	O	N	D
Adult moult	J	F	M	A	M	J	J	A	S	O	N	D
Juvenile moult	J	F	M	A	M	J	J	A	S	O	N	D
Primaries 10 feathers	18	36	40	45	48	47	47	45	45	45		
Secondaries 9 feathers	45	45	44	43	41	37	32	28	24			
Tail 12 feathers	36	40	42	45	47	49						

LITTLE STINT The central pair of tail feathers has black-brown centres with broad chestnut margins on both webs; the remainder are a pale grey-brown, narrowly edged white. The primaries have dark brown outer webs and tips, with paler, white-based inner webs; the shafts are white with browner bases and tips; P1–P6 have a white edge to the basal half of the outer webs. The secondaries are brown, narrowly tipped white, with a white base (more extensive on the inner web); the inner web on the inner secondaries is almost entirely off-white. The tertials are blackish-brown, with broad chestnut to pale buff edges.

	J	F	M	A	M	J	J	A	S	O	N	D	
Adult moult	J	F	M	A	M	J	J	A	S	O	N	D	
Primaries 11 feathers	26	88	87	82	74	68	60	55	50	45	40	M	
Secondaries	40	40	40	40	40	42	45	48	50	55	50	45	M
Tail 12 feathers	38	38	40	41	42	44	M						

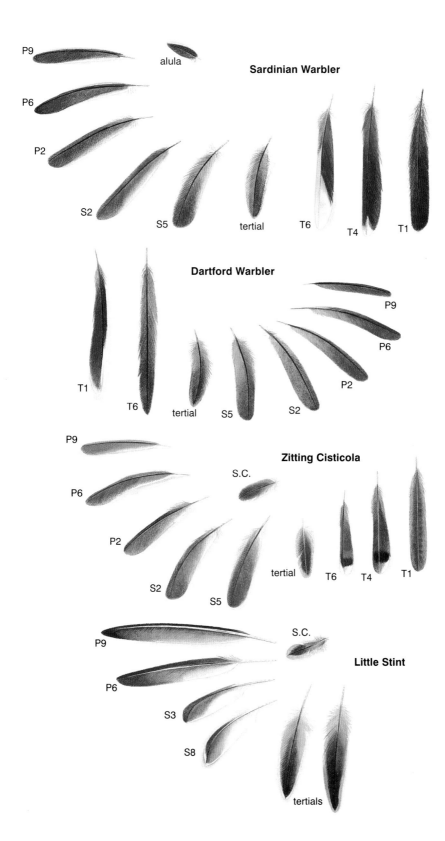

P9
alula
Sardinian Warbler
P6
P2
S2
S5
tertial
T6
T4
T1

Dartford Warbler
P9
P6
P2
T1
T6
tertial
S5
S2

P9
Zitting Cisticola
P6
S.C.
P2
tertial
T6
T4
T1
S2
S5

P9
S.C.
Little Stint
P6
S3
S8
tertials

II

LONG-TAILED TIT The tail feathers are black, the two outer pairs with the outer webs and a large wedge-shaped mark at the tip of the inner web white; the next pair is the same, but only the distal half of the outer web is white. The primaries are brown-black with the inner webs fringed white. The secondaries are the same, but the outer webs are also fringed white or buffish-white, narrowly on outer feathers and broadly on the four innermost ones, which are paler and browner than others. The outer webs of P5–P8 are emarginated.

	J	F	M	A	M	J	J	A	S	O	N	D
Adult moult	J	F	M	A	M	J	J	A	S	O	N	D
Juvenile moult	J	F	M	A	M	J	J	A	S	O	N	D
Primaries 10 feathers	24	45	55	61	62	61	57	54	51	48	M	
Tail 12 feathers	63	73	81	86	88	91	M					

GREAT TIT The tail feathers are blue-grey on outer webs and brown-black on inner webs, but the central pair with most of the inner webs blue-grey and shafts black, the outer pair with outer web white and a wedge of white on distal portion of inner web; next pair has a small white tip, and the following pair often with a small white spot at tip. The flight feathers are black, fringed blue-grey on outer and white on inner webs. P10–P9 not fringed, P8–P4 with distal emarginated portion of outer webs dull white and basal half fringed blue-grey. The inner secondaries have the outer webs broadly fringed greenish-yellow. The outer webs of P4–P8 are emarginated.

	J	F	M	A	M	J	J	A	S	O	N	D
Adult moult	J	F	M	A	M	J	J	A	S	O	N	D
Juvenile moult	J	F	M	A	M	J	J	A	S	O	N	D
Primaries 10 feathers	21	49	61	64	66	66	62	60	57	57		
Secondaries 9 feathers	58	56	55	53	52	48	45	37	25			
Tail 12 feathers	60	64	65	65	65	64						

BLUE TIT The tail feathers are greyish-blue with the central pair and outer webs of rest bright blue, the outer pair is narrowly fringed white on the outer web. The flight feathers are black-brown, the outer webs are blue and the inner webs are narrowly fringed white. P10-P9 are uniform black-brown, P8–P4 with distal emarginated portion of outer webs dull white and basal half bright blue. Inner secondaries tinged greenish on outer webs and tipped dull white. The outer webs of P4-P8 are emarginated.

	J	F	M	A	M	J	J	A	S	O	N	D
Adult moult	J	F	M	A	M	J	J	A	S	O	N	D
Juvenile moult	J	F	M	A	M	J	J	A	S	O	N	D
Primaries 10 feathers	19	45	53	55	57	57	55	52	50	50		
Secondaries 9 feathers	50	49	48	47	45	43	39	33	25			
Tail 12 feathers	52	53	53	53	52	50						

KINGFISHER The tail feathers have dark blue upper surfaces with black shafts, and are dull black on under surface. The flight feathers have outer webs of dull blue or greenish-blue, but the tips of the primaries and the outer web of P10 are a dull black; the inner webs and the narrow lines along the shafts are dull black and the basal inner borders have a variable amount of buff or a creamy tinge. The inner web of P10 is slightly emarginated.

	J	F	M	A	M	J	J	A	S	O	N	D		
Adult moult	J	F	M	A	M	J	J	A	S	O	N	D		
Juvenile moult	J	F	M	A	M	J	J	A	S	O	N	D		
Primaries 10 feathers	58	62	65	64	64	63	62	61	60	58				
Secondaries 13 feathers	58	56	55	53	52	51	50	48	46	44	39	30	23	
Tail 12 feathers	39	42	41	41	41	39								

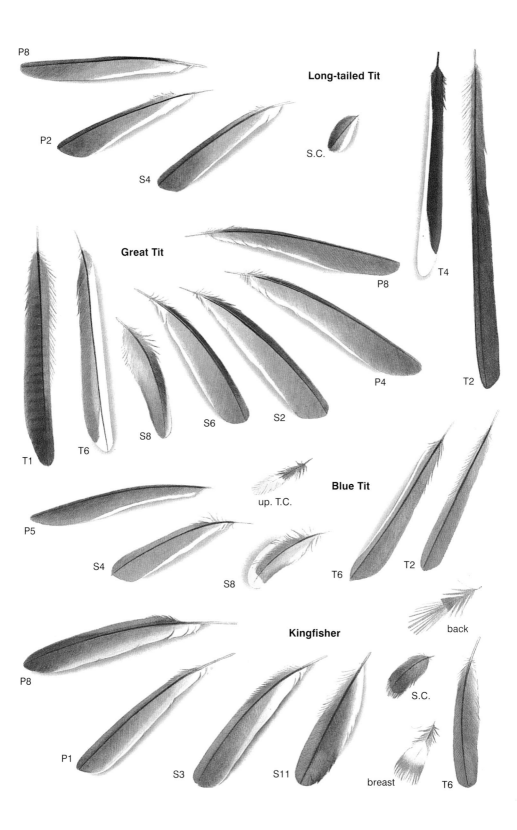

P8

Long-tailed Tit

P2

S4

S.C.

T4

P8

Great Tit

P4

T2

S6

S2

S8

T6

P5

up. T.C.

Blue Tit

S4

S8

T6

T2

T1

back

Kingfisher

S.C.

P8

P1

S3

S11

breast

T6

II

LESSER WHITETHROAT The tail feathers are dark greyish-brown with greyish-white fringes and tips; the outermost pair has the outer web white and a varying amount of white or brownish-white on the inner web. The flight feathers are dark brown, the inner webs narrowly fringed white, and the outer webs fringed pale greyish-brown, the innermost secondaries are greyish-brown. The outer webs of P6–P8 are emarginated.

	J	F	M	A	M	J	J	A	S	O	N	D
Adult moult	J	F	M	A	M	J	J	A	S	O	N	D
Juvenile moult	J	F	M	A	M	J	J	A	S	O	N	D
Primaries 10 feathers	27	60	65	64	60	58	56	54	53	52	M	
Secondaries 9 feathers	50	45	45	45	45	42	40	32	24	M		
Tail 12 feathers	50	55	58	58	60	60	M					

BLACKCAP The tail feathers are greyish-black with the outer webs fringed olive-brown. The flight feathers are greyish-black, fringed white, with the outer webs olive-brown, those of the outer primaries being more greyish. The outer webs of P6–P8 are emarginated.

	J	F	M	A	M	J	J	A	S	O	N	D
Adult moult	J	F	M	A	M	J	J	A	S	O	N	D
Juvenile moult	J	F	M	A	M	J	J	A	S	O	N	D
Primaries 10 feathers	26	63	72	72	70	68	65	58	58	56	M	
Secondaries 9 feathers	55	50	50	45	45	42	42	36	27	M		
Tail 12 feathers	61	62	62	62	62	62	M					

WILLOW WARBLER The tail feathers and the flight feathers are dark brown, with the inner webs very narrowly dull white and outer webs more broadly olive-green or olive-brown. The flight feathers have small whitish tips. The outer webs of P6–P8 are emarginated.

	J	F	M	A	M	J	J	A	S	O	N	D
Adult moult	J	F	M	A	M	J	J	A	S	O	N	D
Juvenile moult	J	F	M	A	M	J	J	A	S	O	N	D

This is the only European passerine in which adults have two complete moults a year.

Primaries 10 feathers	17	50	56	57	57	53	51	50	49	48
Secondaries 9 feathers	47	47	45	44	42	40	38	30	21	
Tail 12 feathers	53	54	54	54	53	51				

CHIFFCHAFF All feathers as Willow Warbler. The outer webs of P5–P8 are emarginated.

	J	F	M	A	M	J	J	A	S	O	N	D
Adult moult	J	F	M	A	M	J	J	A	S	O	N	D
Juvenile moult	J	F	M	A	M	J	J	A	S	O	N	D

REED WARBLER The tail feathers are dark brown with very narrow whitish-cream tips and fringes to the inner webs. The flight feathers are darker brown, with very narrow pale brown tips and narrow pale brown fringes to the outer webs and whitish fringes to the inner webs. The outer web of P8 is emarginated.

	J	F	M	A	M	J	J	A	S	O	N	D
Adult moult	J	F	M	A	M	J	J	A	S	O	N	D
Juvenile moult	J	F	M	A	M	J	J	A	S	O	N	D
Primaries 10 feathers	19	57	61	60	58	56	55	53	51	50	M	
Secondaries 9 feathers	48	48	46	45	45	42	41	36	24	M		
Tail 12 feathers	48	51	51	54	56	58	M					

SEDGE WARBLER Dark brown tail; narrow pale brown edge. Blackish-brown flight feathers with inner webs narrowly edged white. Outer webs pale brown. Whitish-brown tips. Broad, pale brown edge on innermost secondaries.

	J	F	M	A	M	J	J	A	S	O	N	D
Adult moult	J	F	M	A	M	J	J	A	S	O	N	D
Juvenile moult	J	F	M	A	M	J	J	A	S	O	N	D
Primaries 10 feathers	64	63	62	60	58	55	54	53	52		M	
Secondaries 9 feathers	50	50	48	47	44	42	40	34	27	M		
Tail 12 feathers	49	49	49	50	51	51	M					

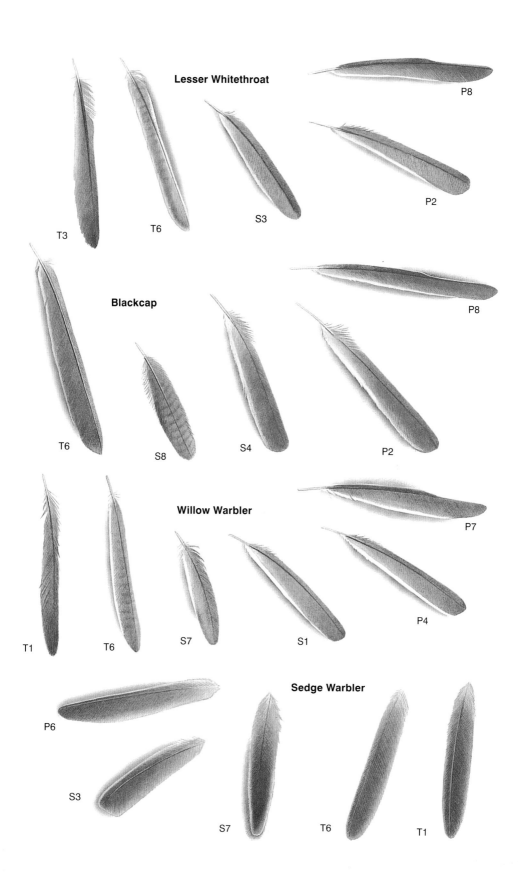

Lesser Whitethroat

T3 T6 S3 P8 P2

Blackcap

T6 S8 S4 P8 P2

Willow Warbler

T1 T6 S7 S1 P7 P4

Sedge Warbler

P6 S3 S7 T6 T1

II

SPOTTED FLYCATCHER The tail feathers are dark brown. The primaries are dark brown with greyish-white margins to the inner webs. The secondaries are the same, but also with a narrow buff edging to the outer webs. The outer webs of P7–P8 are emarginated, and P6 slightly so.

Adult moult: J F M A M J J A S O N D
Juvenile moult: J F M A M J J A S O N D

	J	F	M	A	M	J	J	A	S	O	N	D
Primaries 10 feathers	20	70	73	74	71	66	62	61	60	58		
Secondaries 9 feathers	56	55	54	52	50	48	46	37	28			
Tail 12 feathers	60	61	62	61	59	57						

PIED FLYCATCHER The tail feathers are black to black-brown, the outer pair with the whole or most of the outer webs white or creamy-white and often some white on the inner web, especially on the basal portion; the next pair usually with most of the outer web white or creamy, but sometimes without any white; the third pair from outside usually without white on the outer webs. The primaries are brown-black to dark brown, the inner webs narrowly edged whitish, P1–P5 with a varying amount of white at bases. The secondaries have a larger patch of white or more usually cream colour at base, three innermost with white or creamy-white margins of varying width on the outer webs and the two longer ones with most of their bases white or creamy. The outer webs of P6–P8 are emarginated.

Adult moult: J F M A M J J A S O N D
Juvenile moult: J F M A M J J A S O N D

	J	F	M	A	M	J	J	A	S	O	N	D
Primaries 10 feathers	26	62	70	71	66	59	55	50	48	44	M	
Secondaries 9 feathers	44	43	40	40	40	38	35	28	20	M		
Tail 12 feathers	50	50	52	52	50	50	M					

STONECHAT The tail feathers are brown-black with narrow buff fringes and tips. The flight feathers are brown-black with the inner webs edged dull white; the outer webs of the primaries are narrowly edged buff and those of the secondaries are more broadly edged rufous-buff, the innermost secondary with the basal half, and the next with the third of the outer web white. The outer webs of P5-P8 are emarginated.

Adult moult: J F M A M J J A S O N D
Juvenile moult: J F M A M J J A S O N D

	J	F	M	A	M	J	J	A	S	O	N	D
Primaries 10 feathers	27	53	58	58	57	56	51	50	49	46	M	
Secondaries 9 feathers	46	45	46	44	44	45	45	37	28	M		
Tail 12 feathers	50	50	50	50	50	50	M					

WHINCHAT The central pair of tail feathers has the basal quarter, and the rest have the basal half, white; the distal portions are brown-black with pale buff edgings, and the tips and most of the outer web of the outer pair whitish. The primaries are brown-black with the outer webs and tips narrowly edged buff, and the inner webs edged white or pale buff extending at extreme base to the outer webs. The secondaries are the same, but are more broadly edged on the outer webs and only the tertials have white at the base of the outer webs. The outer webs of P6–P8 are emarginated.

Adult moult: J F M A M J J A S O N D
Juvenile moult: J F M A M J J A S O N D

	J	F	M	A	M	J	J	A	S	O	N	D
Primaries 10 feathers	21	67	70	70	67	64	60	57	55	53	M	
Secondaries 9 feathers	50	48	45	45	42	45	47	42	35	M		
Tail 12 feathers	48	48	49	49	48	46	M					

TREECREEPER The tail feathers are pale brown with pale shafts, but the central portions alongside the shafts are a darker brown. The primaries are dark brown with P5–P10 uniform, but the rest and the secondaries have a broad buff band across their centres margined above and below with black, the outer webs towards tips are duller buff, and the tips whitish; the innermost secondaries without a buff transverse band. The outer webs of P5–P7 are emarginated.

Adult moult: J F M A M J J A S O N D
Juvenile moult: J F M A M J J A S O N D

	J	F	M	A	M	J	J	A	S	O	N	D
Primaries 10 feathers	27	53	60	62	62	57	54	51	51	48	M	
Secondaries 9 feathers	46	45	40	40	40	38	38	35	27	M		
Tail 12 feathers	51	57	59	61	61	63	M					

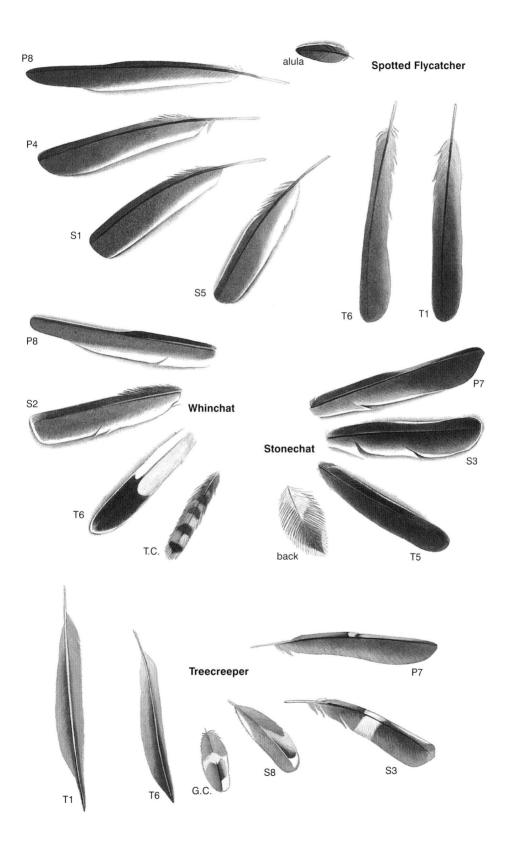

P8

alula

Spotted Flycatcher

P4

S1

S5

T6

T1

P8

S2

Whinchat

Stonechat

P7

S3

T6

T.C.

back

T5

Treecreeper

P7

T1

T6

G.C.

S8

S3

II–III

HOUSE SPARROW The tail feathers are black-brown, fringed buff. The primaries are black-brown, fringed chestnut-buff on the outer and white on the inner webs. The secondaries are the same, but the innermost are broadly fringed on both webs and tipped chestnut-buff. The outer webs of P6–P8 are emarginated.

	J	F	M	A	M	J	J	A	S	O	N	D
Adult moult												
Juvenile moult												
Primaries 10 feathers	14	63	65	66	66	63	60	59	57	55		
Secondaries 9 feathers	55	55	55	54	52	50	49	41	31			
Tail 12 feathers	61	62	62	62	56	56						

TREE SPARROW The tail feathers are dark brown, fringed buff. The primaries are black-brown with the inner webs fringed pale buff, and the outer webs fringed chestnut-brown, broadly at bases and at the ends of the emarginations. The secondaries are the same, but with more even fringes to the outer webs, and the inner feathers more broadly fringed and tipped. The outer webs of P6–P8 are emarginated.

	J	F	M	A	M	J	J	A	S	O	N	D
Adult moult												
Juvenile moult												
Primaries 10 feathers	14	64	65	65	63	60	55	54	51	50	M	
Secondaries 9 feathers	45	45	40	41	43	45	49	44	35	M		
Tail 12 feathers	54	55	55	55	54	54	M					

DUNNOCK Tail feathers black-brown, fringed rufous-brown on the outer webs. The flight feathers are the same, but the inner webs are fringed greyish-white and the innermost secondaries have broader rufous brown fringes on both webs and small buff marks at tips. The outer webs of P5–P8 are emarginated.

	J	F	M	A	M	J	J	A	S	O	N	D
Adult moult												
Juvenile moult												
Primaries 10 feathers	16	54	59	61	62	63	59	58	58	57		
Secondaries 9 feathers	56	56	55	53	51	49	46	36	28			
Tail 12 feathers	64	66	66	66	66	63						

BLUETHROAT Central pair of tail feathers black-brown, narrowly edged, tipped buff; the rest are the same, but with the basal half of each feather bright chestnut. Flight feathers are dark brown, with the inner webs narrowly edged whitish and the outer webs pale brown. The outer webs of P6–P8 are emarginated.

	J	F	M	A	M	J	J	A	S	O	N	D
Adult moult												
Juvenile moult												
Primaries 10 feathers	31	63	70	70	68	64	58	54	54	53	M	
Secondaries 9 feathers	52	50	50	45	45	46	50	46	36	M		
Tail 12 feathers	56	59	59	60	59	58	M					

NIGHTINGALE The tail feathers are a uniform chestnut-brown with the central pair rather duller. The flight feathers' inner webs are black-brown, edged pale brown, and the outer webs are rufous-brown, with the innermost secondaries rufous-brown on both webs. The outer webs of P7–P8 are emarginated.

	J	F	M	A	M	J	J	A	S	O	N	D
Adult moult												
Juvenile moult												
Primaries 10 feathers	24	81	85	80	76	72	70	65	65	62	M	
Secondaries 9 feathers	60	55	55	54	50	50	54	46	36	M		
Tail 12 feathers	66	70	70	70	69	72	M					

ROBIN The tail feathers are dark brown, with a tinge of rufous especially on the outer webs. In the flight feathers, the outer webs are brown with the inner webs black-brown narrowly edged pale buff; the innermost secondaries are more olive-brown, usually with a small buff mark or edging at the tip. The outer webs of P5–P8 are emarginated.

	J	F	M	A	M	J	J	A	S	O	N	D
Adult moult												
Juvenile moult												
Primaries 10 feathers	26	51	60	64	65	65	62	60	59	59		
Secondaries 9 feathers	57	56	56	53	51	48	45	37	27			
Tail 12 feathers	62	64	64	64	62	62						

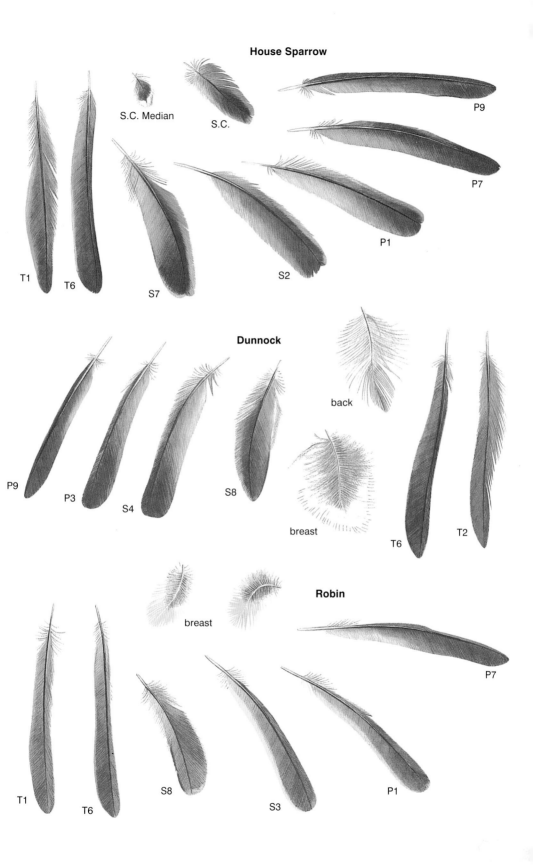

House Sparrow

S.C. Median

S.C.

P9

P7

P1

T1

T6

S7

S2

Dunnock

back

breast

P9

P3

S4

S8

T6

T2

Robin

breast

P7

T1

T6

S8

S3

P1

II–III

TWITE The tail feathers are brown-black, with the two central pairs edged buff, and the rest fringed white on the outer webs and more broadly whitish-buff on the inner webs. The flight feathers are brown-black, tipped buff, and edged white on the inner webs; the inner primaries are conspicuously edged white on the outer webs. The secondaries are narrowly, the innermost broadly, edged buffish-brown. The outer webs of P6–P8 are emarginated.

	J	F	M	A	M	J	J	A	S	O	N	D
Adult moult	J	F	M	A	M	J	J	A	S	O	N	D
Juvenile moult	J	F	M	A	M	J	J	A	S	O	N	D

Primaries 10 feathers	15	63	65	65	64	58	55	54	52	51
Secondaries 9 feathers	49	49	48	47	46	45	43	35	27	
Tail 12 feathers	64	64	63	61	58	55				

LINNET The tail feathers are brown-black, with the central pair edged buff, the rest with narrow white edgings to the outer webs and broad ones to the inner webs. The primaries are as the tail feathers with the white edgings to P1–P5 conspicuous. The secondaries are the same, but the outer webs are fringed buff not white; the innermost secondaries are chestnut with blackish-brown streaks and dark buff edges. The outer webs of P6–P8 are emarginated.

	J	F	M	A	M	J	J	A	S	O	N	D
Adult moult	J	F	M	A	M	J	J	A	S	O	N	D
Juvenile moult	J	F	M	A	M	J	J	A	S	O	N	D

Primaries 10 feathers	16	43	49	53	53	53	52	51	50	47
Secondaries 9 feathers	48	46	45	45	44	42	49	36	24	
Tail 12 feathers	58	56	55	54	52	51	M			

CHAFFINCH The central pair of tail feathers is slate-grey, fringed green; the rest are mostly black, the inner ones fringed green; the outer pair is mostly white with a slanting black mark on the outer part of the distal half and at base of the inner web; the next pair is the same, but with more black at the base, and the next pair sometimes has a white mark on the tip of the inner web. The flight feathers are brown-black, fringed on outer webs greenish-yellow; inner webs fringed white and with the basal portions yellowish-white. P7–P9 have no white at the base of the outer webs. The two innermost secondaries are without white and are fringed greenish-buff. The outer webs of P5–P8 are emarginated.

	J	F	M	A	M	J	J	A	S	O	N	D
Adult moult	J	F	M	A	M	J	J	A	S	O	N	D
Juvenile moult	J	F	M	A	M	J	J	A	S	O	N	D

Primaries 10 feathers	10	65	67	69	70	66	61	58	57	56
Secondaries 9 feathers	57	56	55	55	53	51	48	40	29	
Tail 12 feathers	69	69	69	69	67	65				

HAWFINCH The central pair of tail feathers is black at the base, with the distal part grey and rufous-brown, and tipped white; the other tail feathers have black basal and white distal halves, with the outer webs black, fringed rufous. The primaries are jet-black, tipped glossy green and purple, with the middle portion of the feathers white on the inner webs. The secondaries are the same, but with less white and with the outer webs fringed glossy purple; the inner secondaries are brown. The outer webs of P6–P8 are emarginated. P5–P2 are notched and curled at tip.

	J	F	M	A	M	J	J	A	S	O	N	D
Adult moult	J	F	M	A	M	J	J	A	S	O	N	D
Juvenile moult	J	F	M	A	M	J	J	A	S	O	N	D

Primaries 10 feathers	24	98	100	99	97	86	80	76	74	71	M
Secondaries 9 feathers	70	64	60	56	56	55	58	52	36	M	
Tail 12 feathers	57	57	58	59	54	53	M				

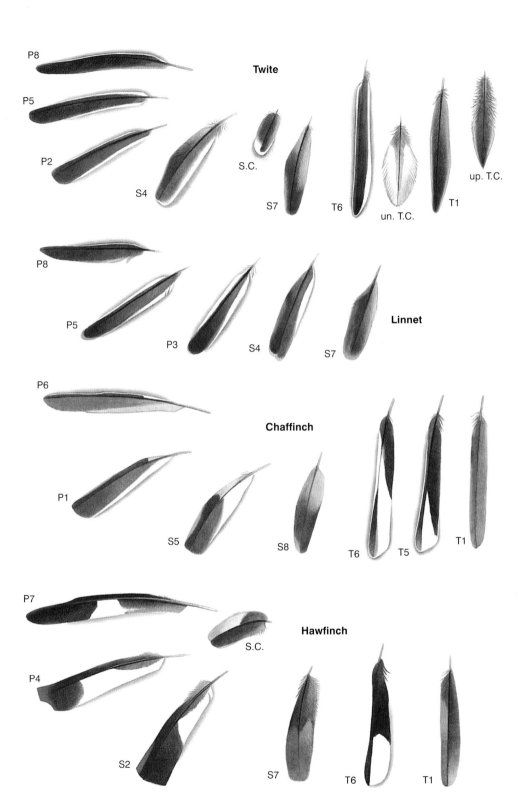

P8
P5
P2
S4
Twite
S.C.
S7
T6
un. T.C.
T1
up. T.C.

P8
P5
P3
S4
S7
Linnet

P6
Chaffinch
P1
S5
S8
T6
T5
T1

P7
S.C.
Hawfinch
P4
S2
S7
T6
T1

II–III

GOLDFINCH The tail feathers are black with small white dots, and with large irregular oval marks on the middle of the inner webs of the two outer pairs and often a small mark on the next pair. The flight feathers are black, with the inner webs fringed white and the basal half of the outer webs bright yellow (P9 has no yellow), all with white tips becoming larger on the innermost secondary. The outer webs of P6–P8 see emarginated.

	J	F	M	A	M	J	J	A	S	O	N	D
Adult moult	**J**	**F**	**M**	**A**	**M**	**J**	**J**	**A**	**S**	**O**	**N**	**D**
Juvenile moult	**J**	**F**	**M**	**A**	**M**	**J**	**J**	**A**	**S**	**O**	**N**	**D**
Primaries 10 feathers	12	63	67	68	67	60	57	55	55	50		
Secondaries 9 feathers	50	50	50	49	48	47	47	36	28			
Tail 12 feathers	55	56	55	54	51	50						

GREENFINCH The tail feathers are brown-black becoming greenish-yellow proximally, the four outer pairs with about the proximal half of the feathers greenish-yellow. The primaries are brown-black, tipped grey, and fringed greenish-yellow on the outer webs. The secondaries are the same, but fringed brownish-grey on the distal and greenish on the proximal halves. The outer webs of P6–P8 are emarginated.

	J	F	M	A	M	J	J	A	S	O	N	D
Adult moult	**J**	**F**	**M**	**A**	**M**	**J**	**J**	**A**	**S**	**O**	**N**	**D**
Juvenile moult	**J**	**F**	**M**	**A**	**M**	**J**	**J**	**A**	**S**	**O**	**N**	**D**
Primaries 10 feathers	11	74	75	76	74	67	64	62	60	58		
Secondaries 9 feathers	58	58	57	56	56	54	52	42	32			
Tail 12 feathers	60	60	59	57	55	52						

SISKIN The central pair of tail feathers is brown-black, fringed yellow; the rest are yellow with brown-black tips and shafts, the outer pair with brown-black outer webs. The flight feathers are black-brown, fringed yellow, P1–P6 and all secondaries with basal parts of outer webs bright yellow and the inner webs pale yellow. The secondaries are tipped greyish-white. The outer webs of P7–P8 are emarginated; P6 slightly emarginated.

	J	F	M	A	M	J	J	A	S	O	N	D
Adult moult	**J**	**F**	**M**	**A**	**M**	**J**	**J**	**A**	**S**	**O**	**N**	**D**
Juvenile moult	**J**	**F**	**M**	**A**	**M**	**J**	**J**	**A**	**S**	**O**	**N**	**D**
Primaries 10 feathers	18	68	68	67	64	58	54	52	49	47	M	
Secondaries 9 feathers	45	44	45	44	44	44	43	37	28	M		
Tail 12 feathers	48	46	46	43	40	38	M					

SERIN The tail feathers are black-brown, tipped and fringed on the inner webs whitish and on the outer webs yellowish-green. The flight feathers are the same, but the inner secondaries have browner fringes and larger white tips. The outer webs of P6–P8 are emarginated.

	J	F	M	A	M	J	J	A	S	O	N	D
Adult moult	**J**	**F**	**M**	**A**	**M**	**J**	**J**	**A**	**S**	**O**	**N**	**D**
Juvenile moult	**J**	**F**	**M**	**A**	**M**	**J**	**J**	**A**	**S**	**O**	**N**	**D**
Primaries 10 feathers	16	70	70	68	61	57	54	53	52	51	M	
Secondaries 9 feathers	48	47	46	43	42	42	42	35	29	M		
Tail 12 feathers	52	51	50	48	48	46	M					

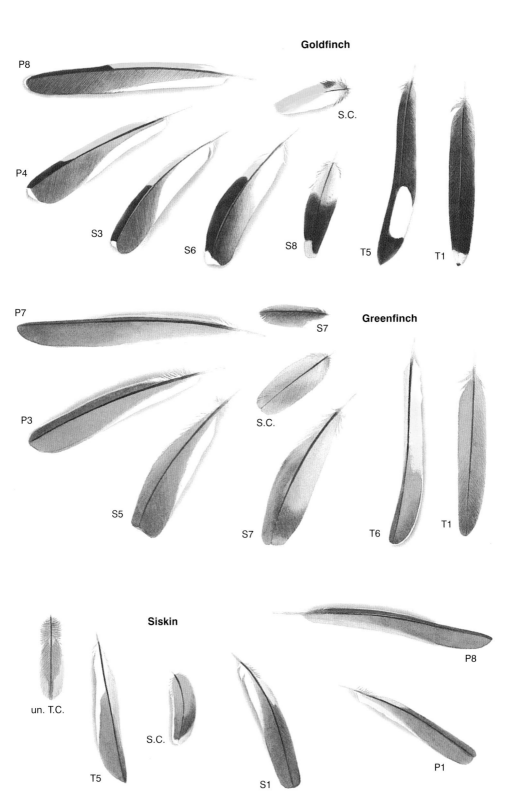

Goldfinch

P8

P4

S3

S6

S.C.

S8

T5

T1

Greenfinch

P7

S7

P3

S.C.

S5

S7

T6

T1

Siskin

un. T.C.

S.C.

T5

S1

P8

P1

II–III

BULLFINCH The tail feathers are black, with the central pair and the outer webs of the rest glossy. The primaries are greyish-black, fringed black on the outer and greyish-white on the inner webs. The secondaries are same, but the outer webs are fringed glossy blue-black; the two inner secondaries are all glossy blue-black and the innermost has the outer web grey, usually marked pinkish-red. The outer webs of P5–P8 are emarginated.

	J	F	M	A	M	J	J	A	S	O	N	D
Adult moult	J	F	M	A	M	J	J	A	S	O	N	D
Juvenile moult	J	F	M	A	M	J	J	A	S	O	N	D
Primaries 10 feathers	11	62	67	67	69	68	62	60	60	60		
Secondaries 9 feathers	60	59	58	56	54	52	48	39	27			
Tail 12 feathers	72	72	70	68	68	68	M					

NUTHATCH The central pair of tail feathers is blue-grey; the rest are black tipped grey, the three outermost pairs with a white patch on the inner web above a grey tip and the outermost pair with a similar white patch on the outer web. The primaries are black-brown, very narrowly fringed blue-grey on the outer webs and more broadly white on the inner webs; the outer feathers with white bases, and with a slight ashy mark on the outer web where the emarginations begin. The secondaries are black-brown with the outer webs more broadly edged blue-grey than the primaries, and the innermost feathers are mostly blue-grey. The outer webs of P6–P8 are emarginated.

	J	F	M	A	M	J	J	A	S	O	N	D
Adult moult	J	F	M	A	M	J	J	A	S	O	N	D
Juvenile moult	J	F	M	A	M	J	J	A	S	O	N	D
Primaries 10 feathers	32	68	74	74	72	67	63	62	60	57	M	
Secondaries 9 feathers	57	58	56	56	55	56	55	44	34	M		
Tail 12 feathers	46	47	47	46	46	45	M					

DIPPER The tail feathers are blackish slate-grey with a brownish tinge. The flight feathers are black-brown, very narrowly tipped brownish-white; the inner webs are narrowly edged greyish-white and the outer webs slate-grey, edgings being rather more broad on the innermost secondaries. The outer webs of P6–P8 are emarginated.

	J	F	M	A	M	J	J	A	S	O	N	D
Adult moult	J	F	M	A	M	J	J	A	S	O	N	D
Juvenile moult	J	F	M	A	M	J	J	A	S	O	N	D
Primaries 10 feathers	34	82	82	81	80	73	70	67	64	60	M	
Secondaries 9 feathers	59	53	48	47	48	50	48	42	33	M		
Tail 12 feathers	52	52	52	53	55	55	M					

GREY WAGTAIL The three central pairs of tail feathers are black with the outer webs fringed yellow-green, broadly at base and narrowly at tip; the three outer pairs are mostly white, with the outermost quite white and the other two pairs with the inner web and tip white and the rest of the outer web black, fringed yellow-green. The primaries are black, with the basal portion of the inner web whitish on P6 and white on P5–P1. The secondaries are the same, but white at the base of both webs; the innermost secondaries are fringed yellowish-white to white on the outer webs. The outer webs of P7–P8 are emarginated; P6 slightly so.

	J	F	M	A	M	J	J	A	S	O	N	D
Adult moult	J	F	M	A	M	J	J	A	S	O	N	D
Juvenile moult	J	F	M	A	M	J	J	A	S	O	N	D
Primaries 10 feathers	15	78	78	79	74	68	66	63	60	58	M	
Tail 12 feathers	103	105	104	104	104	105	M					

PIED WAGTAIL The tail feathers are glossy jet-black, with the central pair narrowly fringed white on the outer webs, and the outer pair mostly white with three-quarters of the inner web edged black; the next pair is the same, but with wider edging of black which reaches the shaft at the base, and with a varying amount of black on the outer web. The primaries are black, fringed white narrowly on the outer webs and tips, broadly on the inner webs. The secondaries are the same, but the inner feathers are more broadly fringed white on the outer webs, and the innermost feathers are browner. The outer webs of P6–P8 are emarginated.

	J	F	M	A	M	J	J	A	S	O	N	D
Adult moult	J	F	M	A	M	J	J	A	S	O	N	D
Juvenile moult	J	F	M	A	M	J	J	A	S	O	N	D
Primaries 10 feathers	12	74	76	76	75	67	63	61	60	58		
Secondaries 9 feathers	58	57	56	57	55	57	69	51	38			
Tail 12 feathers	91	92	92	92	93	93						

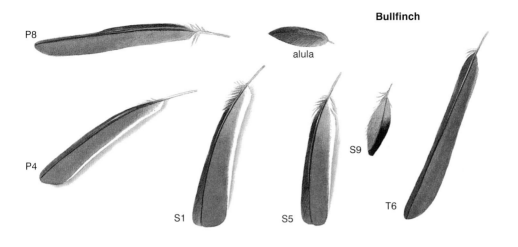

Bullfinch

P8

alula

P4

S1

S5

S9

T6

Nuthatch

P8

S2

S.C.

T5

T2

T1

un. T.C.

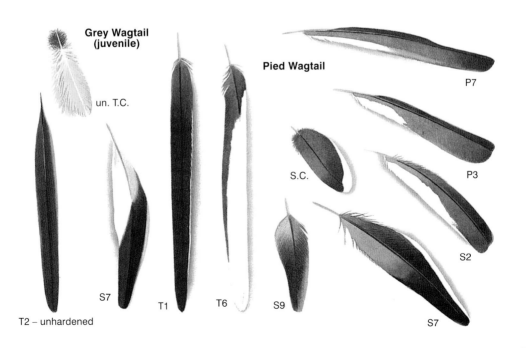

Grey Wagtail (juvenile)

un. T.C.

Pied Wagtail

P7

S.C.

P3

S2

S7

S9

T2 – unhardened

S7

T1

T6

II–III

BARRED WARBLER Tail feathers are medium grey sometimes with traces of darker growth bars. The feathers are narrowly edged white on the inner web, more broadly fringed white on tip. The white fringe along the tip widens into a larger white blob on the inner web on T3–T4. The flight feathers are dark grey, with narrow off-white fringes along the outer web. Outer webs of P7–P9 are emarginated. The inner web of P9 has a distinct notch. P8 is sometimes slightly notched.

	J	F	M	A	M	J	J	A	S	O	N	D
Adult moult	J	F	M	A	M	J	J	A	S	O	N	D
Juvenile moult	J	F	M	A	M	J	J	A	S	O	N	D
Primaries 10 feathers	19	78	86	82	74	70	68	65	58	58		
Secondaries 9 feathers	58	59	58	56	54	50	42	36	25			
Tail 12 feathers	77	77	77	77	77	77						

AZURE TIT Central tail feathers cyanine-blue with a small white spot or wedge on the tip. T2–T4 cyanine-blue with duller and greyer inner webs and gradually more white on tips. T5–T6 are largely white. Flight feathers are dark grey with the outer webs cyanine-blue. The emarginated parts of the outer webs of P4–P8 and the entire border of the outer webs of P9–P10 are white.

	J	F	M	A	M	J	J	A	S	O	N	D
Adult moult	J	F	M	A	M	J	J	A	S	O	N	D
Juvenile moult	J	F	M	A	M	J	J	A	S	O	N	D
Primaries 10 feathers	23	50	57	60	60	62	62	57	55	55		
Secondaries 9 feathers	58	55	55	54	50	45	40	35	28			
Tail 12 feathers	63	65	68	69	68	68						

MELODIOUS WARBLER Tail is greyish-black with very pale yellow or white fringes along the sides and tips. Flight feathers are greyish-black or dull black. The primaries are narrowly fringed pale grey-green along the outer web and white along tip. Outer webs of P5–P8 are emarginated. Inner webs of P7–P9 are notched.

	J	F	M	A	M	J	J	A	S	O	N	D
Adult moult	J	F	M	A	M	J	J	A	S	O	N	D
Juvenile moult	J	F	M	A	M	J	J	A	S	O	N	D
Primaries 10 feathers	17	50	56	57	56	53	51	50	49	48		
Secondaries 9 feathers	48	48	45	44	41	40	38	30	26			
Tail 12 feathers	54	54	54	54	53	51						

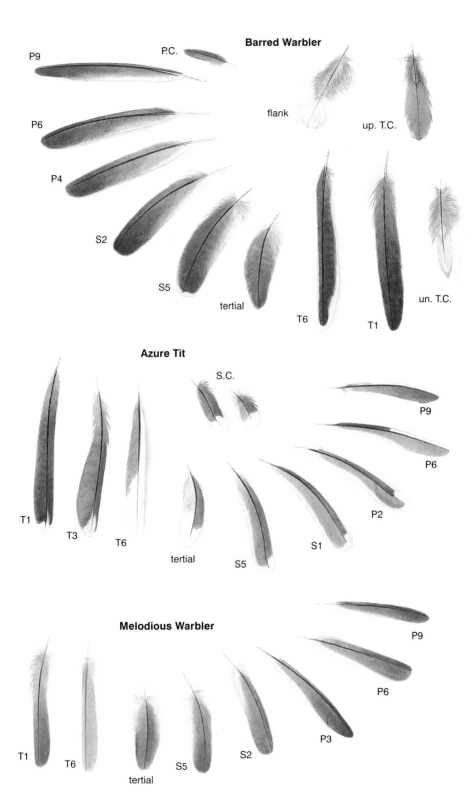

Barred Warbler

P9 P.C. flank up. T.C.

P6

P4

S2

S5 tertial T6 T1 un. T.C.

Azure Tit

S.C. P9

P6

T1 T3 T6 P2

tertial S5 S1

Melodious Warbler

P9

P6

P3

T1 T6 S2

tertial S5

II–III

GREAT REED WARBLER Tail feathers are dark brown, sometimes with faint and narrow dusky bars, outer webs with slightly paler and ill-defined olive-brown fringes, tips with faint pale rufous to pink-white fringe. The flight feathers are black-brown, tips narrowly fringed pink-buff to off-white. The outer webs are narrowly fringed olive-brown or dull cinnamon-brown. The fringes are wider but less sharply defined towards the bases of the secondaries, the basal inner webs are broadly fringed pink-buff. The outer webs of P7–P8 are emarginated. Inner web of P9 is notched.

	J	F	M	A	M	J	J	A	S	O	N	D
Adult moult							J	A	S	O		
Juvenile moult							J	A	S	O		

Primaries 10 feathers	22	84	92	87	84	83	80	75	71	70
Secondaries 9 feathers	70	69	65	60	59	55	50	45	35	
Tail 12 feathers	76	80	82	84	86	86				

RUFOUS BUSH ROBIN Tail feathers bright rufous-cinnamon. The central pair uniform or with ill-defined dusky olive-brown spot on tip T2 with larger and more distinct dark ochre-brown or black band on tip. T3–T5 have similar band subterminally, distally bordered by pale cream or white tip. On T6 the white tip is more extensive along the outer edge. The flight feathers are dark brown-grey, outer webs with narrow cinnamon-rufous fringe widening towards feather base. Tips of secondaries and inner primaries narrowly and sharply fringed pale buff-grey or off-white. Outer webs of P5–P8 and the inner webs of P6–P9 are emarginated.

	J	F	M	A	M	J	J	A	S	O	N	D
Adult moult							J	A	S	O		
Juvenile moult							J	A	S	O		

Primaries 10 feathers	30	76	78	79	82	76	74	72	73	70
Secondaries 9 feathers	68	70	70	65	60	60	62	56	42	
Tail 12 feathers	80	80	80	80	80	76				

REDSTART Central pair of tail feathers dull black or brown-black narrowly fringed rufous-chestnut round tip, broad at base. T2–T6 deep rufous-cinnamon or rufous-chestnut, outer web of T6 and tips of some other feathers sometimes tipped olive-brown. Flight feathers greyish-black, outer web of flight feathers narrowly and sharply edged grey or pale grey-buff. Outer web of P6–P8 and inner web of P7–P9 are emarginated.

	J	F	M	A	M	J	J	A	S	O	N	D
Adult moult						J	J	A	S	O		
Juvenile moult						J	J	A	S	O		

Primaries 10 feathers	22	75	82	82	81	73	68	64	61	58
Secondaries 9 feathers	56	56	56	55	55	53	51	45	35	
Tail 12 feathers	56	56	56	53	52	48				

Great Reed Warbler

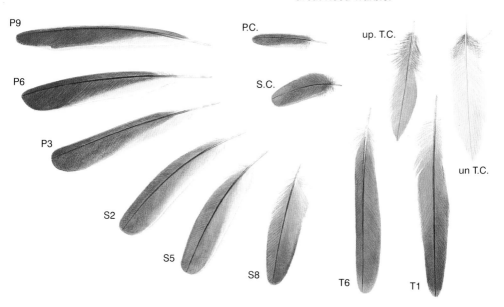

P9

P6

P3

S2

S5

S8

P.C.

S.C.

up. T.C.

un T.C.

T6

T1

Rufous Bush Robin

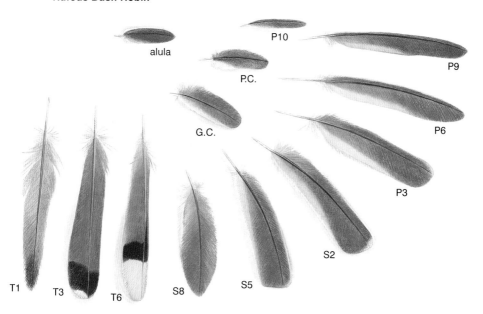

alula

P10

P.C.

G.C.

P9

P6

P3

S2

T1

T3

T6

S8

S5

II–III

PARROT CROSSBILL The feather description is very similar to that of Crossbill on page 180, except that there are no emarginations.

	J	F	M	A	M	J	J	A	S	O	N	D
Adult moult	J	F	M	A	M	J	J	A	S	O	N	D
Juvenile moult	J	F	M	A	M	J	J	A	S	O	N	D
Primaries 10 feathers	20	93	96	96	93	85	80	76	73	70		
Secondaries 9 feathers	68	68	68	67	67	65	63	58	47			
Tail 12 feathers	80	80	80	78	78	75						

CIRL BUNTING Central pair of tail feathers brown to grey-brown with greenish, brownish, yellowish or whitish edges, wider on outer webs. T2–T4 dark grey with narrow greenish, yellowish or whitish edge. T4 occasionally with white tip. T5 dark grey with white wedge about one-third of distal part of inner web. Tip of outer web white. T6 as T5 but white wedge longer. Outer web with narrow white fringe. Flight feathers dark brownish-grey, outer webs with greenish, yellowish or whitish edge. P4–P8 emarginated.

	J	F	M	A	M	J	J	A	S	O	N	D
Adult moult	J	F	M	A	M	J	J	A	S	O	N	D
Juvenile moult	J	F	M	A	M	J	J	A	S	O	N	D
Primaries 10 feathers	18	67	75	73	70	68	65	63	62	62		
Secondaries 9 feathers	62	62	62	60	59	55	50	48	35			
Tail 12 feathers	76	76	76	76	76	76						

REDPOLL The tail feathers are black-brown, narrowly fringed whitish on the inner and buff on the outer webs. The flight feathers are the same, the inner secondaries with broader buff fringes on the outer webs. The outer webs of P6–P8 are emarginated.

	J	F	M	A	M	J	J	A	S	O	N	D
Adult moult	J	F	M	A	M	J	J	A	S	O	N	D
Juvenile moult	J	F	M	A	M	J	J	A	S	O	N	D
Primaries 10 feathers	17	66	68	66	64	58	54	52	50	47	M	
Secondaries 9 feathers	45	45	43	42	42	43	42	35	27	M		
Tail 12 feathers	63	63	61	58	56	53	M					

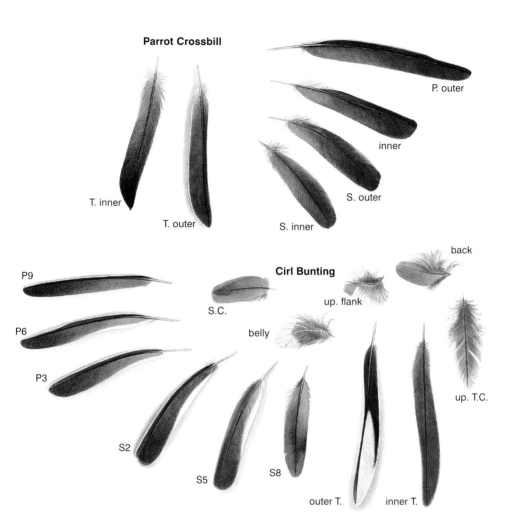

Parrot Crossbill

T. inner

T. outer

P. outer

inner

S. outer

S. inner

back

Cirl Bunting

up. flank

P9

S.C.

belly

up. T.C.

P6

P3

S2

S5

S8

outer T.

inner T.

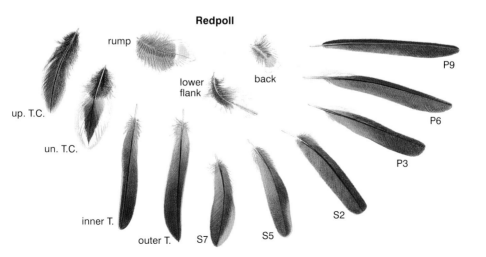

Redpoll

rump

back

P9

lower flank

P6

up. T.C.

P3

un. T.C.

S2

inner T.

outer T.

S7

S5

II–III

REED BUNTING The central pair of tail feathers is mostly brown with a mesial black line and outer webs of chestnut-brown; the rest are black, narrowly edged brown, the outmost pair with a large wedge of white occupying most of the feather, the penultimate pair with a smaller wedge on distal half of the inner web. The flight feathers are brown-black, with the inner webs fringed white and the outer webs bright bay. The inner secondaries are broadly margined and tipped the same, with an outer fringe of buff. The outer webs of P5–P8 are emarginated.

	J	F	M	A	M	J	J	A	S	O	N	D
Adult moult	J	F	M	A	M	J	J	A	S	O	N	D
Juvenile moult	J	F	M	A	M	J	J	A	S	O	N	D
Primaries 10 feathers	9	62	66	67	69	68	64	62	61	59		
Secondaries 9 feathers	59	59	58	57	55	56	54	43	32			
Tail 12 feathers	65	67	67	66	66	64						

YELLOWHAMMER The tail feathers are brown-black, with the central pair fringed yellowish or chestnut-brown; two outer pairs narrowly fringed greenish-yellow on the outer webs, and with large wedge-shaped white marks on the distal two-thirds of the inner webs. The primaries are black-brown, with the outer webs narrowly fringed greenish-yellow and the inner greyish-white. The secondaries are the same, but with more brownish fringes, and the innermost with broad chestnut fringes and tips. The outer webs of P5–P8 are emarginated.

	J	F	M	A	M	J	J	A	S	O	N	D
Adult moult	J	F	M	A	M	J	J	A	S	O	N	D
Juvenile moult	J	F	M	A	M	J	J	A	S	O	N	D
Primaries 10 feathers	8	68	71	72	73	70	65	63	61	63		
Secondaries 9 feathers	60	61	61	60	58	56	55	37	27			
Tail 12 feathers	73	74	74	74	72	67						

CROSSBILL Male tail feathers and flight feathers are black-brown with a very narrow pinkish fringe on the outer webs. **Female** as the male, but the fringe is greenish. The outer webs of P6–P8 are emarginated.

	J	F	M	A	M	J	J	A	S	O	N	D
Adult moult	J	F	M	A	M	J	J	A	S	O	N	D
Juvenile moult	J	F	M	A	M	J	J	A	S	O	N	D
Primaries 10 feathers	11	81	84	84	81	73	68	64	61	58		
Secondaries 9 feathers	56	56	56	55	55	53	51	45	35			
Tail 12 feathers	66	66	66	63	62	58						

MEADOW PIPIT The tail feathers are black-brown with the central pair fringed olive, greenish-brown or buffish-brown; the outer pair with dusky white outer web and a large white wedge-shaped mark on the inner web; the penultimate pair has a small wedge-shaped white mark at the tip of the inner web, the next pair usually with a very small white mark at the tip. The flight feathers are black-brown, fringed on the inner webs dusky grey and on the outer webs greenish or greyish-buff; the inner secondaries have paler buff edgings and tips. The outer webs of P6–P8 are emarginated.

	J	F	M	A	M	J	J	A	S	O	N	D
Adult moult	J	F	M	A	M	J	J	A	S	O	N	D
Juvenile moult	J	F	M	A	M	J	J	A	S	O	N	D
Primaries 10 feathers	10	78	79	79	65	64	60	58	56	56		
Secondaries 9 feathers	54	54	54	53	53	52	56	46	35			
Tail 12 feathers	65	66	66	65	64	64						

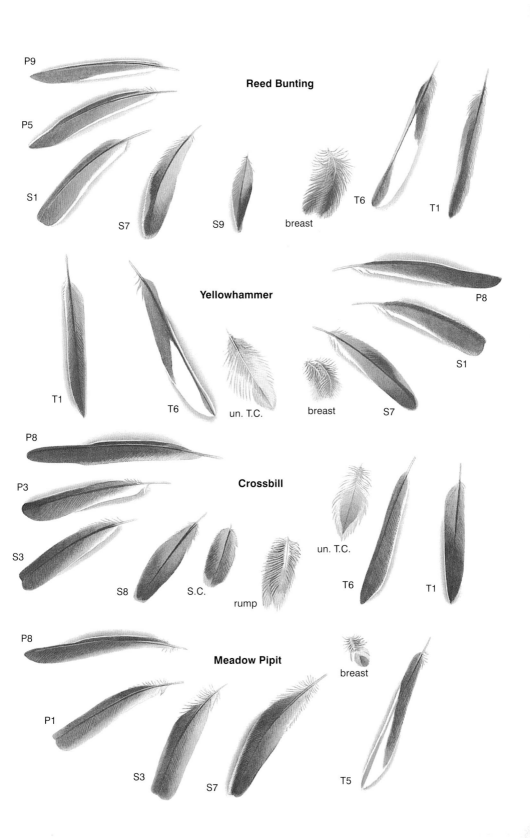

Reed Bunting

P9

P5

S1

S7

S9

breast

T6

T1

Yellowhammer

P8

S1

T1

T6

un. T.C.

breast

S7

Crossbill

P8

P3

S3

S8

S.C.

rump

un. T.C.

T6

T1

Meadow Pipit

P8

P1

S3

S7

breast

T5

II–IV

WOODCHAT SHRIKE The central pair of tail feathers (T1–T4) are black with the tips fringed white. base of T2–T4 are white gradually increasing to approx half the feather length on T4. The tip of T5 is white as well as the base, leaving the black as a subterminal band. T6 is white with a black subterminal band on the inner web, this band is sometimes broken into bars and T6 is frequently completely white. Flight feathers are black with the tips of the secondaries and inner primaries narrowly fringed white or pink-buff. The base of primaries white or pale cream, absent on P10. The outer webs of P6–P8 are emarginated. the inner webs of P7–P9 have a distinct notch.

	J	F	M	A	M	J	J	A	S	O	N	D
Adult moult	J	F	M	A	M	J	J	A	S	O	N	D
Juvenile moult	J	F	M	A	M	J	J	A	S	O	N	D
Primaries 10 feathers	28	73	85	84	82	78	75	72	68	65		
Secondaries 9 feathers	65	63	60	58	55	50	45	39	30			
Tail 12 feathers	74	80	82	82	82	82						

BLACK WHEATEAR The central tail feathers have the basal half white and the distal half brown-black; the rest of the feathers are white with black tips. The flight feathers are blackish-brown, with the outer webs very narrowly edged pale brown and the inner webs edged greyish-white. The outer webs of P5–P8 are emarginated.

Primaries 10 feathers	35	73	81	81	74	70	68	68	67	68	M
Secondaries 9 feathers	68	68	67	65	65	62	58	54	47	M	
Tail 12 feathers	77	79	79	80	80	79	M				

WALLCREEPER The tail is black with the central 3 pairs (T1–T3) with medium grey tips, T4–T5 with grey tips and white subterminal patch or bar, T6 with terminal white bordered by narrow grey fringe on tip. Flight feathers have black tips of secondaries and inner primaries fringed pale grey or off-white. large square or round white spot subterminally on inner web of P5–P9 and another white spot near base. Basal outer web of secondaries and P1–P7 bright reddish-pink. Outer webs of P5–P8 are emarginated. Inner web of P6–P9 with faint notch.

	J	F	M	A	M	J	J	A	S	O	N	D
Adult moult	J	F	M	A	M	J	J	A	S	O	N	D
Juvenile moult	J	F	M	A	M	J	J	A	S	O	N	D
Primaries 10 feathers	34	70	78	96	94	88	85	85	84	84		
Secondaries 9 feathers	80	76	70	63	57	56	56	48	42			
Tail 12 feathers	62	60	60	60	60	59						

ALPINE ACCENTOR The tail feathers are black-brown, narrowly edged grey-brown, the tips of the outer webs have buff edging, and the tips of the inner webs of the central feathers have large buff edging; a much clearer, paler and often whitish, semi-circular tip on the inner webs of the rest of the tail feathers. The primaries are dark brown, with the outer and the inner webs narrowly edged buff and with a rather broader and paler mark at the tips of the feathers. The secondaries are blacker, the brown more broadly edged rufous-buff, the inner feathers with glossy black centres broadly edged rufous-brown and with a whitish mark at the tip. The outer webs of P5–P8 are emarginated.

	J	F	M	A	M	J	J	A	S	O	N	D
Adult moult	J	F	M	A	M	J	J	A	S	O	N	D
Primaries 10 feathers	25	96	100	100	98	91	85	81	78	75		
Secondaries 9 feathers	72	68	67	65	63	59	54	49	36			
Tail 12 feathers	74	75	75	74	73	73						

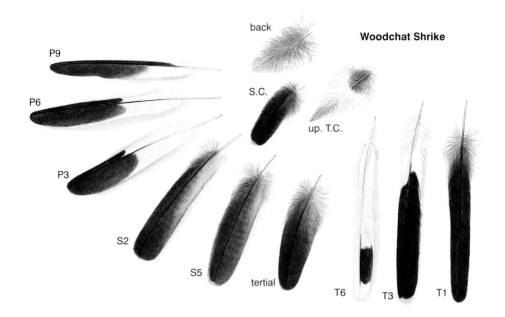

Woodchat Shrike

back

P9

P6

S.C.

up. T.C.

P3

S2

S5

tertial

T6   T3   T1

Black Wheatear

P7

P4

S2

tertial

outer T.   inner T.

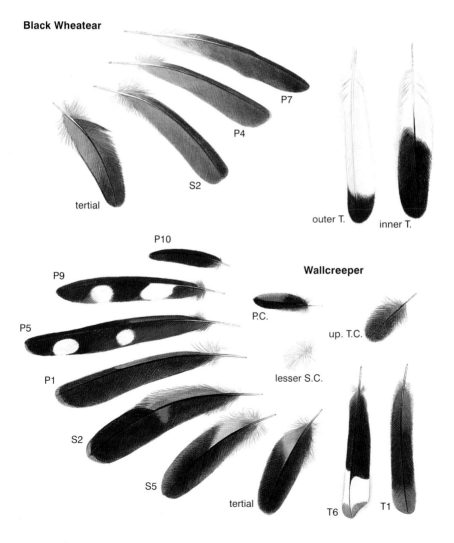

Wallcreeper

P10

P9

P.C.

P5

up. T.C.

P1

lesser S.C.

S2

S5

tertial

T6   T1

III

EUROPEAN BEE-EATER The tail feathers are a dull bluish-green with black shafts. The primaries are cerulean-blue, the inner webs broadly tipped dull black and with a grey inner border, the outer webs with a narrow dusky fringe at the tip and a narrow grass-green edge at the base. The secondaries are bright rufous-cinnamon, with a broad black tip, the outermost and the innermost with a green tinge on the outer webs, the tertials are bluish-green, the outer one tipped dusky. The primaries are not emarginated, but the tips of P1–P7 and of all the secondaries have a shallow notch.

Adult moult	J	F	M	A	M	J	J	A	S	O	N	D
Primaries 10 feathers	37	111	100	91	85	82	78	75	74	73	M	
Secondaries 9 feathers	70	71	70	70	73	70	60	50	40	M		
Tail 12 feathers	96	96	96	96	96	113	M					

QUAIL The tail feathers are sepia, browner towards the sides and tips; the narrow shaft streaks, edges and bars on each feather are pale buff. The primaries are dark sepia-grey with the tips bordered pale buff; the outer webs are mottled buff, forming irregular barring; P10 is uniform grey, with the outer edge narrowly pale buff. The secondaries are as the primaries, but the bars are more distinct and bordered by dull black; the inner webs have buff barring near the tips. The outer webs of P8–P9 and the inner web of P10 are emarginated.

	J	F	M	A	M	J	J	A	S	O	N	D
Adult moult	J	F	M	A	M	J	J	A	S	O	N	D
Juvenile moult	J	F	M	A	M	J	J	A	S	O	N	D
Primaries 10 feathers	80	80	78	77	73	75	72	70	68	65		
Secondaries 14 feathers	63	61	60	59	57	56	54	58	57	57	57	56	53	48
Tail 10 feathers	33	39	38	40	40							

LESSER SPOTTED WOODPECKER The central pairs of tail feathers (T1–T2) are black; T3 is black, with a lot of white on the outer web and some on the tip; T4–T5 are mostly white or cream, with the basal halves of the inner webs black and two or three black bars across the tips, and the outer webs of T4–T5 mainly white; T6 is black with some white spotting. The flight feathers are black or blackish-brown, the outer webs of P5–P9 with four to six fairly small and equally spaced white spots, spots progressively fewer towards the inner primaries; three or four slightly larger spots on the outer webs of the secondaries; similar but larger and rounder spots on the inner webs of flight feathers, but not reaching the shafts. The tertials are as the secondaries except that the white spots of both webs meet across the shafts, forming contrasting bars (see p203).

	J	F	M	A	M	J	J	A	S	O	N	D
Adult moult	J	F	M	A	M	J	J	A	S	O	N	D
Juvenile moult	J	F	M	A	M	J	J	A	S	O	N	D
Primaries 10 feathers	27	68	83	86	86	85	75	69	67	65	M	
Secondaries 10–12 feathers	63	63	63	60	58	55	52	50	46	36	28	M
Tail 12 feathers	41	48	53	55	60	64	M					

WRYNECK The central pair of tail feathers is closely speckled grey or cream and dark grey, with four or five narrow and irregular black bars, each bordered by a fairly broad and almost uniform grey band towards the base and by a yellow-buff band with some dusky speckling distally (either of the bordering bands may be faint or absent); the remainder are similar, but black bars are equally spaced slightly wider and more distinct. The flight feathers are greyish-black or brownish-black, the outer webs having rufous cinnamon spots about the same width as the intervening black, the spots partly speckled black on the secondaries and sometimes a little on the primaries; the inner webs have rounder and paler pink-buff or cream spots along the border. The outer webs of P7–P8 and the inner webs of P7–P9 are emarginated.

Adult moult	J	F	M	A	M	J	J	A	S	O	N	D
Primaries 10 feathers	20	71	76	76	73	71	68	67	66	64		
Secondaries 10 feathers	62	62	60	59	58	57	58	53	43	34		
Tail 12 feathers	55	56	60	63	65	65	M					

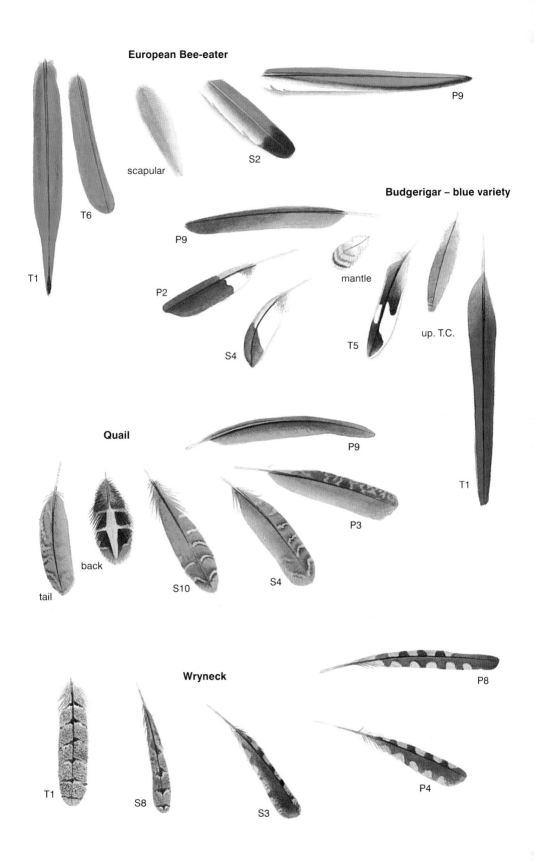

European Bee-eater

P9

S2

scapular

T6

T1

Budgerigar – blue variety

P9

P2

mantle

S4

T5

up. T.C.

T1

Quail

P9

P3

back

S10

S4

tail

Wryneck

P8

T1

S8

S3

P4

III

CORN BUNTING The tail feathers are dark brown with buff tips and fringes. The primaries are black-brown with the inner webs narrowly fringed whitish, the outer webs fringed buffish-brown. The secondaries are the same, but with more rufous fringes, especially on the innermost which have wider fringes and pale tips. The outer webs of P6–P8 are emarginated.

	J	F	M	A	M	J	J	A	S	O	N	D
Adult moult	J	F	M	A	M	J	J	A	S	O	N	D
Primaries 10 feathers	13	83	86	87	87	80	75	73	73	72		
Secondaries 9 feathers	70	70	68	65	64	63	63	61	52	M		
Tail 12 feathers	81	81	81	81	81	80	M					

SKYLARK The tail feathers are black-brown, narrowly fringed brown, the central pair broadly fringed brown; the outer pair with outer web and a large wedge-shaped mark on the inner web white; in the next pair the outer web is white. The flight feathers are dark brown with tips, and fringes of inner and outer webs of the outer primaries buffish-white; the outer webs of the inner primaries and the secondaries are fringed more reddish-buff, and the innermost secondaries are paler brown on distal portions. The outer webs of P6–P8 are emarginated.

	J	F	M	A	M	J	J	A	S	O	N	D
Adult moult	J	F	M	A	M	J	J	A	S	O	N	D
Juvenile moult	J	F	M	A	M	J	J	A	S	O	N	D
Primaries 10 feathers	16	85	88	89	85	79	74	72	70	69		
Secondaries 10 feathers	69	69	68	68	68	67	56	50	46	31		
Tail 12 feathers	63	63	63	63	60	58	M					

WHEATEAR The tail feathers are black, tipped greyish-white, with white bases extending in the central pair to one-third or less but in the rest to two-thirds of the length. The flight feathers are black, tipped greyish-white, with the outer webs edged pale to rich buff, narrowly on the primaries and more broadly on the secondaries.

	J	F	M	A	M	J	J	A	S	O	N	D
Adult moult	J	F	M	A	M	J	J	A	S	O	N	D
Juvenile moult	J	F	M	A	M	J	J	A	S	O	N	D
Primaries 10 feathers	18	82	85	84	77	69	63	60	57	54	M	
Secondaries 9 feathers	54	53	52	53	52	53	53	46	35	M		
Tail 12 feathers	63	65	66	65	64	59	M					

SNOW BUNTING The two central pairs of tail feathers are black, fringed white or buff; the next pair are black and white, the two outer pairs are white, tipped black on the outer webs; the next pair have larger black tips. The primaries are black, narrowly edged and tipped white or buffish-white, with bases white; P2 usually has only the distal quarter black, and P1 only a black patch on the outer web at the tip. The secondaries are white, often with black marks on the outer webs at the tip. The tertials are black with long tawny-buff tips and fringes. The outer webs of P7–P8 are emarginated.

	J	F	M	A	M	J	J	A	S	O	N	D
Adult moult	J	F	M	A	M	J	J	A	S	O	N	D
Juvenile moult	J	F	M	A	M	J	J	A	S	O	N	D
Primaries 10 feathers	26	103	102	100	90	76	73	70	66	66	M	
Secondaries 9 feathers	66	65	65	65	67	68	70	63	52	M		
Tail 12 feathers	77	77	79	79	76	75	M					

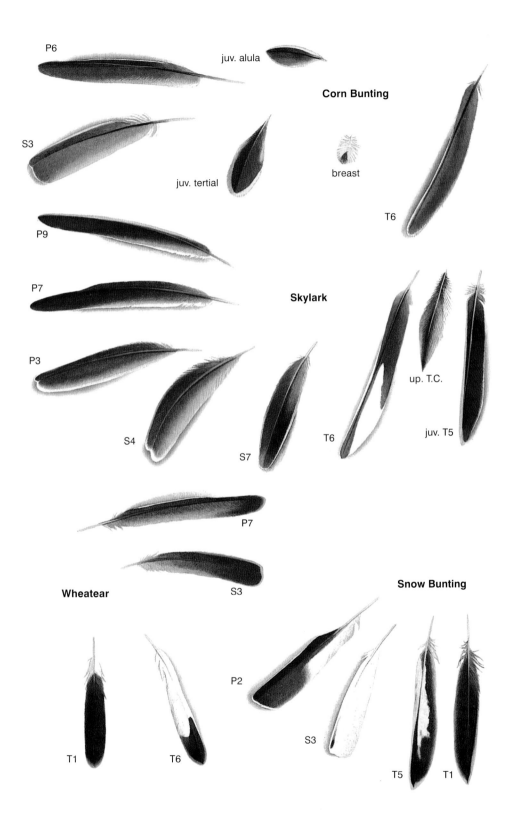

P6

juv. alula

Corn Bunting

S3

juv. tertial

breast

T6

P9

P7

Skylark

P3

up. T.C.

S4

T6

juv. T5

S7

P7

S3

Wheatear

Snow Bunting

P2

S3

T1

T6

T5

T1

III–IV

PINE GROSBEAK Tail dark greyish or fuscous-brown, outer webs and tips of feathers faintly edged off-white, shading to faint pale brown or pink-brown on bases. Flight feathers dark fuscous-brown, outer webs narrowly and rather indistinctly edged dull pink or pink-brown, off-white along terminal part and tip of primaries, more buff or off-white along outer webs of inner secondaries. Outer webs of P5–P8 are emarginated. Inner webs of P7–P0 with slight notch.

	J	F	M	A	M	J	J	A	S	O	N	D
Adult moult	J	F	M	A	M	J	J	A	S	O	N	D
Juvenile moult	J	F	M	A	M	J	J	A	S	O	N	D
Primaries 10 feathers	22	102	120	115	108	100	96	90	86	94		
Secondaries 9 feathers	82	80	80	75	75	70	60	40	35			
Tail 12 feathers	106	106	104	100	100	96						

BRAMBLING The tail feathers are black, narrowly edged yellowish, with the central pair mostly grey tipped buff and edged yellowish; the outer pair is white at the base of the outer and at the tip of the inner webs, and with white or whitish diagonal streak at base. The flight feathers are black, with distal halves of outer webs fringed yellowish and basal parts of inner webs fringed white; the inner secondaries are tipped and edged chestnut-buff. The outer webs of P6–P8 are emarginated.

	J	F	M	A	M	J	J	A	S	O	N	D
Adult moult	J	F	M	A	M	J	J	A	S	O	N	D
Juvenile moult	J	F	M	A	M	J	J	A	S	O	N	D
Primaries 10 feathers	20	83	84	84	80	71	67	65	62	61	M	
Secondaries 9 feathers	61	57	55	55	57	58	59	52	43	M		
Tail 12 feathers	68	68	67	65	64	62	M					

CALANDRA LARK The central pair of tail feathers are olive-brown with black centre and rufous fringe. T2–T4 olive-black to black with white tips and narrow cream-pink or off-white edges. T5 black with white tip and a broad cream-pink or off-white fringe along outer web. T6 cream-pink or white with dusky grey wedge on base of inner web. Flight feathers greyish-black, secondaries with off-white tip. P1–P3 with somewhat narrower tip, replaced by rufous-buff fringe on tip of P4–P7. Outer edge of secondaries and of outer primaries fringed pink-buff, remainder of feathers faintly edged grey-buff, outer web of P9 rather broadly fringed pale buff or off-white. Outer webs of P6–P8 and the inner webs of P6–P9 are emarginated.

	J	F	M	A	M	J	J	A	S	O	N	D
Adult moult	J	F	M	A	M	J	J	A	S	O	N	D
Juvenile moult	J	F	M	A	M	J	J	A	S	O	N	D
Primaries 10 feathers	22	109	112	108	105	98	90	80	79	78		
Secondaries 9 feathers	78	78	78	76	76	76	76	58	36			
Tail 12 feathers	72	72	70	70	65	65						

BLUE ROCK THRUSH Tail feathers black, both sides of central pair and outer webs of others fringed slate-blue. Flight feathers black, tips faintly edged white, outer webs narrowly fringed slate-blue. Outer webs of P6–P8 and inner webs of P7–P9 are emarginated.

	J	F	M	A	M	J	J	A	S	O	N	D
Adult moult	J	F	M	A	M	J	J	A	S	O	N	D
Juvenile moult	J	F	M	A	M	J	J	A	S	O	N	D
Primaries 10 feathers	20	97	98	96	96	96	90	88	87	80		
Secondaries 9 feathers	80	79	75	75	73	70	65	58	35			
Tail 12 feathers	87	87	86	86	86	86						

Pine Grosbeak

P9
P7
P3
S1
S5
S7
T6
T1
P.C.
S.C.
body

Brambling

P9
P7
P3
P1
S2
S4
S8
T6
T1
S.C.

III–IV

DUNLIN The tail feathers are grey, narrowly edged white when fresh; the inner web of T1 is black, and T5–T6 have some white along the shafts near the base. The flight feathers are grey, becoming black on the outer webs and the tips of P7–P10; P1–P6 have a white border to the basal and central section of the outer webs. The secondaries have a lot of white at the base of the inner webs, with the inner webs of S8–S10 being almost completely white. The tips of the secondaries and inner primaries are narrowly edged white; the shafts are white, except for a horn-brown tinge to the base of the primaries, increasing towards P9, absent on P10.

	J	F	M	A	M	J	J	A	S	O	N	D
Adult moult												
Juvenile moult												
Primaries 11 feathers	31	105	103	99	93	84	77	70	63	57	52	M
Secondaries	50	50	50	48	47	50	50	54	55	59	M	
Tail 12 feathers	44	44	45	45	50	54	M					

TEMMINCK'S STINT The central tail feathers are brown, sometimes narrowly edged buff; T2 has a dark grey outer web and a pale grey inner web, and T4–T6 are wholly white or a very pale grey. The primaries are dark brown, paler at the base of the inner webs (white on inner primaries); the shafts are pale brown, that of P10 white. The secondaries are dark brown, the outer ones narrowly and the inner ones more broadly tipped white; the inner webs have pale grey or white bases, the outer webs have white margins.

SNIPE The central tail feathers are black with a broad area of cinnamon towards the tip, and with a black-brown subterminal band and a broad buff tip; T2–T5 are similar, but the cinnamon becomes progressively wider and the bases are dark brown; T6 is pale buff to white, with three to five dark brown bars. The primaries are dark brown, narrowly tipped white; the inner webs are paler and tinged grey, with white mottling at the base, and the outer web of P10 is mostly white. The secondaries are as the primaries, but have broader white tips and the inner webs are mottled white or pale buff.

	J	F	M	A	M	J	J	A	S	O	N	D			
Adult moult															
Juvenile moult															
Primaries 10 feathers	42	105	105	101	94	87	83	78	72	66	64	M			
Secondaries 14 feathers	64	64	64	65	64	65	66	65	68	70	75	65	62	58	58	M
Tail 10 feathers	64	66	66	68	68	70	M								

JACK SNIPE The central tail feathers are dark brown with broad rufous edges and markings, the rest a paler brown with broad buff to white edges and markings; the undersides of the tail feathers are a pale brownish-grey with pale rufous or buff edges. The primaries are dark brown, with the shaft and outer web of P10 pale brown to white, and the outer webs of P1–P9 with a faint green gloss; the inner webs are pale brown; P1–P7 are tipped white. The secondaries are dark grey-brown, broadly tipped white; the outer webs have a faint green gloss and the inner webs are pale grey-brown.

	J	F	M	A	M	J	J	A	S	O	N	D
Adult moult												
Juvenile moult												
Primaries 11 feathers	36	105	105	101	96	90	82	76	71	65	60	M
Tail 12–18 feathers	48	49	50	50	52	54	61	M				

KNOT The tail feathers are grey with indication of narrow white fringes; they may be a slightly darker grey-brown subterminally. The inner primaries are grey, gradually becoming black on P8–P10; P1–P7 have lateral white margins. The secondaries are grey, narrowly fringed white. The shafts of all flight feathers are white, P8–P10 horn-grey at the base.

	J	F	M	A	M	J	J	A	S	O	N	D			
Adult moult															
Primaries 11 feathers	31	123	125	119	109	101	93	85	78	72	66				
Secondaries 15 feathers	65	65	66	65	65	66	69	69	71	73	77	81	85	74	54
Tail 12 feathers	76	75	74	74	76	76	M								

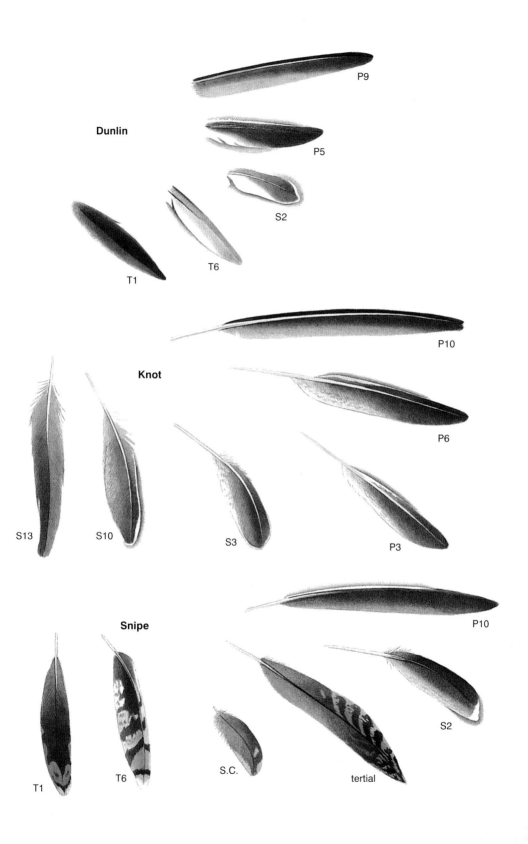

Dunlin

P9

P5

S2

T1

T6

Knot

P10

P6

S13

S10

S3

P3

Snipe

P10

T1

T6

S.C.

tertial

S2

III–IV

GUILLEMOT The tail and the flight feathers are black or blackish-brown. The primaries have pale brown inner webs, these becoming whitish towards the edge and base and increasingly black towards the tip; shafts of outermost primaries horn-coloured, becoming pale brown towards the tip, those of inner primaries black-brown, of secondaries and tail feathers black. The secondaries are broadly tipped white, with the inner webs pale brown. P11 is minute.

	J	F	M	A	M	J	J	A	S	O	N	D
Adult moult												
Primaries 11 feathers	38	130	133	132	127	123	117	113	106	99	91	
Secondaries 20 feathers	80 75	71	68 68	69	70 70	69	69 68	66	64 61	59 57	55 53	49 44
Tail 12 feathers	55	59	61	61	62	60						

BLACK GUILLEMOT The tail is black. The flight feathers have black outer webs; the distal half of inner webs is black, tapering along shaft and margin, the rest of web being white; a few inner secondaries may be narrowly tipped white; all flight feathers have black shafts, becoming horn-coloured towards the base. P11 is minute.

	J	F	M	A	M	J	J	A	S	O	N	D
Adult moult												
Primaries 11 feathers	35	150	148	143	137	130	122	116	107	100	96	M
Secondaries 18 feathers	85	80	80	76	75	75	70	60	60	45	M	
Tail 12 feathers	57	57	58	60	60	60	M					

RAZORBILL The tail feathers are entirely black. The flight feathers are black, with the inner webs of the primaries grading to dull grey on the edge and base. The secondaries have a conspicuous white tip. The shafts are black or brown-black, lightening to a pale horn colour towards the base. P11 minute.

	J	F	M	A	M	J	J	A	S	O	N	D
Adult moult												
Primaries 11 feathers	42	131	134	132	126	120	115	108	100	92	82	
Secondaries 20 feathers	74 76	65	65 66	66	66 66	65	64 62	60	58 56	55 53	51 52	50 48
Tail 12 feathers	71	74	77	79	80	84						

PUFFIN The tail feathers are black. The flight feathers are black above, with grey-brown inner webs and the shafts dark horn grading to brown towards the tip; the under surfaces are a dark silver-grey, P10 with a black outer web. P11 minute.

	J	F	M	A	M	J	J	A	S	O	N	D
Adult moult												
Juvenile moult												
Primaries 11 feathers	41	114	118	118	114	108	103	96	90	85	77	
Secondaries	68	64	63	65	68	66	67	66	65	64	60	57	55	51
Tail 16 feathers	59	59	60	60	60	59	60	60				

LITTLE AUK The tail feathers are black; often the tips of the outermost ones (and occasionally of others) have a white spot or white edges. The primaries have black-brown outer webs and tip, paler on inner webs and towards base. The secondaries are similar, but have a prominent white tip. The shafts of the flight feathers are largely black, but horn-coloured towards the base. P11 minute.

	J	F	M	A	M	J	J	A	S	O	N	D
Adult moult												
Primaries 11 feathers	30	92	93	91	87	85	81	76	70	66	60	
Secondaries	57	53	51	52	53	53	53	52	51	50	49	47	46
Tail 12 feathers	46	47	48	47	47	43						

STARLING The tail feathers and primaries are black-brown, edged and tipped buff, with a very slight green gloss inside the buff on the outer webs. The secondaries are the same, but with wider and more brilliant edging of blue-green gloss. The outer webs of P8–P9 are emarginated.

	J	F	M	A	M	J	J	A	S	O	N	D
Adult moult												
Juvenile moult												
Primaries 10 feathers	18	107	108	104	98	93	89	86	83	80		
Secondaries 9 feathers	77	76	75	72	70	68	65	56	43			
Tail 12 feathers	72	72	72	71	70	67						

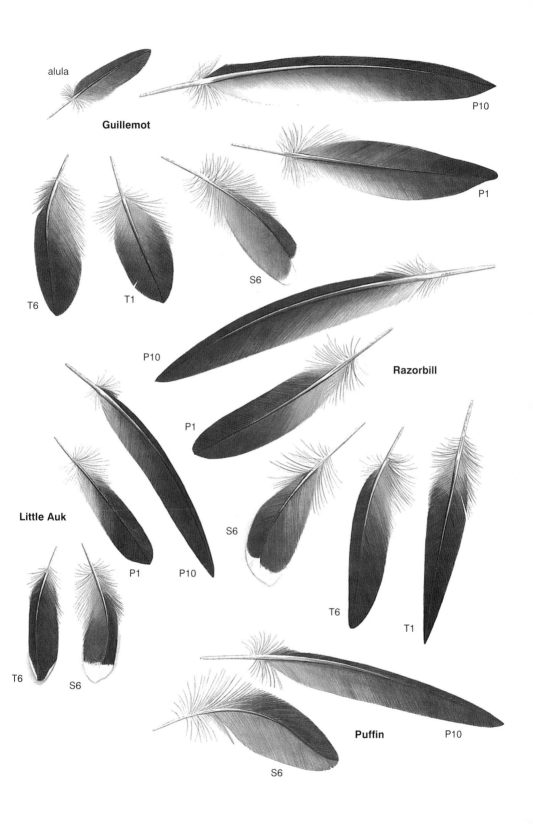

alula

Guillemot

P10

P1

T6

T1

S6

P10

Razorbill

P1

Little Auk

S6

P1

P10

T6

S6

T6

T1

Puffin

P10

S6

III–V

PIN-TAILED SANDGROUSE The central tail feathers are long and pointed, black barred buff and brown towards the base. Others are grey brown, broadly tipped white, their outer webs barred buff towards the tail; becoming paler towards the outer feathers, the outer web of T8 distally white. The primaries have pale grey outer webs and brown inner webs narrowly margined with white, with a pale area near the shaft, prominent on the inner feathers and extending to the tip on P1 & P2. Secondaries are dark brown, their tips and outer webs edged with white and the inner webs with white bases. Inward from S10 the feathers have an increasingly large yellow-olive patch on the outer web. The inner webs are pale brown-grey, the innermost with a yellow spot at the tip. No marked emargination.

Adult moult	J	F	M	A	M	J	J	A	S	O	N	D		
Primaries 11 feathers	36	168	160	150	145	142	140	120	110	94	85			
Secondaries c. 18 feathers	85	85	85	82	83	83	85	85	88	85	85	83	86	85
Tail 16–18 feathers	72	90	120	155	155	158	158	158						

BLACK-WINGED STILT The tail feathers are pale grey, with the tips narrowly fringed white; the outer feathers and the bases of the remainder are white. The flight feathers are black with a green gloss.

	J	F	M	A	M	J	J	A	S	O	N	D
Adult moult	J	F	M	A	M	J	J	A	S	O	N	D
Juvenile moult	J	F	M	A	M	J	J	A	S	O	N	D
Primaries 10 feathers	42	487	181	177	164	154	140	135	124	117	109	M
Secondaries	98	99	95	95	96	95	97	100	94	M		
Tail 12 feathers	91	89	88	90	90	95	M					

COLLARED PRATINCOLE Inner tail feathers dark grey with sooty centres, narrow white tips and broad white bases. Outers with much white at the base reaching nearly to the tip on the outer webs. Primaries black becoming grey towards the inners. The inner webs dark grey. Shaft of P10 white. Secondaries grey broadly tipped white, the innermost nearly black. There are no emarginations.

	J	F	M	A	M	J	J	A	S	O	N	D			
Adult moult	J	F	M	A	M	J	J	A	S	O	N	D			
Juvenile moult	J	F	M	A	M	J	J	A	S	O	N	D			
Primaries 11 feathers	35	168	150	140	135	125	120	110	90	84	70				
Secondaries 14–16 feathers	64	64	65	65	65	63	65	66	67	65	65	65	61	55	46
Tail 12 feathers	114	110	110	105	63	61									

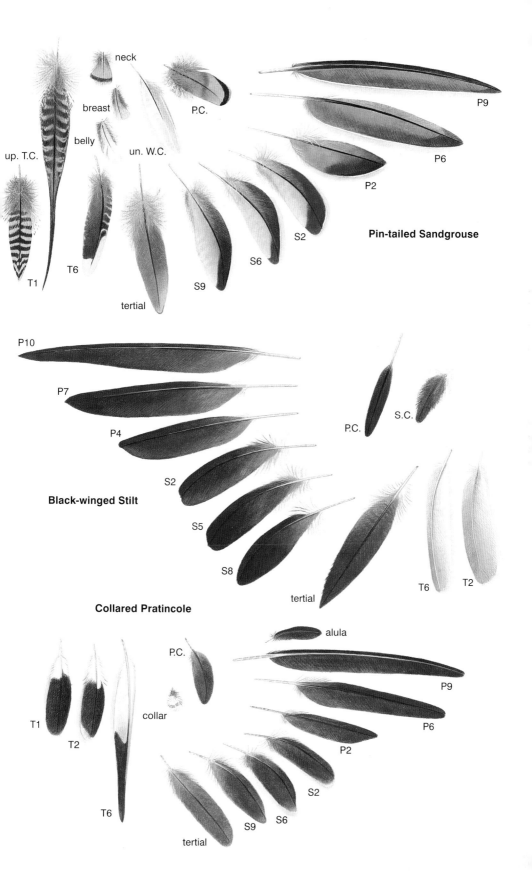

Pin-tailed Sandgrouse

neck

breast

belly

up. T.C.

un. W.C.

P.C.

P9

P6

P2

S2

S6

S9

tertial

T6

T1

Black-winged Stilt

P10

P7

P4

S2

S5

S8

P.C.

S.C.

tertial

T6

T2

Collared Pratincole

alula

P.C.

collar

T1

T2

T6

P9

P6

P2

S2

S6

S9

tertial

III–V

SWALLOW The tail feathers are black-brown, glossed metallic green, with the central pair being uniform and the remainder with a broad white patch on the inner web; on the outer pair, white extends up the shaft to a point. The flight feathers are black-brown, glossed dark metallic green on outer webs and tips; the innermost secondaries are dark metallic blue, and the inner primaries and the outer secondaries often have some metallic blue.

Primaries 10 feathers	9	105	105	98	90	83	77	71	64	57
Secondaries 9 feathers	54	53	51	51	50	48	45	37	25	
Tail 12 feathers	73	63	59	55	52	50				

RED-RUMPED SWALLOW The tail feathers are black-brown, glossed green-blue, with the outer pair sometimes having a grey mark on the inner webs. The flight feathers are the same, with the inner webs very narrowly edged buff; the innermost secondaries are more glossed, and the tertials are tipped white or pale buff.

Primaries 10 feathers	9	105	105	98	90	83	77	71	62	55	M
Secondaries 9 feathers	45	45	45	45	46	43	40	35	24	M	
Tail 12 feathers	86	65	56	50	46	43	M				

HOUSE MARTIN The tail feathers are black-brown with a slight green gloss. The flight feathers are the same with pale brown edges to inner webs, and S7 has a white tip.

Adult moult	J	F	M	A	M	J	J	A	S	O	N	D
Primaries 10 feathers	14	95	96	89	83	76	69	62	56	52		
Secondaries 9 feathers	47	45	44	44	43	42	38	33	29			
Tail 12 feathers	68	65	54	49	46	45						

SAND MARTIN The tail feathers are dark brown with a very faint green gloss, the inner and outer webs very narrowly edged white. The primaries are black-brown with a very faint green gloss, the inner webs very narrowly edged white. The secondaries are the same, but the outer webs are also very narrowly edged grey-brown to white.

Adult moult	J	F	M	A	M	J	J	A	S	O	N	D
Primaries 10 feathers	15	102	102	98	90	84	76	65	58	49	M	
Secondaries 9 feathers	43	43	43	46	47	49	47	40	31	M		
Tail 12 feathers	51	51	48	46	44	42	M					

SWIFT The tail feathers are olive-brown with a slight oily-bronze sheen. The outer webs and tips of the outer 4-5 primaries are black with a blue-green or bronze green gloss; both webs of the inner primaries and the inner webs of the outer primaries are a dark olive-brown with a slight bronze-green gloss. The secondaries and tertials are blackish olive-brown with a slight bluish-green sheen. The primaries are very narrow, curved backwards, have pointed tips and no emarginations.

Adult moult	J	F	M	A	M	J	J	A	S	O	N	D
Primaries 10 feathers	141	146	139	127	113	98	84	72	61	52		
Secondaries 9 feathers	45	46	47	47	46	47	44	34	30			
Tail 10 feathers	86	78	67	58	55							

ALPINE SWIFT The tail feathers are olive-black with a slight bronzy lustre; the base of the outer web of T5 has a grey-brown tinge and is narrowly fringed off-white. The flight feathers have olive-black outer webs and tips (deep black on outermost primaries); the inner webs are a paler grey-brown, the outer web of P10 narrowly edged off-white. The primary shape is as the Swift.

Adult moult	J	F	M	A	M	J	J	A	S	O	N	D
Primaries 10 feathers	195	201	190	170	147	123	104	84	68	61	M	
Tail 10 feathers	78	76	71	66	63	M						

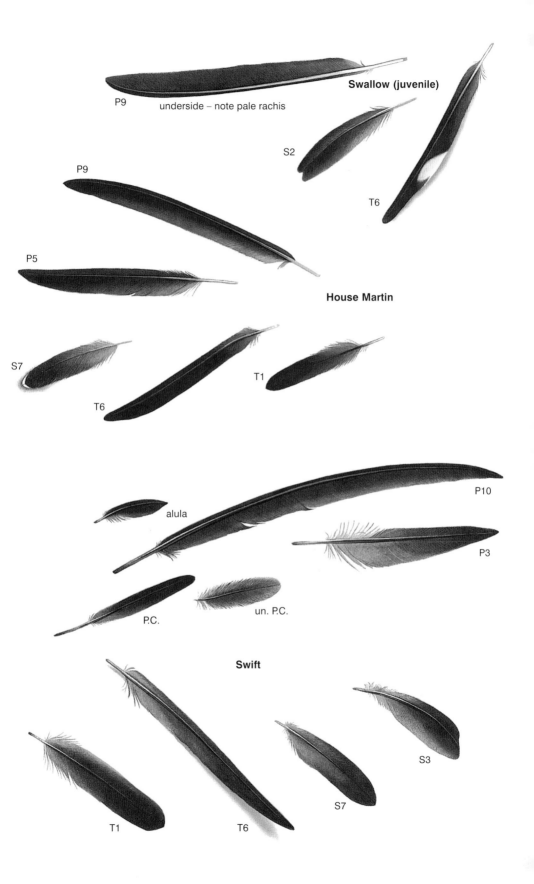

P9

Swallow (juvenile)

underside – note pale rachis

S2

T6

P9

P5

House Martin

S7

T6

T1

P10

alula

P3

P.C.

un. P.C.

Swift

T1

T6

S7

S3

III–V

BLACK TERN The tail feathers are medium grey, with the outer web of T6 sometimes paler. The flight feathers are slate-grey, with the inner webs of primaries darker and with an ill-defined dark smoke-grey wedge towards the base. The P4-P7 outer primaries are almost black when worn.

	J	F	M	A	M	J	J	A	S	O	N	D
Adult moult												
Primaries 11 feathers	44	192	184	175	161	145	130	115	100	90	86	M
Secondaries 15 feathers	85	80	80	78	75	75	70	70	M			
Tail 12 feathers	88	86	78	77	75	75	M					

LITTLE TERN The tail feathers are white, usually with a faint grey tinge on T1 and on the outer webs of T2-T3. The primary base colour varies from pale grey to silvery grey, with the outer primaries black; the shaft of P10 is white to pale horn, of the others dark horn to black. The secondaries are light grey, with white tips and inner borders.

	J	F	M	A	M	J	J	A	S	O	N	D
Adult moult												
Primaries 11 feathers	30	154	144	139	126	121	106	98	86	75	60	M
Secondaries 15 feathers	55	55	55	54	52	50	50	50	M			
Tail 12 feathers	78	60	55	55	50	50	M					

RINGED PLOVER The central tail feathers are olive brown, shading towards the tips to black-brown, the tips narrowly edged white. Outer feathers with lessening subterminal bar and increasing white tip. Outermost completely white sometimes with dark spot on inner web. Primaries dark brown fading to white on base of inner web. Shafts of P7 – P10 subterminally white. Basal portions of inners < P6 increasingly white. Secondaries dark brown with white bases and narrow tips, inners completely white. There are no emarginations.

	J	F	M	A	M	J	J	A	S	O	N	D			
Adult moult															
Juvenile moult															
Primaries 11 feathers	30	115	118	116	115	110	109	98	95	96	96				
Secondaries 14–19 feathers	96	95	95	95	95	90	90	90	90	90	90	85	84	78	56
Tail 12 feathers	68	68	68	68	68	68									

TURNSTONE The central tail feathers are black with a white base and a narrow white tip; on the other feathers the white areas became gradually more extensive towards T6, which is mostly white with a narrow black subterminal dot or bar. The primaries are dark grey-brown, the outer ones almost black; the inner 6 have mainly white bases to the outer web. The outer secondaries are white with a fairly broad dark tip, the white gradually increasing towards the inner secondaries; the innermost S1–S3 are wholly white or with a small dark subterminal dot on the outer web.

	J	F	M	A	M	J	J	A	S	O	N	D
Adult moult												
Juvenile moult												
Primaries 11 feathers	32	136	134	129	118	110	98	92	84	78	70	M
Secondaries	64	64	64	65	65	65	65	68	70	M		
Tail 12 feathers	71	75	77	77	77	80	M					

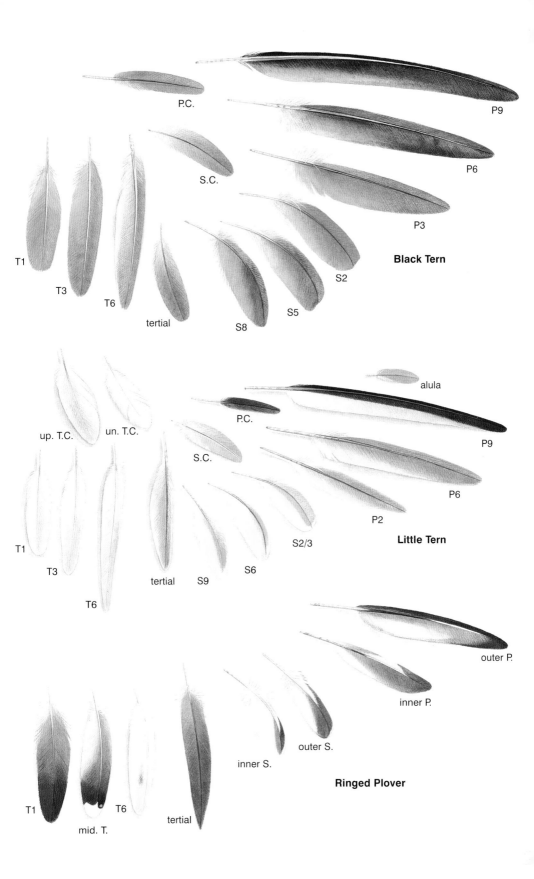

P.C.

P9

P6

P3

S.C.

Black Tern

T1

T3

T6

tertial

S8

S5

S2

alula

up. T.C.

un. T.C.

P.C.

P9

S.C.

P6

P2

Little Tern

S2/3

T1

T3

S6

tertial

S9

T6

outer P.

inner P.

outer S.

inner S.

Ringed Plover

T1

mid. T.

T6

tertial

III–VA

WAXWING The tail feathers are grey at the base, shading into black with bright yellow tips; the shafts at the tip are red and occasionally slightly thickened and with small 'wax' tips. The primaries are black with the inner webs broadly edged greyish; P9 has a small white spot at the tip; P8 and P7 have a white V-shaped margin at the tip, P6 is the same but with the side of the V on the outer web yellowish, the rest are as P6 but with the side of the V on the outer web bright yellow. The secondaries are more greyish-black with the tips of the outer webs white; the tips of the shafts are elongated, flattened and 'waxy' bright red; the three innermost secondaries are brownish-grey, with no white on the outer web and usually without waxy tips. The outer webs of P7–P8 are emarginated. The waxy tips are formed by the fusion of the shaft of the feather with the tip of its outer vane.

	J	F	M	A	M	J	J	A	S	O	N	D
Adult moult	J	F	M	A	M	J	J	**A**	**S**	**O**	**N**	D
Juvenile moult	J	F	M	A	M	J	J	**A**	**S**	**O**	**N**	D
Primaries 10 feathers	24	101	103	97	94	86	83	78	73	68		
Secondaries 10 feathers	63	63	65	65	65	60	60	56	43	34		
Tail 12 feathers	62	64	64	64	64	64						

GOLDEN ORIOLE The tail feathers are velvety-black, tinged yellow at the base; the central pair is narrowly tipped yellow, and the rest have the distal half or third yellow. The primaries are velvety-black, tipped yellowish-white; the inner webs are fringed grey, and the outer webs of P6-P8 are fringed whitish on the distal half. The secondaries are velvety-black with broader yellowish-white tips. The outer webs of P7–P8 are emarginated.

	J	F	M	A	M	J	J	A	S	O	N	D
Adult moult	**J**	**F**	**M**	**A**	**M**	**J**	**J**	A	S	O	**N**	**D**
Primaries 10 feathers	68	119	130	128	115	105	99	94	90	87	M	
Secondaries 11 feathers	83	83	78	73	71	68	65	60	55	45	32	M
Tail 12 feathers	83	86	86	88	88	88	M					

RED-BACKED SHRIKE Tail variable. The central pair of tail feathers is usually black with small whitish tips, the next pair the same but with the basal half white, the rest with the basal two-thirds white, the shafts are black and they have longer white tips. The flight feathers are brown-black with narrow edgings, rufous on the outer webs and whitish on the inner webs; the inner primaries have white bases; the inner secondaries have broader rufous edgings, and the innermost are still more rufous and with whitish tips. The outer webs of P7–P8 are emarginated.

	J	F	M	A	M	J	J	A	S	O	N	D
Adult moult	**J**	**F**	**M**	**A**	**M**	**J**	**J**	**A**	**S**	**O**	**N**	**D**
Juvenile moult	**J**	**F**	**M**	**A**	**M**	**J**	**J**	**A**	**S**	**O**	**N**	**D**
Primaries 10 feathers	31	80	92	81	85	79	75	71	68	65	M	
Secondaries 10 feathers	65	60	56	53	50	50	50	45	41	32	M	
Tail 12 feathers	83	87	89	90	90	90	M					

GREAT GREY SHRIKE The central pair of tail feathers is black with white bases and small dull white marks at the tips; the second pair is the same, but with 5–10mm of white at the tip; the third pair has 10–20mm white at the tip; the fourth pair has 20–40mm white at tip, but occasionally is mostly white, with only part of the shaft and an irregular mark on both webs black; the fifth pair has 30–40mm white at the tip, but occasionally is all white, with only part of the shaft black; the sixth pair sometimes all white, sometimes with part of the shaft black, and sometimes with the base of the inner web or a mark of varying size black. The primaries are black with white bases, and with the tips of the inner feathers white, the outer feathers have the outer webs narrowly fringed whitish. The secondaries are as the primaries, but with longer white tips and rather less white at the base; the inner secondaries have no white at the base. The outer webs of P6–P8 are emarginated.

	J	F	M	A	M	J	J	A	S	O	N	D
Primaries 10 feathers	55	92	106	106	104	96	90	90	91	88	M	
Secondaries 10 feathers	88	85	80	74	67	60	60	60	56	45	M	
Tail 12 feathers	90	102	105	105	106	108	M					

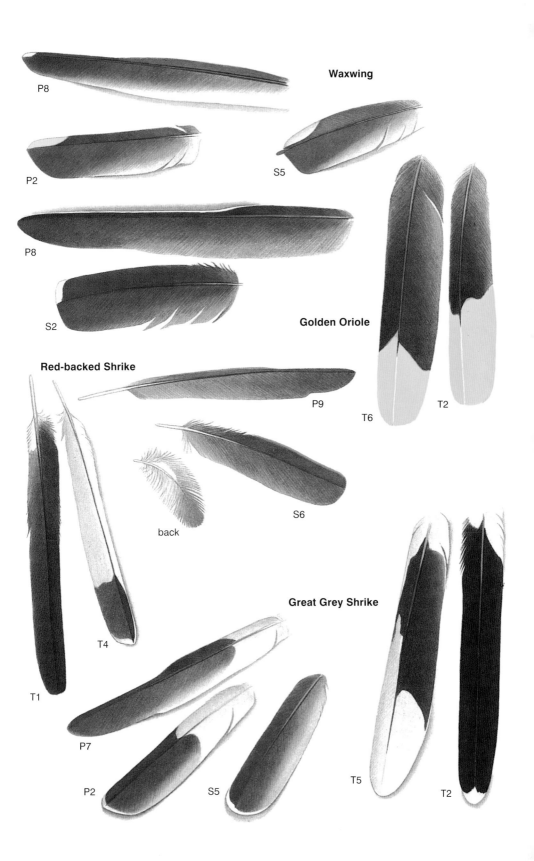

Waxwing

P8

P2

S5

P8

S2

Golden Oriole

T6

T2

Red-backed Shrike

P9

S6

back

Great Grey Shrike

T4

T1

P7

P2

S5

T5

T2

III–VA

GREAT SPOTTED WOODPECKER The central pair of tail feathers (T1) is black; T2 is similar or with some yellow-buff or off-white bars at the very tip; T3 has a large yellow-buff spot at the tip and one or two subterminal off-white bars or spots; T4–T5 are off-white with black at base of inner webs, usually with black bars across tip; T6 black. The primaries are black; the outer web of P9 has two or three shallow white spots along the basal margin, the outer webs of P6–P8 have four to six large and equally spaced white spots, P1–P5 have three to five large white spots on the outer webs and a small white spot on the tip, the inner webs of the primaries are similar, but the white spots along the borders are larger and the distal parts are uniform black. The secondaries are black, with three to five large white spots along the borders of both webs; the tips of the outer secondaries have a small white fringe or spots. The tertials are more glossy black, the longer ones having two or three white spots on the middle portion and a black tip. The outer webs of P5–P8 are emarginated, the inner webs of P5–P9 slightly emarginated.

Adult moult	J	F	M	A	M	J	J	A	S	O	N	D
Primaries 10 feathers	57	118	124	138	135	128	116	111	98	98	M	
Secondaries 11–12 feathers	95	95	90	90	88	85	85	80	73	60	56	M
Tail 12 feathers	72	80	88	95	100	105	M					

HOOPOE The tail feathers are black with a broad white transverse band: the band on T1 is about 12mm wide with 40–45mm of the tip black; the band gradually gets slightly wider and closer to the tip towards the outer feathers, on T5 being about 15mm wide with 25–35mm of the tip black on the inner web, widening on the outer web. The primaries are black with a broad white band on P2–P9, reduced to a white subterminal spot on the inner web of P10 and on P1–P3. The secondaries are black with five broad white transverse bands, these reduced to broken bars or spots on S2–S3 and S1 having only a small white subterminal spot on the inner web; the white bands are partly tinged cream or may have cinnamon edges at the border with the black, especially on the inner secondaries. The outer webs of P5–P8 and the inner webs of P6–P9 are emarginated.

Adult moult	J	F	M	A	M	J	J	A	S	O	N	D
Primaries 10 feathers	80	132	148	149	148	144	134	123	118	117	M	
Secondaries 11–12 feathers	117	115	115	114	115	111	106	98	86	64	M	
Tail 12 feathers	106	106	106	107	107	107	M					

LITTLE GREBE The tail-tuft feathers are black. The primaries and outer webs of the secondaries are brownish-grey, the inner webs of the secondaries having a variable amount of white. The tertials are dark brown. The outer webs of P9–P10 are emarginated, with P8 slightly so, and the inner webs of P10 and P11 are emarginated.

Adult moult	J	F	M	A	M	J	J	A	S	O	N	D
Juvenile moult	J	F	M	A	M	J	J	A	S	O	N	D
Primaries 12 feathers	8	68	73	75	75	73	71	71	70	70	69	66
Secondaries	68	68	67	67	64	61	61	61	60	60	59	56

WATER RAIL The tail feathers have large black centres and are broadly fringed olive-brown. The primaries and outer secondaries are black, with an olive-brown tinge to the outer webs of the secondaries. The inner secondaries are like the tail, but the black is more restricted.

Adult moult	J	F	M	A	M	J	J	A	S	O	N	D
Juvenile moult	J	F	M	A	M	J	J	A	S	O	N	D
Primaries 10 feathers	78	94	100	103	103	95	90	87	85	80		
Secondaries 13 feathers	85	84	84	81	81	80	80	88	96	94	84	70	57
Tail 12 feathers	47	49	50	53	55	56						

CORNCRAKE The tail feathers are buff-brown with large black centres, the fringes tinged grey at the tips. The flight feathers are a dark rufous-brown, the primaries with a dull black tinge near the tips and on the inner webs; the outer web of P10 is pale cream and is narrow.

Adult moult	J	F	M	A	M	J	J	A	S	O	N	D
Juvenile moult	J	F	M	A	M	J	J	A	S	O	N	D
Primaries 10 feathers	111	126	122	119	115	110	101	94	85	82	M	
Tail 12 feathers	50	50	52	52	55	58	M					

Great Spotted Woodpecker (*Lesser)

un. T.C.

T2

T5

S4

P9

P6

*S1

Hoopoe

T1

T6

S3

P12

P4

P9

Little Grebe

P1

S3

S7

Water Rail

P10

P8

S1

S10

S13

up. T.C.

flank

IV

RING OUZEL The tail feathers are brown-black, with the outer feathers very narrowly fringed greyish-white. The flight feathers are black-brown, tinged greyish; the outer webs are narrowly margined dull greyish-white (rather more widely on the secondaries), the inner margins of the inner webs are grey. The outer webs of P6–P8 are emarginated.

Adult moult	J	F	M	A	M	J	J	A	S	O	N	D
Primaries 10 feathers	29	100	114	113	109	105	100	98	98	96	M	
Tail 12 feathers	111	115	116	118	120	120	M					

BLACKBIRD The tail feathers are brown-black. The flight feathers are brown-black, with greyish margins to the inner webs and deep umber outer webs. The outer webs of P5–P8 are emarginated.

Adult moult	J	F	M	A	M	J	J	A	S	O	N	D
Primaries 10 feathers	29	98	110	112	114	112	105	100	99	97		
Secondaries 9 feathers	96	95	92	90	86	81	78	66	49			
Tail 12 feathers	112	116	117	118	117	116						

REDWING The tail feathers are dark brown, with a very narrow buffish-white edging at the tip of the inner webs of the outer feathers. The flight feathers are dark brown, edged paler. The outer webs of P6–P8 are emarginated.

Adult moult	J	F	M	A	M	J	J	A	S	O	N	D
Primaries 10 feathers	18	93	100	101	97	88	84	82	80	78		
Secondaries 9 feathers	76	75	73	70	67	64	62	52	40			
Tail 12 feathers	85	84	87	86	84	80						

SONG THRUSH The tail feathers are reddish-brown. The flight feathers are black-brown with most of the basal portion of the inner webs buff; the outer webs except at tips are reddish-brown with darkish centres. The outer webs of P6–P8 are emarginated.

Adult moult	J	F	M	A	M	J	J	A	S	O	N	D
Primaries 10 feathers	20	92	99	100	99	91	87	85	83	81		
Secondaries 9 feathers	79	78	76	75	72	70	67	57	42			
Tail 12 feathers	91	92	92	91	91	88						

MISTLE THRUSH The tail feathers are greyish-brown, narrowly edged greyish-buff on the outer webs and greyish-white on the inner webs; the outermost pair has white tips and a varying amount of white on the inner webs; the next two pairs have much smaller white tips on the inner webs. The primaries are dark brown with the outer webs narrowly edged greyish-buff, becoming white towards the tips; the basal portion of the inner webs is white. The secondaries are the same, but the outer webs are more widely fringed creamy-buff and the innermost feathers have white tips. The outer webs of P6–P8 are emarginated, P5 slightly emarginated.

Adult moult	J	F	M	A	M	J	J	A	S	O	N	D
Primaries 10 feathers	25	114	126	128	124	114	106	103	99	96		
Secondaries 9 feathers	95	94	91	88	85	81	76	67	48			
Tail 12 feathers	88	103	113	118	119	119						

FIELDFARE The tail feathers are brown-black with the outer webs fringed greyish at the base, the outer pair with a narrow whitish margin at the tip of the inner webs. The primaries are brown-black with the inner webs greyish at base; the outer webs of the outer feathers are fringed grey, those of the inner feathers are browner. The secondaries are brown-black with the outer webs fringed more broadly and with more chestnut-brown, but greyish at tips. The outer webs of P6–P8 are emarginated.

Adult moult	J	F	M	A	M	J	J	A	S	O	N	D
Primaries 10 feathers	24	116	123	124	120	109	102	99	97	94		
Secondaries 9 feathers	93	91	89	88	85	83	80	67	50			
Tail 12 feathers	114	120	121	123	123	121						

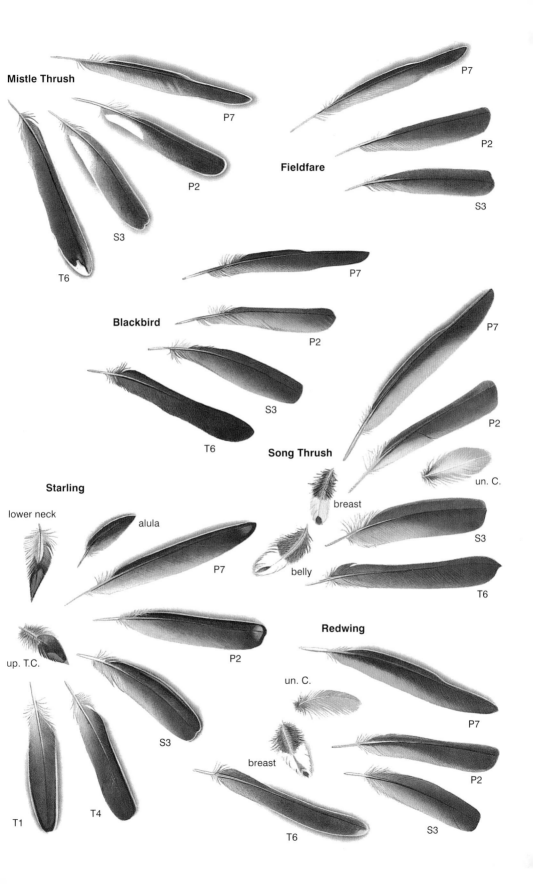

Mistle Thrush

P7

P2

S3

T6

Fieldfare

P7

P2

S3

Blackbird

P7

P2

S3

T6

Song Thrush

P7

P2

un. C.

breast

belly

S3

T6

Starling

lower neck

alula

P7

P2

up. T.C.

S3

T1

T4

Redwing

un. C.

breast

P7

P2

T6

S3

IV–V

GREAT CRESTED GREBE The tail is black above and buff and white below. The primaries are dark brown-grey, paler below, and with white bases; the innermost are tipped white. The secondaries are white, the outmost with a mainly brown-grey outer web and a brown-black inner web. P12 hidden by primary coverts. The outer webs of P9–P10 are emarginated, as are the inner webs of P10–P11.

	J	F	M	A	M	J	J	A	S	O	N	D	
Adult moult													
Juvenile moult													
Primaries 12 feathers	46	162	161	158	147	139	130	122	112	106	100	93	M
Secondaries 22 feathers	92	92	90	90	90	85	80	74	70	65	65	M	

BLACK-NECKED GREBE The tail tuft feathers are black on the upper half and dirty white below. The outer primaries are dark brownish-grey; P6 often has a white spot at the tip, P5 with inner web mottled white and P4–P1 increasingly white. The secondaries are white, becoming increasingly darker grey towards the inner ones. P12 is concealed by primary coverts. The outer web of P10 is emarginated, P9 slightly so; and the inner web of P11 is emarginated, with P10 slightly so.

	J	F	M	A	M	J	J	A	S	O	N	D	
Adult moult													
Juvenile moult													
Primaries 12 feathers	24	116	115	113	105	99	93	87	81	75	70	60	M
Secondaries 18–19 feathers	55	55	54	54	54	50	50	M					

SLAVONIAN GREBE The tail tuft is of black feathers. The primaries are grey; the secondaries are largely white, with the outer two partly grey and the innermost entirely grey. P12 hidden by primary coverts. P9–P11 emarginated on both webs.

	J	F	M	A	M	J	J	A	S	O	N	D	
Adult moult													
Juvenile moult													
Primaries 12 feathers	30	124	124	121	113	107	102	95	89	83	79	73	M
Secondaries	75	76	75	75	76	74	M						

RED-NECKED GREBE Tail tuft of black feathers, partly white below. The primaries are brown-grey with black shafts; the outermost secondary is similar, with the next two or three increasingly spotted white, the next ten or so mostly white with black bases to shafts, the next three or so brown-grey with white or rufous at the base, and the innermost brown-black. P12 hidden by primary coverts. The outer webs of P9–P10 and the inner webs of P9–P11 are emarginated.

	J	F	M	A	M	J	J	A	S	O	N	D	
Adult moult													
Juvenile moult													
Primaries 12 feathers	42	161	162	160	152	145	137	112	106	103	96	92	M
Secondaries 20 feathers	90	90	88	86	86	85	84	M					

COOT The tail feathers are dark slate-grey, tipped black, with a green gloss. The flight feathers are dark brown-grey, with the inner webs paler grey and the outer webs tinged slate, P10 sometimes edged white; the tips of the secondaries are white with dark horn-brown shafts, the white most extensive on the inner webs and on the central secondaries.

	J	F	M	A	M	J	J	A	S	O	N	D	
Adult moult													
Juvenile moult													
Primaries 11 feathers	24	135	144	156	159	157	154	149	141	136	129		
Secondaries 17–20 feathers	125	118	112	112	116	125	135	129	114	105	103	96	93
Tail 12–16 feathers	68	70	72	72	72	71	71						

MOORHEN The tail feathers are black with a faint green gloss and a tinge of olive-brown. The flight feathers are dull black, the outer webs with an olive-brown tinge; the outer edge of P10 is white.

	J	F	M	A	M	J	J	A	S	O	N	D	
Adult moult													
Juvenile moult													
Primaries 11 feathers	18	116	141	144	144	142	138	133	128	122	114		
Secondaries 12–14 feathers	109	107	103	100	97	97	100	108	111	105	93	77	63	63
Tail 12 feathers	67	78	82	83	84	84							

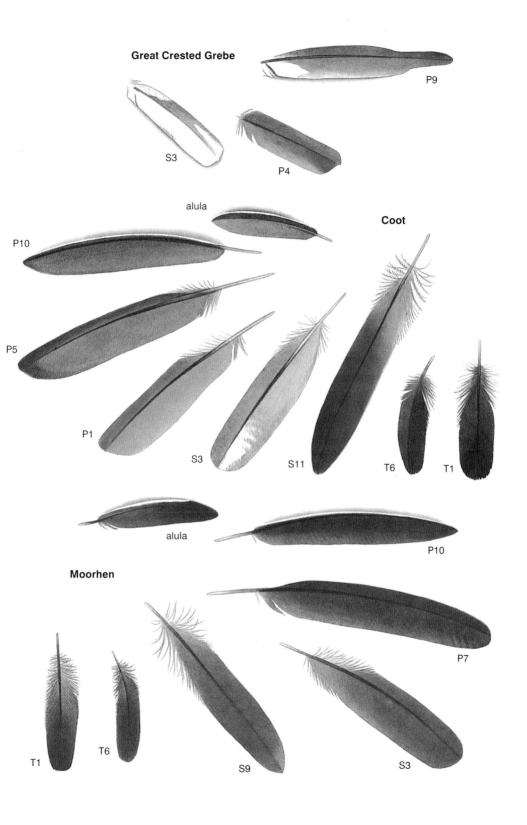

Great Crested Grebe

P9

S3

P4

alula

Coot

P10

P5

P1

S3

S11

T6

T1

alula

P10

Moorhen

T1

T6

S9

S3

P7

IV–V

MERLIN The tail feathers are slate blue and with black partial bars, a broad black subterminal band and an off-white tip. The primaries are grey-black to brown-black with narrow off-white tips, their inner webs with pale grey to white comb-like bars which on the inner primaries, extend onto the outer webs. Outer secondaries are slate blue on the outer webs, the grey-brown inner webs with white partial bars. Inner secondaries are grey to grey-brown. The outer webs of P8 and P9, and the inner webs of P9 and P10, are emarginated.

	J	F	M	A	M	J	J	A	S	O	N	D
Adult moult	J	F	M	A	M	J	J	A	S	O	N	D
Juvenile moult	J	F	M	A	M	J	J	A	S	O	N	D

Primaries 11 feathers	36	158	185	189	175	162	150	153	145	120	112			
Secondaries 14 feathers	107	103	103	98	97	97	97	96	96	95	90	87	77	67
Tail 12 feathers	142	150	150	148	145									

SCOPS OWL Tail feathers cream-buff to cream-white with fine grey speckling, with 5–8 almost unspeckled buff or cream bars each with irregular narrow black border basally. Flight feathers with cream and buff bars, (8 on largest primaries to 4 on inners and secondaries). Pale bars partly broken at shafts, all bars speckled with dusky grey particularly on inner webs obscuring the barred pattern, distinct large spots with buff or white-cream on outer edges of outer primaries. Tips of flight feathers pale buff to cream with narrow black-brown shaft streak and close dusky speckling. Outer webs of P8–P9 and inner webs of P8–P10 emarginated.

	J	F	M	A	M	J	J	A	S	O	N	D
Adult moult	J	F	M	A	M	J	J	A	S	O	N	D
Juvenile moult	J	F	M	A	M	J	J	A	S	O	N	D

Primaries 10 feathers	118	124	130	114	110	110	105	105	103	100		
Secondaries 12 feathers	100	101	100	96	96	96	94	94	94	92	90	87
Tail 12 feathers	69	70	70	72	72	72						

TURTLE DOVE The central tail feathers are dull greyish olive-brown; the remainder black with a grey bloom, and tipped white; tip of T2 often partly suffused bluish-grey and olive-brown, outer web of T6 white Underside of tail feathers black with broad white tips, outer web of T6 white. Flight feathers greyish-black; tips of secondaries have slight olive-brown tinge and outer webs of secondaries and inner primaries are tinged grey. Outer webs of P8–P9 and inner webs of P10 slightly emarginated.

	J	F	M	A	M	J	J	A	S	O	N	D
Adult moult	J	F	M	A	M	J	J	A	S	O	N	D
Juvenile moult	J	F	M	A	M	J	J	A	S	O	N	D

Primaries 10 feathers	147	149	146	136	130	123	112	107	100	98	M			
Secondaries 13 feathers	95	84	84	85	85	81	81	81	80	80	76	76	70	M
Tail 12 feathers	94	104	106	110	114	118	M							

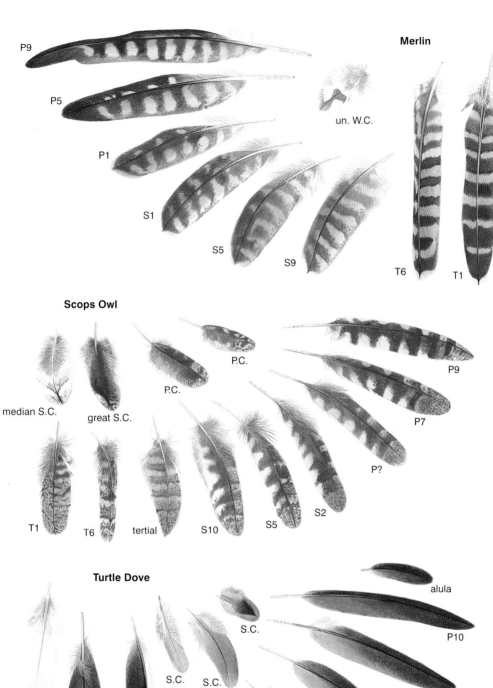

Merlin

P9

P5

P1

S1

S5

S9

un. W.C.

T6 T1

Scops Owl

median S.C.

great S.C.

P.C.

P.C.

P9

P7

P?

T1

T6

tertial

S10

S5

S2

Turtle Dove

alula

S.C.

P10

S.C.

S.C.

P8

un. T.C.

tertial

mid. S.

P3

T1

T6

IV–VA, VIII

GREY PARTRIDGE The central tail feathers are closely vermiculated pale grey and dull black, the outer ones deep chestnut with black-freckled pale buff tips. The primaries are dark sepia with a few short buff bars, the bars widely separated on the outer webs and narrow and broken (often reduced to spots) on the inner webs; the tips and a narrow line on the outer edges are pale buff. The secondaries are black with white or pale buff shaft streaks, and with fine buff and dusky vermiculation on the tips and edges, the outer webs have some pale buff bars bordered by dark sepia. The outer webs of P4–P9 are emarginated near the base, and the inner webs of P6–P10 are emarginated.

	J	F	M	A	M	J	J	A	S	O	N	D
Adult moult												
Juvenile moult												
Primaries 10 feathers	110	127	132	134	134	135	122	112	104	97		
Secondaries 15 feathers	98	103	101	100	100	100	100	99	99	99	93	
Tail 14 feathers	82	84	84	85	86	86	90					

RED-LEGGED PARTRIDGE The central pair of tail feathers is dark olive-grey, the remainder are chestnut. The primaries are dark sepia or black; the outer webs have a distinct yellow-buff distal edge (lacking on P10) and the bases washed buff-brown and finely speckled dusky. The secondaries are dark olive-grey, the outer webs of the outer ones with buff margins and with dusky speckling towards the centre. The outer webs of P4–P9 and the inner webs of P7–P10 are emarginated.

	J	F	M	A	M	J	J	A	S	O	N	D
Adult moult												
Primaries 10 feathers	110	121	126	130	130	127	121	112	108	100		
Secondaries 15 feathers	100	105	105	110	110	110	110	109	104	100	88	73
Tail 14 feathers	93	93	95	95	95	97	100					

RED GROUSE The tail feathers are black with slightly paler tips. The primaries are a dark greyish-brown, the outer feathers with a silver-grey cast near the base of the outer webs and the inner ones with grey tips of variable extent. The secondaries are also dark grey-brown, the inner ones with black centres and narrow and irregular tawny-buff bars and white edges. The outer webs of P5–P9 are basally emarginated, the inner webs of P6–P9 slightly so.

	J	F	M	A	M	J	J	A	S	O	N	D
Adult moult												
Primaries 10 feathers	118	154	166	166	164	151	126	116	113	110		
Tail 16 feathers	114	113	113	113	112	112	111	112				

HAZEL HEN The central tail feathers are brown-grey, with black and white vermiculations tending to form irregular bars; the remainder are similar, but have a broad subterminal black band and a white tip. The primaries are dark grey-brown, with well-defined narrow buff at the tips and along the edge of the inner webs; the distal part of the outer webs of P4–P10 are white to pale buff, with a number of inconspicuous grey-brown bars (reduced on P5–P7); P9 rarely has more than seven bars, but often has a dark distal part to the outer web. The secondaries are grey-brown, with irregularly pale buff bars and margins; the tips of the inner ones are a pale cream-grey, with a dark brown subterminal spot on the outer web and a white margin. The outer webs of P4–P9 and the inner webs of P6–P10 are emarginated.

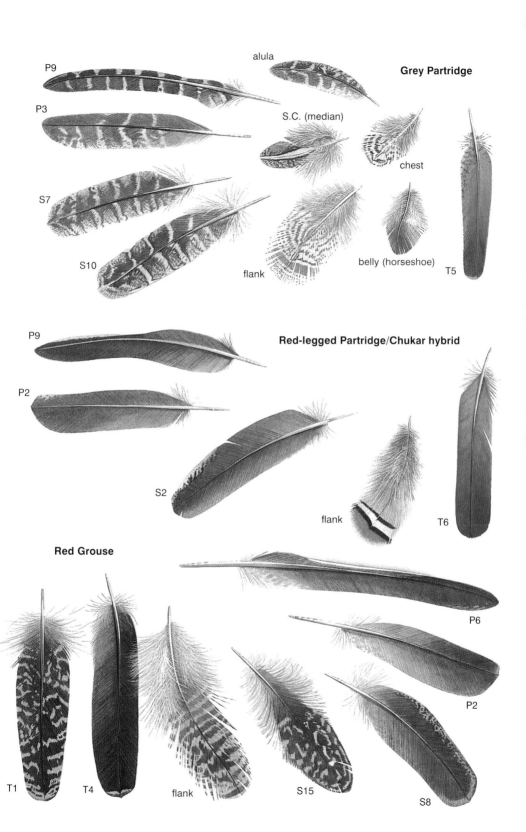

P9

alula

Grey Partridge

P3

S.C. (median)

chest

S7

belly (horseshoe)

S10

flank

T5

P9

Red-legged Partridge/Chukar hybrid

P2

S2

flank

T6

Red Grouse

P6

P2

T1

T4

flank

S15

S8

V

BLACK-TAILED GODWIT The tail feathers are black, with the basal half of T1 white, the white gradually increasing towards the outer feathers; the tips are narrowly fringed white. The flight feathers have black outer webs and tips and dark grey inner webs; the basal two-thirds of P1–P6 and of all secondaries are white; the shafts white.

Adult moult	J	F	M	A	M	J	J	A	S	O	N	D
Primaries 11 feathers	54	480	479	171	164	158	144	135	121	112	103	M
Secondaries	100	100	98	97	95	96	100	110	115	M		
Tail 12 feathers	95	95	95	92	92	91	M					

BAR-TAILED GODWIT The tail feathers are broadly barred black and white, and narrowly tipped white. The flight feathers are dark grey, becoming black on the tips and the outer webs of the outer primaries; the secondaries and innermost primaries have narrow white fringes; all flight feathers have the bases of the inner webs partly white and partly mottled grey and white.

Adult moult	J	F	M	A	M	J	J	A	S	O	N	D
Primaries 11 feathers	45	163	162	153	141	128	113	102	90	85	82	M
Secondaries	80	80	80	78	78	78	76	75	75	M		
Tail 12 feathers	83	84	84	85	90	90	M					

GREY PLOVER The central tail feathers have even black and white bands, the white gradually increasing to the outer feathers, T6 being white except for a black subterminal bar and dots. The primaries are black, the inner webs with white bases; there are large white subterminal patches on the outer webs of P1–P6. The secondaries are dark grey, the inner webs with broad white fringes.

Adult moult	J	F	M	A	M	J	J	A	S	O	N	D
Primaries 11 feathers	42	156	153	148	140	130	118	106	98	90	80	M
Secondaries	78	78	78	76	78	80	80	80	85	88	M	
Tail 12 feathers	72	74	77	78	80	81	M					

GOLDEN PLOVER The tail feathers are dull black or sepia-grey, with narrowish regular straight bars or chevrons which are a golden-yellow or pale yellow on T1 and off-white towards T6. The flight feathers are dark grey, becoming black on the outer webs and tips of the outer primaries; the tips of the secondaries and innermost primaries have narrow white edges.

Adult moult	J	F	M	A	M	J	J	A	S	O	N	D
Primaries 11 feathers	40	169	164	159	148	142	131	121	109	99	86	M
Secondaries	80	79	80	80	78	76	76	75	75	75	74	70	M
Tail 12 feathers	96	80	81	83	83	85	M					

REDSHANK The tail feathers are closely barred blackish-brown and white; the central feathers are often suffused grey or buff-brown. The primaries are black-brown, their inner webs sepia with a brown-speckled broad white base; the shafts are sepia, but that of P10 is white. The secondaries are white with ash-brown bases.

Adult moult	J	F	M	A	M	J	J	A	S	O	N	D
Primaries 11 feathers	31	125	128	125	119	114	104	98	91	85	81	
Secondaries	79	79	80	79	77	77	78	78	80	81	82	90	99	10	93
Tail 12 feathers	68	68	68	68	68	70	M					

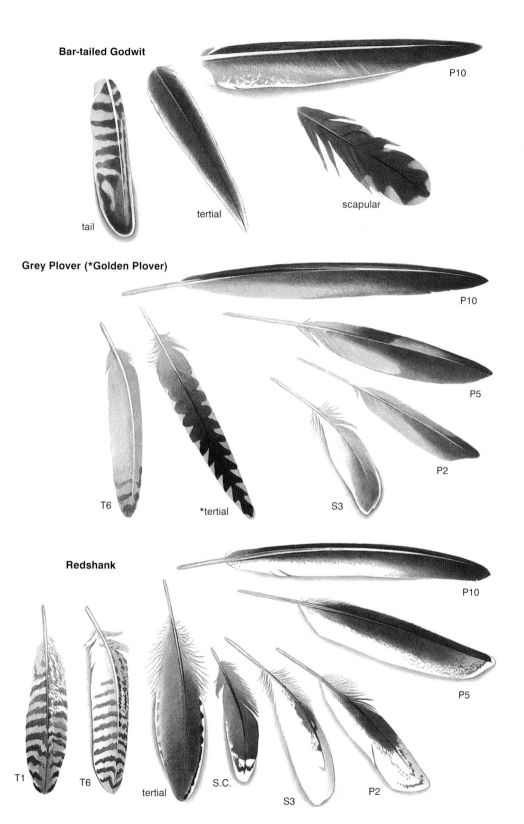

Bar-tailed Godwit

P10

scapular

tail

tertial

Grey Plover (*Golden Plover)

P10

P5

P2

T6

*tertial

S3

Redshank

P10

P5

T1

T6

tertial

S.C.

S3

P2

V

TUFTED DUCK The tail feathers are dull black. The primaries are grey, with the outer edges of the outer four to five feathers and all the tips black; the outer webs of inner primaries are white, except for tips and bases. The secondaries are white, broadly tipped black on outer web and dark grey on inner. The outer web of P9 and the inner web of P10 are emarginated.

	J	F	M	A	M	J	J	A	S	O	N	D
Adult moult	J	F	M	A	M	J	J	A	S	O	N	D
Juvenile moult	J	F	M	A	M	J	J	A	S	O	N	D
Primaries 11 feathers	43	148	153	149	141	132	124	116	108	101	97	
Secondaries 14 feathers	93	92	88	88	88	91	96	101	109			
Tail 14 feathers	61	65	67	68	69	68	67					

MANDARIN The tail feathers are dark grey-brown. The flight feathers are sepia, with the outer webs of primaries edged silvery white and the tips glossed blue-green. The secondaries are broadly tipped white, with a subterminal black border, about five secondaries have a strong blue-green gloss on outer webs. The central tertial, or 'sail', has an extremely wide warm cinnamon inner web and narrow purple-blue outer web; the tip of the inner web is bordered black and the border at the base and the narrow shaft streak is white. The outer web of P9 and the inner web of P10 are emarginated.

	J	F	M	A	M	J	J	A	S	O	N	D
Adult moult	J	F	M	A	M	J	J	A	S	O	N	D
Juvenile moult	J	F	M	A	M	J	J	A	S	O	N	D
Primaries 11 feathers	44	191	191	183	174	170	167	161	150	135	126	M
Secondaries	120	120	115	115	110	M						
Tail 16 feathers	101	105	108	112	114	115	115	120	M			

GOLDENEYE Tail feathers are black with a dark grey bloom. Primaries and S1–S4 are black with white tips, remaining secondaries are white. Outer web of P9 and inner web of P10 are emarginated.

	J	F	M	A	M	J	J	A	S	O	N	D
Adult moult	J	F	M	A	M	J	J	A	S	O	N	D
Juvenile moult	J	F	M	A	M	J	J	A	S	O	N	D
Primaries 11 feathers	56	205	205	195	183	171	161	152	141	129	119	M
Tail 16 feathers	48	65	75	80	94	100	105	110	M			

POCHARD The tail feathers are dark grey. The primaries are pale ash, with the tips of all and the outer edges of P8–P11 sooty black, all finely speckled white at tips. The secondaries are pale ash, darker near tip, a few inner ones blue-grey with a narrow black outer edge; all are narrowly tipped white. The outer web of P9 and the inner web of P10 are emarginated.

	J	F	M	A	M	J	J	A	S	O	N	D
Adult moult	J	F	M	A	M	J	J	A	S	O	N	D
Primaries 11 feathers	36	153	152	150	146	139	130	124	119	109	104	M
Tail 14 feathers	49	53	55	55	56	55	56	M				

RED-BREASTED MERGANSER The tail feathers are dark slate, sometimes with tips and edges vermiculated dark grey and white. The primaries and inner tertials are sooty black. A few outer secondaries are black, greyer near the tip and on the inner web, the other secondaries are white with broad black bases; the innermost secondary and the outer tertials are white, bordered with black on the outer web and suffused grey on the inner web.

	J	F	M	A	M	J	J	A	S	O	N	D
Adult moult	J	F	M	A	M	J	J	A	S	O	N	D
Juvenile moult	J	F	M	A	M	J	J	A	S	O	N	D
Primaries 11 feathers	56	176	174	172	170	166	165	158	144	134	123	M
Secondaries	120	120	120	115	110	100	M					
Tail 18 feathers	61	70	81	85	88	94	100	103	103	M		

LONG-TAILED DUCK White outer tail feathers. Central pair black, next pair with white sides. Primaries and primary coverts sepia. Dark secondaries with outer webs of outer secondaries olive tinged and inner secondaries warm brown.

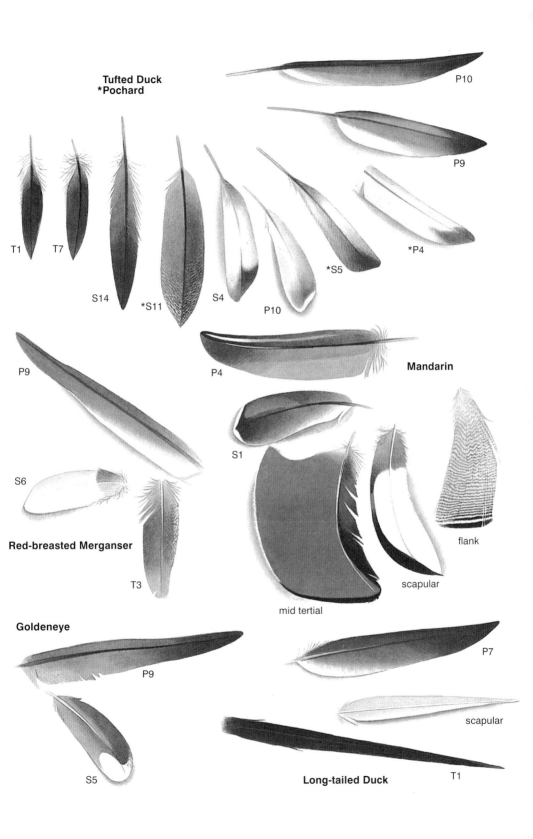

Tufted Duck
*Pochard

P10

P9

T1

T7

S14

*S11

S4

P10

*S5

*P4

P9

P4

Mandarin

S1

flank

S6

Red-breasted Merganser

T3

mid tertial

scapular

Goldeneye

P9

P7

scapular

S5

Long-tailed Duck

T1

V

SPARROWHAWK The tail feathers are grey-brown, narrowly tipped off-white, and have a broad dark brown subterminal band and four or five dark brown bars; the cental feathers are tinged slate. The underside of the tail is pale grey with are dark brown bars. The primaries are brown with the inner webs proximally white with four to six brown to grey bars; the outer webs are tinged grey, and are paler below with more pronounced bars. The secondary outer webs are grey, and the inner webs are white with dark brown bars. The inner webs of P6–P10 and the outer webs of P5–P9 emarginated.

Adult moult	J	F	M	A	M	J	J	A	S	O	N	D
Primaries 11 feathers	100	146	176	191	196	190	166	155	148	142		
Secondaries 12–14 feathers	145	142	140	134	130	124	120	117	115	112	109	100	91	84
Tail 12 feathers	191	190	193	190	193	189						

NIGHTJAR The central pair of tail feathers is coarsely vermiculated pale buff-grey or cream-white and black with six to eight narrow and partly broken black bars; the remaining feathers have broad and rather irregular black bands coarsely speckled or vermiculated cinnamon-buff or grey-buff and black in between; tip of T4–T5 uniform white. The primaries are black, tipped grey, and with coarse black vermiculation and traces of dark bars; P1–P7 and bases of P8–P10 with broken cinnamon bars, large rounded triangular patch of white on inner webs of P8–P10 (not on female). The secondaries are brownish-black, with broken cinnamon bars, dusky and freckled. The outer webs of P8–P9 and inner webs of P9–P10 are slightly emarginated. The edges of inner webs of primaries slightly serrated.

	J	F	M	A	M	J	J	A	S	O	N	D
Adult moult	J	F	M	A	M	J	J	A	S	O	N	D
Juvenile moult	J	F	M	A	M	J	J	A	S	O	N	D
Primaries 10 feathers	158	167	165	144	134	116	108	101	97	94	M	
Secondaries 13 feathers	90	91	94	91	90	88	86	84	83	M		
Tail 10 feathers	132	139	141	142	144	M						

RED-NECKED NIGHTJAR The tail feathers as in Nightjar, but T1 often with narrower and sharper bars. The flight feathers are as in Nightjar, but barring often deeper rufous, more chestnut than cinnamon, and the white spots on P8–P10 relatively larger. The outer webs of P8–P9 and inner webs of P9–P10 are emarginated, and the edge of the emarginated portion is slightly serrated.

	J	F	M	A	M	J	J	A	S	O	N	D
Adult moult	J	F	M	A	M	J	J	A	S	O	N	D
Juvenile moult	J	F	M	A	M	J	J	A	S	O	N	D
Primaries 10 feathers	186	196	196	193	169	142	129	115	104	93	M	
Tail 10 feathers	163	169	173	179	176	M						

CUCKOO The tail feathers are black with small white tips; there are rows of irregular white spots along the shafts and edges, occasionally absent on T1 and often absent along outer webs of T2–T5; spots on inner webs sometimes form short bars and occasionally join spots along shafts to form irregular bands, especially on T4–T5. The flight feathers are dark grey, with the outer primaries a dull olive-black, and the inner webs of primaries have a row of large white triangular or squarish spots extending from the base to 50mm from the tip (spots largest and squarest near base). The secondaries are bluish, and the flight feathers have a narrow white fringe and tip.

	J	F	M	A	M	J	J	A	S	O	N	D
Adult moult	J	F	M	A	M	J	J	A	S	O	N	D
Juvenile moult	J	F	M	A	M	J	J	A	S	O	N	D
Primaries 10 feathers	163	201	211	201	186	164	148	134	118	112	M	
Secondaries 9 feathers	94	94	94	100	104	110	94	85	80	M		
Tail 10 feathers	120	153	157	165	165	M						

GREAT SPOTTED CUCKOO The tail feathers are black with an olive-brown bloom and white tips. The flight feathers are grey-brown, with a faint green or bronze gloss subterminally and white tips. The inner webs of P7–P10 are slightly emarginated.

	J	F	M	A	M	J	J	A	S	O	N	D
Adult moult	J	F	M	A	M	J	J	A	S	O	N	D
Juvenile moult	J	F	M	A	M	J	J	A	S	O	N	D
Primaries 10 feathers	128	180	196	201	187	173	160	147	136	126	M	
Secondaries 11 feathers	113	112	116	115	114	118	125	110	94	82	M	
Tail 10 feathers	118	168	185	195	204	M						

Sparrowhawk

alula

P10

P7

P2

S4

T4

Nightjar

P9

P5

T1

T6

Cuckoo (juv)

P8

P2

breast

S5

T3

un T.C.

up T.C.

V–VI

STONE CURLEW The central pair of tail feathers is grey to medium brown with dark shafts and buff-brown sides, and with dark sepia bars bordered by pale grey near the tip; T2 has a grey base, separated from a broad white subterminal band by irregular dark bars, and a broad black tip, the amount of grey at the base decreasing and being replaced by white from T2 to T6. The flight feathers are black, becoming grey on the bases of the inner webs; P10 has a broad white subterminal patch, P9 (and sometimes on P8) a smaller one; the tips of P2–P4 may frequently show a variable amount of white.

	J	F	M	A	M	J	J	A	S	O	N	D
Adult moult	J	F	**M**	**A**	**M**	**J**	**J**	**A**	**S**	**O**	N	D
Juvenile moult	J	F	M	A	M	J	J	A	S	O	N	D
Primaries 11 feathers	45	230	246	241	228	217	196	179	158	146	138	M
Secondaries	130	130	128	128	128	126	125	125	120	M		
Tail 12–14 feathers	88	98	107	115	120	124	M					

OYSTERCATCHER The tail feathers are white with a broad black subterminal band (narrow white tips when fresh). The primaries are black to black-brown with a variable amount of white, all with the proximal three-quarters of inner webs white; in P9–P10 a small part of the shaft on the distal half of the feather is white, this widening to a narrow shaft streak on P8, and extending progressively farther on to the outer webs on P7–P5; P1–P4 have mainly white outer webs. The secondaries are white, their tips with an irregular black-brown patch; the tertials are black-brown, with bases paler brown to white.

	J	F	M	A	M	J	J	A	S	O	N	D
Adult moult	**J**	**F**	**M**	**A**	**M**	**J**	**J**	**A**	**S**	**O**	N	D
Juvenile moult	J	F	M	A	M	J	J	A	S	O	N	D
Primaries 11 feathers	52	190	193	188	183	174	161	149	138	128	119	
Secondaries 20 feathers	112	110	106	107	108	112	122	130	115	129	116	
Tail 12 feathers	113	114	114	114	113	108						

AVOCET Tail feathers white; T1 and the tips of a variable number of others are pearl-grey, narrowly fringed white, while tips of central feathers may be dull black. Outer 6 primaries are black, with white on the bases increasing towards the innermost, especially on the inner webs; P4 has the tip and outer web black, P3 has a solid black tip to at least the outer web, sometimes whole outer web and much of the tip of the inner are black; P1 and P2 are white. Secondaries are white, some inner tertials dark grey.

	J	F	M	A	M	J	J	A	S	O	N	D
Adult moult	**J**	**F**	**M**	**A**	**M**	**J**	**J**	**A**	**S**	**O**	**N**	**D**
Juvenile moult	**J**	**F**	M	A	M	J	J	A	S	O	N	D
Primaries 11 feathers	36	190	188	185	181	174	160	149	136	128	118	M
Secondaries	115	115	115	110	110	108	108	110	M			
Tail 12 feathers	94	94	94	94	94	94	M					

LAPWING The tail feathers are white at the base, and have a very broad subterminal band, often glossed green, and buff/white tips; the width of the band decreases outwards from T1. The primaries are black; P8–P10 have an off-white patch towards the tip, which is smoke-brown; P7 is uniform black or with a pale patch at the tip of the outer web. The secondaries are black, with the bases, especially on the inner webs, white, the white increasing in extent towards the inner feathers. The outer webs of P7–P9 and the inner webs of P7–P10 are emarginated.

	J	F	M	A	M	J	J	A	S	O	N	D
Adult moult	J	**F**	**M**	**A**	**M**	**J**	**J**	**A**	**S**	**O**	N	D
Juvenile moult	J	**F**	**M**	**A**	**M**	J	**J**	**A**	**S**	**O**	**N**	D
Primaries 11 feathers	46	181	189	189	187	182	177	168	153	140	132	M
Secondaries	128	124	125	125	125	125	125	124	120	118	M	
Tail 12 feathers	110	113	113	113	112	113	M					

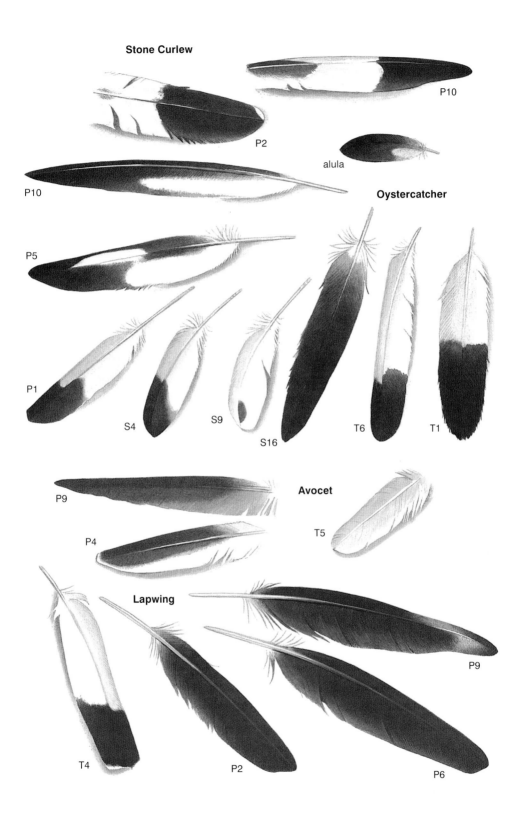

Stone Curlew

P10

P2

alula

P10

P5

P1

S4

S9

S16

Oystercatcher

T6

T1

P9

P4

Avocet

T5

Lapwing

T4

P2

P9

P6

V–VI

ARCTIC TERN Very similar to the Common Tern, but the white wedge to the inner webs of the primaries is more extensive, thus leaving a narrower grey streak at the shaft. The secondaries are more broadly tipped white, and the white on the inner webs is more extensive.

	J	F	M	A	M	J	J	A	S	O	N	D
Adult moult												
Primaries 11 feathers	50	220	211	192	173	153	135	119	105	92	84	
Secondaries 18 feathers	78	76	80	81	81	82	83	80	72			
Tail 12 feathers	185	134	111	93	88	84						

COMMON TERN The tail feathers are white, with the outer webs grey; on T6 the outer web is dark grey and the inner web has a pale grey tinge towards the tip. The outer webs of the primaries are a pale silver-grey; the inner webs with an extensive white wedge, and a narrow grey streak along shafts and at tip; the inner edges of the inner primaries are bordered white; the outer web of P10 and tips and inner edges of other primaries become dusky grey, tinged blackish. The secondaries are light grey, with white tips and the inner webs broadly bordered white.

	J	F	M	A	M	J	J	A	S	O	N	D
Adult moult												
Juvenile moult												

LITTLE GULL The tail is white. The primaries are blue-grey, becoming a lead-grey on the inner half of the inner web, and with broad white tips; all primaries except P9 and P10 have a white edge on the distal inner web. The secondaries are pale blue-grey with dark shading on the inner webs, broad white tips and a white edge on outer webs. The under surfaces of all flight feathers (and of the under primary coverts) are black or blackish. P11 minute.

	J	F	M	A	M	J	J	A	S	O	N	D
Adult moult												
Primaries 11 feathers	34	184	184	178	172	162	150	132	115	97	92	M
Secondaries 18–19 feathers	92	92	90	90	94	94	95	M				
Tail 12 feathers	99	99	98	98	99	99	M					

PTARMIGAN The central tail feathers are white, with the remainder black with white tips. The flight feathers are white, apart from the inner secondaries which are dark grey-brown vermiculated and speckled with grey-buff; the bases are grey-brown. The outer webs of P5–P9 are basally emarginated, the inner webs of P6–P9 are slightly emarginated.

	J	F	M	A	M	J	J	A	S	O	N	D
Adult moult												
Primaries 10 feathers	138	181	185	185	185	165	145	134	125	120	M	
Secondaries 18–19 feathers	120	120	115	115	115	110	110	M				
Tail 16 feathers	110	119	119	120	121	125	125	128	M			

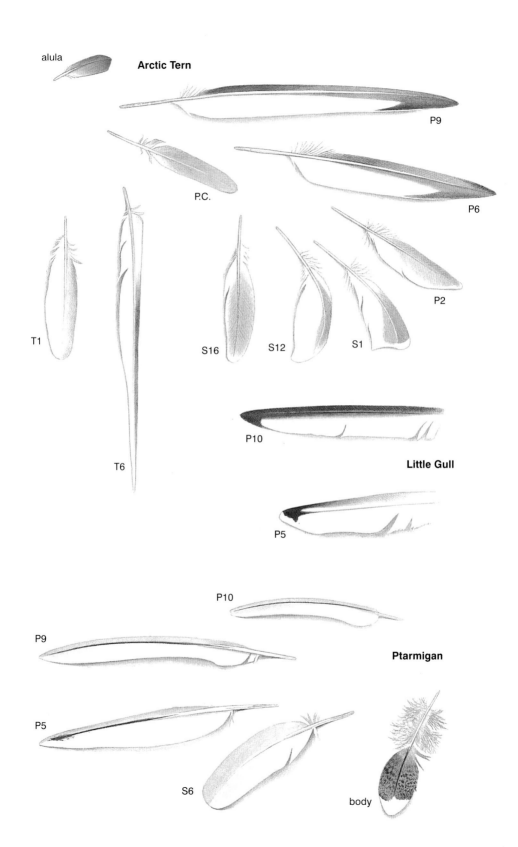

alula

Arctic Tern

P9

P.C.

P6

P2

T1

S16   S12   S1

P10

Little Gull

P5

T6

P10

P9

Ptarmigan

P5

S6

body

V–VI

GULL-BILLED TERN The tail feathers are pale grey, the outers even paler. The flight feathers are grey, the outer webs of the inner primaries and the secondaries narrowly edged with white, while the inner webs of the primaries have a white basal area. No emargination.

	J	F	M	A	M	J	J	A	S	O	N	D
Adult moult												
Primaries 11 feathers	57	278	265	247	247	211	204	163	142	136	107	
Secondaries 20–24? feathers	107	105	97	97	97	97	97	98	97	97	99	99
Tail 12 feathers	142	140	121	110	102	100						

CATTLE EGRET The tail feathers are white as are the primary and secondary flight feathers. The outer webs of P7–P9 (slightly) and the inner webs of P9 and P10, are emarginated.

	J	F	M	A	M	J	J	A	S	O	N	D			
Adult moult															
Juvenile moult															
Primaries 10 feathers	175	190	196	197	195	185	178	164	158	M					
Secondaries 15 feathers	150	155	150	140	148	148	148	151	151	149	149	143	143	133	131
Tail 12 feathers	106	105	98	103	100	97									

SANDWICH TERN The tail feathers are white, the outer webs of the outer feathers often shaded very pale grey. The primaries are pale silvery grey, with the outer web of P10 and a streak along the shafts of the inner webs of the outer P4–P5 a darker grey; the inner webs of all primaries have broad white margins and white tips. The secondaries are pale grey with the inner webs white.

	J	F	M	A	M	J	J	A	S	O	N	D
Adult moult												
Primaries 11 feathers	57	278	265	247	226	204	184	163	142	123	107	M
Secondaries	105	105	105	100	100	M						
Tail 12 feathers	165	115	113	100	91	87	M					

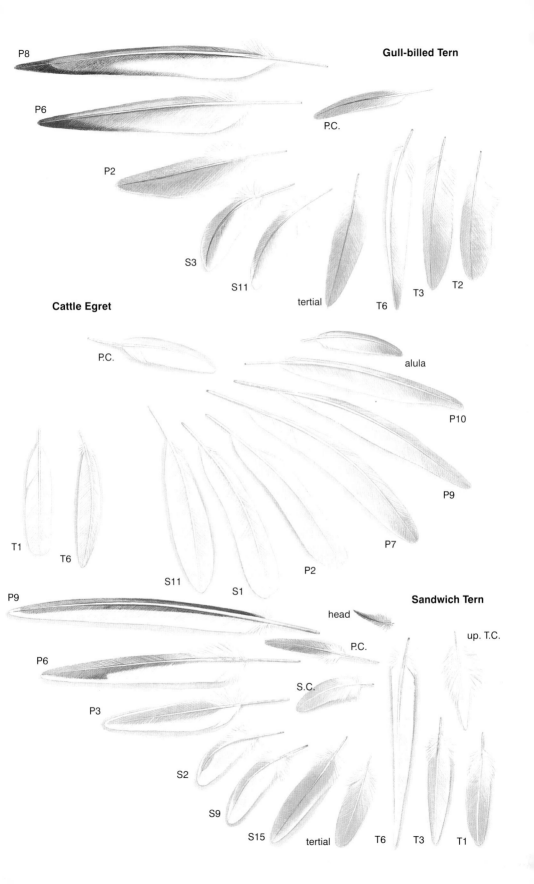

Gull-billed Tern

P8

P6

P2

P.C.

S3

S11

tertial

T6

T3

T2

Cattle Egret

P.C.

alula

P10

P9

T1

T6

P7

S11

S1

P2

P9

Sandwich Tern

head

up. T.C.

P6

P.C.

S.C.

P3

S2

S9

S15

tertial

T6

T3

T1

V–VIA

MAGPIE The tail feathers are black below; above, both webs of central pair and outer webs of the remainder are brilliant bronze-green, with a distal band of red-purple merging into blue-purple and green-purple at tip. The primaries have purple outer webs and tips glossed blue-green; the inner webs are mostly white except at base and tip; in outer primaries the white comes to a point near shaft, in the inner ones it is squarer at tip and extends less towards base. The secondaries have the outer webs glossed bright blue, with an inner line of bronze-green on basal half of outer feathers; the tips are blue-green and the inner webs black, except those of innermost feathers which are blue-green. The outer webs of P4–P8 are emarginated.

	J	F	M	A	M	J	J	A	S	O	N	D
Adult moult	J	F	M	A	M	J	J	A	S	O	N	D
Juvenile moult	J	F	M	A	M	J	J	A	S	O	N	D
Primaries 10 feathers	65	127	160	169	173	173	170	162	158	153		
Secondaries 10 feathers	149	149	148	144	141	136	130	114	92	76		
Tail 12 feathers	136	159	173	189	210	244						

AZURE-WINGED MAGPIE The tail feathers are azure-blue, the two central ones with broad white tips, the remainder with only a slight margin of white. The flight feathers are azure-blue; P8–P9 are blue-black and P3–P7 have a varying amount of white on the outer webs. The outer webs of P4–P7 are emarginated.

Primaries 9 feathers	78	105	130	135	140	140	140	136	130	M
Secondaries 10 feathers	125	120	118	115	115	115	110	99	86	70	M
Tail 12 feathers	100	120	136	158	164	216	M			

BLACK GROUSE The lyre-shaped tail feathers are black, often with a faint dark blue to green-blue tinge, the central pairs usually narrowly tipped white; the undersides are a shiny brown-black. The primaries are brown, paler on the shafts, the outer webs mottled pale or white; the inner primaries have white bases; the under surfaces are shiny grey on the inner webs (except for dull grey edges) and shiny grey-brown on the outer webs. The secondaries are white, with a broad dark brown subterminal band and narrow white tips.

	J	F	M	A	M	J	J	A	S	O	N	D
Adult moult	J	F	M	A	M	J	J	A	S	O	N	D
Primaries 10 feathers	167	208	218	224	224	211	189	162	145	140	M	
Secondaries	140	140	144	143	140	138	126	115	M			
Tail 18 feathers	143	145	140	136	125	120	118	114	109	M		

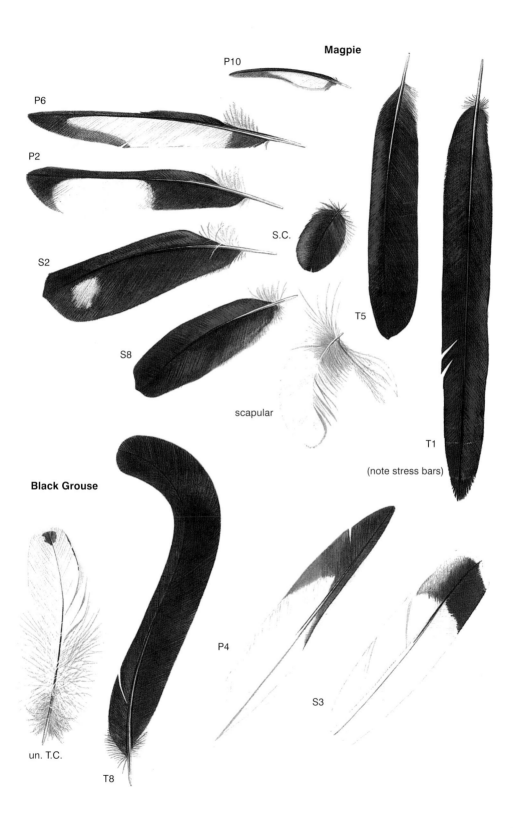

Magpie

P10

P6

P2

S.C.

S2

S8

T5

scapular

T1

(note stress bars)

Black Grouse

P4

S3

un. T.C.

T8

V–VIA

MALLARD Male The central pair of tail feathers is black; the others with centres of sepia or grey broadly edged white, the outers mainly white. The primaries are brown-grey, with paler inner webs and the outer edges of the outer webs pale grey. The secondaries are brown-grey, broadly tipped white, with the outer webs strongly glossed purple-blue or blue-green, and with a black bar bordering white tip. **Female** The tail feathers are buff, irregularly streaked, barred and spotted sepia or black, the outer feathers edged white. The flight feathers are the same as the male. The outer webs of P9 emarginated and P8 slightly so, and the inner web of P10 emarginated and P9 slightly so.

	J	F	M	A	M	J	J	A	S	O	N	D
Adult moult	J	F	M	A	M	J	**J**	**A**	**S**	**O**	N	D
Juvenile moult	J	F	M	A	M	**J**	**J**	**A**	**S**	**O**	N	D
Primaries 11 feathers	57	204	217	217	208	201	189	177	167	156	147	
Secondaries 17 feathers	141	140	136	136	142	151	160	170	161	115	120	94
Tail 20 feathers	103	11	114	115	119	119	115	110	110	105		

PINTAIL Male The tail feathers are dark grey on the outer web and paler grey on inner; narrowly edged off-white; the central feathers are black, conspicuously elongated. The primaries are sepia on the outer webs and paler ash on the inner. The secondaries have glossy green or bronze-green outer webs with narrow black subterminal bars and broad white tips, but four or so outer secondaries are dull black; the inner webs of secondaries dark grey. **Female** All feathers as male but paler. The outer web of P9 and the inner web of P10 are emarginated.

	J	F	M	A	M	J	J	A	S	O	N	D
Adult moult	J	F	M	A	M	J	**J**	**A**	**S**	**O**	N	D
Juvenile moult	**J**	F	M	A	M	J	J	A	S	**O**	**N**	**D**
Primaries 11 feathers	60	234	234	222	211	200	187	169	156	143	131	M
Tail 16 feathers	79	91	102	106	111	120	123	135	M			

WIGEON Male The central tail feathers are black with a grey bloom; the others are pale brown-grey, edged white. The primaries are dark grey, browner on the outer web. The outer webs of the secondaries are black, with the basal half glossed metallic green; the inner webs are dark grey, edged white at tips; the outer web of the innermost secondary is white, narrowly margined black. **Female** All feathers as male except paler. The outer web of P9 and the inner web of P10 are emarginated.

	J	F	M	A	M	J	J	A	S	O	N	D
Adult moult	**J**	F	M	A	M	**J**	**J**	**A**	S	O	N	D
Juvenile moult	J	F	M	A	M	J	J	A	**S**	**O**	N	D
Primaries 11 feathers	42	197	208	205	195	184	170	155	139	126	118	
Secondaries 16 feathers	110	113	114	112	113	120	135	115	99			

TEAL Male The tail feathers are dark grey, narrowly edged off-white. The primaries are sepia, with the inner webs paler. The secondaries are grey-brown, narrowly tipped white or pink-buff; the outer webs of S3-S6 metallic green; the others velvety black, partly glossed green towards the base. **Female** The tail feathers are dark grey, narrowly edged white, and there is a variable number of buff-marked feathers. The flight feathers are as the male, except the white tips of the secondaries are wider, the outer secondaries arc often mottled white, and the green gloss is less extensive. The outer web of P9 and the inner web of P10 are emarginated.

	J	F	M	A	M	J	J	A	S	O	N	D
Adult moult	**J**	F	M	A	M	J	**J**	**A**	**S**	**O**	N	D
Juvenile moult	J	F	M	A	M	J	J	A	**S**	**O**	N	D
Primaries 11 feathers	38	156	160	153	150	145	139	128	118	108	97	M
Tail 16 feathers	74	79	83	86	87	88	88	90	M			

SHOVELER Male The central tail feathers are dark olive-sepia, narrowly edged off-white and buff, the rest suffused and broadly edged white. The flight feathers are dark sepia, with the inner webs of primaries dark grey and the outer webs of secondaries, apart from one outer feather, strongly glossed metallic green. **Female** The tail feathers are sepia, broadly barred pink-buff, with the central feathers narrowly and the outer feathers broadly edged pale buff or off-white. The flight feathers are as the male, but the green gloss on the secondaries is fainter. The outer web of P9 and the inner web of P10 are emarginated

	J	F	M	A	M	J	J	A	S	O	N	D
Adult moult	**J**	F	M	A	M	**J**	**J**	**A**	S	O	N	**D**
Primaries 11 feathers	42	208	208	197	190	174	164	149	135	120	111	M
Tail 14 feathers	90	90	95	96	96	103	111	M				

Eider described on page 238.

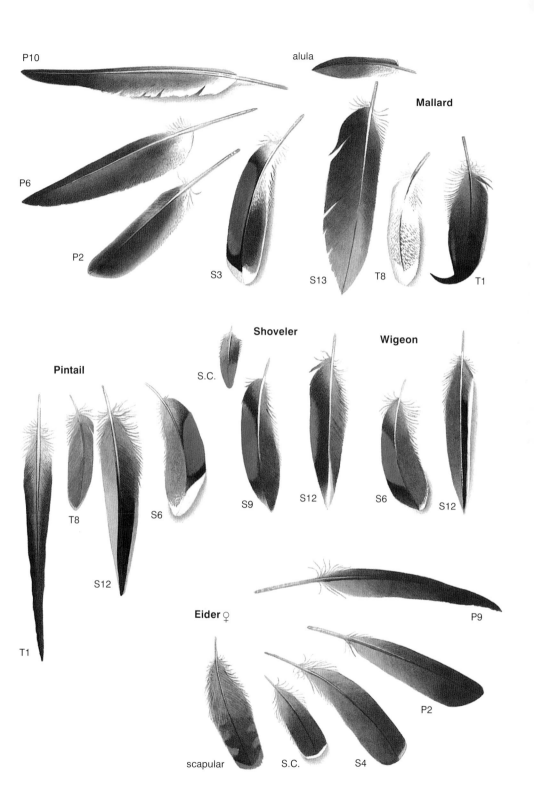

P10

alula

Mallard

P6

P2

S3

S13

T8

T1

Shoveler

Wigeon

Pintail

S.C.

T8

S6

S9

S12

S6

S12

S12

T1

Eider ♀

P9

P2

scapular

S.C.

S4

V–VIA

WOODPIGEON Upper surface of tail feathers pale grey with ill-defined greyish-black tips and bases, pale centres showing as a broad ill-defined band only when tail spread; under surface of feathers has sharply demarcated greyish-white band and shiny black base and tip. Primaries black with slight tinge of grey, bases or inner feather and outer webs others greyish; P3–P9 have distinct white margin, margins of P1–P2 and P10 narrower, often mostly pale grey. Secondaries medium grey, outers slightly darker towards tips; S1 has white margin along outer web, while S2–S4 have a greyish-white or light grey margin; inner secondaries have a slight brown tinge. Inner web of P9–P10 and outer web of P8–P10 emarginated.

	J	F	M	A	M	J	J	A	S	O	N	D
Adult moult	J	F	M	A	M	J	J	A	S	O	N	D
Juvenile moult	J	F	M	A	M	J	J	A	S	O	N	D
Primaries 10 feathers	187	208	214	201	190	176	163	152	147	146		
Secondaries 13 feathers	143	141	138	135	132	128	126	122	120	116	105	89	76
Tail 12 feathers	183	180	180	179	177	175						

ROCK DOVE/FERAL PIGEON Tail medium grey with black tip, often slightly grey at extreme tip; T6 has the middle part of outer web white. The primaries are medium grey, slightly darker towards the tips and paler towards the base. Outer secondaries medium grey with greyish-black or black tips; outer webs of inner secondaries black with ash-grey tips. Black forming band across spread wing.

	J	F	M	A	M	J	J	A	S	O	N	D
Adult moult	J	F	M	A	M	J	J	A	S	O	N	D
Juvenile moult	J	F	M	A	M	J	J	A	S	O	N	D
Primaries 10 feathers	183	193	191	179	163	152	143	134	126	118		
Secondaries 13 feathers	119	118	115	115	109	106	106	102	99	96	89	80	76
Tail 12 feathers	123	126	134	136	135	134						

STOCK DOVE The tail is bluish-grey with a black tip. The outer primaries are brownish-black, with the outer webs of P6–P9 having a narrow off-white outer border; the inner primaries and secondaries are light bluish-grey with a black tip. The base and middle part of the inner webs of the primaries is dark grey; light bluish-grey of middle part of outer web extends to P5 or P7. The inner web of P10 is emarginated.

	J	F	M	A	M	J	J	A	S	O	N	D
Adult moult	J	F	M	A	M	J	J	A	S	O	N	D
Juvenile moult	J	F	M	A	M	J	J	A	S	O	N	D
Primaries 10 feathers	183	193	191	179	163	152	143	134	126	118		
Secondaries 13 feathers	119	118	115	115	109	106	106	102	99	96	89	80	76
Tail 12 feathers	123	126	134	136	135	134						

COLLARED DOVE Upper surface of central tail feathers dusky greyish, may have silvery grey bloom along shaft; remainder greyish, with off-white tips, inner web of T6 black or greyish-black with straight greyish-white tip. From below, tail contrastingly glossy black on basal three-fifths white on remainder, with black pattern on T6 similar to upper surface. Primaries dark olive-brown, inner webs shading to white at base; outer webs and tips have narrow pale grey edge. Secondaries pale grey, with tips and outer webs variably washed dusky olive. Inner webs of P9–P10 and outer webs of P7–P9 emarginated.

	J	F	M	A	M	J	J	A	S	O	N	D
Adult moult	J	F	M	A	M	J	J	A	S	O	N	D
Juvenile moult	J	F	M	A	M	J	J	A	S	O	N	D
Primaries 10 feathers	138	153	155	147	138	130	124	118	113	110		
Secondaries 11 feathers	110	110	110	103	99	96	92	95	91	85	70	
Tail 12 feathers	138	138	145	146	145	143						

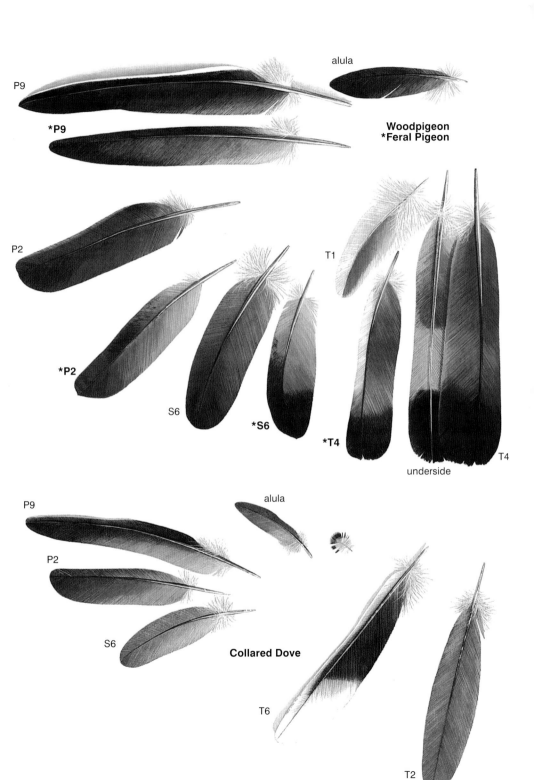

P9

alula

*P9

Woodpigeon
*Feral Pigeon

P2

T1

*P2

S6

*S6

*T4

T4

underside

P9

alula

P2

S6

Collared Dove

T6

T2

VA

GREEN WOODPECKER The central pair of tail feathers is black with green sides, the black at each side is broken by a row of pale green or cream-white spots; T2–T4 are black, with sides faintly greenish and sometimes with traces of pale spots near the bases of centres; T5 is dull black, with indistinct dull grey-green bars on the upper surface, and more contrastingly barred pale grey-green and black on under surface; T6 is green, with variable black marks on the centre and the inner web. The outer webs of P7–P10 and emarginated areas of the outer webs of P5–P6 are dull black faintly tinged greenish interrupted by a row of off-white spots but with terminal part uniform black; the outer webs of P1–P4 and the base of the outer webs of P5–P6 have a row of dull black and off-white blobs along the shafts and a broad uniform green fringe. The inner webs of the primaries are greyish-black, the basal halves of P7–P10 with broad incomplete off-white bars this barring becoming gradually more extensive towards the inner primaries (almost reaches the tip on P1). The outer webs of the secondaries are grass-green, often with a slight tinge of brass or golden colour; a narrow streak along the shaft is dull black occasionally bordered by a row of indistinct pale green or cream-white specks; the inner webs are similar to those of the inner primaries. The outer webs of P4–P8 and the inner webs of P5–P10 are emarginated. P10 is deeply emarginated.

	J	F	M	A	M	J	J	A	S	O	N	D
Adult moult						■	■	■	■	■		
Juvenile moult							■	■	■	■		
Primaries 10 feathers	43	105	132	139	141	139	132	123	120	115		
Secondaries 11–12 feathers	114	115	115	110	110	106	103	98	83	67	52	
Tail 12 feathers	34	83	95	98	103	111						

LITTLE OWL The ground colour of the tail is dark olive-brown or slightly paler olive, rather poorly defined fringes along tips white, rather narrow and usually broken bars buff to cream-buff or white (reduced to spots or short bars on outermost feathers). The flight feathers are dark olive-brown or fuscous brown darkest along shafts and on outer primaries; primaries have three or four well-spaced shallow pale spots along outer webs, and much larger spots or short bars on inner webs. The secondaries have only two or three spots or bars. Outer webs of P6–P9 and inner webs of P6–P10 emarginated. Outer edge of P10 with short serrations.

	J	F	M	A	M	J	J	A	S	O	N	D
Adult moult						■	■	■	■		■	
Juvenile moult							■	■	■		■	
Primaries 10 feathers	103	123	130	134	131	122	115	112	111	110		
Secondaries 14 feathers	107	109	108	108	106	102	102	99	98	94	91	86	77	63
Tail 12 feathers	89	90	90	90	90	91						

WOODCOCK The tail feathers are brown-black with outer webs incompletely barred orange-cinnamon; the inner webs also occasionally have a few incomplete bars, the tips are pale brown-grey on upper and bright white on under surface. The primaries are black-brown, narrowly tipped buff and incompletely barred pink-buff to rufous; the bars on the outer webs are darker than those on the inner, and those on P9–P10 paler than on other primaries. The secondaries are the same as the inner primaries. P11 is concealed by the primary coverts.

	J	F	M	A	M	J	J	A	S	O	N	D
Adult moult		■	■	■	■		■		■		■	■
Primaries 11 feathers	33	156	160	157	151	146	140	133	128	123	116	
Secondaries	118	121	120	118	116	116	115					
Tail 12 feathers	77	78	80	84	84	87	M					

Green Woodpecker

P9

P1

S1

rump

flank

T1

T5

S11

P10

alula

P7

Little Owl

S2

S8

flank

T6

alula

P10

T4

underside

S4

Woodcock

P6

VB–VI

ROOK The tail feathers are black underneath, glossed red and green-purple above. The primaries are black underneath, and glossed purple-green above, especially on the outer webs and tips. The secondaries are the same, but glossed red-purple on outer webs and green on inner. The outer webs of P6–P9 are emarginated.

	J	F	M	A	M	J	J	A	S	O	N	D
Adult moult	J	F	M	A	M	J	J	A	S	O	N	D
Juvenile moult	J	F	M	A	M	J	J	A	S	O	N	D

Primaries 10 feathers	164	270	292	292	283	255	230	212	196	188	M	
Secondaries 11 feathers	180	176	176	176	175	165	160	155	152	138	108	M
Tail 12 feathers	170	177	181	185	188	188	M					

CARRION CROW The tail feathers are black underneath, glossed green and blue-purple above. The primaries are black underneath, and glossed purple-green above. The secondaries are the same, but glossed red-purple on outer web and green on inner. The outer webs of P5–P9 are emarginated.

	J	F	M	A	M	J	J	A	S	O	N	D
Adult moult	J	F	M	A	M	J	J	A	S	O	N	D
Juvenile moult	J	F	M	A	M	J	J	A	S	O	N	D

Primaries 10 feathers	142	228	256	266	268	252	221	205	197	196
Secondaries 11 feathers	184	186	185	178	173	167	165	155	128	92	84
Tail 12 feathers	174	182	182	182	183	183				

HOODED CROW The tail feathers are black, with the outer ones glossed blue-green and the inner red-purple. The outer primaries are black, glossed green-blue, and the inner primaries and secondaries are black, glossed red-purple. The outer webs of P5–P9 are emarginated.

	J	F	M	A	M	J	J	A	S	O	N	D
Adult moult	J	F	M	A	M	J	J	A	S	O	N	D
Juvenile moult	J	F	M	A	M	J	J	A	S	O	N	D

Primaries 10 feathers	147	236	271	284	284	269	234	215	204	199
Secondaries 11 feathers	190	191	187	182	179	175	170	156	130	95	83
Tail 12 feathers	182	188	191	196	194	190				

JACKDAW The tail feathers are black, glossed blue-green on the outer webs, with the inner webs glossed blue. The primaries are black, glossed blue-green, and the secondaries are black, glossed red-purple. The outer webs of P6–P9 are emarginated.

	J	F	M	A	M	J	J	A	S	O	N	D
Adult moult	J	F	M	A	M	J	J	A	S	O	N	D

Primaries 10 feathers	107	204	226	226	215	193	175	162	154	142	M
Secondaries 10 feathers	142	135	135	135	135	135	135	130	125	112	M
Tail 12 feathers	138	138	140	142	142	144	M			

GLOSSY IBIS Tail feathers are black with strong purple gloss, more metallic green towards the edges of the feathers. Flight feathers are black, glossed dark metallic green, strongly tinged purple on the centres of the inner secondaries and tertials. Outer webs of P8–P9 and inner webs of P9–P10 are emarginated.

	J	F	M	A	M	J	J	A	S	O	N	D
Adult moult	J	F	M	A	M	J	J	A	S	O	N	D
Juvenile moult	J	F	M	A	M	J	J	A	S	O	N	D

Primaries 11 feathers	46	205	213	211	202	191	183	171	160	152	142	M
Secondaries	140	140	138	138	138	135	130	M				
Tail 12 feathers	104	102	96	95	95	95	M					

BLACK WOODPECKER The tail feathers are black with a slight grey tinge. The primaries are black, tinged sepia-brown. The secondaries are black, tinged grey. The outer webs of P4–P7 and the inner webs of P4–P10 are emarginated.

	J	F	M	A	M	J	J	A	S	O	N	D
Adult moult	J	F	M	A	M	J	J	A	S	O	N	D
Juvenile moult	J	F	M	A	M	J	J	A	S	O	N	D

Primaries 10 feathers	72	156	198	208	222	218	218	205	185	174	M
Secondaries	168	158	155	150	150	140	140	136	123	M	
Tail 12 feathers	127	156	171	175	179	201	M				

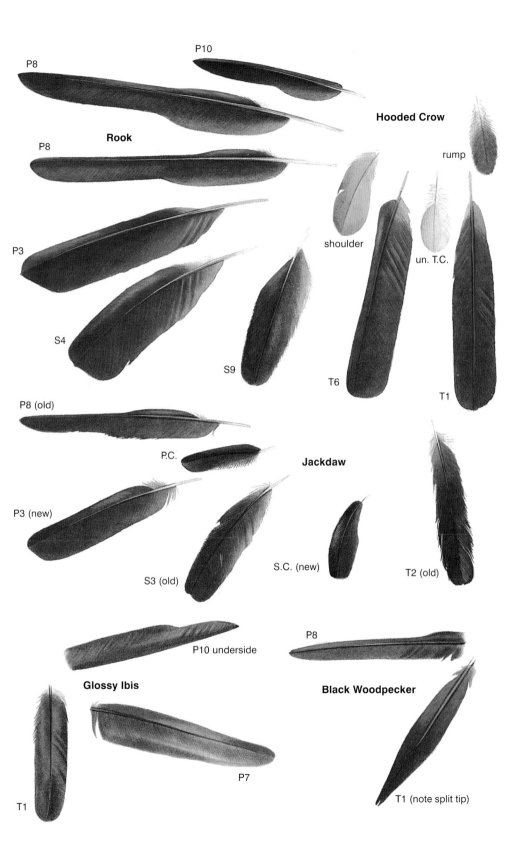

P10

P8

Hooded Crow

rump

P8

Rook

shoulder

un. T.C.

P3

S4

S9

T6

T1

P8 (old)

P.C.

Jackdaw

P3 (new)

S3 (old)

S.C. (new)

T2 (old)

P10 underside

P8

Glossy Ibis

Black Woodpecker

P7

T1

T1 (note split tip)

VB–VI

CORMORANT The tail feathers are black with the shafts dark horn. The flight feathers are black, the secondaries having bronze outer webs. The outer webs of P7–P9 and the inner webs of P8–P10 are emarginated.

	J	F	M	A	M	J	J	A	S	O	N	D	
Adult moult	J	F	M	A	M	J	J	A	S	O	N	D	
Juvenile moult	J	F	M	A	M	J	J	A	S	O	N	D	
Primaries 11 feathers	56	269	282	280	277	268	255	239	226	218	212	M	
Tail 16 feathers	148	165	173	190	198	205	210	M					

SHAG The tail feathers are black, glossed purple-green. The flight feathers are dull black, slightly glossed green on the outer webs; the inner webs are brown. The outer webs of P7–P9 and the inner webs of P8–P10 are emarginated.

	J	F	M	A	M	J	J	A	S	O	N	D
Adult moult	J	F	M	A	M	J	J	A	S	O	N	D
Juvenile moult	J	F	M	A	M	J	J	A	S	O	N	D
Primaries 11 feathers	65	193	200	203	192	186	182	177	176	172	167	
Secondaries 18 feathers	170	170	168	165	155	143	141	134	120	106		
Tail 12 feathers	126	146	156	160	164	166						

RED-THROATED DIVER The tail feathers are dark brown. The primaries and secondaries are dark brown, paler below; the secondaries show a little white at the tips. P11 minute.

	J	F	M	A	M	J	J	A	S	O	N	D	
Adult moult	J	F	M	A	M	J	J	A	S	O	N	D	
Juvenile moult	J	F	M	A	M	J	J	A	S	O	N	D	
Primaries 11 feathers	54	174	184	187	177	165	162	155	140	132	125	M	
Secondaries 23 feathers	120	118	120	120	115	110	107	102	99	95	85	85	M

BLACK-THROATED DIVER The tail feathers are brownish-black. The primaries are glossy black, paler below and at the bases of inner webs; the secondaries have black tips, are pale grey on the lower halves and have white margins to the inner webs. P11 minute.

	J	F	M	A	M	J	J	A	S	O	N	D
Adult moult	J	F	M	A	M	J	J	A	S	O	N	D
Juvenile moult	J	F	M	A	M	J	J	A	S	O	N	D

GREAT NORTHERN DIVER The tail feathers are black, paler below. The primaries are black with dark brown shafts; the secondaries are similar, and the inner ones have one or two white spots. P11 minute.

	J	F	M	A	M	J	J	A	S	O	N	D	
Adult moult	J	F	M	A	M	J	J	A	S	O	N	D	
Juvenile moult	J	F	M	A	M	J	J	A	S	O	N	D	
Primaries 11 feathers	60	250	248	245	230	214	204	196	183	172	160	M	
Secondaries 23 feathers	168	168	172	168	164	150	150	150	110	100	108	97	M

MANX SHEARWATER The tail feathers are black. The flight feathers are black, paler below. P10 with a narrow outer web.

	J	F	M	A	M	J	J	A	S	O	N	D
Adult moult	J	F	M	A	M	J	J	A	S	O	N	D
Primaries 11 feathers	54	177	183	178	170	161	151	140	123	113	100	
Secondaries 22 feathers	91	84	84	85	86	86	86	86	86	86	83	80
Tail 12 feathers	85	88	88	89	90	88	M					

GREAT SHEARWATER The tail feathers are dark brown. The primaries are dark brown, the inner webs paler with a white wedge on the inner two-thirds. The outer webs of the secondaries are grey; the inner webs are white with a grey spot at the tips. P10 with a narrow outer web.

	J	F	M	A	M	J	J	A	S	O	N	D	
Adult moult	J	F	M	A	M	J	J	A	S	O	N	D	
Juvenile moult	J	F	M	A	M	J	J	A	S	O	N	D	
Primaries 11 feathers	60	262	262	245	222	201	185	169	143	131	115	M	
Tail 12 feathers	111	116	119	122	127	127							

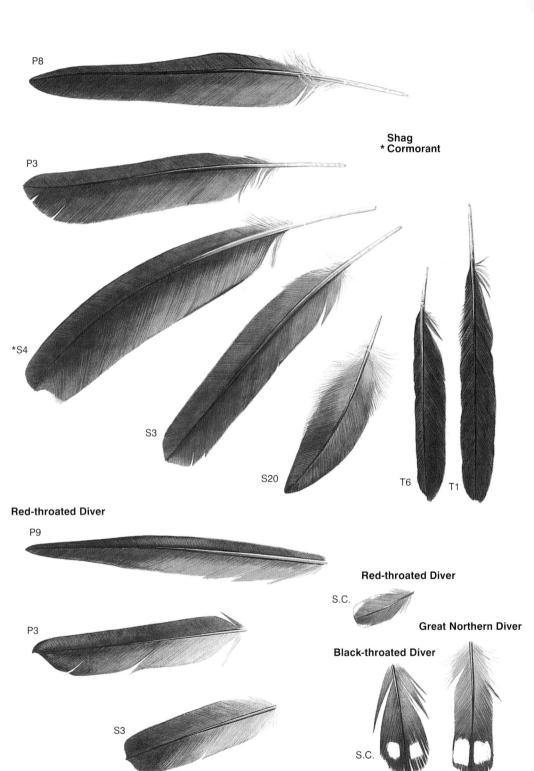

P8

Shag
* Cormorant

P3

*S4

S3

S20

T6   T1

Red-throated Diver

P9

Red-throated Diver

S.C.

Great Northern Diver

P3

Black-throated Diver

S3

S.C.

S.C.

VB–VI

CURLEW Central tail feathers grey, with dark sepia and a buff or cinnamon tinge to the edges or centre; grey ground colour changes to white with buff tinge less extensive towards outer feathers. Secondaries and inner five to six primaries dull black, both webs deeply notched white, tips narrowly edged white. Outer primaries a uniform deep black on outer webs and variably notched or irregularly mottled white on basal and median parts of inner webs. P10 has a white rachis.

Adult moult	J	F	M	A	M	J	J	A	S	O	N	D
Primaries 11 feathers	46	240	230	210	200	190	170	165	160	155	145	
Secondaries 20 feathers	~~145~~	~~140~~	~~136~~	~~130~~	~~130~~	~~127~~	~~120~~	~~111~~	~~132~~	~~136~~		
Tail 12 feathers	122	124	126	128	129	130	M					

KESTREL Adult male Tail ash-grey with a grey-white tip and a broad black subterminal band, inner webs of feathers unbarred. The primaries are brown-black, the proximal part of inner webs with comb-like white bars, outermost secondaries as primaries, innermost rufous. **Adult female** Tail ash-grey to brown-grey with often incomplete black-brown bars, off-white tip and broad black subterminal band. Primaries as male, but pale bars on inner web tinged rufous. Outer web of P9 emarginated and of P8 slightly. Inner web of P10 notched, that of P9 slightly emarginated.

Adult moult	J	F	M	A	M	J	J	A	S	O	N	D
Primaries 11 feathers	40	170	198	201	188	176	164	152	136	126	118	
Secondaries 13 feathers	114	110	110	105	105	105	102	101	100	99	94	84	75
Tail 12 feathers	144	157	161	162	166	167						

LANNER FALCON The tail feathers are cream to grey, tipped off-white, with nine or ten black bars; under surface shiny and paler grey. The primaries are grey-brown to brown, narrowly tipped off-white, the inner webs with comb-like white bars, often tinged rufous near shaft. Secondaries as primaries or slightly browner; some indistinct pale grey bars on outer webs. Outer webs of P8–P9 and inner web of P9 emarginated; P8 slightly; inner web of P10 notched.

Adult moult	J	F	M	A	M	J	J	A	S	O	N	D

HOBBY The tail feathers are slate to black-brown, barred rufous on the inner webs, with the exception of T1 which is uniform slate; under surfaces shiny grey with pale rufous bars on inner webs. The flight feathers are slate to black-brown, on inner webs elliptical black spots forming incomplete bars. Outer web of P9 emarginated; of P8 slightly. Inner web of P10 notched, that of P9 slightly emarginated.

Adult moult	J	F	M	A	M	J	J	A	S	O	N	D
Primaries 11 feathers	54	236	249	229	210	193	177	158	140	123	117	M
Secondaries 11 feathers	100	100	100	104	120	120	120	120	123	123	125	M
Tail 12 feathers	130	138	138	140	141	146	M					

PEREGRINE FALCON The tail feathers are grey with a narrow off-white tip, a broad ill-defined subterminal dark band and numerous narrow dark bars; underside paler. The primaries are dark grey with a narrow white line at tip, inner web proximally with numerous incomplete white bars. Outer secondaries like primaries, inner secondaries blue-grey with dark bars. The outer web of P9 is marginated, P8 slightly so; the inner web of P9 is slightly emarginated, that of P10 notched.

Adult moult	J	F	M	A	M	J	J	A	S	O	N	D	
Primaries 11 feathers	36	280	287	300	270	252	230	204	182	176	170	M	
Secondaries 13 feathers	168	165	158	158	158	158	158	168	174	184	194	198	198	M
Tail 12 feathers	176	182	180	180	180	181	M						

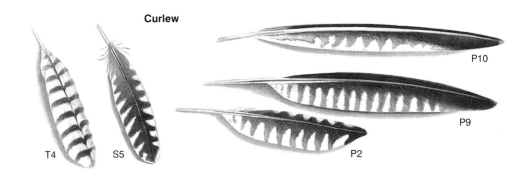

Curlew

T4   S5   P10   P9   P2

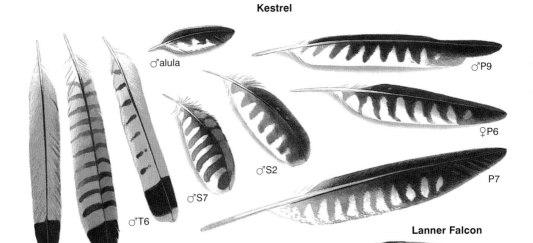

Kestrel

♂alula   ♂P9   ♀P6   ♂S2   ♂S7   P7   ♂T6   ♂T1   ♀T4

Lanner Falcon

P2

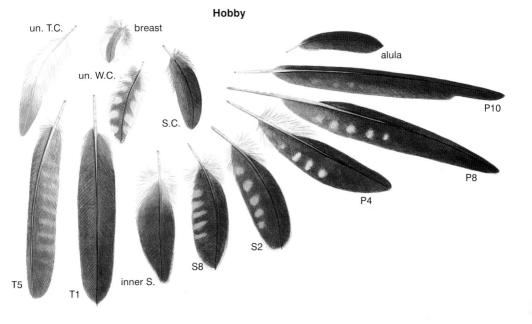

Hobby

un. T.C.   breast   un. W.C.   S.C.   alula   P10   P8   P4   S2   S8   inner S.   T5   T1

VB–VIA

JAY The tail feathers are brown-black, with base grey barred blue-grey. The primaries are brown-black, with outer webs fringed grey-white and inner webs mottled blue at base. The secondaries are black, with the basal half of outer web of the five marked blue and black; the base of the sixth barred blue, white and black; the innermost deep chestnut, tipped black. The outer webs of P4–P7 slightly and P3 very slightly emarginated.

Adult moult	J	F	M	A	M	J	J	A	S	O	N	D
Primaries 10 feathers	77	125	156	169	176	178	176	168	160	151		
Secondaries 10 feathers	153	150	145	139	135	126	120	108	84	75		
Tail 12 feathers	136	170	168	169	169	168						

PURPLE GALLINULE The tail feathers are black with dull violet-blue outer webs. The flight feathers are greyish-violet with black inner webs.

Adult moult	J	F	M	A	M	J	J	A	S	O	N	D
Primaries 10 feathers	175	234	233	228	224	210	208	192	180	165	M	
Secondaries 11 feathers	157	157	157	160	173	173	175	178	173	150	126	M
Tail 10 feathers	56	63	68	72	76	M						

ROLLER The central pair of tail feathers is dusky grey, slightly tinged olive or blue; T2 is a dusky dark blue with a greenish-tinged fringe along the outer web, a broad black fringe along the inner web and a pale blue tip (on under surface, the central parts and base of inner web are a bright violet-blue); all other tail feathers resemble T2; all tail feathers have a black shaft. The flight feathers are black, the outer webs of P7–P9 with slight greenish-blue tinge, extensive on P10; the outer webs of secondaries are tinged a dark violet-blue; the extreme bases of inner primaries and the basal part of secondaries are a pale blue. The under surfaces of the flight feathers are a bright violet-blue except for tips. The outer webs of P7–P9 and the inner webs of P8–P10 are emarginated.

Adult moult	J	F	M	A	M	J	J	A	S	O	N	D
Primaries 10 feathers	175	179	177	166	153	145	135	127	122	120	M	
Secondaries	110	106	106	106	108	110	M					
Tail 12 feathers	146	141	142	144	144	145	M					

EIDER The tail feathers are sooty black. The primaries are dark grey with the outer webs black; the inner primaries are sometimes tipped white. The secondaries are black; the inner secondary is black, with the inner web and tip white; the tertials are white. The outer web of P9 and the inner web of P10 are emarginated.

Adult moult	J	F	M	A	M	J	J	A	S	O	N	D
Primaries 11 feathers	35	190	204	205	190	190	181	172	160	154	146	
Secondaries	140	140	138	130	128	125	130	125	110	89	67	
Tail 14 feathers	72	83	86	90	98	101	103	M				

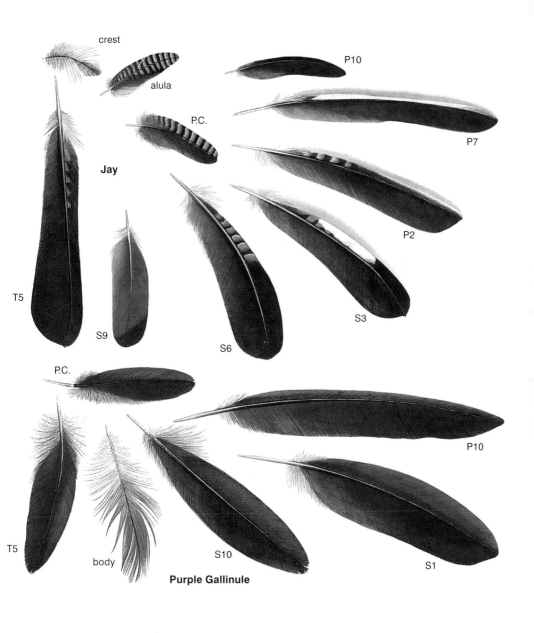

crest

alula

P10

P.C.

P7

Jay

P2

T5

S3

S9

S6

P.C.

P10

T5

S10

S1

body

Purple Gallinule

Roller

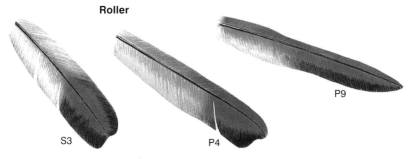

S3

P4

P9

V–VI

PHEASANT The centres and tips of the two central pairs of tail feathers are buff-brown, with narrow, well-spaced black bars, and with loose-webbed sides a uniform copper-red with a purple-pink gloss; the remainder are similar, but the inner edges and tips are vermiculated grey-buff and dull black, the outer feathers being wholly vermiculated. The primaries are dark sepia, with short, curved bars partly mottled pale buff, the bars being vague or absent on the outer webs and tips of the primaries. The secondaries are similar to the primaries, but with the bars more irregular and the outer edges buff-brown with fine black specks.

	J	F	M	A	M	J	J	A	S	O	N	D
Adult moult	J	F	M	A	**M**	J	J	A	**S**	O	**N**	D
Juvenile moult	J	F	M	A	M	J	J	A	**S**	O	**N**	D
Primaries 10 feathers	178	200	206	209	214	213	209	196	183	167		
Secondaries 16 feathers	160	165	170	172	172	172	172	176				
Tail 18 feathers	138	162	185	216	248	286	332	413	560	M		

GOLDEN PHEASANT The central pair of tail feathers has many rounded cinnamon-buff dots, surrounded by a network of black, with the tips almost uniform cinnamon; the next pair is similar, but the inner webs have irregular, shallow V-shaped bars; the rest are cinnamon, paler on the inner web and closely but rather irregularly barred dull black. The primaries are dull black with a broad pink-buff line along the outer edges, slightly mottled cinnamon at the tip and on the inner webs. The secondaries are black, with the outer edges broadly fringed deep cinnamon with fine black specks.

	J	F	M	A	M	J	J	A	S	O	N	D
Adult moult	J	F	M	A	**M**	J	J	A	**S**	O	**N**	D
Juvenile moult	J	F	M	A	M	J	J	A	**S**	O	**N**	D
Primaries 10 feathers	134	158	170	176	178	180	178	171	153	144	M	
Secondaries 16 feathers	145	145	150	150	155	160	M					
Tail 18 feathers	120	158	202	286	400	526	566	685	M			

LADY AMHERST'S PHEASANT The central pair of tail feathers is white, with broad glossy black bars and coarse black vermiculations; the outer webs of the remainder are pale grey with cinnamon-buff outer edges and broad black bars, the inner webs being coarsely vermiculated black and off-white. The primaries and outer secondaries are dark sepia, with white margins to outer edges, except P10 which has no margin; the inner secondaries are black.

	J	F	M	A	M	J	J	A	S	O	N	D
Adult moult	J	F	M	A	**M**	J	J	A	**S**	O	**N**	D
Juvenile moult	J	F	M	A	M	J	J	A	**S**	O	**N**	D
Primaries 10 feathers	158	182	193	201	207	207	206	197	192	174	M	
Secondaries 16 feathers	172	172	170	165	160	M						
Tail 18 feathers	118	166	233	470	686	712	890	1020	M			

REEVES'S PHEASANT The two very long central pairs of tail feathers are silvery-white, with many crescent-like bars of black and deep chestnut along the shaft, and broad cinnamon-yellow margins; the three adjacent pairs are similar, but the yellow margin is very wide and confined to the outer web, the five shorter outer pairs are almost entirely yellowish-cinnamon, vermiculated with dull black on the inner web. The primaries are blackish-brown, barred with rufous-brown. The secondaries are barred white black and chestnut, with a broad buff-yellow tip bordered with black and dark chestnut.

Primaries 10 feathers	187	208	218	219	222	216	202	188	178	160	M
Secondaries 16 feathers	155	155	155	150	150	145	M				
Tail 20 feathers	126	153	187	238	315	406	603	985	1343	M	

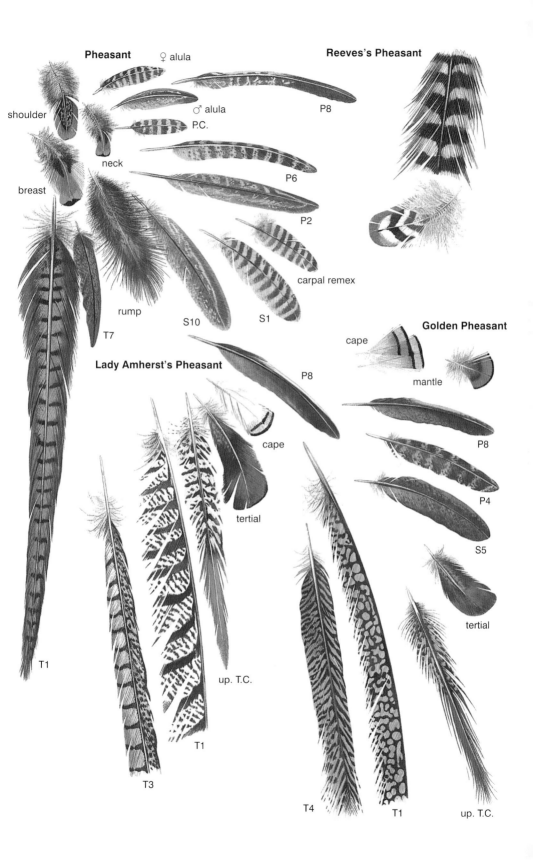

Pheasant

♀ alula

shoulder

♂ alula
P.C.

neck

P8

breast

P6

P2

rump

carpal remex

T7

S10

S1

Reeves's Pheasant

Lady Amherst's Pheasant

P8

cape

tertial

T1

up. T.C.

T1

T3

T4

T1

up. T.C.

Golden Pheasant

cape

mantle

P8

P4

S5

tertial

V–VIII

DOMESTIC FOWL The cock's tail is very compressed, and is composed of 14–16 feathers, the central pair elongated, pointed, soft and curved downwards; the longest tail-covers resemble them but are similar. The feathers of the back and rump are elongated, forming brightly coloured hackles failing on either side of the tail; those of the neck are similar. The hen lacks all the ornamental feathers.

RED JUNGLEFOWL The tail feathers are dark metallic green with white bases. The primaries are blackish-brown. The secondaries are rufous.

Primaries 11 feathers	46	151	180	196	205	212	218	220	222	219	206
Secondaries 15 feathers	190	198	196	190	186	168	150	132	109	93	
Tail 14 feathers	152	160	173	183	196	210	246				

GREEN JUNGLEFOWL The tail feathers are glossy blue-green black. The flight feathers are black.

GUINEAFOWL The tail feathers are dark grey with short white bars basally along the edges; the outer feathers have less grey mottling. The primaries are dark sepia-brown, closely barred with interrupted white lines, forming dots near the tips of the outer webs. The secondaries are black with short white streaks along the shafts, bordered by rows of white dots; there are rows of short white bars along the outer edges.

Primaries 10 feathers	74	204	219	252	261	263	260	255	245	225	M
Secondaries	215	215	210	205	205	200	M				
Tail 14 feathers	163	170	176	178	182	183	192	M			

PEACOCK The tail feathers are blackish-brown, with pale mottlings on the outer border; the upper tail coverts, 100–150 in number, forming the train, have long disintegrated barbs of metallic green with bronzy lilac or purple reflections, and a large subterminal ocellus formed by a deep blue patch surrounded by two broad rings of brilliant cobalt-blue and bronzy brown and two narrow ones of golden-green and bronzy lilac; the outer and the longest central feathers have no ocelli, the outer has a thick velvety blue-green border on the outer web, the longest central ones are terminated with a broad black half moon. The primaries are fulvous. The secondaries are black with a blue tinge on the outer web; the tertials are coarsely and irregularly barred pale buff and brownish-black.

Primaries	261	326	365	380	397	395	390	388	362
Secondaries	330	355	360	360	370	365			
Tail	340	364	396	427	460	490	525	555	555

Domestic Fowl, Cock.

up. T.C. 'sickle'

saddle hack

T3

P8

S4

S5

GuineaFowl

P7

S.C.

S7

S11

up. T.C.

T1

Peacock

VI–VII

TAWNY OWL The tail feathers range from deep rufous-cinnamon on the centre feather to paler cinnamon on outer webs, and paler buff on inner webs of outer feathers, with faint bands on centre feathers to contrasting bands on outer. Primaries with brown-black bands, outer webs with rufous-cinnamon spots, inner webs with greyish-buff bars. Secondaries similar, but black bands narrower. Outer webs of P6–P9 and inner webs of P7–P10 emarginated. Outer web of longest feather of alula, outer web of P10 and emarginated part of outer webs of P8–P9 with rather long and curved serrations.

Adult moult	J	F	M	A	M	J	J	A	S	O	N	D
Primaries 10 feathers	140	185	215	230	230	220	210	195	190	185		
Secondaries 14 feathers	175	180	180	180	170	170	165	160	160	150	140	140	138
Tail 12 feathers	160	160	160	160	165	175	M					

LONG-EARED OWL The central pair of tail feathers are buff, with five rather broad greyish-black bands partly freckled buff; the remainder are similar, but bands gradually become narrower and purer black-brown towards the outer feathers. Basal halves of first six primaries with outer webs uniform golden brown; terminal halves buff with grey wash and speckling, and with four to six well-spaced brown-black bands. Remaining primaries and secondaries pale greyish-buff; broad border of base, and middle portion of inner webs white, outer webs with four well-spaced brown-black bands. Outer web of P9 and inner webs of P9–P10 emarginated. Outer web of longest feather of alula, outer web of P10 and emarginated part of outer web of P9 with long curved serrations.

Adult moult	J	F	M	A	M	J	J	A	S	O	N	D
Primaries 10 feathers	215	250	250	230	220	205	190	175	165	155		
Secondaries 12 feathers	155	150	150	145	140	140	135	130	130	130	130	130
Tail 12 feathers	146	149	150	150	152	150						

SHORT-EARED OWL Central pair of tail feathers with even bands of buff and black-brown, black-brown bands gradually narrower towards outer feathers, also buff paler. Primary ground colour cinnamon-buff on outer webs, pale tawny-buff to white on inner webs; outer five to six primaries have dusky grey tips, two or three black bands on outer webs and a single band on inner webs; outer webs have two or three buff mirrors, inner web usually only one. Secondaries and inner primaries have white tips and white inner webs, outer webs with three or four black-brown bands. Outer webs of P8–P9 and inner web of P10 emarginated. Outer edges of longest feather of alula, outer edge of P10 and emarginated portion of outer web of P9 with short fine serrations.

Adult moult	J	F	M	A	M	J	J	A	S	O	N	D
Primaries 10 feathers	213	246	247	235	219	202	188	175	163	155		
Secondaries 12 feathers	154	150	148	145	140	137	134	132	128	128	128	126
Tail 12 feathers	139	142	142	146	151	158	M					

BARN OWL Tail ground colour ranges from cream-buff to golden-buff with the lighter colour on the outside, having rather dark narrow grey bars reducing outwards to outer feathers. The primaries are golden-buff on outer webs and along shaft on inner webs, with grey and white bars; uniform grey on inner web. Primaries not emarginated. Outer web of P10 with rather short serrations along edge.

Adult moult	J	F	M	A	M	J	J	A	S	O	N	D
Primaries 10 feathers	222	230	228	219	205	191	178	166	158	152		
Secondaries 14 feathers	148	149	148	143	139	137	133	132	130	124	119	112	96	85
Tail 12 feathers	112	114	118	118	118	122						

GOSHAWK The tail feathers are brown to slate-brown and are narrowly tipped off-white, with a broad black-brown subterminal band and three or four broad black-brown bars. The primaries are dark brown, barred black-brown and narrowly tipped off-white; the inner webs have irregular white patterns, the outer webs are tinged slate. The secondaries are as primaries, but with more white. Inner web of P6–P10 and outer web of P5–P9 emarginated.

Adult moult	J	F	M	A	M	J	J	A	S	O	N	D
Primaries 10 feathers	200	273	298	305	300	246	240	233	191	191	M	
Secondaries 14 feathers	193	193	193	195	210	212	218	215	218	218	204	M
Tail 12 feathers	249	285	287	288	288	289	M					

Note Owl feathers are easily identified by their furry upper surface.

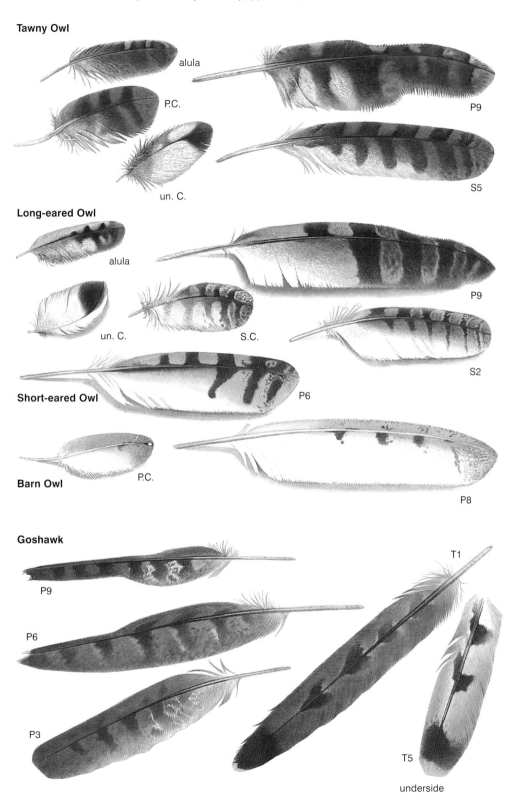

Tawny Owl

alula

P.C.

un. C.

P9

S5

Long-eared Owl

alula

un. C.

S.C.

P9

S2

P6

Short-eared Owl

P.C.

Barn Owl

P8

Goshawk

P9

P6

P3

T1

T5

underside

VI–VII

POMARINE SKUA The tail feathers are black with some white near bases; the central pair is elongated, broad and twisted. The flight feathers are black; the primary shafts are white on the innermost near the bases only; the primary bases are white, reaching higher on the inner webs than on the outer.

Adult moult	J	F	M	A	M	J	J	A	S	O	N	D
Primaries 11 feathers	81	267	265	254	240	222	205	189	171	156	141	
Secondaries	138	140	142	143	146	148	148	146	141	132	114	
Tail 12 feathers	155	155	157	160	160	178						

ARCTIC SKUA The tail feathers are dark slate-grey to dark umber-brown with white bases, the centre pair elongated. The flight feathers are black, the primaries having white at the bases and projecting up the inner web; the shafts of at least three outer primaries are white.

Adult moult	J	F	M	A	M	J	J	A	S	O	N	D
Primaries 11 feathers	54	258	255	243	229	206	188	176	156	136	121	M
Tail 12 feathers	119	118	118	120	123	135	M					

LONG-TAILED SKUA The tail feathers are slate-grey, gradually darker towards the tips, the central pair strongly elongated. The flight feathers are black, with white primary bases; the shafts of P9–P10 are white.

Adult moult	J	F	M	A	M	J	J	A	S	O	N	D
Primaries 11 feathers	60	268	251	235	220	201	177	159	139	125	115	M
Tail 12 feathers	135	135	134	139	140	315	M					

MONTAGU'S HARRIER Central tail grey, other feathers narrowly white tipped. Outer webs grey, inner webs barred pale grey-dark grey brown. Outer primaries black, grey tipped. Inner primaries grey, proximal inner web white, dark brown bars. Grey secondaries, black bars $^1/_3$ and $^2/_3$ from tip. Inner webs proximally white. Inner secondaries grey, unbarred.

Adult moult	J	F	M	A	M	J	J	A	S	O	N	D	
Primaries 10 feathers	224	303	325	310	302	280	240	214	193	174		M	
Secondaries 12 feathers	165	160	160	155	155	154	154	153	153	152	151	150	150	M
Tail 12 feathers	224	229	232	236	243	240	M						

HEN HARRIER The central tail feathers are silvery grey with white at base and tip, slightly mottled darker grey; the remainder become paler with more extensive white outwards, and have seven or eight incomplete dark grey to brown-grey bars. The outer primaries are black with narrow pale grey tips, the outer webs are paler with grey tinge, the inner webs white at base; the inner primaries are grey to brown-grey with paler tips, the outer webs proximally paler, the inner webs with broad white proximal margins. The secondaries are as the inner primaries, but their inner webs have a contrasting dark grey patch near the tip. The outer webs of P6–P9 and the inner webs of P7–P10 are emarginated, the outer P5 and inner P6 slightly so.

Adult moult	J	F	M	A	M	J	J	A	S	O	N	D
Primaries 11 feathers	40	230	294	318	322	310	265	251	231	219	212	M
Secondaries 13 feathers	200	185	180	180	190	195	200	210	220	230	M	
Tail 12 feathers	254	262	263	268	268	270	M					

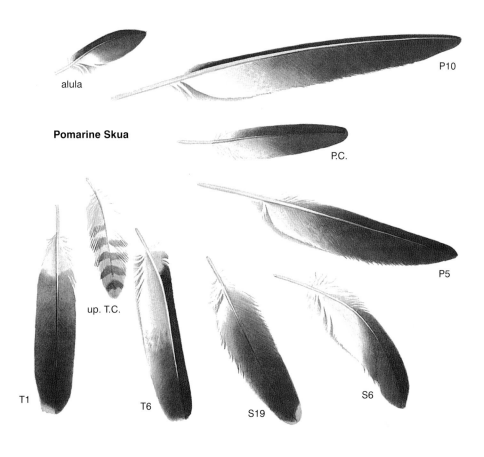

alula

P10

Pomarine Skua

P.C.

up. T.C.

P5

T1

T6

S19

S6

Montagu's Harrier

P9

P5

T1

S5

VI–VII

SHELDUCK The tail feathers are white and broadly tipped black. The primaries and inner webs of the secondaries black, the secondary outer webs with a strong bronze-green gloss; both primaries and secondaries are white towards the base of the inner web. P11 is minute and the inner web of P10 and the outer web of P9 is emarginated. Outer webs of the outer tertials are deep chestnut, separated by a grey shaft streak from white inner webs.

	J	F	M	A	M	J	J	A	S	O	N	D
Adult moult	J	F	M	A	M	J	J	A	S	O	N	D
Juvenile moult	J	F	M	A	M	J	J	A	S	O	N	D

Primaries 11 feathers	62	243	260	253	242	228	212	197	182	170	160			
Secondaries 20 feathers	152	152	150	149	148	147	146	147	148	151	155	158	168	179	174
Tail 14 feathers	128	131	130	128	126	123	120							

EGYPTIAN GOOSE The tail feathers are black. The primaries and inner webs of the secondaries are black (similar to the Shelduck but larger); the outer webs of the secondaries have a dark metallic green or purple gloss, except at tip. P11 is minute, and the inner webs of P10 and P9 and outer webs of P9 and P8 emarginated.

Primaries 11 feathers	75	375	391	384	381	367	345	320	300	282	270	M
Secondaries 20 feathers	268	268	268	270	281	290	292	300	310	315	M
Tail 14 feathers	111	123	125	125	128	133	137	M

ANSER GEESE

The tail feathers range from dark grey to black, all of them margined and tipped white. All flight feathers are black, with the primaries having white shafts, and are basally tinged grey; some secondaries are narrowly bordered and tipped white. On all *Anser* geese, P11 is hidden by the primary coverts and the inner webs of P10 and P9 and the outer webs of P9 and P8 are emarginated.

	J	F	M	A	M	J	J	A	S	O	N	D
Adult moult	J	F	M	A	M	J	J	A	S	O	N	D
Juvenile moult	J	F	M	A	M	J	J	A	S	O	N	D

GREYLAG GOOSE

Primaries 11 feathers	56	410	414	411	385	354	326	301	280	258	230	M
Tail 14 feathers	148	154	156	163	165	168	168	168	170	M

BRANTA GEESE

The tail feathers of both the Brent and the Barnacle Goose are black, as also are the flight feathers, with the outer webs of the Barnacle Goose edged grey. The primary shaft of all *Branta* geese is black, thereby providing a positive distinction from the *Anser* geese. P11 hidden by primary coverts. Inner webs of P10 and P9 and the outer webs of P9 and P8 are emarginated.

	J	F	M	A	M	J	J	A	S	O	N	D
Adult moult	J	F	M	A	M	J	J	A	S	O	N	D
Juvenile moult	J	F	M	A	M	J	J	A	S	O	N	D

BRENT GOOSE

Primaries 11 feathers	56	410	414	411	385	354	326	301	280	258	230	M
Tail 14 feathers	148	154	156	163	165	168	168	168	170	M

BARNACLE GOOSE

Primaries 11 feathers	65	358	361	354	319	286	260	239	200	192	186	M
Secondaries	184	184	190	200	200	212	220	220	230	250	260	264
Tail 16 feathers	132	134	138	138	139	140	140	140	M

CANADA GOOSE The tail feathers are black, and the flight feathers are dark sepia with the primaries edged black at tips. P11 hidden by primary coverts. Inner webs of P10, P9 and P8 and the outer webs of P9, P8 and P7 emarginated.

Primaries 11 feathers	60	438	447	438	414	371	348	322	292	266	250	M
Secondaries	248	250	260	266	274	282	290	292	296	298	298	M
Tail 16 feathers	169	176	180	184	184	186	189	185	M

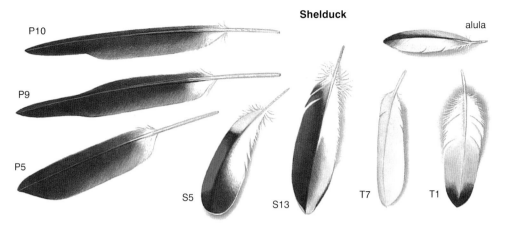

Shelduck

P10

P9

P5

alula

S5

S13

T7

T1

Underside, showing resistance of 'tegmen' to wear.

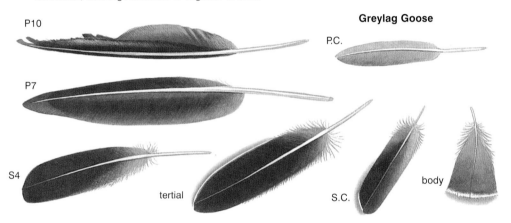

P10

P7

S4

tertial

Greylag Goose

P.C.

S.C.

body

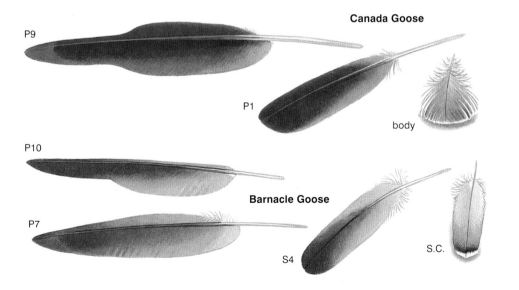

Canada Goose

P9

P1

body

P10

P7

Barnacle Goose

S4

S.C.

VI–VII

FULMAR The tail feathers are pale grey and narrowly tipped white, paler below. The primaries are dark grey, fading to white at the base of the inner webs, paler below; the shafts are off-white with brownish-grey tips. The secondaries are similar, but paler. P11 minute.

	J	F	M	A	M	J	J	A	S	O	N	D
Adult moult	J	F	M	A	M	J	J	A	S	O	N	D
Juvenile moult	J	F	M	A	M	J	J	A	S	O	N	D
Primaries 11 feathers	70	244	246	240	226	210	189	167	147	129	116	
Secondaries 20 feathers	110	105	101	101	102	103	105	107	110	107	95	
Tail 14 feathers	126	128	130	131	134	133	130					

BLACK-HEADED GULL The adult tail is completely white. Outer primaries white: P10 with narrow black outer edging, not reaching shaft or tip, on inner web black tip with widening brown/slaty edging extending down inner edge (variable in width); P9 similar, but black lacking on outer web or reduced to very narrow line and inner web with broader dark edging; P8 similar, but black on outer web extends from black tip and much of inner web is washed grey; P7 has most of the inner web grey, this merging into dark edging, and normally a small white apical spot; P6 similar, but has both webs grey; P5 with larger pale grey spot at apex; P4–P1 grey. Secondaries grey, becoming very pale at base and on inner edge of inner feathers. P11 minute.

	J	F	M	A	M	J	J	A	S	O	N	D
Adult moult	J	F	M	A	M	J	J	A	S	O	N	D
Juvenile moult	J	F	M	A	M	J	J	A	S	O	N	D
Primaries 11 feathers	67	237	239	229	211	193	177	163	149	134	125	
Secondaries 20 feathers	120	120	118	118	118	118	119	118	118	109		
Tail 12 feathers	127	130	128	125	124	120						

KITTIWAKE Adult tail is completely white. Primaries are pale blue-grey, fading to white at tip and on inner edge of inner web, inner primaries being palest: P10 has long black tip and outer web; P9–P7 have progressively shorter black tips, P7 or P8 often with a minute white spot at apex; P6 usually has subterminal black band, sometimes broken into two spots; P5 may have a black subterminal spot on one or both webs. Outer secondaries are as inner primaries, pale blue-grey with broad white tip and inner edge to inner web; inner secondaries have broader white tips and become progressively darker grey. P11 minute.

	J	F	M	A	M	J	J	A	S	O	N	D
Adult moult	J	F	M	A	M	J	J	A	S	O	N	D
Primaries 11 feathers	71	238	240	235	220	205	190	173	156	140	126	
Secondaries 20 feathers	118	116	115	115	120	125	126	126	124	116	95	
Tail 12 feathers	140	142	139	135	132	129						

MEDITERRANEAN GULL The tail feathers are white. The primaries are a very pale grey, almost white, and shade to white at the tips; there is often a black line on the outer web of P10, not extending to the tip and not quite reaching the shaft. The secondaries are very pale grey, with white tips and with most of the inner webs white. P11 is hidden by the primary coverts.

	J	F	M	A	M	J	J	A	S	O	N	D
Adult moult	J	F	M	A	M	J	J	A	S	O	N	D
Juvenile moult	J	F	M	A	M	J	J	A	S	O	N	D
Primaries 11 feathers	70	256	254	247	231	211	187	170	152	134	130	M
Secondaries 20 feathers	130	125	130	125	125	120	120	118	115	106	M	
Tail 12 feathers	123	126	126	126	126	126	M					

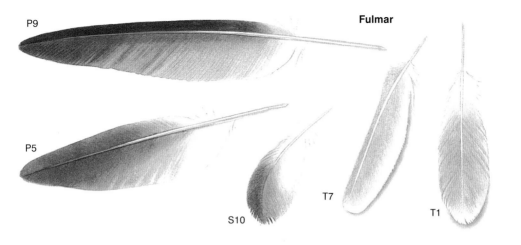

Fulmar

P9

P5

S10

T7

T1

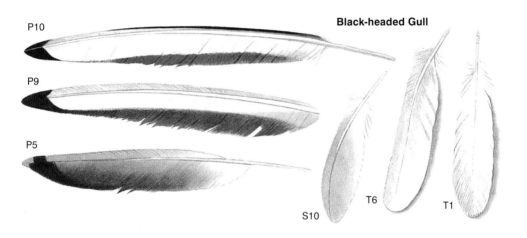

Black-headed Gull

P10

P9

P5

S10

T6

T1

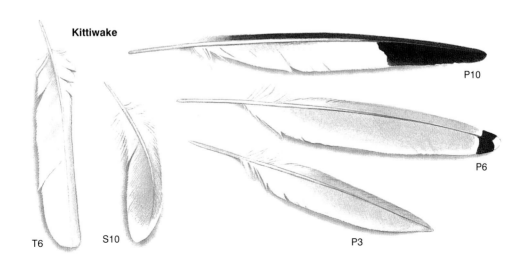

Kittiwake

P10

P6

P3

T6

S10

VI–VIII

HONEY BUZZARD The tail feathers are light brown with a broad dark brown terminal band, irregular pale bars and three dark brown bars towards the base, the inner webs generally paler. Primaries are dark brown at the tip becoming paler towards the base, with dark brown bars. Their inner webs have white bases with grey-brown bars. Secondaries are similar. The outer webs of P5 to P9 and the inner webs of P6 to P10, are emarginated.

Adult moult	J	F	M	A	M	J	J	A	S	O	N	D
Primaries 11 feathers	50	225	298	376	388	322	296	265	260	256	245	
Secondaries 13? feathers	240	236	230	220	213	210	190	186	180	175	170	155	98
Tail 12 feathers	263	265	265	270	270	275						

BITTERN The tail feathers are tawny-buff, mainly black along the shaft and with black speckles on both webs. The flight feathers are black, irregularly barred rufous; the inner secondaries have a buff margin to outer web. Primary webs are not emarginated. P10 pointed.

Adult moult	J	F	M	A	M	J	J	A	S	O	N	D
Primaries 11 feathers	46	258	260	260	254	242	234	221	205	205	195	M
Secondaries 18 feathers	190	190	189	190	188	190	190	190	190	M		
Tail 10 feathers	89	94	96	98	100	M						

MARSH HARRIER The tail feathers are silvery grey with paler tips; the outer feathers have paler inner edges and white bases. The outer primaries are distally black with paler tips, with the outer webs silvery and the inner webs basally white to cream; the inner primaries are pale brown to silvery grey, with the inner webs proximally paler with broad white margins. The outer secondaries are silvery grey, the inner webs paler, white basally; a dark brown patch near the tip increases in width towards the dark brown inner secondaries. The outer webs of P6–P9 and the inner webs of P7–P10 are emarginated.

Adult moult	J	F	M	A	M	J	J	A	S	O	N	D
Primaries 11 feathers	46	253	353	372	371	346	304	273	251	247	230	M
Secondaries 13 feathers	230	230	228	225	225	225	225	220	218	M		
Tail 12 feathers	247	256	259	260	264	264	M					

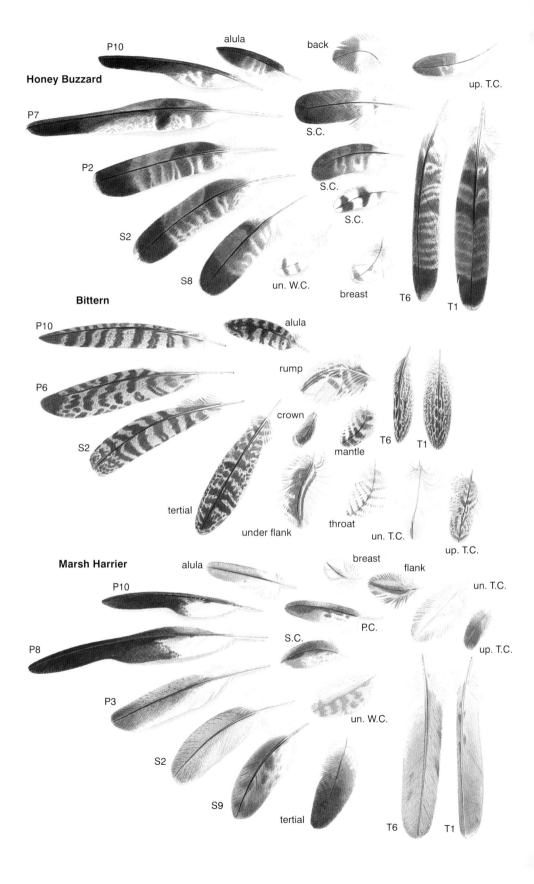

Honey Buzzard

P10
alula
back
up. T.C.
P7
S.C.
P2
S.C.
S.C.
S2
S8
un. W.C.
breast
T6
T1

Bittern

P10
alula
P6
rump
crown
T6
T1
S2
mantle
tertial
under flank
throat
un. T.C.
up. T.C.

Marsh Harrier

breast
alula
flank
un. T.C.
P10
P.C.
S.C.
up. T.C.
P8
P3
S2
un. W.C.
S9
tertial
T6
T1

VI–VIII

GREY HERON The tail feathers are grey, with grey-black tips. The primaries and most of the secondaries are black, with the inner secondaries blue-grey. The undersides of secondaries and of the inner webs of the primaries are grey. The outer webs of P7–P9 (P6 slightly) and the inner webs of P8–P10 (P7 slightly) are emarginated.

Adult moult	J	F	M	A	M	J	J	A	S	O	N	D
Juvenile moult	J	F	M	A	M	J	J	A	S	O	N	D
Primaries 11 feathers	100	284	299	319	328	328	311	292	277	268	261	
Secondaries 19 feathers	256	254	248	246	246	240	230	216	190	168	143	
Tail 12 feathers	168	168	168	168	166	162						

PURPLE HERON The tail feathers are dark grey with a slight gloss. The primaries are brown-black, with paler undersides. The secondaries are slightly paler, with the outer webs glossed grey-green. The outer webs of P7–P9 and the inner webs of P8–P10 are emarginated.

Adult moult	J	F	M	A	M	J	J	A	S	O	N	D
Juvenile moult	J	F	M	A	M	J	J	A	S	O	N	D
Primaries 11 feathers	83	258	282	282	294	296	285	283	270	259	239	M
Secondaries 19 feathers	230	230	226	226	226	M						
Tail 12 feathers	130	136	138	138	140	142	M					

NIGHT HERON The tail feathers are grey. The flight feathers are grey; the outer webs of the outer primaries are darker, the outermost primary with a narrow white marginal line. The outer webs of P7–P9 are slightly emarginated, and the inner webs of P9 (slightly) and P10 (strongly) emarginated.

Adult moult	J	F	M	A	M	J	J	A	S	O	N	D
Primaries 11 feathers	65	216	218	219	214	204	195	189	182	174	172	M
Secondaries 19 feathers	174	174	175	168	165	160	150	M				
Tail 12 feathers	103	104	104	105	111	111	M					

RAVEN The tail feathers are black, glossed green and red-purple. The outer primaries are black, glossed green, with the inner primaries more blue. The secondaries and all wing-coverts are black, glossed red-purple. The feather bases are brownish-white on all flight and tail feathers. The outer webs of P6–P9 are emarginated.

Adult moult	J	F	M	A	M	J	J	A	S	O	N	D
Primaries 10 feathers	271	384	414	416	350	308	288	268	247	M		
Secondaries 11 feathers	245	245	240	230	230	220	210	190	169	158	123	M
Tail 12 feathers	200	224	237	250	259	268	M					

FLAMINGO The tail feathers are pale pink, with the inner webs often white. The flight feathers are black, but the innermost secondaries are rose-pink. The outer webs of P8–P9 and the inner webs of P9–P10 are emarginated.

Adult moult	J	F	M	A	M	J	J	A	S	O	N	D
Juvenile moult	J	F	M	A	M	J	J	A	S	O	N	D
Primaries 10 feathers	275	285	288	268	248	230	212	201	189	185	M	
Secondaries 20 feathers	175	175	173	160	152	152	156	180	190	M		
Tail 14 feathers	120	120	126	128	130	132	135	M				

GANNET The tail is white. The primaries, their coverts and the alula are black, with the shafts of the primaries paler towards the base; the secondaries are white. P11 minute. Inner web of P10 strongly emarginated, those of P8–P9 slightly so. Outer webs of P8–P10 slightly emarginated.

Adult moult	J	F	M	A	M	J	J	A	S	O	N	D	
Primaries 11 feathers	65	274	307	319	301	275	250	246	200	186	164	M	
Secondaries 16 feathers	150	150	154	150	153	154	154	154	157	160	162	164	165	M
Tail 12 feathers	110	188	206	224	238	258	M						

Gannet illustrated on p257

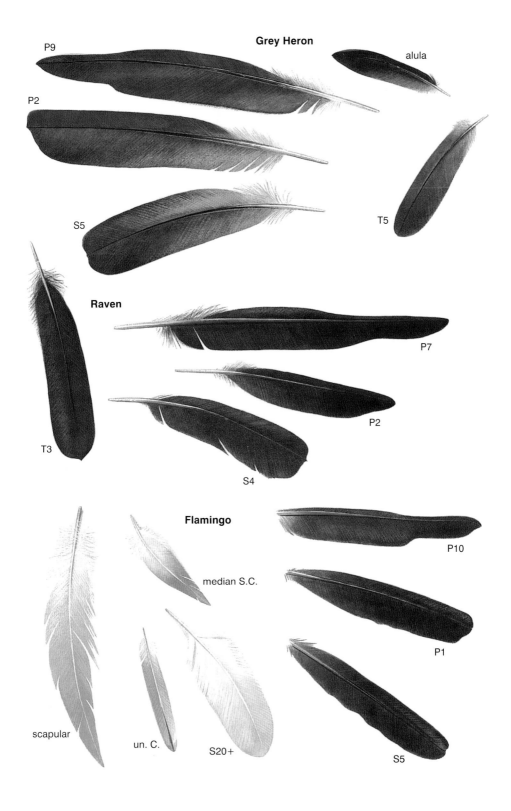

Grey Heron

P9

P2

S5

alula

T5

Raven

T3

P7

P2

S4

Flamingo

scapular

median S.C.

un. C.

S20+

P10

P1

S5

VIB–VIII

COMMON GULL The tail is entirely white. P10 is black, becoming very dark slate at the base of the inner web, with a long subterminal white mirror and a small white spot at the apex (the mirror occasionally extends to tip); P9 is black, with base of both webs grey, mirror smaller and spot larger; P8 has more grey at the base, and lacks the white mirror (though occasionally has a small one); P7 is grey, with a long black tip and a large white spot at apex; P6 has the black tip much restricted; P5 is grey with a white tip, also with a narrow subterminal black band of variable width, often broken (band may be absent on outer or even on both webs); P4–P1 are grey, becoming white at tips, P4 with occasionally a brownish-black mark. The secondaries are blue-grey, with long white tips. P11 narrow and pointed, hidden by primary coverts.

	J	F	M	A	M	J	J	A	S	O	N	D
Adult moult	J	F	M	A	M	J	J	A	S	O	N	D
Juvenile moult	J	F	M	A	M	J	J	A	S	O	N	D
Primaries 11 feathers	84	282	284	268	249	227	207	196	173	157	143	
Secondaries 20 feathers	138	138	139	140	140	140	142	142	140	129	132	
Tail 12 feathers	149	150	148	146	144	143						

HERRING GULL The tail is completely white. P10 is black, with the base of inner web ashy blue-grey, the tip white, and usually with a black (often broken) subterminal band; P9 is black, with base of both webs grey, white at extreme tip, and usually with a white subterminal mirror; P8 is similar, but lacks mirror and blue-grey extends farther towards tip; P7 has even more extensive blue-grey, becoming almost white on inner web; P6 has black restricted to a subterminal band; P5 is grey, tipped white, usually with a black subterminal spot; P4–P1 are grey, tipped white, P4 occasionally with a black subterminal spot. The secondaries are pale blue-grey, tipped white. P11 hidden by primary coverts.

	J	F	M	A	M	J	J	A	S	O	N	D
Adult moult	J	F	M	A	M	J	J	A	S	O	N	D
Juvenile moult	J	F	M	A	M	J	J	A	S	O	N	D
Primaries 11 feathers	96	305	310	299	278	259	267	247	228	211	194	
Secondaries 20 feathers	163	145	140	134	136	136	135	130	124	125		
Tail 12 feathers	168	168	168	168	169	166						

LESSER BLACK-BACKED GULL The tail is completely white. P10 is black, with the base of inner web dull grey and a white tip with black subterminal band, inner web of the tip sometimes clouded grey; the rest of the primaries are as Herring Gull, but the grey is much darker and with a more prominent white line where grey meets black on inner web; P9 usually has a smaller white mirror, P5 has a black subterminal band, P4 a variable amount of black, and P3 may have a black dot. The secondaries are slate-grey with long white tips. P11 hidden by primary coverts.

	J	F	M	A	M	J	J	A	S	O	N	D
Adult moult	J	F	M	A	M	J	J	A	S	O	N	D
Primaries 11 feathers	96	310	320	310	290	274	255	238	216	193	175	
Secondaries 20 feathers	175	170	166	165	165	165	168	167	169	160		
Tail 12 feathers	158	158	158	158	158	158						

GREAT BLACK-BACKED GULL The tail is completely white. P10 is black, tipped white, with grey base to inner web extending along inner edge, inner web narrowly edged white; P9 is the same but grey of inner web extends farther towards tip, base of outer web is fringed grey, and tip usually has less white and shows subterminal black band of variable width; P8 has a small white tip and may have a white subterminal spot on inner web; P7–P6 are slate-grey to grey-black, tipped white and with subterminal band extending up outer web, and with a white line or patch where grey meets black; P5 is similar, but subterminal band is broken, often reduced to a spot (may even be absent); P4–P1 are slate grey to grey -black tipped white. The secondaries are slate-grey to grey-black, with long white tips. P11 hidden by primary coverts.

	J	F	M	A	M	J	J	A	S	O	N	D
Adult moult	J	F	M	A	M	J	J	A	S	O	N	D
Juvenile moult	J	F	M	A	M	J	J	A	S	O	N	D
Primaries 11 feathers	90	442	440	435	408	375	351	321	310	298	285	M
Tail 12 feathers	190	193	194	195	198	200	M					

Gannet description see p254

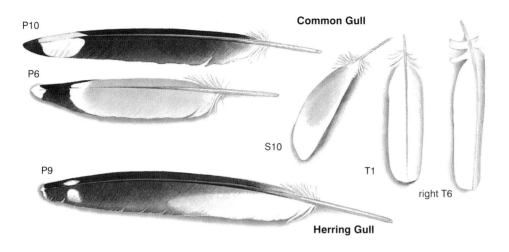

P10

P6

Common Gull

S10

T1

right T6

P9

Herring Gull

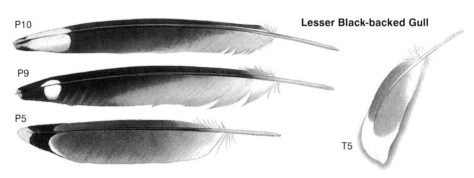

P10

P9

P5

Lesser Black-backed Gull

T5

Great Black-backed Gull

P10

P4

T5

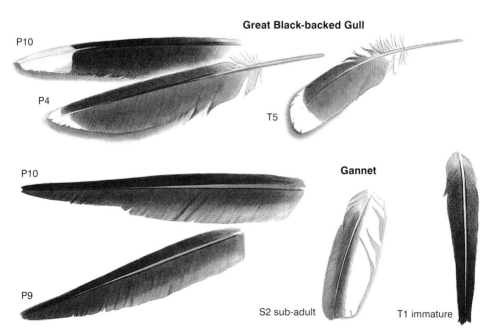

P10

Gannet

P9

S2 sub-adult

T1 immature

VIB–VIII

ICELAND GULL The tail feathers are white. The primaries are pale grey, tipped white, with pale straw shafts; the outer web of P10 is almost white. The secondaries are pale grey, tipped white.

	J	F	M	A	M	J	J	A	S	O	N	D
Adult moult	**J**	**F**	**M**	**A**	**M**	**J**	**J**	**A**	**S**	**O**	**N**	D
Primaries 11 feathers	54	305	317	308	292	273	254	236	218	202	187	
Secondaries 24 feathers	180	180	175	170	172	172	172	172	170	165	155	
Tail 12 feathers	175	178	178	178	178	174						

GLAUCOUS GULL All tail and flight feathers are as in Iceland Gull.

	J	F	M	A	M	J	J	A	S	O	N	D
Adult moult	**J**	**F**	**M**	**A**	**M**	**J**	**J**	**A**	**S**	**O**	**N**	**D**
Juvenile moult	**J**	**F**	**M**	**A**	**M**	**J**	**J**	**A**	**S**	**O**	**N**	**D**
Primaries 11 feathers	95	335	340	330	308	289	297	277	258	241	224	M
Secondaries 24 feathers	193	170	170	164	166	166	166	160	M			
Tail 12 feathers	188	188	188	188	188	188	M					

IVORY GULL The whole plumage is pure white, with the shafts of the tail and flight feathers pale yellow. The outer web of P10 is emarginated.

	J	F	M	A	M	J	J	A	S	O	N	D
Adult moult	**J**	**F**	**M**	**A**	**M**	**J**	**J**	**A**	**S**	**O**	**N**	**D**
Primaries 11 feathers	75	268	270	265	250	235	220	203	186	170	156	M
Secondaries	150	146	145	145	150	155	158	158	154	M		
Tail 12 feathers	160	162	159	155	152	149	M					

SLENDER-BILLED GULL The tail feathers are white. P10 is white, with a narrow black edging along at least the basal three-quarters of the outer edge but not reaching the shaft or the tip, with a small black area at tip and with a narrow brown-black inner edging to the inner web; P6 is similar, but black on the outer web is absent or reduced to a very short and narrow distal line and inner web has a broader dark edging; P8 is similar, with the black on the outer web reduced to a short and narrow extension of the black of the tip, the black on the inner web is broader, and the white area of the inner web is tinged grey at the base; P7 is similar, but on the inner web much of the light area is grey and merges into the dark edging; P6 is similar, but has all the pale areas of the webs grey, this sometimes becoming a light grey near the shaft; P5 is similar, with paler, smaller dark tip and grey spot at apex; P1–P4 are grey. The secondaries are light blue-grey, the inner ones having the base and the inner edge of the inner web slightly paler grey. The tertials are grey.

	J	F	M	A	M	J	J	A	S	O	N	D
Adult moult	J	F	**M**	**A**	**M**	J	**J**	**A**	**S**	**O**	N	D
Juvenile moult	J	F	**M**	**A**	**M**	J	**J**	**A**	**S**	**O**	N	D
Primaries 11 feathers	75	252	254	238	219	197	177	166	143	140	120	M
Secondaries	118	118	118	118	120	120	M					
Tail 12 feathers	129	130	128	128	124	123	M					

GYR FALCON Highly variable; white morph described here. The tail feathers are white, with some incomplete and irregular dark bars and spots. The primaries are white, with shafts black-brown; a broad irregular subterminal band and some broken bars near the tip usually present, inner webs have comb-like bars. The secondaries are white with irregular brown barring, bars near tip shaped like arrowheads. The outer webs of P8–P9 and the inner web of P9 are emarginated.

	J	F	M	A	M	J	J	A	S	O	N	D
Adult moult	**J**	F	**M**	**A**	**M**	**J**	**J**	**A**	**S**	**O**	**N**	**D**

Iceland Gull (sub-adult)

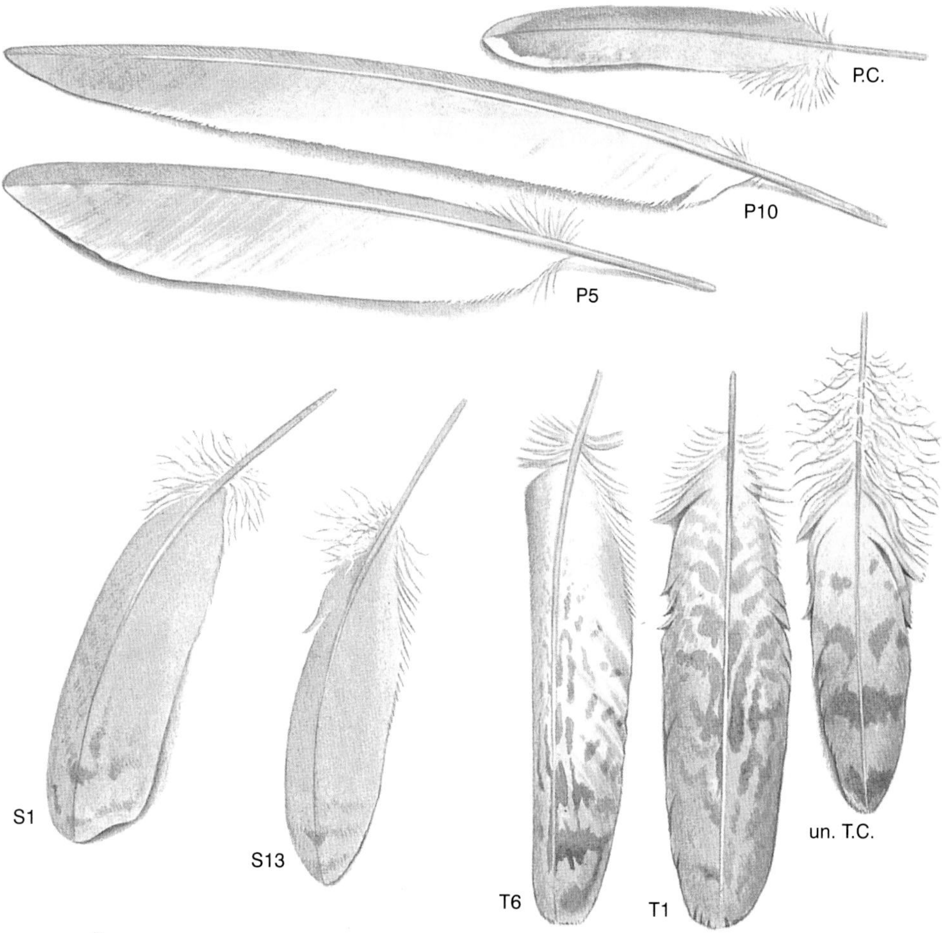

P.C.

P10

P5

S1

S13

T6

T1

un. T.C.

Gyr Falcon ♀

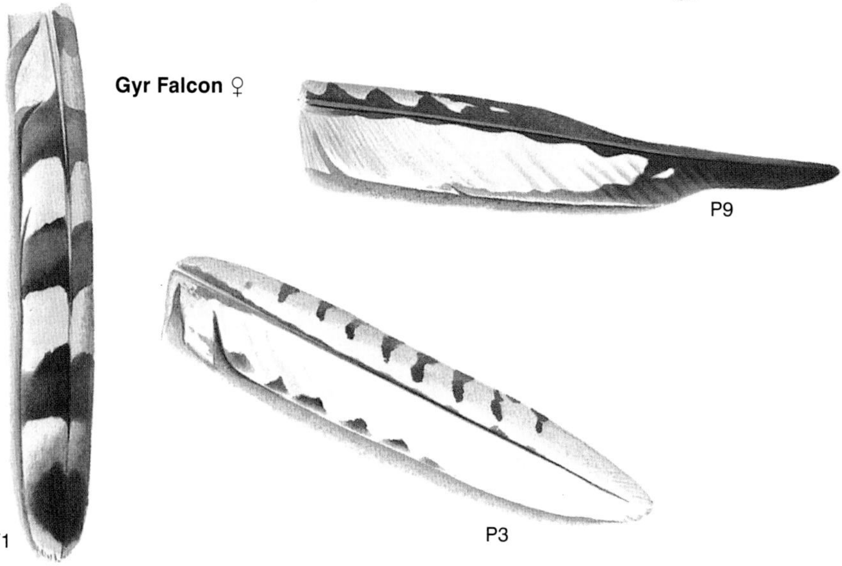

P9

T1

P3

VII–VIII

OSPREY Tail feathers are dark brown, narrowly tipped cream-buff; inner webs, with the exception of T1, are white with brown barring on proximal half and brown near tip. Outer primaries are black-brown with inner webs paler brown and white at base; inner primaries and outer secondaries are a paler brown, their inner webs being pale brown near the shaft and white near the edge, and have incomplete brown bars; the inner secondaries are almost uniform brown, with little white. The outer webs of P6–P9 and inner webs of P7–P9 are emarginated; inner web of P10 has a notch 130–153mm from tip.

Adult moult	J	F	M	A	M	J	J	A	S	O	N	D
Primaries 11 feathers	64	319	381	406	397	373	330	292	263	238	235	
Secondaries 20 feathers	235	230	230	230	230	228	215	210	210	180	156	
Tail 12 feathers	196	205	205	210	212	214						

CAPERCAILLIE The tail feathers are black, slightly paler below; the central feathers have indistinct pale grey vermiculations, the remainder have irregular white mottling just below the tips. The primaries are brown, with pale grey or pale buff vermiculations near tips (very indistinct on P1 and P2); the proximal areas of the outer webs of P4–P9 are off-white. The secondaries are brown, narrowly tipped white, and with pale vermiculations on the outer webs. The outer webs of P4–P10 are emarginated, the inner webs of P5–P10 slightly so.

Adult moult	J	F	M	A	M	J	J	A	S	O	N	D
Primaries 10 feathers	222	263	295	295	302	294	276	230	213	186	M	
Secondaries 18–19 feathers	186	186	195	195	190	180	176	168	164	152	M	
Tail 18–24 feathers	185	188	194	198	202	206	209	214	215	M		

RED KITE The tail feathers are cinnamon-rufous, the inners with dark brown spots along the shaft, others more distinctly barred with narrow dark brown bars on the inner webs. The outer tail feathers are browner, the outermost with a dark brown tip. The primaries have dark brown tips and outer webs, the inner webs being extensively white towards the base. The inner primaries are lighter brown with partial bars on the light parts of the inner webs. Secondaries are dark brown becoming paler with bars towards the base. The outer webs of P6 to P9 and the inner webs of P6 to P10, are emarginated.

Adult moult	J	F	M	A	M	J	J	A	S	O	N	D
Primaries 11 feathers	46	268	359	408	425	410	347	303	277	260	244	
Secondaries 14? feathers	241	244	240	237	228	227	223	225	226	225	226	205	165
Tail 12 feathers	350	364	338	325	320	307						

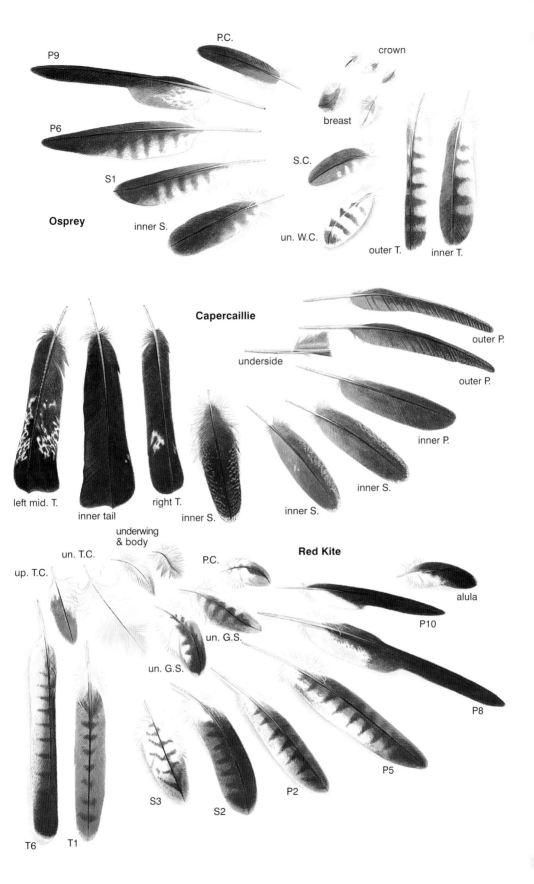

P9

P.C.

crown

P6

breast

S.C.

S1

Osprey

inner S.

un. W.C.

outer T.

inner T.

Capercaillie

outer P.

underside

outer P.

inner P.

left mid. T.

right T.

inner S.

inner S.

inner tail

inner S.

inner S.

underwing
& body

un. T.C.

P.C.

Red Kite

up. T.C.

alula

P10

un. G.S.

un. G.S.

P8

S3

P5

S2

P2

T6

T1

VII–IX

EAGLE OWL The central pair of tail feathers is dark grey with about six narrow, somewhat irregular buff bands, or buff with about five olive-grey bands; the broad olive-grey bands gradually become narrower and blacker towards T6, which is tawny-buff with up to nine fairly narrow greyish-black bars. The flight feathers are tawny-buff, the outer webs with four to six evenly spaced broad olive-black bands on the outer webs; the inner webs have similar but narrower and less regular bars, reduced towards the inner edge. Both webs of P6–P9 and inner web of P10 deeply emarginated; outer web of longest feather of alula, outer web of P10 and emarginated parts of outer webs of P8–P9 serrated.

Primaries 10 feathers	232	358	386	390	390	370	338	316	298	292	M
Tail 12 feathers	269	275	286	294	300	306	M				

BUZZARD The tail feathers are a rufous-tinged greyish-brown with white bases; they have eight to ten, often asymmetrical, dark brown bars, a wider dark brown subterminal band, and are pale grey/pale rufous at the tips. The outer primaries are black-brown, becoming paler towards the base, with white inner webs which are mottled and have incomplete brown bars; the inner primaries and secondaries have the same pattern, but are paler brown. The outer webs of P5–P9 are emarginated, P4 slightly so; the inner webs of P8–P10 are notched or emarginated (P7 always emarginated, P6 slightly).

Adult moult	J	F	M	A	M	J	J	A	S	O	N	D
Primaries 11 feathers	54	253	320	374	377	372	329	286	269	256	230	M
Secondaries 13 feathers	230	230	230	228	228	210	200	186	185	180	180	170	160	M
Tail 12 feathers	221	228	231	240	244	246	M					

ROUGH-LEGGED BUZZARD The tail feathers have white bases, with black-brown spots proximally near shafts; the distal part has a grey tinge, and has some black-brown bars, a broad subterminal band and white to pale grey tips. The outer primaries are brown to blackish-brown, with the base of the outer webs white with brown mottling, the base of the inner webs extensively white; the white decreases in extent towards the inner primaries, which are paler and greyer and have incomplete black-brown bars. The secondaries are grey-brown, with black-brown bars and subterminal band; the proximal area of inner webs is white with some brown barring. The outer webs of P6–P9 and inner webs of P7–P10 are emarginated, outer web of P5 and inner web of P6 slightly so.

Adult moult	J	F	M	A	M	J	J	A	S	O	N	D
Primaries 11 feathers	51	247	313	398	405	394	344	319	290	267	247	M
Secondaries 13 feathers	245	230	220	220	218	216	210	210	200	195	186	170	156	M
Tail 12 feathers	230	235	236	238	244	247	M					

BLACK KITE The tail feathers are barred pale and dark brown, the barring being faint on the inner webs of the outermost feathers and absent on the outer webs. The primaries are black-brown, the inner ones paler; the inner webs have off-white bases and irregular brown bars or mottling. The secondaries are brown, with area near the base of the inner webs paler and barred; inner webs of inner secondaries are almost wholly barred brown and white. The inner webs of P6–P10 and the outer webs of P6–P9 are emarginated.

Adult moult	J	F	M	A	M	J	J	A	S	O	N	D
Primaries 11 feathers	54	340	430	450	435	378	314	277	243	219	210	M
Tail 12 feathers	306	300	284	280	280	275	M					

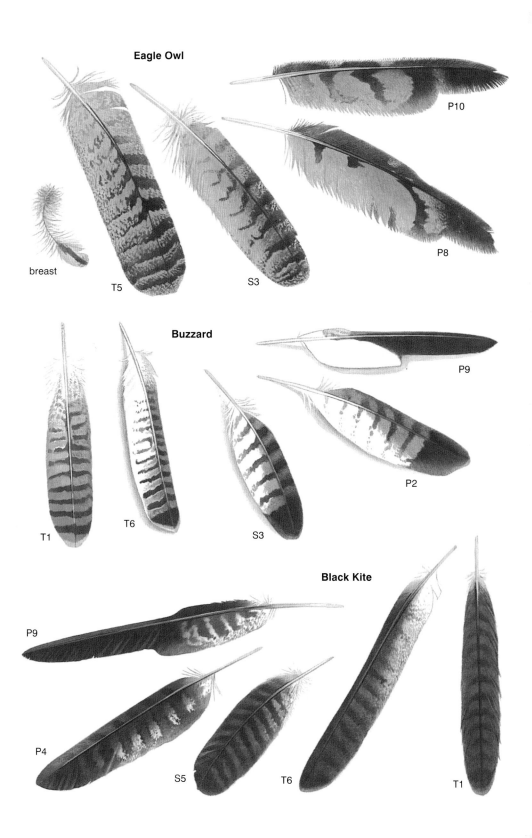

Eagle Owl

breast   T5   S3   P10   P8

Buzzard

T1   T6   S3   P9   P2

Black Kite

P9   P4   S5   T6   T1

VIII–IX

SNOWY OWL Adult male Tail is wholly white or with single dark broken bar on T1–T3. Flight feathers are white, outer primaries having one to three dark broken bars on tips; each or any of the inner primaries and secondaries may have a small dark spot. **Adult female** Tail is white, T1 with three broken dark brown bars on distal half, reducing outwards to become spots on tips of T4–T5; T6 all white. Flight feathers white, with two to four dark brown distal bars; Inner primaries and secondaries may show a trace of single subterminal bar. **Both sexes** Outer webs of P6–P9, inner webs of P6–P10 deeply emarginated. Outer web of P10 and emarginated portions of other outer primaries slightly serrated.

Adult moult	J	F	M	A	M	J	J	A	S	O	N	D
Primaries 10 feathers	287	340	350	347	309	273	245	240	235	235		
Secondaries 19 feathers	230	230	230	225	225	225	225	225	220	230		
Tail 12 feathers	270	275	285	295	300	310						

ALL SWANS

Tail primaries and secondaries entirely white. P11 reduced, concealed by primary coverts. Outer webs of P7-P9 and inner webs of P8-P10 emarginated.

MUTE SWAN

Adult moult	J	F	M	A	M	J	J	A	S	O	N	D
Primaries 11 feathers	113	423	428	414	403	388	377	376	352	334	321	
Secondaries 22–28 feathers	318	316	316	310	308	308	305	300	295	296	294	292
Tail 20–24 feathers	142	156	165	175	188	203	223	226	230	234		

WHOOPER SWAN

Adult moult	J	F	M	A	M	J	J	A	S	O	N	D
Primaries 11 feathers	118	420	465	470	426	395	375	356	340	335	324	
Secondaries 22–28 feathers	324	322	322	320	320	320	317	315	315	310		
Tail 20 feathers	137	145	165	177	187	190	196	199	210	215		

BEWICK'S SWAN

Adult moult	J	F	M	A	M	J	J	A	S	O	N	D
Primaries 11 feathers	76	317	332	346	322	291	270	252	245	230	224	
Secondaries 20 feathers	224	224	230	230	226	226	226	220	220	216	215	215	210	210
Tail 20 feathers	169	174	189	197	196	198	198	200	204	206		

GREAT WHITE EGRET Tail, primaries and secondaries entirely white. The feathers of the nape are slightly elongated; during courtship and breeding scapulars contain 30–50 long aigrettes (up to 500mm), reaching well past tip of tail. P11 minute. Inner web of P10 strongly emarginated, P8–P9 slightly so. P7–P9 slightly emarginated on outer webs.

Adult moult	J	F	M	A	M	J	J	A	S	O	N	D
Primaries 11 feathers	64	320	332	339	348	330	313	300	296	290	280	
Secondaries	272	272	270	270	270	270	270	265	266	260		
Tail 12 feathers	178	180	183	186	188	192						

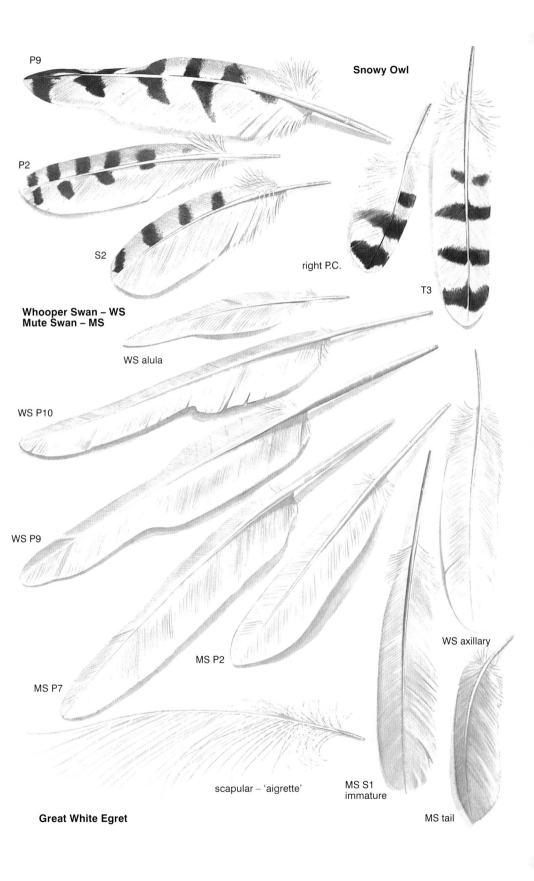

P9

P2

S2

Snowy Owl

right P.C.

T3

Whooper Swan – WS
Mute Swan – MS

WS alula

WS P10

WS P9

MS P7

MS P2

WS axillary

scapular – 'aigrette'

MS S1
immature

MS tail

Great White Egret

VIII–IX

LAMMERGEIER The tail feathers are grey with black or dark sepia edges, and with tinge of silver near the white shafts. The flight feathers are grey, with the shafts white and the outer edges dark. The under surfaces of both tail and flight feathers are grey-brown. The inner webs of P6–P10 are emarginated, the outer webs are all fairly narrow and with indistinct emarginations.

Adult moult	J	F	M	A	M	J	J	A	S	O	N	D
Primaries 10 feathers	587	670	676	673	620	531	483	479	449	420	M	
Secondaries	390	385	375	360	360	M						
Tail 12 feathers	415	458	479	480	485	510	M					

WHITE PELICAN The tail feathers are white. The primaries are dark grey, the tips and the edges of the inner webs silvery grey and the bases of the inner webs paler dull grey. The outer secondaries are dark grey at the centre with the tips and edges of the inner webs paler and the edges of the outer webs broadly white with narrow dark margins. The inner secondaries are increasingly white. The outer webs of P6–P9, and the inner webs of P6–10 are emarginated, (P6–7 only slightly). Moults are poorly known.

Primaries 11 feathers	380	430	520	470	420	370	340	325	310	300	M				
Secondaries 30 feathers*	330	340	350	340	340	340	335	330	320	310	325	340	345	350	350
Tail 24 feathers	150	155	160	165	170	175	175	180	180	185	185	190			

*each entry represents 2 feathers

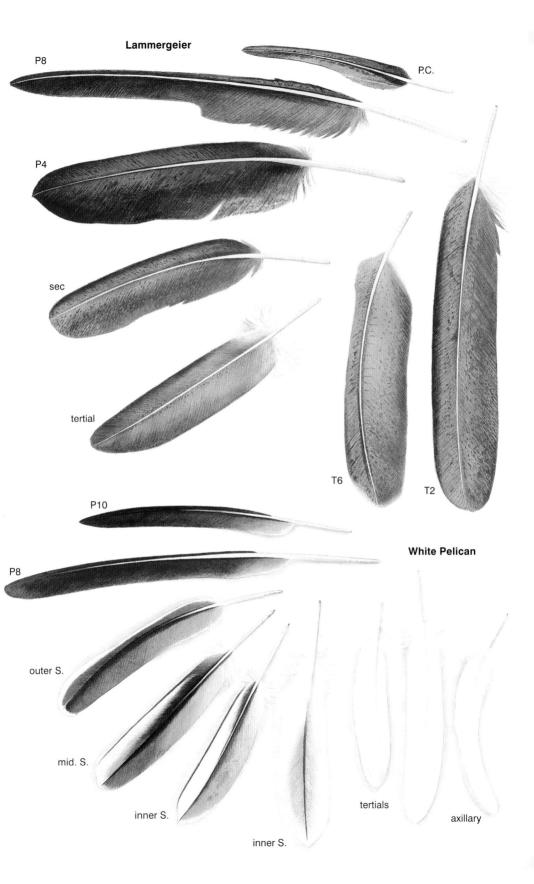

Lammergeier

P8

P.C.

P4

sec

tertial

T6

T2

P10

White Pelican

P8

outer S.

mid. S.

inner S.

inner S.

tertials

axillary

VIII–IX

BLACK STORK The tail and flight feathers are black, with a strong purple and green gloss; the tail feathers are also tinged brown. The outer webs of P6–P10 and the inner webs of P7–P11 are emarginated.

	J	F	M	A	M	J	J	A	S	O	N	D
Adult moult	J	F	M	A	M	J	J	A	S	O	N	D
Juvenile moult	J	F	M	A	M	J	J	A	S	O	N	D
Primaries 12 feathers	65	359	404	420	436	405	364	324	293	290	280	M
Secondaries 22 feathers	280	280	280	275	275	270	M					
Tail 12 feathers	268	281	298	298	300	300	M					

WHITE STORK The tail feathers are white. The flight feathers are black, glossed green or purple; the outer webs of the secondaries and the inner primaries are frosted grey. The outer webs of P6–P10 and the inner webs of P7–P11 are emarginated.

	J	F	M	A	M	J	J	A	S	O	N	D
Primaries 12 feathers	70	350	399	441	442	439	419	360	315	294	280	258	M
Secondaries 22 feathers	250	250	250	240	240	M						
Tail 12 feathers	177	190	210	230	243	250	M					

COMMON CRANE The tail feathers are grey, with a dark slate or black tinge on the tips of the central feathers and slate tips to the inner webs of the outer feathers. The primaries are black with grey bases. The secondaries are black with grey bases to the inner webs.

	J	F	M	A	M	J	J	A	S	O	N	D
Adult moult	J	F	M	A	M	J	J	A	S	O	N	D
Primaries 11 feathers	46	384	412	420	428	426	405	317	295	290	286	M
Secondaries	280	280	280	270	260	250	M					
Tail 12 feathers	201	204	205	212	215	216	M					

DEMOISELLE CRANE Tail feathers pale with dark slate tips. Primaries and alula black. Inner webs of primaries basally grey. Secondaries black, showing increasing amount of grey on inner webs towards tertials.

	J	F	M	A	M	J	J	A	S	O	N	D
Adult moult	J	F	M	A	M	J	J	A	S	O	N	D

GREAT BUSTARD The tail feathers are white with a subterminal black bar, on most black broadly bordered by cinnamon at base, paler on the inner web; the central feathers are deep cinnamon with a broad subterminal black bar and some narrower barring, often broken, towards the base. The primaries are black or dark sepia, the shafts pale horn and the inner webs becoming paler towards the bases; the outer webs are white at the base; the primaries are white on under surface, with broad dark sepia margins. The secondaries are black or dark sepia, with the basal half white and with black tips. The tertials are white with a black margin at the tip; the innermost have broad black and deep cinnamon bars. The outer webs of P5–P9 and the inner webs of P6–P10 are emarginated.

	J	F	M	A	M	J	J	A	S	O	N	D
Adult moult	J	F	M	A	M	J	J	A	S	O	N	D
Primaries 10 feathers	533	582	581	585	565	546	450	410	385	380	M	
Secondaries	395	395	395	400	M							
Tail 20 feathers	217	220	240	247	251	251	256	259	259	260	M	

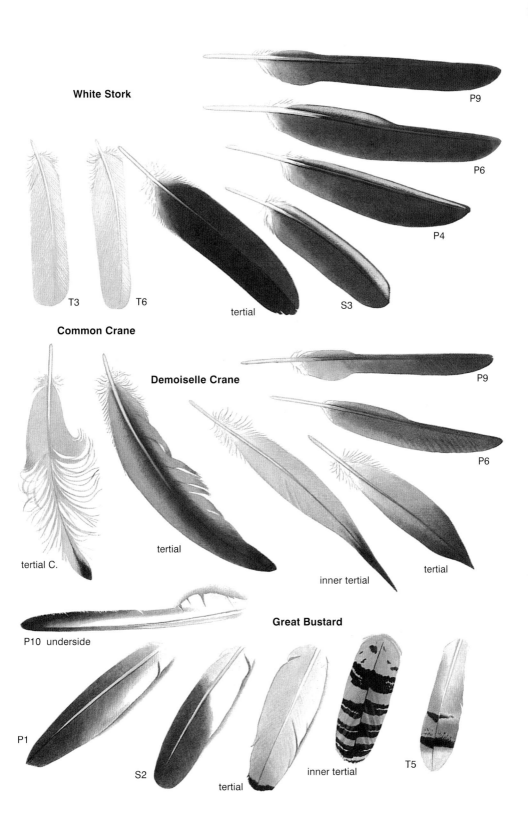

White Stork

T3

T6

tertial

S3

P9

P6

P4

Common Crane

tertial C.

tertial

Demoiselle Crane

P9

P6

inner tertial

tertial

P10 underside

Great Bustard

P1

S2

tertial

inner tertial

T5

IX

BLACK VULTURE The tail feathers are sooty-black. The flight feathers are sooty-black with brown outer edges. The outer webs of P4–P9 and the inner webs of P5–P10 are emarginated.

Primaries 10 feathers	370	411	418	419	413	396	350	319	300	285	M
Secondaries	280	280	280	275	270	M
Tail 12 feathers	221	225	233	242	243	250	M

WHITE-TAILED EAGLE The tail feathers are white, mottled dark brown at the bases. The flight feathers are dark brown, paler proximally and with shafts almost pure white; the tips of the primaries are black-brown, darker than the tips of the secondaries.

Adult moult	J	F	M	A	M	J	J	A	S	O	N	D
Primaries 11 feathers	76	381	480	573	580	590	562	533	480	445	430	M
Secondaries	430	430	425	420	420	M
Tail 12 feathers	280	286	300	308	330	330	M

GOLDEN EAGLE The tail feathers have broad black-brown tips, the proximal area is paler and greyer with irregular black-brown marks, and the base pale grey to pale brown; the central feathers can be uniform grey-brown, tipped black-brown; the shafts are black with white bases. The primaries are blackish-brown; the inner webs are paler and with white mottling, the latter more profuse on the inner feathers. The secondaries have dark brown tips; grey-brown proximal area mottled brown and with white base to the inner web. The outer webs of P4–P9 and the inner webs of P5–P10 are emarginated.

Adult moult	J	F	M	A	M	J	J	A	S	O	N	D
Juvenile moult	J	F	M	A	M	J	J	A	S	O	N	D
Primaries 11 feathers	65	405	552	589	593	597	583	502	453	420	400	M
Secondaries 17 feathers	380	380	375	370	370	M
Tail 12 feathers	330	346	361	364	365	370	M

GRIFFON VULTURE The tail feathers are black. The flight feathers are black, with the outer webs of the secondaries tinged bronze-brown. The tertials are black, tinged bronze-brown and tipped silver-grey. The outer webs of P4–P9 and the inner webs of P4–P10 are emarginated.

Adult moult	J	F	M	A	M	J	J	A	S	O	N	D
Primaries 10 feathers	465	576	581	581	575	572	415	390	386	386	M
Secondaries	385	385	380	390	390	M
Tail 14 feathers	277	300	350	350	350	352	352	M

EGYPTIAN VULTURE The tail feathers are white. The primaries are black, with a pearl-gray bloom to the bases of outer webs. The secondaries are pale grey with the tips, inner webs and bases black; sides of the outer webs are washed white. The tertials are pale brownish-grey, tipped dull sepia and with a submarginal off-white tinge. The outer webs of P6–P9 and the inner webs of P7–P10 are emarginated.

Adult moult	J	F	M	A	M	J	J	A	S	O	N	D
Juvenile moult	J	F	M	A	M	J	J	A	S	O	N	D
Primaries 10 feathers	388	401	410	410	406	365	310	296	257	230	M
Tail 14 feathers	311	315	320	325	325	325	330	M

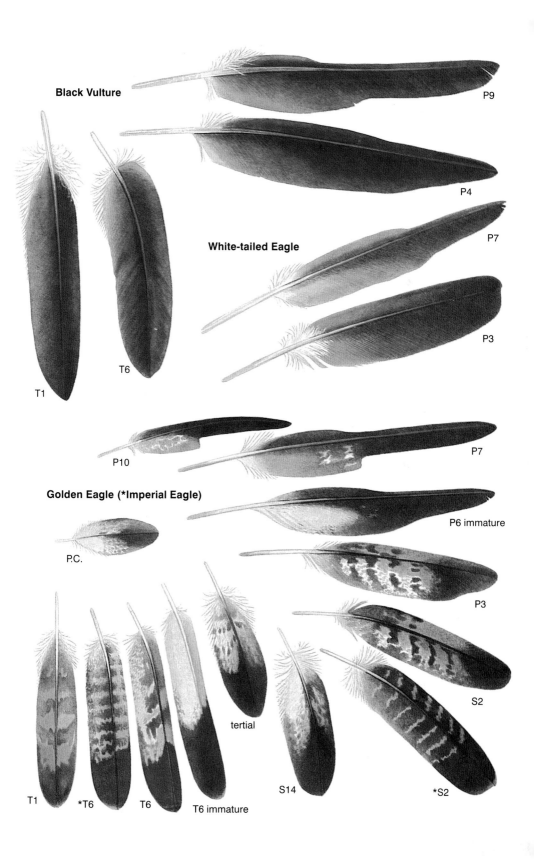

Black Vulture

P9

P4

T1

T6

White-tailed Eagle

P7

P3

P10

P7

Golden Eagle (*Imperial Eagle)

P6 immature

P.C.

P3

T1

*T6

T6

T6 immature

tertial

S14

S2

*S2

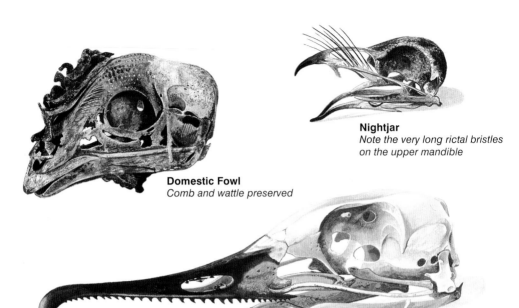

Domestic Fowl
Comb and wattle preserved

Nightjar
Note the very long rictal bristles on the upper mandible

Goosander
Note the 'saw teeth' of bill sheath

Swift
Sclerotic plate in orbit still in place

Barn Owl
Elongated skull unlike other owls

Green Woodpecker
Note tongue and hyoid apparatus

Skulls as found in the field, showing some well preserved anatomical and diagnostic features.

Chapter 9

SKULLS

The remains of bird skeletons are common, especially along the shoreline where storm-driven corpses have accumulated, in the remains of predators' meals or even below nest sites. Skulls are the most readily identifiable part of the skeleton and the following series of annotated skull drawings is designed to make identification of all the families, if not individual species, possible. Other vertebrate skulls may be confused with those of birds, but can be distinguished by distinct characteristics.

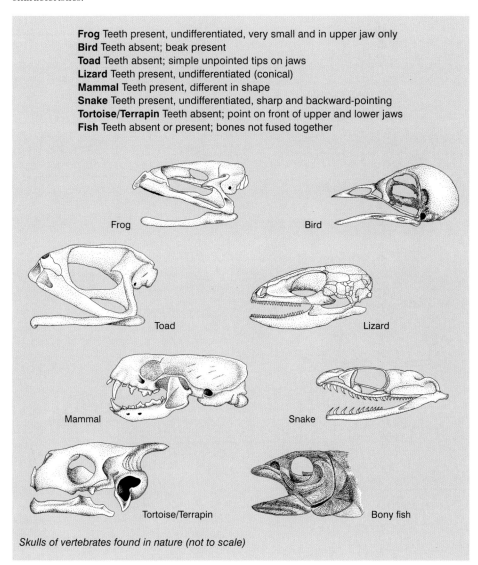

Frog Teeth present, undifferentiated, very small and in upper jaw only
Bird Teeth absent; beak present
Toad Teeth absent; simple unpointed tips on jaws
Lizard Teeth present, undifferentiated (conical)
Mammal Teeth present, different in shape
Snake Teeth present, undifferentiated, sharp and backward-pointing
Tortoise/Terrapin Teeth absent; point on front of upper and lower jaws
Fish Teeth absent or present; bones not fused together

Frog

Bird

Toad

Lizard

Mammal

Snake

Tortoise/Terrapin

Bony fish

Skulls of vertebrates found in nature (not to scale)

Bird Skulls

The diagrams of the Raven, gull and Long-eared Owl skulls illustrate the structures and technical terms used in their description. The skulls of different species vary greatly in shape, particularly in the form of the bill and its horny sheath, which may be considerably different from the underlying bony structure. These differences reflect the great variety in adaptation to diet and habitat.

In the field many skulls will be found incomplete, with the bill sheath and the pterygoid, quadrate, inter-orbital septum and lachrymal bones commonly damaged or missing. Frequently the cranium itself will be damaged, but, provided the general structure of the cranium and bill are intact, the basic features and adaptations remain obvious. One important diagnostic measurement is the ratio of bill length to cranium length. The ranges in this ratio, and the percentage of the overall skull length occupied by the bill, are given for each species illustrated and some of their close relatives. Examples of the three main categories of ratio are:

A. Bill greater than length of cranium
B. Bill approximately equal to length of cranium
C. Bill less than length of cranium

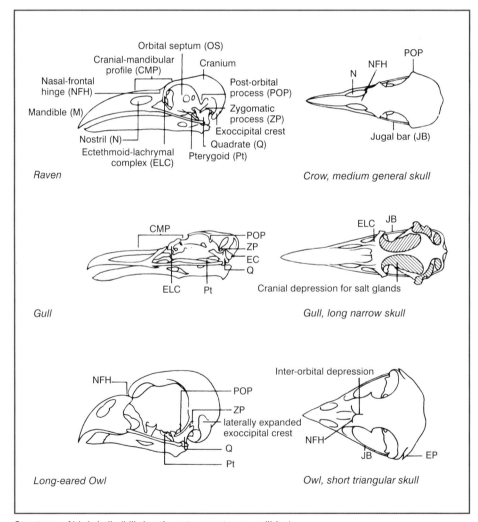

Structures of bird skulls (bill sheaths not present on mandibles)

There are many variations in this basic pattern, ranging from the pelicans, where the bill is four times the length of the cranium, to the tiny Scops Owl, where the bill is little more than one-third the length of the cranium. The skulls are grouped here according to form and function of the bill, and this displaces normal taxonomic relationships in terms of skull anatomy in many, although not all, cases. The grouping of skulls and the classification of the bill may seem arbitrary in some cases, particularly since some bills could be assigned to more than one category: the Magpie, for example, fits equally well into 'dagger-shaped' or 'general'. The layouts are, however, designed for ease of reference in a field situation and have been kept as simple as possible.

A large number of skulls are illustrated, but many closely related species have variations in size rather than form. Where this is so, a representative species is illustrated and described, and measurements of skulls, bills and the percentage ratio for closely related species are tabulated.

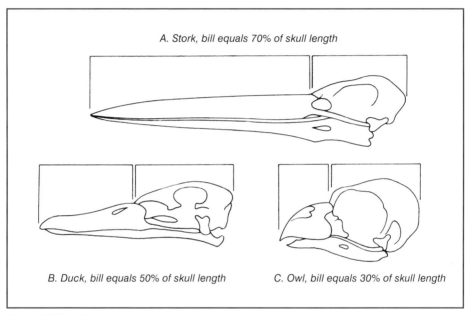

A. Stork, bill equals 70% of skull length

B. Duck, bill equals 50% of skull length

C. Owl, bill equals 30% of skull length

Ratio of bill length to cranium length

Measures and Illustrations

To aid identification, the details in the drawing, the tabulated size charts and the verbal description should be carefully examined. To compare a specimen in the hand, first locate which of the ten general groups it belongs to. Take the measurements from the bill tip to the back of the cranium to give the overall length; and the bill tip to the nasal-frontal hinge to give the bill length. In the case of a strongly curved bill the measurement should be linear, rather than following the curve, for purpose comparison with the measurements here. In all cases, the measurements refer to adult skulls; where there is a marked difference in skull size between male and female, a sufficiently large number of specimens have been measured to cover the range in all but exceptionally large or small specimens.

Tables of measurements show the following information:

Species examples	Range of overall length of skull (mm)	Range of bill length (mm)	Range of the bill length expressed as % of total skull length
Raven	119/109mm	69/64mm	58%
Grey Partridge	56/44mm	22/18mm	41/39%

Bill Shapes

A. General Bills (small) p.278
Smaller skulls, with bill length
equal to, or less than, length of
cranium but less robust than A.
Includes larks, wagtails, pipits,
wren, tits, warblers, flycatchers,
thrushes, chats, wheatears,
sandgrouse, starlings.

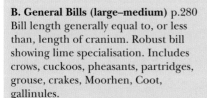

B. General Bills (large–medium) p.280
Bill length generally equal to, or less
than, length of cranium. Robust bill
showing lime specialisation. Includes
crows, cuckoos, pheasants, partridges,
grouse, crakes, Moorhen, Coot,
gallinules.

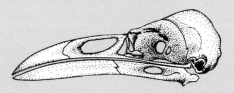

C. Slender Bills (long) p.284
Bills generally at least twice
length of cranium. Bill very
slender. Includes sandpipers,
shanks, godwits, Woodcock,
Oystercatcher, Snipe, Bee-eater,
Hoopoe, Glossy Ibis, Curlew,
Whimbrel.

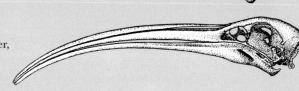

D. Slender Bills (medium–small) p.286
Bill length equal to, or slightly
greater than, cranium. Bill very
slender. Includes rails, plovers,
sandpipers (part), phalaropes,
pigeons, doves, mergansers,
Shag, Cormorant, Chough.

E. Seed-eaters p.290
Small rounded skulls, less than
40mm long. Bill length less than
cranium. Three types:
(i) Finches, characterised by a
heavy conical bill. (ii) Buntings,
characterised by generally less
robust bill with an acute angle
in the upper mandible. Also
includes sparrows.
(iii) Other, including quails,
waxbills and some larks.

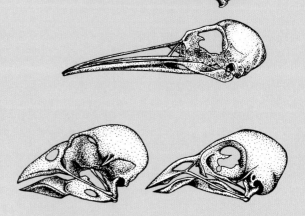

F. Duck Bills p.291
Bill length equal to, or slightly less than, cranium. Bill flattened and laterally extended. Includes ducks, geese, swans.

G. Spear- or Dagger-shaped Bills p.300
Bill length generally greater than cranium. Bill robust and tapering. Includes herons, bitterns, egrets, Kingfisher, woodpeckers, terns, storks, cranes, divers, grebes, Gannet, guillemots.

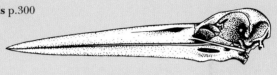

H. Highly Modified Bills p.306
Wide range of bill shapes, highly adapted for feeding purposes. Includes, for example, crossbills, Puffin, Spoonbill, flamingoes, pelicans, auks, martins, swallows, swifts, nightjars, parrots, shearwaters and petrels.

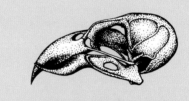

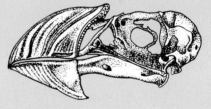

I. Hooked Bills (short) p.310
Bill distinctly hooked, but generally less than the length of the cranium. Includes owls, hawks, falcons, harriers, kites, buzzards, Osprey, Honey Buzzard, some eagles.

J. Hooked Bills (long) p.314
Bill distinctly hooked, and greater than or equal to length of cranium. Includes vultures, some eagles, gulls, skuas, Capercaillie.

A. General Bills (small)

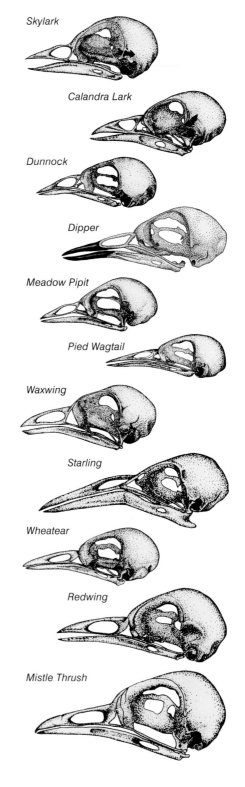

Skylark

Calandra Lark

Dunnock

Dipper

Meadow Pipit

Pied Wagtail

Waxwing

Starling

Wheatear

Redwing

Mistle Thrush

Larks

Bills markedly less than length of cranium. Large orbits with post-orbital and zygomatic processes fused.

Skylark	37/35mm:17/15mm	46/43%
Calandra Lark	38/35mm:18/15mm	47/43%

Calandra Lark Post-orbital/zygomatic process is complicated and bifurcated, with a large foremen.

Skylark Post-orbital/zygomatic process simple, with large foremen.

Dunnock 34/30mm:16/13mm 47/43%
Curved and angular bill markedly less than length of cranium. Marked angle between upper mandible and jugal bar. CMP straight, with a step. Cranium rounded and smooth.

Pipits and Wagtails

Meadow Pipit	34/31mm:15/13mm	44/42%
Pied Wagtail	36/32mm:17/14mm	47/44%

Meadow Pipit Bill markedly shorter than cranium. Very long nostril in slender mandible. CMP straight, with a slight indentation. Upper mandible slightly convex above nostril.

Pied Wagtail Long slender skull, with bill slightly shorter than cranium. Bill narrow, fine and pointed, with a marked nasal-frontal hinge. Cranium almost egg-shaped.

Waxwing 38/36mm:18/15mm 48/42%
Bill slightly shorter than cranium. Bill curved, orbit very large with prominent orbital ridge. Cranium rounded, and CMP slightly notched.

Starling 56/49mm:31/24mm 55/49%
Bill equal to or slightly longer than cranium. Bill tapers gradually, hut is pointed at the tip. Acute inflection in both upper and lower mandibles. Orbit deep. Back of skull angular, and CMP concave.

Robins, Chats & Blue Rock Thrush

Bill slightly less than length of cranium. Bill slender, with slightly angled lower mandible. Long nostril. Rounded cranium.

Redstart	33/30mm:14/13mm	42/43%
Stonechat	33/30mm:14/12mm	42/40%
Whinchat	33/32mm:14/13mm	42/41%
Wheatear	39/36mm:19/16mm	49/44%
Blue Rock Thrush	51/51mm:27/26mm	53/51%

Wheatear Bill slightly shorter than cranium. Elliptical cranium, which is rounded. Bill slender and slightly angled. CMP deeply and convexly stepped.

Robin   34/32mm:15/13mm   44/41%
Slender bill, much shorter than cranium. Very large nostril. CMP convex and stepped. Lower mandible very narrow. Cranium surface smooth, but back is angular.

Typical Thrushes

Unspecialised bills ranging from equal to down to considerably less than length of cranium. CMP with step, and bill curving towards tip. Cranium relatively deep, with the back slightly angular.

Redwing	47/45mm:23/21mm	49/47%
Song Thrush	48/45mm:23/21mm	48/47%
Fieldfare	51/50mm:24/21mm	47/42%
Blackbird	52/47mm:27/23mm	52/49%
Mistle Thrush	54/49mm:25/22mm	46/45%

Wren   32/29mm:16/13mm   50/45%
Very slender bill equal to or slightly less than cranium in length. Upper and lower mandibles angled. Orbit large. Cranium oval in outline and smooth.

Red-backed Shrike   38/33mm:18/15mm   47/45%
Deep bill only slightly shorter than cranium. Bill rounded, deeply convex towards pointed tip. If sheath present on upper mandible, there is a depression followed by a prominent process. The lower mandible is pointed, and the orbital ridge is large.

Wryneck   34mm:12mm 35% (one only)
The bill is little more than half the length of the cranium. The lower mandible is very slender and the nostril is more than half bill length. Orbit half the cranium length. Cranium elliptical and smooth. In this specimen the hyoid apparatus and elongated tongue attached to the top of the skull have been preserved; this structure is also seen in other woodpeckers.

Tits

Blue Tit	25/24mm:10/9mm	40/37%
Bearded Tit	27/24mm:13/9mm	48/37%
Great Tit	32/28mm:13/10mm	40/36%

Blue Tit The slender, conical bill is much shorter than the cranium. The bill tip forms a straight line with the top of the orbit and the nasal-frontal hinge is marked. Cranium smooth and rounded. Orbit small.

Warblers

Bill markedly shorter than cranium. Mandibles narrow and finely pointed, with nostrils approximately half the length of the upper mandible. Acute concave angle at nasal-frontal hinge.

Goldcrest	25/24mm:12/11mm	48/46%
Willow Warbler	28/27mm:13/12mm	46/44%

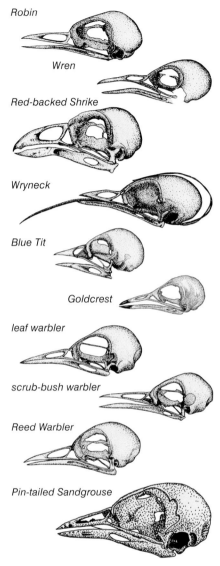

Robin

Wren

Red-backed Shrike

Wryneck

Blue Tit

Goldcrest

leaf warbler

scrub-bush warbler

Reed Warbler

Pin-tailed Sandgrouse

Melodious Warbler	30mm:14mm 47% (one only)	
Whitethroat	31/28mm:14/12mm	45/43%
Grasshopper Warbler	31/30mm:14/14mm	47/45%
Reed Warbler	33/31mm:17/15mm	51/48%

Flycatchers

Spotted Flycatcher	34/32mm:17/15mm	50/47%
Pied Flycatcher	30/28mm:13/11mm	43/39%
Collared Flycatcher	29/28mm:12/11mm	41/39%

Sandgrouse and Buttonquails

Pin-tailed Sandgrouse	44/42mm:21/20mm	50/48%
Black-bellied Sandgrouse	48/42mm:23/20mm	48/48%
Small Buttonquail	36mm:16mm	44%

B. General Bills (medium)

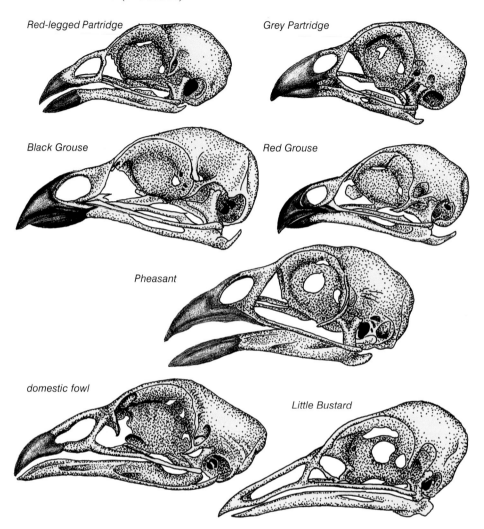

Red-legged Partridge

Grey Partridge

Black Grouse

Red Grouse

Pheasant

domestic fowl

Little Bustard

Gamebirds

Quail	36/34mm:15/14mm	42%
Hazel Hen	50/49mm:23/21mm	46/43%
Willow/Red Grouse	54/49mm:24/21mm	44/43%
Red-legged Partridge	55/48mm:28/20mm	51/42%
Grey Partridge	56/44mm:22/18mm	41/39%
Rock Partridge	58/51mm:26/21mm	43/41%
Pheasant	76/59mm:49/30mm	64/51%

Red-legged Partridge Bill less than or equal to length of cranium, which is rounded at the back with a prominent orbital ridge. The lower surface of the upper mandible and the whole of the lower mandible are angular.

Grey Partridge Bill much shorter than cranium. Upper mandible distinctly curved, lower mandible slender. Orbit large. Cranium undulating, but not angular.

Pheasant Bill varies from approximately equal to well over length of cranium. Upper mandible convex, with a depression just in front of the nostrils. Bill pointed. Orbit large, surface of cranium undulating.

Domestic fowl Bill markedly less than length of cranium (no measurements given as there is great variation with breed). Large orbit, without prominent ridge. The elongated cranium is concave behind the orbit.

Little Bustard   68/65mm:37/30mm   58/46%

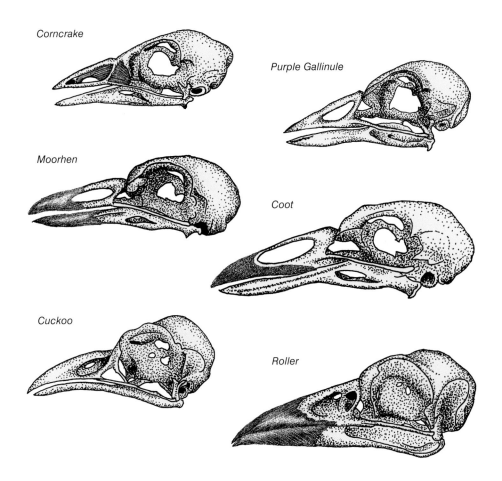

Corncrake

Purple Gallinule

Moorhen

Coot

Cuckoo

Roller

Rails

Little Crake	44mm:21mm	48% (one only)
Corncrake	50/50mm:23/21mm	46/42%
Purple Gallinule	56/47mm:27/21mm	48/46%
American Purple		
Gallinule	57mm:28mm	49% (one only)
Moorhen	60/58mm:29/27mm	48/46%
Coot	75/72mm:40/36mm	53/50%

Corncrake Bill markedly shorter than cranium. Bill sharply pointed from the base. CMP with a slight notch. Nasal-frontal hinge obvious. Back of cranium smooth but angular.

Purple Gallinule Bill less than cranium length. Bill is pointed and tapers distinctly from the base. Nasal-frontal hinge prominent. Cranium rounded and smooth.

Moorhen Bill less than cranium length. Bill less tapered than in the Coot.

Coot Bill slightly longer than cranium. Bill tapering, with elongated nostril. Large orbit, but without ridging. Nasal-frontal hinge distinct.

Roller   69/66mm:43/41mm 62%
Bill longer than cranium. Both upper and lower mandibles are heavy, and the bill tapers gently to a slight, curved point. The orbit has a prominent ridge, and there is a depression in the cranium between the extended post-orbital process and exoccipital crest.

Cuckoo	54/48mm:28/23mm	52/48%
Great Spotted Cuckoo	60/55mm:31/29mm	53/52%

Cuckoo Bill approximately equal to cranium length. Bill very broad at base, tapering to a point. Lower mandible narrow, with a laterally displaced process half way along length. Cranium angular, with a prominent orbital ridge, large orbit and small inter-orbital depression.

(medium/large)

Jay

Magpie

Rook

Carrion Crow

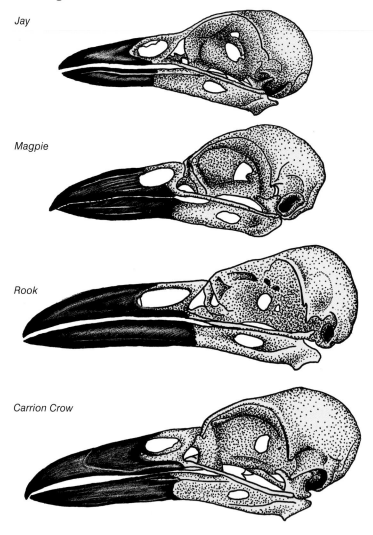

Crow family

Cranium generally smooth and rounded

Siberian Jay	55/51mm:28/23mm	51/54%
Alpine Chough	67/59mm:36/28mm	54/47%
Jay	69/61mm:37/31mm	53/51%
Jackdaw	69/62mm:37/29mm	52/47%
Magpie	75/65mm:42/34mm	63/56%
Carrion Crow/Rook	92/81mm:58/45mm	63/55%
Raven	119/109mm:69/64mm	58%

Jay Bill approximately equal to cranium length. Bill robust and less curved than in Magpie, but more pointed. Cranium smooth and rounded. CMP convex and slightly depressed.

Magpie Bill longer than cranium. Top and bottom of bill parallel at base, but distinctly hooked at tip. Although the cranium is smoothed, it is also rather undulating. CMP is convex, with a marked nasal-frontal hinge.

Rook Bill longer than cranium, which is flattened and rather angular. Bill deep, heavy and laterally compressed. Bill markedly pointed. CMP stepped.

Carrion Crow Bill longer than rounded cranium. Bill rather blunt towards tip. CMP stepped.

Raven Massive heavy bill, well over the length of the cranium. Bill laterally flattened, strongly convex at tip. Orbit prominent. CMP stepped.

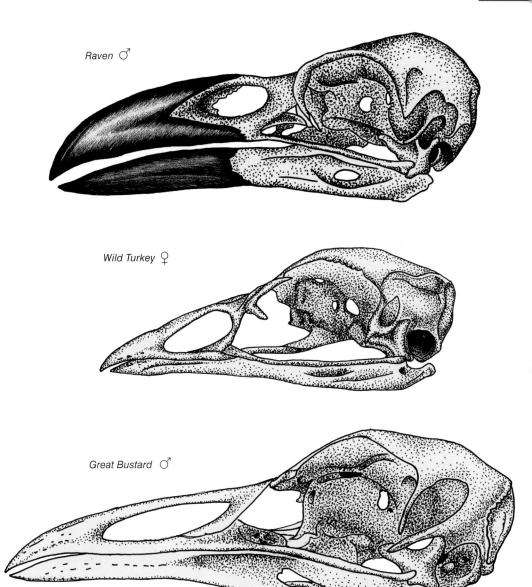

Raven ♂

Wild Turkey ♀

Great Bustard ♂

Wild Turkey				
Wild Turkey	♂	111/102mm:69/59mm	62/58%	
	♀	98/93mm:53/50mm	54%	

Great Bustard		
Great Bustard	Ad. 138/118mm:70/84mm	61/60%
	Juv. 108:66mm	one only 61%

Bill longer than cranium. Male considerably larger than female. Postorbital and zygomatic processes fused forming a hole. Nostril large, over half of bill length.

Bill longer than cranium. Male much larger than female. Zygomatic process long and slender. Bill tapers gently and nostril with bill sheath absent, long and narrow.

C. Slender Bills (long)

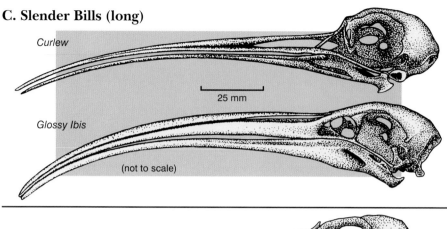

Curlew

Glossy Ibis

25 mm

(not to scale)

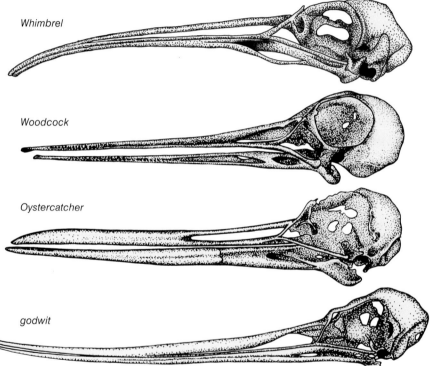

Whimbrel

Woodcock

Oystercatcher

godwit

Curlews and other large waders

| Curlew | 210/149mm:175/115mm | 83/77% |
| Whimbrel | 125/110mm:90/78mm | 72/71% |

Curlew Very slender, downcurving bill more than three times the length of the cranium. CMP stepped.

Glossy Ibis 163/145mm:130/110mm 80/76%
Robust, downcurved bill more than three times the length of the cranium. CMP slightly concave.

Woodcock 110/105mm:80/77mm 73%
Very slender, tapering bill almost three times

the length of the cranium. There are tubercules on the bill. The orbit is completely enclosed and the quadrate is positioned below the anterior area of the orbit.

Oystercatcher 112/96mm:75/64mm 67%
Robust bill over twice length of cranium. Bill tapers gradually towards tip, the tapering most marked in the upper mandible.

Bar-tailed Godwit 136/120mm:105/90mm 77/75%
Slightly upturned, slender bill about three times length of cranium.

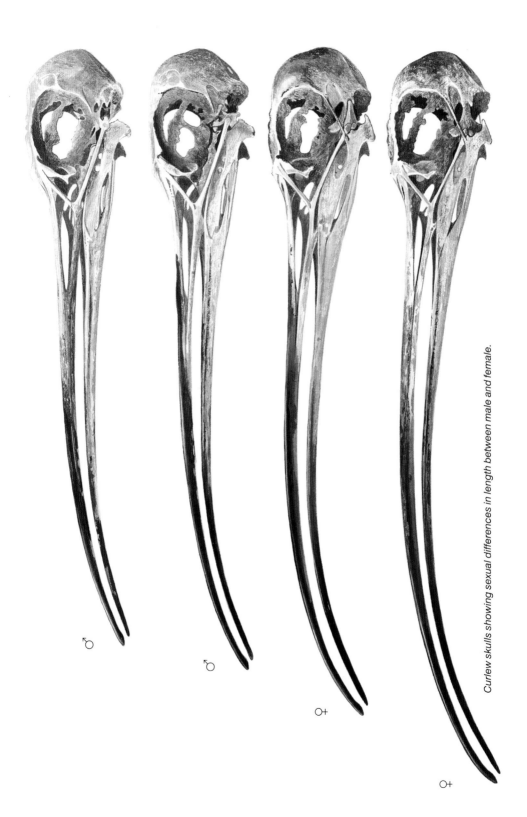

♂

♂

♀

♀

Curlew skulls showing sexual differences in length between male and female.

Snipe	95/94mm:76/72mm	80/76%
Avocet	105/94mm:83/72mm	79/76%

Long, slender, upturned bill about three times length of cranium.

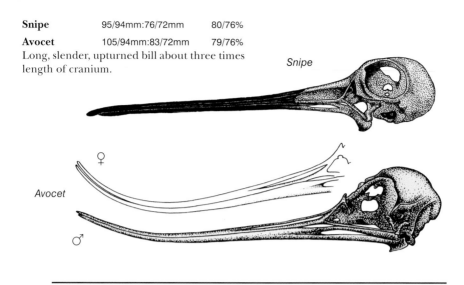

Snipe

Avocet ♀ ♂

D. Slender Bills (medium)

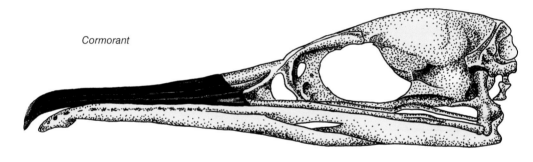

Cormorant

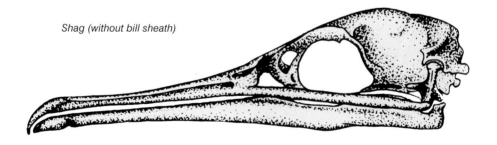

Shag (without bill sheath)

Shags and Cormorants

Cormorant	154/131mm:85/71mm	55/54%
Shag	127/118mm:73/67mm	57%

Shag Robust bill, longer than cranium. Upper mandible slightly concave and hooked at tip. Lower mandible flat. CMP smoothly concave. Occipital-sagittal crest prominent, jugal bar very strong.

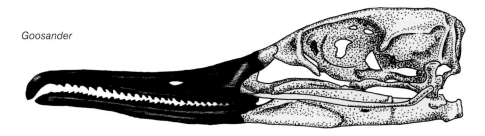

Goosander

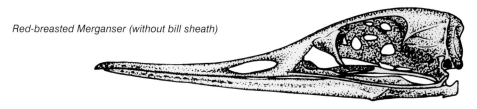

Red-breasted Merganser (without bill sheath)

Large Sawbills

Goosander	121/118mm:71/67mm	59/57%
Red-breasted Merganser	112/100mm:67/57mm	60/57%

Red-breasted Merganser Slender concave bill markedly longer than cranium. If the bill sheath is present, it may be saw-toothed. CMP is a smooth transition from convex to concave.

Slender Bills (small)

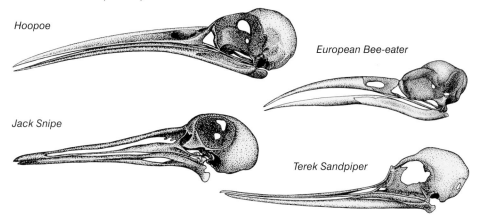

Hoopoe

European Bee-eater

Jack Snipe

Terek Sandpiper

Hoopoe   88/70mm:65/45mm   74/64%
Slender, downcurved bill at least twice length of cranium. Orbit large, with a prominent orbital ridge. Marked inter-orbital depression. CMP concave. In dorsal view, the skull has a 'tear-drop' outline.

European Bee-eater 56/46mm:34/29mm 63/61%
Slender, downturned bill about twice length of cranium. Prominent orbital ridge with inter-orbital depression. CMP deeply notched. Deep depressions in cranium behind post-orbital process. In dorsal view, skull has 'tear-drop' outline.

Terek Sandpiper	77/68mm:53/45mm	69/66%
Curlew Sandpiper	62/59mm:44/40mm	71/68%

Terek Sandpiper Slightly upturned bill more than twice the length of the cranium. CMP deeply concave.

Jack Snipe   68/66mm:49/46mm   72/69%
Slender bill, broad at base, more than twice length of cranium. CMP concave. Cranium rounded and smooth. Orbit completely encircled, with quadrate below central portion.

Treecreeper	32/26mm:19/12mm	59/46%
Wallcreeper	45/41mm:24/21mm	53/51%

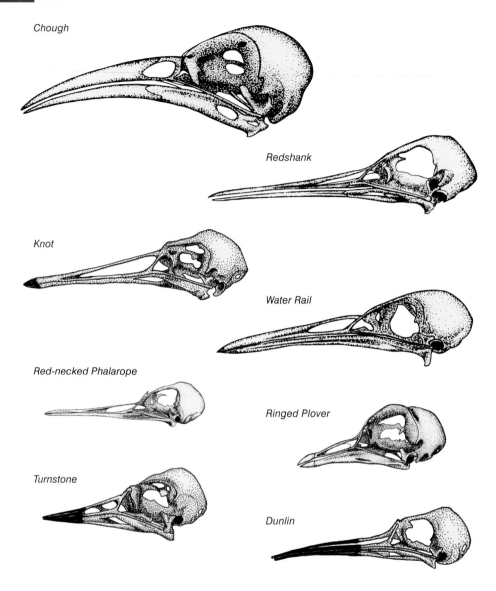

Chough

Redshank

Knot

Water Rail

Red-necked Phalarope

Ringed Plover

Turnstone

Dunlin

Chough   89/73mm:55/41mm   62/56%
Bill robust and distinctly downward-curved and pointed. The bill is longer than the cranium.

Redshank   76/73mm:51/47mm   67/74%
Pointed, elongated bill much longer than the cranium. Bill tapers rapidly. CMP slightly concave.

Knot   64/61mm:41/39mm   64/61%
The bill has a shallow downward curve and is almost twice the length of the cranium. CMP stepped. Marked angular orbital ridge.

Water Rail   72/67mm:44/40mm   58/55%
Distinctly pointed bill, with slight downward curvature and marginally longer than cranium. Cranium smooth, but CMP notched. Nasal-frontal hinge distinct. Back of lower mandible with distinct downward-projecting process.

Other Waders

Ringed Plover	43/41mm:21/20mm	49%
Red-necked Phalarope	46/42mm:29/26mm	63/62%
Turnstone	48/45mm:26/24mm	54/53%
Dotterel	50/47mm:24/23mm	49/48%

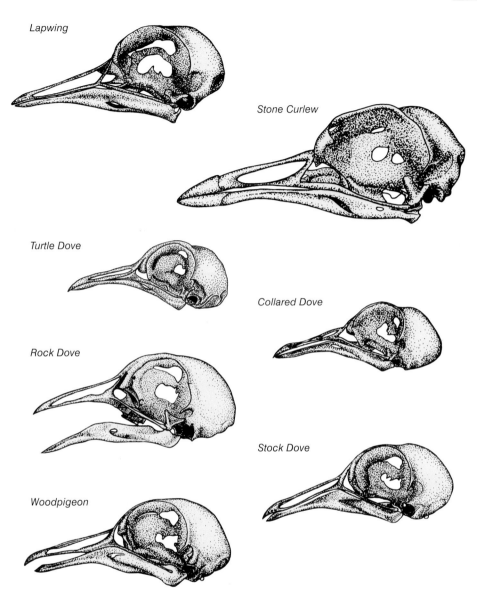

Lapwing

Stone Curlew

Turtle Dove

Collared Dove

Rock Dove

Stock Dove

Woodpigeon

Common Sandpiper	51/48mm:32/30mm	63/62%
Golden Plover	61/54mm:31/27mm	51/50%
Lapwing	61/59mm:34/31mm	56/52%
Stone Curlew	84/78mm:43/38mm	51/49%

Lapwing Bill slightly longer than skull. The orbit is very prominent, as is the orbital ridge. There is a deep inter-orbital depression in dorsal view.

Stone Curlew The bill is approximately the same length as the cranium. Orbit is enormous, with a deep inter-orbital depression. The expanded orbit gives the CMP a deep-stepped appearance.

Pigeons and Doves

In all species the bill is markedly shorter than the cranium. The angle between the upper mandible and jugal bar is acute. The cranium is smooth, and the orbit is prominent. The orbital ridge is particularly pronounced in the genus *Streptopelia* (Turtle and Collared Doves).

Turtle Dove	46/43mm:21/18mm	46/42%
Collared Dove	49/46mm:23/22mm	48/47%
Stock Dove	54/51mm:25/22mm	46/43%
Woodpigeon	60/55mm:28/26mm	47%

E. Seed-eaters

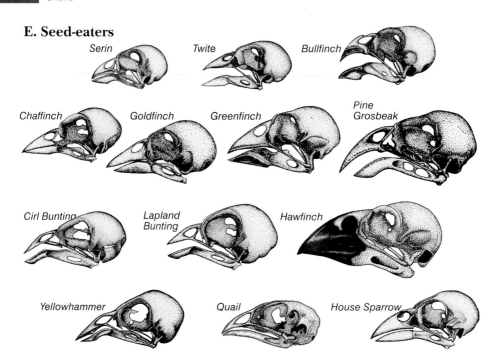

Serin · Twite · Bullfinch · Chaffinch · Goldfinch · Greenfinch · Pine Grosbeak · Cirl Bunting · Lapland Bunting · Hawfinch · Yellowhammer · Quail · House Sparrow

Finches

Citril Finch	23/21mm: 6/5mm	27/25%
Redpoll	25/23mm: 13/11mm	51/46%
Siskin	27/23mm: 15/13mm	56/51%
Linnet	28/24mm:14/9mm	51/39%
Bullfinch	28/27mm:12/11mm	43/41%
Snow Finch	35/32mm: 27/25mm	27/25%
Brambling	38/28mm: 16/14mm	50/49%
Pine Grosbeak	39/38mm:20/18mm	51/47%

Goldfinch   30/28mm:16/14mm   53/50%
Delicate, conical bill, approximately same length as cranium. CMP almost straight.

Greenfinch   32/31mm:16/14mm   50/45%
The robust bill, which is deep at the base, is slightly shorter than the cranium. The orbit is prominent, and the CMP is slightly concave.

Serin   22/21mm:917mm   41/33%
Bill often only slightly over half cranium length. Lower mandible has an acute angle. Orbit prominent, but does not project above lie of cranium. CMP is convex, nasal-frontal hinge marked.

Twite   25mm:10mm   40% (one only)
Bill curved and markedly shorter than the cranium. Acute angle between the jugal bar and upper mandible. CMP straight, but with a distinct notch.

Chaffinch   30/26mm:14/12mm   47/46%
Bill shorter then cranium. Bill broad and peg-like curving gently. Orbit prominent, with marked shallow inter-orbital depression. Cranium smooth.

Buntings

Bill generally markedly shorter than cranium. There is a distinct inflection and acute angle in both upper and lower mandibles. There is also an acute angle between the upper mandible and jugal bar. Cranium generally rounded

Rock Bunting	27/26mm:9/7mm	34/30%
Cirl Bunting	29/28mm:11mm	39/37%
Reed Bunting	29/28mm: 12/11mm	41/39%
Ortolan Bunting	30/28mm:13/10mm	43/36%
Yellowhammer	31/28mm:14/10mm	45/36%
Snow Bunting	32/27mm: 15/11mm	47/40%
Corn Bunting	32/30mm: 19/11mm	59/37%

Lapland Bunting 30/29mm:14/12mm   45/44%
Bill barely half the length of cranium. The bill is angular, as with the other buntings, and there is a prominent ridge in the lower mandible.

Sparrows

Tree Sparrow	30/28mm:14/10mm	47/38%
House Sparrow	31/29mm:15/14mm	48%
Rock Sparrow	32mm:15mm	46%(one only)

House Sparrow Non-angular bill slightly shorter than cranium. Gives the impression of a more elongated skull than other finch-like birds. The lower mandible is straight, while the upper mandible is convex like the cranium. Nasal-frontal hinge obvious.

F. Duck Bills

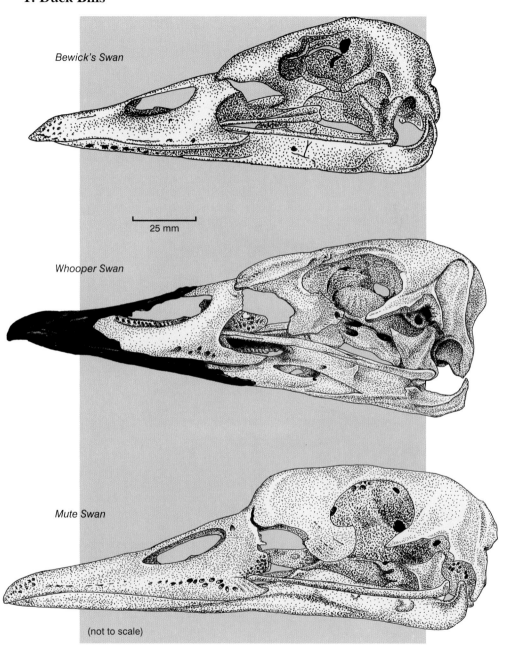

Bewick's Swan

25 mm

Whooper Swan

Mute Swan

(not to scale)

Swans

Bill equal to cranium in length. Heavy wedge-shaped skull in profile. Orbit small, lachrymal bones robust. CMP slightly stepped. In male Mute Swan there is an inflation of the lachrymal bones immediately behind upper mandible.

Bewick's Swan	160/149mm:78/74mm	49%
Whooper Swan	186/161mm:92/83mm	51/49%
Mute Swan	192/167mm:97/86mm	51/50%

Egyptian Goose 135/104mm:70/52mm   52/50%
Bill approximately same length as cranium. Bill
slightly concave towards tip, with a heavy lower
mandible. CMP convex.

Egyptian Goose

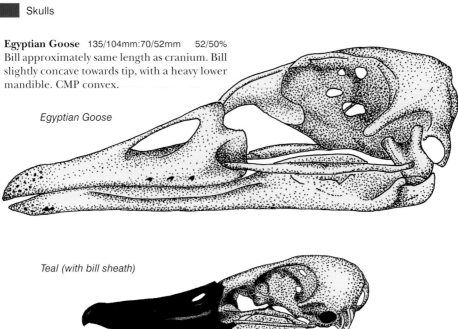

Teal (with bill sheath)

Garganey (with bill sheath)

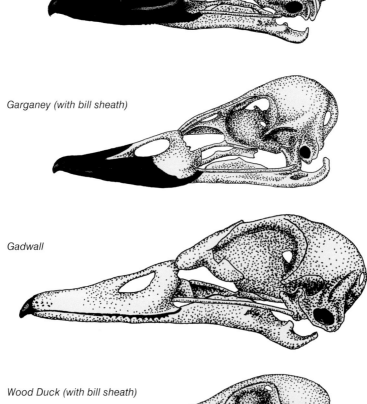

Gadwall

Wood Duck (with bill sheath)

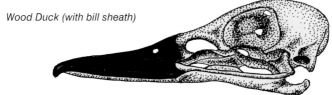

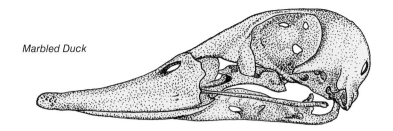

Marbled Duck

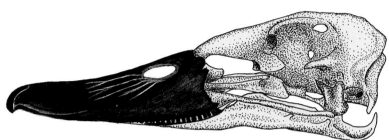

Mallard (with bill sheath)

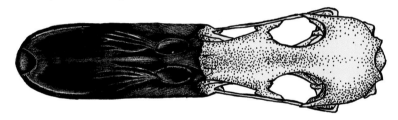

Shoveler (with bill sheath)

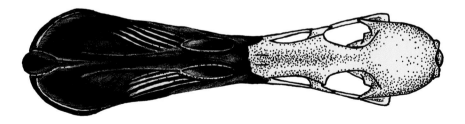

Mainly surface-feeding ducks

The bill ranges from just under to markedly over cranium length. Skull shallow, lachrymals robust. CMP slightly concave.

Garganey	82/75mm:40/35mm	49/47%
Wigeon	87/80mm:42/37mm	48/46%
Gadwall	98/91mm:51/45mm	52/49%
Pintail	106mm:56mm	53% (one only)
Mallard	112/105mm:62/50mm	55/48%
Teal	79/76mm:41/38mm	52/50%
Shoveler	118/110mm:72/62mm	61/56%

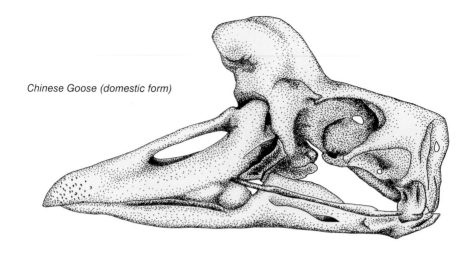

Chinese Goose (domestic form)

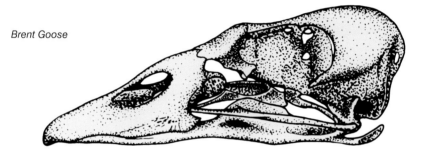

Brent Goose

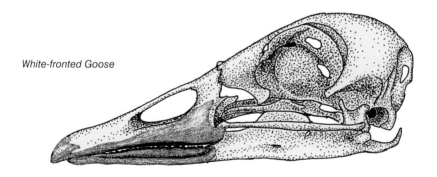

White-fronted Goose

Geese

Barnacle Goose	86/78mm:39/34mm	45/43%
Brent Goose	101mm:47mm (one only)	47%
White-fronted Goose	109/94mm:56/45mm	51/48%
Chinese Goose	112mm:59mm (one only)	52%
Bean Goose	125/100mm:68/48mm	54%
Greylag Goose	148/120mm:80/65mm	54%

Brent Goose Bill distinctly shorter than cranium (in *Anser* geese is equal to or slightly longer than cranium). Raised lachrymal-frontal area gives a double convex CMP. Upper mandible curves down at tip.

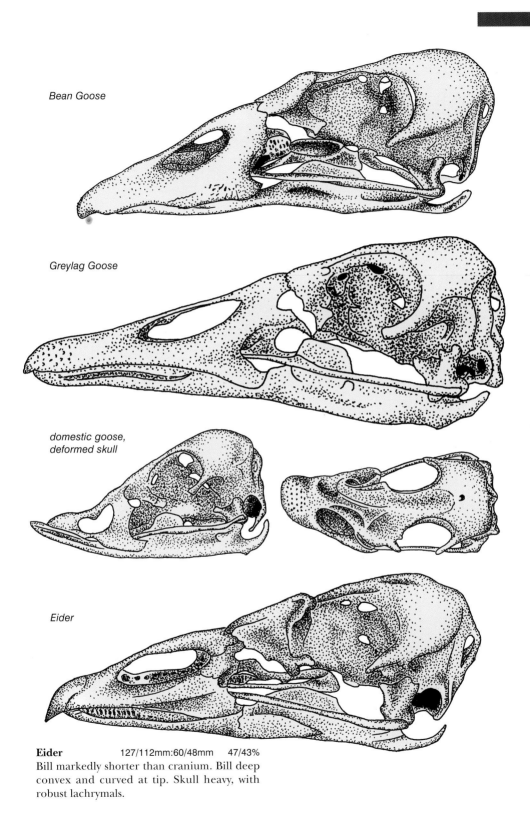

Bean Goose

Greylag Goose

*domestic goose,
deformed skull*

Eider

Eider   127/112mm:60/48mm   47/43%
Bill markedly shorter than cranium. Bill deep
convex and curved at tip. Skull heavy, with
robust lachrymals.

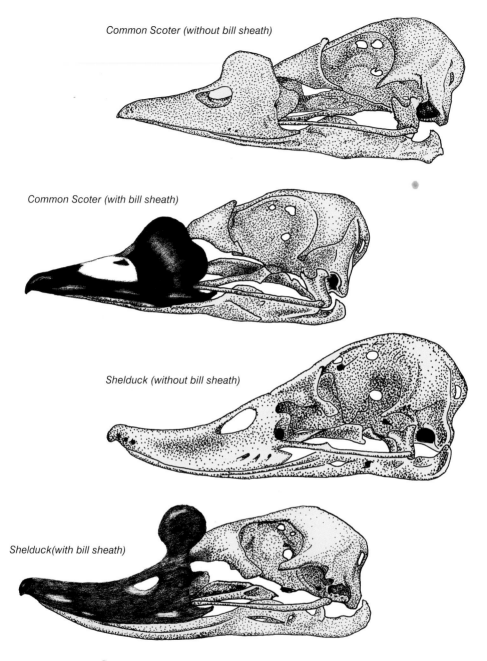

Common Scoter (without bill sheath)

Common Scoter (with bill sheath)

Shelduck (without bill sheath)

Shelduck(with bill sheath)

Scoters

Bill approximately equal to cranium. Bill very deep, with a rounded tip, and enlarged at the base of the upper mandible in the male. Cranium deep and lachrymals robust.

Common Scoter	97/91mm:47/44mm	48%
Velvet Scoter	111/103mm:58/51mm	52/49%

Shelduck 101/96mm:47/40mm 46/42%

Bill distinctly shorter than cranium. Whole bill upturned, upper mandible distinctly concave with a hooked tip.

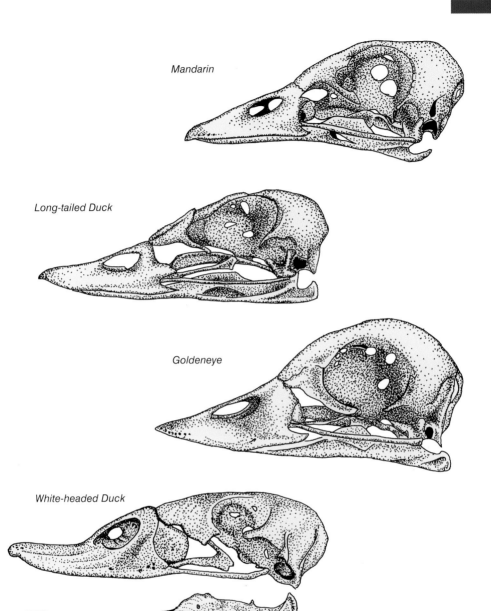

Mandarin

Long-tailed Duck

Goldeneye

White-headed Duck

Mandarin   77/75mm:35/31mm   45/41%
Bill much shorter than cranium. Cranium flat on top, curving at back, with a straight CMP from top of orbit to tip of beak.

Long-tailed Duck 81/73mm:34/33mm   45/42%
Bill markedly shorter than cranium. Concave depression towards the tip on the underside of the bill. Cranium deep, skull distinctly wedge-shaped in profile.

White-headed Duck 88mm:42mm (one only)   48%
Barrow's Goldeneye 89/82mm:39/35mm   44/42%
Goldeneye   90/76mm:38/32mm   42%

Goldeneye Bill markedly shorter than cranium. Bill deep at base, slightly concave and pointed. Skull deep relative to length.

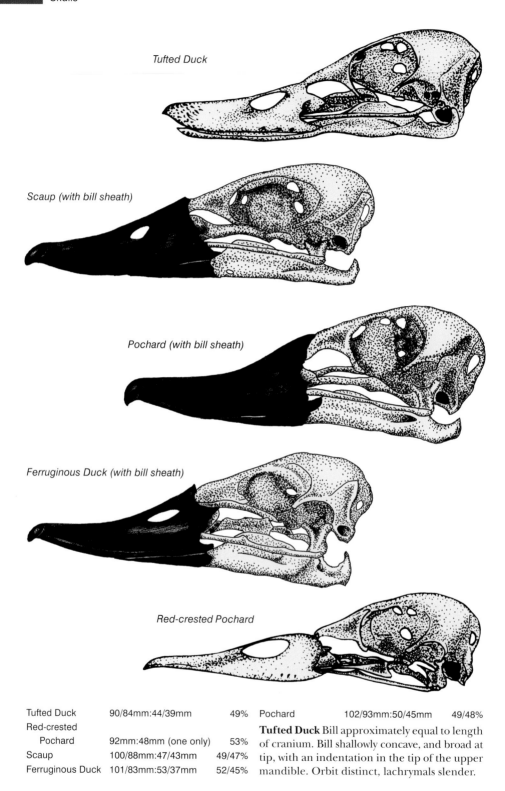

Tufted Duck

Scaup (with bill sheath)

Pochard (with bill sheath)

Ferruginous Duck (with bill sheath)

Red-crested Pochard

Tufted Duck	90/84mm:44/39mm	49%
Red-crested Pochard	92mm:48mm (one only)	53%
Scaup	100/88mm:47/43mm	49/47%
Ferruginous Duck	101/83mm:53/37mm	52/45%

Pochard 102/93mm:50/45mm 49/48%

Tufted Duck Bill approximately equal to length of cranium. Bill shallowly concave, and broad at tip, with an indentation in the tip of the upper mandible. Orbit distinct, lachrymals slender.

Mallard

 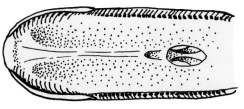

gently undulating ventral profile   parallel sided, ventral view

Shoveler

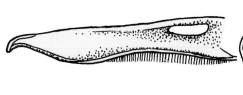 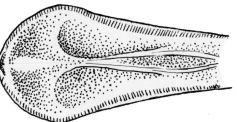

strongly undulating ventral profile   diverging fan-shaped, ventral view

Comparison between Mallard and Shoveler

Anser geese

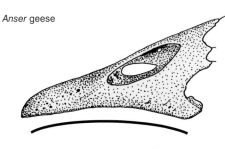 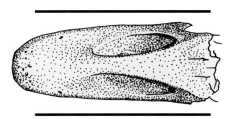

concave ventral profile   parallel sided

Branta geese

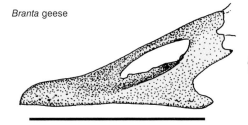 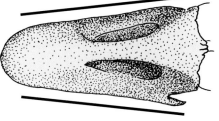

'straight' ventral profile   diverging

Comparison between Anser *and* Branta *Geese*

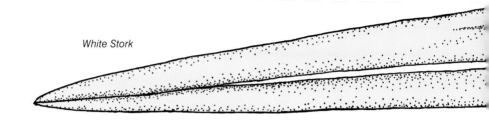

White Stork

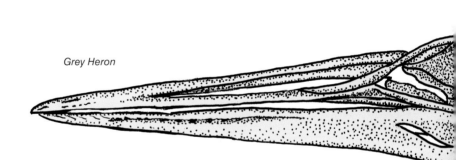

Grey Heron

G. Spear- or Dagger-shaped Bills

Storks

Black Stork	232/229mm:178/170mm	77/75%
White Stork	254/231mm:193/140mm	76/74%

White Stork Very heavy bill three times length of cranium. Bill almost as deep as cranium at base. Cranium smooth and rounded.

Cranes

Demoiselle Crane	127/110mm:71/58mm	59/56%
Crane	185/166mm:119/97mm	65/61%

Crane Bill markedly longer than cranium. Bill slender and pointed. CMP concave.

Herons, Egrets and Bitterns

Bill twice length of cranium. Bill robust and deep. CMP straight. Cranium rounded. Whole skull profile is dagger-blade-shaped.

Little Bittern	79/72mm:47/42mm	59/58%
Cattle Egret	92/103mm:59/63mm	64/61%
Squacco Heron	97/90mm: 60/53mm	62/59%
Black-crowned Night Heron	132/110mm:78/62mm	59/56%
Bittern	132/120mm:77/69mm	58/57%
Little Egret	135/117mm:94/77mm	69/66%
Great White Egret	172/149mm:119/99mm	69/66%
Purple Heron	175/165mm:126/103mm	72/62%
Grey Heron	185/168mm:125/111mm	67/66%

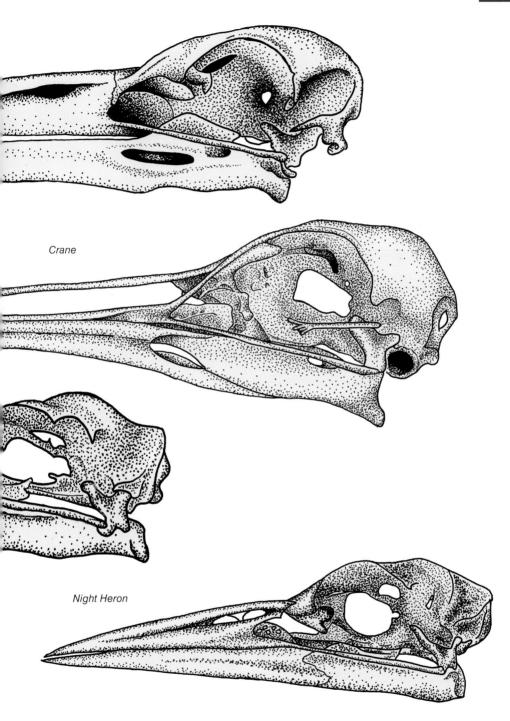

Crane

Night Heron

Grey Heron Robust bill twice length of cranium. Cranium undulating, with marked exoccipital ridge. CMP slightly notched. Lower mandible very heavy at base.

Black-crowned Night Heron Bill markedly longer than cranium. CMP distinctly concave.

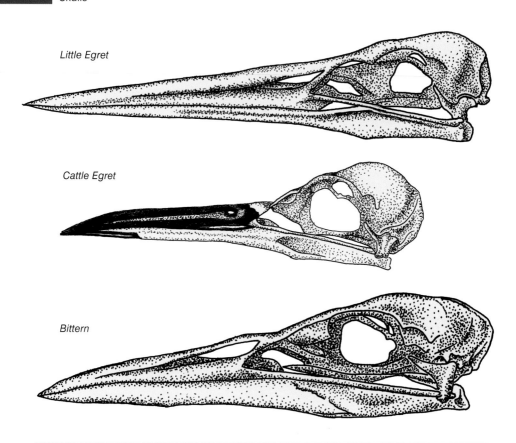

Little Egret

Cattle Egret

Bittern

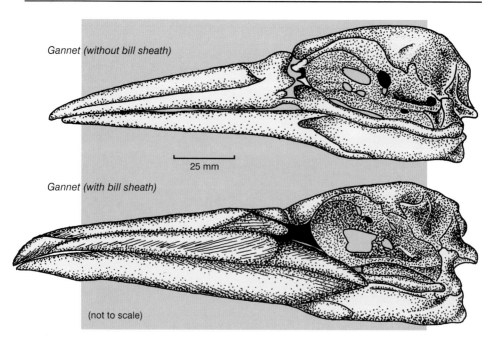

Gannet (without bill sheath)

├─── 25 mm ───┤

Gannet (with bill sheath)

(not to scale)

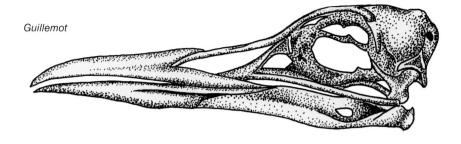

Guillemot

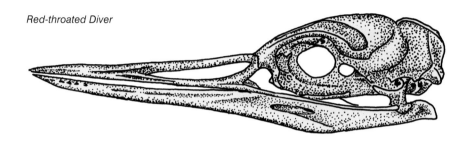

Red-throated Diver

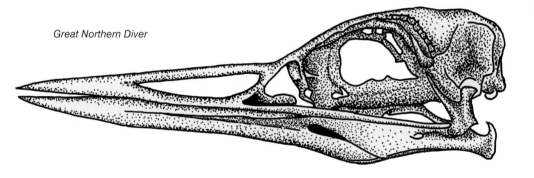

Great Northern Diver

Bittern Bill markedly longer than cranium. Bill robust. CMP with a slight notch. Cranium undulating, with a marked sagittal crest.

Gannet	182/170mm:110/95mm	60/56%

The robust bill is markedly longer than the cranium. The diagnostic feature is a distinct lateral groove running along the entire length of the upper mandible, with or without the bill sheath.

Black Guillemot	79/72mm:43/37mm	54/51%
Guillemot	115/95mm:70/53mm	61/56%

Guillemot The slender, curved bill is markedly longer than the cranium. CMP concave. Sagittal crest prominent.

Divers

Bill robust, tapering gently. Bill markedly longer than cranium. Hook-like process at back of lower mandible. CMP distinctly concave. Exoccipital and sagittal crest areas well developed.

Black-throated Diver	120mm:69mm	57% (one only)
Red-throated Diver	124/100mm:73/60mm	60/59%
Great Northern Diver	167/139mm:100/76mm	60/55%

Greater Spotted Woodpecker

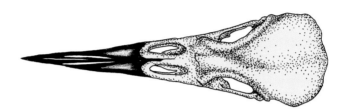

Green Woodpecker

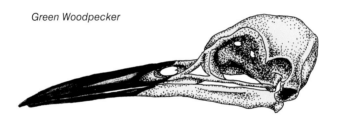

Kingfisher

Woodpeckers

Bill length varies from approximately equal to almost twice cranium length. Bill broad at base. Groove for hyoid apparatus and greatly extensible tongue sometimes apparent on back of cranium. Orbit large and prominent. CMP with convex notch.

Great Spotted Woodpecker	59/41mm:35/22mm	59/53%
Grey-headed Woodpecker	61mm:29mm (one only)	48%
Green Woodpecker	83/65mm:49/30mm	59/46%
Black Woodpecker	88/78mm:52/45mm	59/58%

Lesser Spotted Woodpecker	34/28mm:18/12mm	67/53%
Three-toed Woodpecker	48/56mm:25/33mm (two only)	52/59%

Kingfisher 69/52mm:46/32mm 67/61%

The very narrow bill is approximately twice the length of the cranium. The lower mandible is extremely thin. CMP with distinct notch.

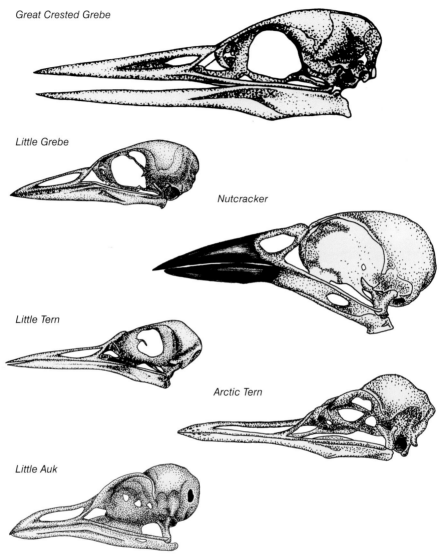

Great Crested Grebe

Little Grebe

Nutcracker

Little Tern

Arctic Tern

Little Auk

Grebes

Little Grebe	53/45mm:27/20mm	51/44%
Slavonian Grebe	67/57mm:35/27mm	52/47%
Great Crested Grebe	105/86mm:63/47mm	60/55%

Great Crested Grebe Bill longer than cranium. Bill tapering. Cranium oval in shape. CMP concave.

Nutcracker 78/76mm:48/45mm 61/59%
Bill longer than cranium. Mandibles curved, lower mandible distinctly concave. CMP notched.

Terns

Bill equal to or slightly longer than cranium. Bill slender and pointed. Large orbit with prominent lachrymal area.

Little Auk	53/48mm:32/25mm	60/52%
Little Tern	58/53mm:29/26mm	50/49%
Black Tern	60/52mm:35126mm	58/50%
Whiskered Tern	60/58mm:31/30mm	60/52%
Common Tern	70/65mm:44/34mm	62/52%
Arctic Tern	73/61mm:40/32mm	58/53%
Sandwich Tern	92/75mm:54/44mm	61/59%
Caspian Tern	130mm:75mm (one only)	58%

H. Highly-modified Bills

The following section of species covers a range of skull with bills highly modified for particular activities, especially feeding.

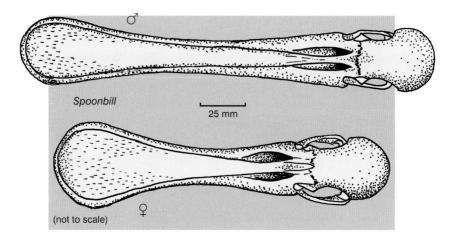

Spoonbill

25 mm

(not to scale)

Spoonbill   239/228mm:231/168mm 96/73%
The enormous spatula-shaped bill is at least three to four times the cranium length. The bill is adapted for sifting aquatic invertebrates.

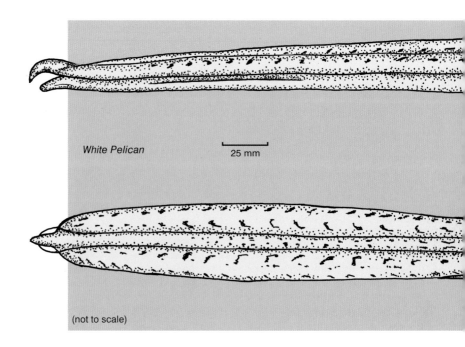

White Pelican

25 mm

(not to scale)

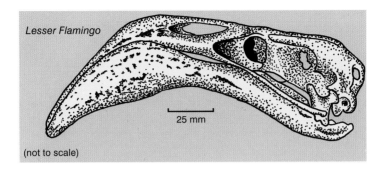

Lesser Flamingo

25 mm

(not to scale)

Greater Flamingo   154/167mm:128/140mm   83%
Lesser Flamingo   134mm:109mm (one only) 74%

Flamingo Massive downturned bill, with the lower mandible much larger than the upper. Adaptation for feeding on invertebrates sucked into the bill and sifted through fine lamellae as the bird moves slowly through the water with the bill upside down. (Note: the bill measurements were taken diagonally from bill tip to nasal frontal hinge.)

Dalmation Pelican 508/512mm:457/458mm   89%
White Pelican   408/423mm:342/347mm 83/82%

Pelican This enormously elongated bill, which is laterally extended, is at least four times the length of the cranium. The lower mandible supports the greatly enlarged pouch in which water and fish are swept up.

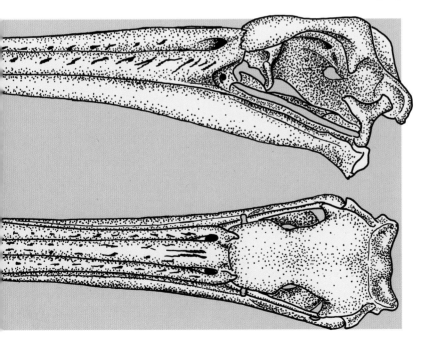

Parrot Bills

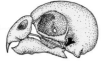
Budgerigar

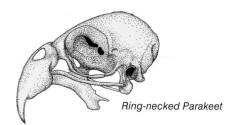
Ring-necked Parakeet

Bugerigar 30/23mm:15/10mm 50/43%
Ring-necked Parakeet 48/43mm:29/22mm 60/51%

Gape Bills

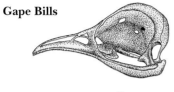

Nightjar

Swallow

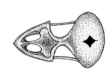
House Martin – juvenile

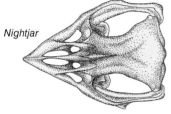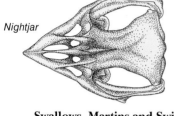

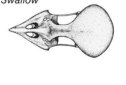
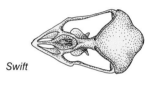
Swift

Swallows, Martins and Swifts

Swallow	30/28mm:11mm	39/37%
House Martin	26/23mm:10/8mm	38/35%
Swift	32/30mm:12/10mm	37/33%
Alpine Swift	36mm:15mm (one only)	43%

Swallow The bill is adapted for catching insect prey on the wing. It is little more than half the length of the cranium, although it is very wide at the base. Viewed dorsally, the base of the bill is equal to the width of the cranium and extends beyond the jugal bar. There is a marked inter-orbital constriction.

Crossbills

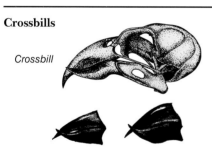
Crossbill

Crossbill 39/34mm:16/15mm 44/41%
Without the bill sheath, the skull is finch-like with straight mandibles. With the sheath present, the mandibles appear to cross over, enabling the bird to split cone scales and seeds.

| Two-barred (larch) | Common (spruce & pine) | Scottish (Scots Pine) | Parrot (mainly pine) |

Bill sheaths of crossbills (after Beaman & Madge 1988).

Tubenoses

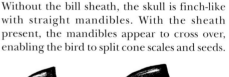
Cory's Shearwater without bill sheath

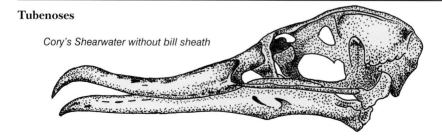

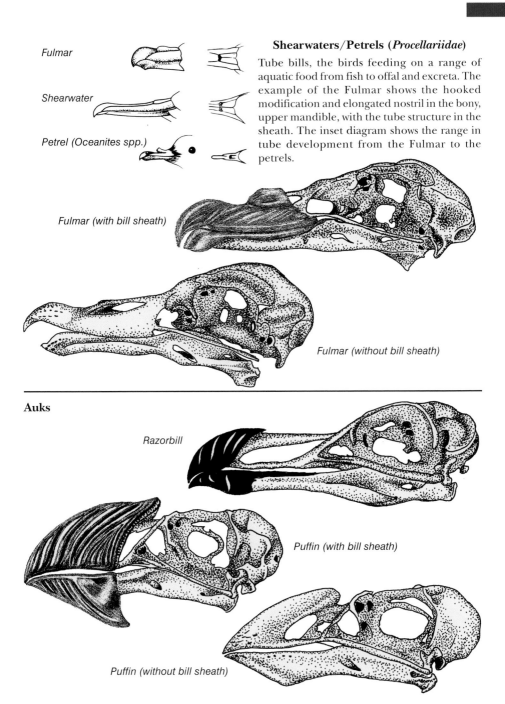

Fulmar

Shearwater

Petrel (Oceanites spp.)

Shearwaters/Petrels (*Procellariidae*)

Tube bills, the birds feeding on a range of aquatic food from fish to offal and excreta. The example of the Fulmar shows the hooked modification and elongated nostril in the bony, upper mandible, with the tube structure in the sheath. The inset diagram shows the range in tube development from the Fulmar to the petrels.

Fulmar (with bill sheath)

Fulmar (without bill sheath)

Auks

Razorbill

Puffin (with bill sheath)

Puffin (without bill sheath)

Razorbill   96/83mm:52/46mm   55/54%
Elongated skull, bill markedly longer than cranium and possessing a black and white hooked sheath. Bill adapted for catching fish which the bird pursues by diving from the surface and swimming underwater.

Puffin   75/72mm:42/38mm   56/53%
The bill is laterally compressed and is as deep as the cranium, or even deeper if the brightly coloured sheath is still attached. The bill is adapted for catching fish, digging and display.

I. Hooked Bills (short)

Owls Short, hooked bills generally much shorter than the cranium. In dorsal view the skull is triangular in outline, with a rounded back to the cranium. Orbits very large. Prominent exoccipital process. Internal bones of the nostrils expanded into a bulbous mass at back of bill.

Pygmy Owl	36/35mm:13/12mm	36/34%
Scops Owl	42/38mm:15/14mm	37/36%
Tengmalm's Owl	49mm/20mm (one only)	40%
Little Owl	50/46mm:17/14mm	34/30%
Long-eared Owl	58/53mm:24/22mm	41%
Short-eared Owl	59/55mm:24/22mm	40%
Hawk Owl	60/56mm:23/21mm	38/37%
Barn Owl	68/65mm:31/28mm	45/43%
Tawny Owl	71/63mm:27/22mm	38/35%
Ural Owl	80/76mm:40/33mm	50/43%
Snowy Owl	90/85mm:45/35mm	50/41%
Eagle Owl	108/95mm:50/40mm	46/42%

Scops Owl Short, deeply curved bill little more than half the length of the cranium.

Little Owl Bill less than half the cranium length and deeply curved. Flat cranium with enormous orbit.

Barn Owl Bill markedly shorter than cranium. Orbit large. CMP concave above the orbit, then convex into marked nasal-frontal hinge.

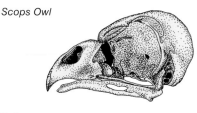

Scops Owl

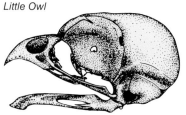

Little Owl

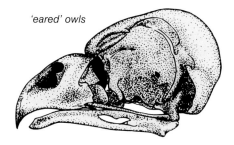

'eared' owls

Barn Owl

Tawny Owl

Ural Owl
(with bill sheath)

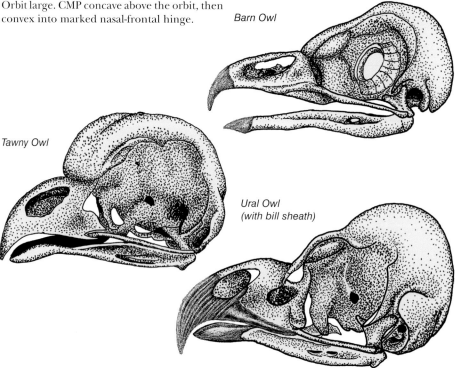

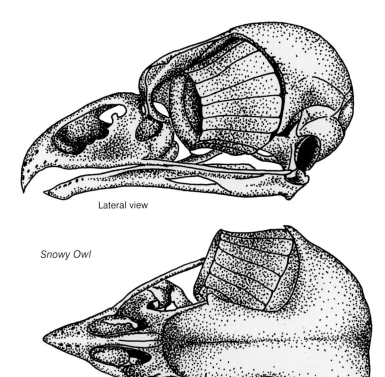

Lateral view

Snowy Owl

Dorsal view

Snowy Owl The sclerotic rings supporting the eyes are intact in this specimen, a rare occurrence.

Eagle Owl Cranium flat, CMP straight with a deep convex step.

Eagle Owl

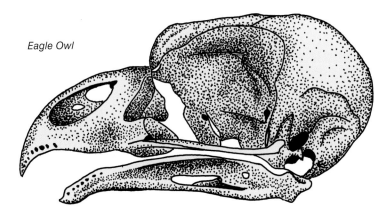

Buzzard 80/73mm:33/25mm 41/34%

Bill often little more than half length of cranium. Bill hooked, with large nostril. Orbit enormous CMP straight, with slight notching at nasal-frontal hinge.

Rough-legged
Buzzard 83/79mm: 33/29mm 40/39%

Sparrowhawk 51/44mm:20/13mm 39/29%
Goshawk 76/69mm:32/25mm 42/36%

Goshawk The bill, which is strongly curved at the tip, is little more than half the length of the cranium. Nostril small. Orbit large. CMP straight with a slight notch.

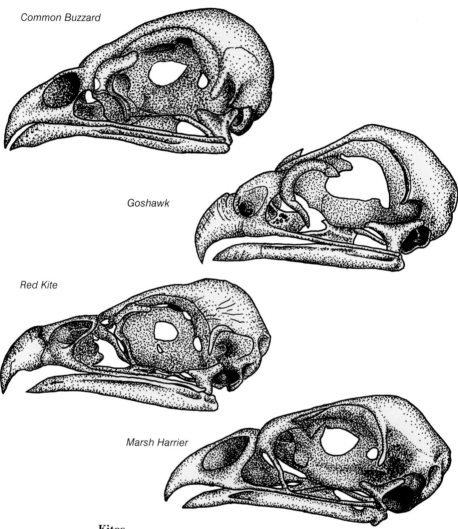

Common Buzzard

Goshawk

Red Kite

Marsh Harrier

Kites

Bill markedly shorter than cranium. Strongly hooked bill, with indentation behind the tip of the upper mandible. Nostril elongated. Orbit large. CMP undulating.

Black-shouldered Kite 57/53mm:30/21mm 52/40%
Black Kite 75/70mm:31/28mm 41/40%
Red Kite 83/78mm:36/32mm 43/41%

Montagu's Harrier 58/57mm:24/23mm 41/40%
Hen Harrier 66/60mm:28/22mm 42/37%
Marsh Harrier 79/71mm:35/29mm 44/41%

Marsh Harrier Strongly hooked bill, markedly shorter than cranium. Nostril very large. CMP straight, with a slight concavity. Back of cranium angular and slightly concave.

Osprey   80/74mm:38/33mm   47/44%

Bill slightly shorter than cranium, very strongly hooked. Nostril less than half bill length. Orbit large.

Honey Buzzard   77172mm:28128mm   38/36%

Bill pointed, but not so deeply as in hawks and falcons, little more than half length of cranium. Nostril large and elongated. Orbit very large.

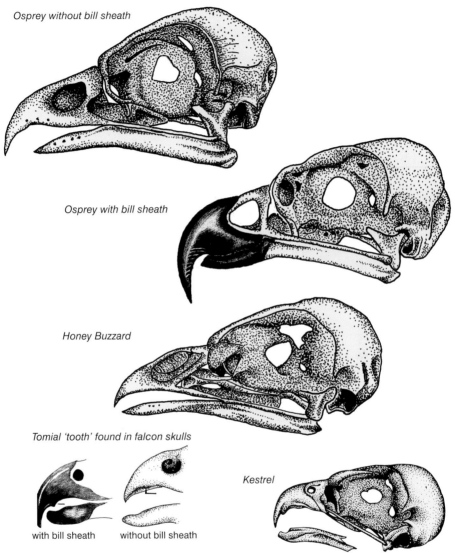

Osprey without bill sheath

Osprey with bill sheath

Honey Buzzard

Tomial 'tooth' found in falcon skulls

with bill sheath   without bill sheath

Kestrel

Lesser Kestrel	38mm:17mm (one only)	44%
Red-footed Falcon	44/38mm:17/16mm	43/39%
Merlin	47mm:16mm (one only)	34%
Hobby	49/44mm:17/13mm	34/29%
Eleonora's Falcon	49mm:20mm (one only)	41%
Kestrel	50/46mm:18/15mm	36/33%
Lanner Falcon	68/60mm:28/22mm	44/37%
Peregrine Falcon	70/63mm:28/23mm	40/36%
Saker Falcon	71/66mm:32/26mm	50/49%
Gyr Falcon	81/75mm:32/29mm	39%

Kestrel Skull structure typical of the other falcons. Bill little more than half the length of the cranium. Bill curved, with a prominent notch and peg on the underside of the upper mandible and a corresponding notch in the lower mandible. Orbit large. The jugal bar forms an angle with the top of the flat cranium.

J. Hooked Bills (long)

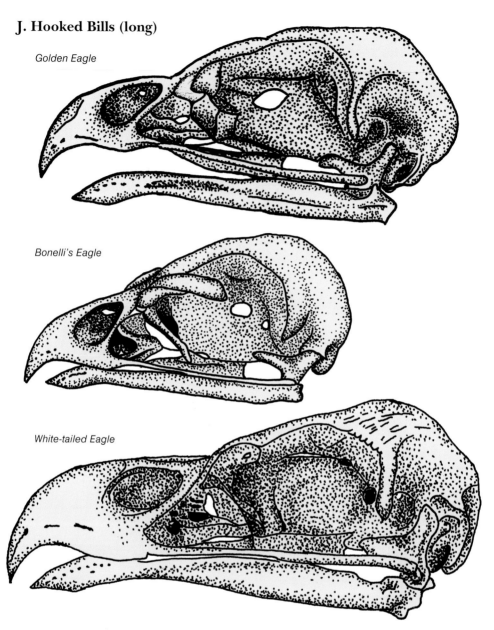

Golden Eagle

Bonelli's Eagle

White-tailed Eagle

Golden Eagle 125/104mm:59/42mm 47/40%
The thick, heavy bill is markedly shorter than the cranium and has a simple hook at the tip. The post-orbital process is strong, and the cranium is flat, but irregular.

Bonelli's Eagle 100/85mm:41/36mm 42/41%
Bill markedly shorter than cranium, thick at base and strongly curved. Nostril large. Orbit large and rounded. Post-orbital process strong, but short and rounded. CMP concave.

Lesser Spotted Eagle 90mm:41mm (one only) 45%
Greater Spotted Eagle 102/96mm:54/50mm 56/50%
Short-Toed Eagle 103/99mm:54/42mm 53/43%
Imperial Eagle 111/109mm:59/57mm 53/52%

White-tailed Eagle 138/122mm:65/58mm 47%
Long, heavy bill slightly shorter than cranium. Very deep at base, nostrils large. Bill deeply curved. Orbit large and deep, with strong post-orbital process. CMP flat, almost concave.

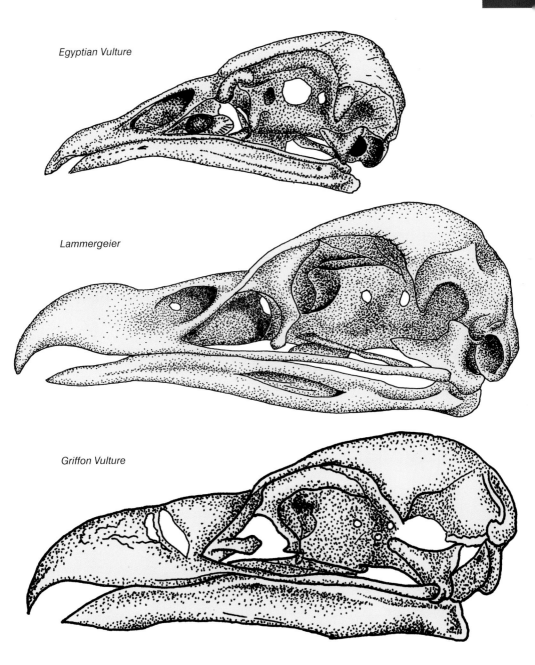

Egyptian Vulture

Lammergeier

Griffon Vulture

Egyptian Vulture	105/196mm:60/51mm	57/53%
Lammergeier	145/136mm:80/68mm	55/50%
Griffon Vulture	147/125mm:74/65mm	52/50%
Black Vulture	149/135mm:79/65mm	53/48%

Egyptian Vulture Bill markedly longer than cranium. Bill generally very narrow, with a distinct hook if the sheath is present. Nostril very long. CMP convex.

Lammergeier Bill slightly longer than cranium, heavy and hooked, expanding towards tip (expansion very marked if sheath is present).

Griffon Vulture Bill longer than cranium. Powerful, relatively narrow bill, with nostrils pointing forward. Post-orbital and exoccipital processes give rise to a ridge.

Black Vulture Heavy, thick bill markedly longer than cranium. Upper mandible parallel-sided, bill curving strongly to tip. CMP concave.

Capercaillie   120/100mm:62/56mm 52/56%
The heavy bill is longer than the cranium, and is strongly curved at the tip. Angular processes at back of lower mandible very prominent. Cranium convex, but flattened towards back. Prominent orbital ridge, with very deep inter-orbital depression.

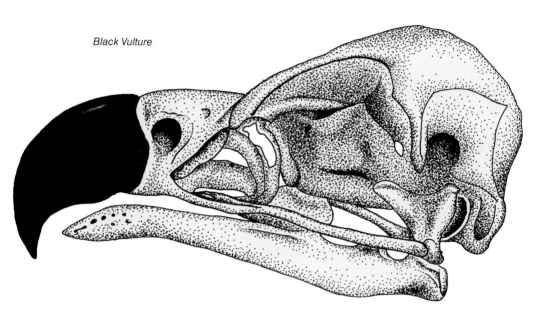

Black Vulture

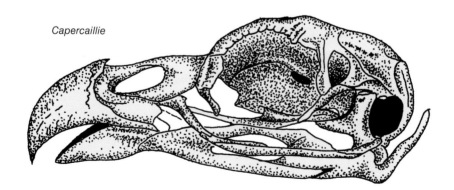

Capercaillie

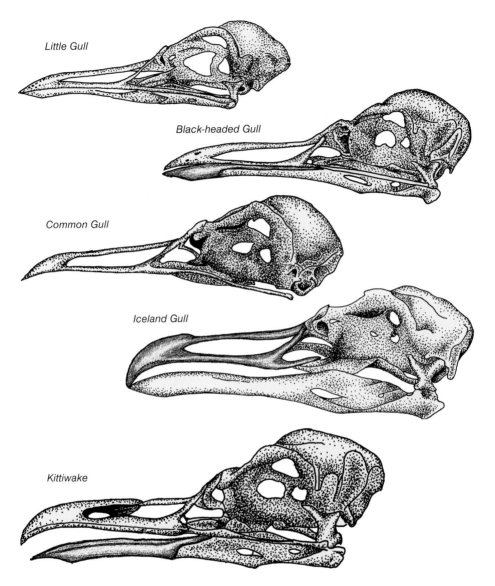

Little Gull

Black-headed Gull

Common Gull

Iceland Gull

Kittiwake

Gulls (*Larus*)

Elongated skulls with large, powerful bills at least as long as cranium. In dorsal view, there are depressions behind the lachrymals which contain salt glands. In the absence of a bill sheath, the nostril is very long. Bill top and bottom generally parallel, but expanded at the tip. Bill laterally compressed. Main differences are in size, although the cranium is rounded in the Common and Black-headed Gulls, but tends to be more angular in other species.

Little Gull	59/58mm:31/30mm	52%
Mediterranean Gull	85mm:47mm (one only)	26%
Black-headed Gull	92/80mm:51/41mm	55/51%
Common Gull	93/87mm:50/42mm	54/48%
Iceland Gull	101/92mm:54/46mm	53/50%
Kittiwake	110/89mm:61/45mm	55/50%
Herring Gull	118/111mm:65/60mm	55/54%
Glaucous Gull	140/121mm:83/72mm	62/59%
Great Black-backed Gull	145/131mm:81/72mm	56/55%

Kittiwake Similar to other gulls, but with strongly developed post-orbital process and angular cranium.

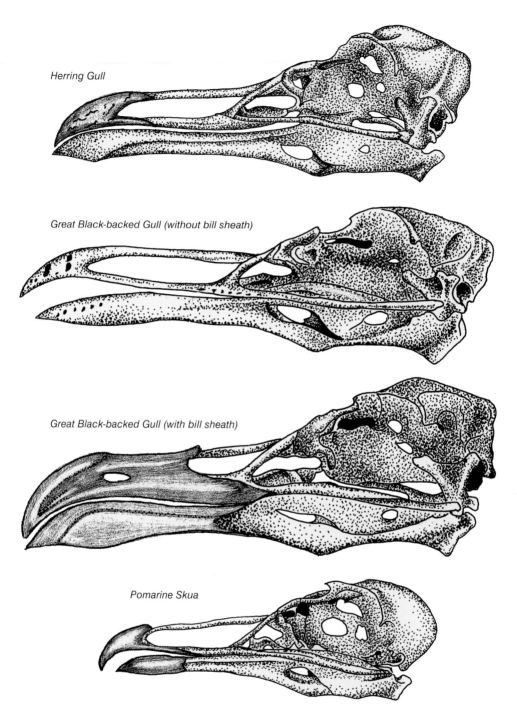

Herring Gull

Great Black-backed Gull (without bill sheath)

Great Black-backed Gull (with bill sheath)

Pomarine Skua

Pomarine Skua	92mm:48mm	52% (one only)	
Arctic Skua	80/74mm:42/38mm	52/51%	

Pomarine Skua Bill slightly longer than cranium. Very curved tip at the end of the bill. Back of cranium rounded.

European Bird Protection and Study Organisations

Austria Österreichische Geselschah für Vogelkunde, Naturhistorisches Museum, A-1014 Vienna 1.

Belgium Institut Royal des Sciences Naturelles de Belgique, rue Vautier 31, Bruxelles 4.

Denmark Dansk Ornithologisk Forening, Faelledvej 9 Mezz, Dk 2200, Copenhagen N.

Eire Irish Society for the Protection of Birds, Department of Lands, 24 Upper Merrien Street, Dublin 2.

Finland Societas pro Fauna et Flora Fennica, Zoological Museum of the University, Novra Jarnvagsgaten 13, Helsinki 10.

France Ligue pour la Protection des Oiseaux, 57 rue Cuvier, BP505, 75005 Paris.

Germany (West) Deutscher Bund für Vogelschutz, 705 Waiblingen, Lange Strasse 34, Bonn.

Great Britain British Trust for Ornithology, Beech Grove, Tring, Herts. HP23 5NR.

Royal Society for the Protection of Birds, The Lodge, Sandy, Beds. SG19 2DL.

Scottish Ornithologists Club, 21 Regent Terrace, Edinburgh EH7 5BT.

Italy La Lega Italiana per la Protezione degli Uccelli, Lungano Guicciardina 9, 50125 Firenze.

Luxembourg Ligue Luxembourgeoise pour L'Etude et la Protection des Oiseaux, 32 rue de la Foret, Luxembourg.

Netherlands Nederlandse Vereniging Tot Berscherming Van Vogels, Dreibergseweg 16 B. Zeist 2740.

Norway Zoologisk Museum, Sarsgatan 1 Oslo 5.

Portugal Sociedada Portuguese de Ornitologia, Seccao de Zoologica, Faculdade Ciencas, Oporto.

Spain Sociedad Espanola de Ornitologica, Castellana 80, Madrid.

Sweden Svenska Naturskydd-sföreningen Kungsholms Strand 125, 112 34 Stockholm.

Sveriges Ornitologiska Förening, Runesbergsgatan 8, 114 29 Stockholm.

Switzerland Schweizerische Vogelwarte, 6204 Sempach, Lucerne.

Bibliography

Bang, P. and Dahlstrom, P (1974). *Animal Tracks and Signs*. Collins, Glasgow.

Brown, RW, Lawrence, MJ, and Pope, J (1984). *The Country Life Guide to Animals of Britain and Europe; their tracks, trails and signs*. Country Life, London.

Bruun, B, *et al*. (1986). *Birds of Britain and Europe*. Country Life, London.

Cramp, S. *et al*. (eds.) (1977 85). *Handbook of the Birds of Europe, the Middle East and North Africa*. Vols I-IV. Oxford University Press.

Delacour, J (1964). *The Pheasants of the World*.

Farmer and King (eds.) (1972). *Avian Biology Vol. 11* (in particular chapter by P Stettenheim on feather development).

Fitter, R. *et al*. (1969). *Book of British Birds*. Drive Publications Ltd. Basingstoke.

Ginn, HB, and Melville, DS (1983). *Moult in Birds*. British Trust for Ornithology, Guide no. 19.

Gooders, J (1970). *Where to watch Birds*. Deutsch, London.

Goodwin, D (1976). Crows of the World. British Museum (Natural History).

Harrison, C (1975). *A Field Guide to the Nests, Eggs and Nestlings of British and European Birds*. Collins, Glasgow.

Harrison, P (1983). *Seabirds. An identification guide*. Croom Helm.

Hayman, P, and Burton, P (1'37h). *The Bird life of Britain*. Mitchell Beazley with RSPB.

Hayman, P. Marchant, J and Prater, T (1986). *Shorebirds. An identification guide to the waders of the world*. Croom Helm.

Howard, R. and Moore, A (1984). *A Complete Checklist of the Birds of the World*. Macmillan, London.

Kaufman, J (1970). *Birds in Flight*. World's Work, Kingswood.

Keith, S. and Gooders, J (1980). *Collins Bird Guide*. Collins, London.

Lloyd, C (1981). *Birdwatching on Estuaries, Coast and Sea*. Severn House, London.

Lovegrove, R. and Barret, P (1982). *Birdwatcher's Diary*. Hutchinson, London.

Madge, S (1980). *Birdwatching*. Ward Lock, London.

Peterson, R. Mountfort, G. and Hollom, PAD (1983). *A Field Guide to the Birds of Britain and Europe*. Collins, London.

Simms, E (1983). *A Natural History of British Birds*. Dent, London.

Stidworthy, J (1983). *Bird Spotting and Studying*. Nature Detective Series, Macdonald, London.

Storer, JH (1948). 'The flight of birds analysed through slow-motion photography'. Cranbrook Institute of Science, Bulletin No. 28.

Svensson, L (1984). *Identification Guide to European Passerines*. Stockholm.

Tuck, GS (1978). *A Field Guide to the Seabirds of Britain and Europe*. Collins, London.

Van Tyne, J. and Berger, AJ (1959). *Fundamentals of Ornithology*. John Wiley & Sons Inc. USA.

Witherby, HF, *et al*. (1938-41). *The Handbook of British Birds*. 5 Vols. London.

Index